Time, like tide,
will not wait for dreams.

Running
with the
Tide

To Linda & George,
Happy boating.

Marlene B. Allen

Marlene B. Allen

Book and cover design by Lumina Designworks, San Rafael, CA
Photographs by Robert Allen

Copyright 1998
First Printing 1998

Library of Congress Cataloging-in Publication Data
Allen, Marlene B.
Running With the Tide: Time, Like Tide, Will Not Wait For Dreams
1. Allen, Marlene
2. Realization of a Dream
3. Voyaging and Relationship
1997   97-093345
ISBN 0-9656839-0-7

Published by:
GIMCRACK PRESS
301 E. Strawberry Dr.
Mill Valley, CA 94941

This book is dedicated to my husband Bob.
His patience and love made
a dream blossom into a reality.

TABLE OF CONTENTS

FOREWARD

Sea Chanties, or sometimes spelled Shanties, have played an important part of the history of a sailor's life at sea, making his work a little easier when pulling on the halyards, or pushing the capstan to raise the anchor. Each type of song needs its own rhythm. The songs and dancing of the hornpipe helped sailors pass time when off watch, reminding them of the fun they had with lusty gals in foreign ports, or the excitement of going home and collecting their pay. It took many months for them to get their wages, and once on land, money quickly leaked from their pockets into a bartender's till. If any money was left the same pockets were later picked by infamous ladies of the night. Sailors also sang about cruel captains and first mates who created a hell ship for the crew.

Bob and I have collected a variety of Sea Chanties over that last forty-six years. They have been entwined through out our married life, weaving old time histories and fun into our boating. Because of their importance in our lives I felt a Sea Chantey should begin each chapter in the book.

Chapter 1

THE DAMN BOAT

"A bully ship and a bully crew, Doo da, doo da.
A bully mate and a captain too, oh doo da day."
(Sea Chantey, "Sacramento")

"How in blue blazes did I let myself get talked into going sailing," I muttered, shivering despite the warm California weather. "I hate water. I don't even like to drink it."

Jamming my hands into the pockets of my faded blue jeans I paced the living room, startled when the tap of mother's high heels paused at the hall doorway. A wry grin framed her mouth as her hazel eyes held mine. My friends told me she looked like my older sister, not the mother of an eighteen year old. I liked that. One could hope the genes would be on my side when forty rolled around, even though it was hard to imagine being *that* old.

"You're wearing holes in the rug," mom said with a chuckle. If you didn't want to go out with Bob, or what ever his name is, you should have told him so."

Easy for her to say, I thought. She's not the one who'd die of embarrassment. I offered up my most earnest face, "Get me out of this please mom. I'll even spend the day cleaning my room."

1

"No way, though Lord knows it needs it. Now open the door. I think your nice guy just rang the doorbell."

We both looked at my clothes. The scuffed tennis shoes looked properly careworn, the broken left lace knotted into a single piece. The right lace hung in quiet desperation, ready to surrender at any moment. I smoothed the faded jeans and straightened my father's old dress shirt that I had rescued from the rag bag the week before. Mother wagged her head. She had teased me earlier saying I looked like a clone of one of my teen-aged friends; but this was 1950, we didn't have to dress up in prissy little outfits like our parents. "Maybe when he sees me he'll change his mind about taking me out on his boat," I whispered. "

No such luck. The big smile on Bob's face told it all when the door was opened. I could have been wearing sack cloth and ashes and he wouldn't have noticed.

"Don't worry Mrs. Clabby, I'll take good care of her," Bob said.

"Somehow I don't think I'm the one who's worried," she replied.

Signaling a sigh toward mom I clasped her in a quick bear hug and plodded out the door, looking like a shanghaied sailor facing two years before the mast.

Bob held open the wood trimmed door of his green 1947 Ford Sportsmans, gripping my elbow a tad too long. I'm going to keep my eye on him, I thought, and moved a little closer to my door. "Nice car," my voice cracked. "It must take a lot of varnishing to keep the wood up."

He laughed, nodding his head while he put the car in gear. He turned on the radio. "How High The Moon" blared out. We both hummed along, but his off key voice ran a small shiver up my spine. Wait until I tell grandma about him, I thought. She said she could teach anyone to sing, but I'll bet she's never heard a voice this far off. The song ended and a news commentator reported the latest developments in the Korean conflict.

I blinked when Bob audibly bristled, exclaiming the so called conflict was a war, whether it had been declared or not. "When I graduate from UCLA I'll be an officer, fighting for my country from the deck of a navy ship."

Only one boy from my class abandoned school to join the army. This new war had an ambiguous feeling to it, unlike the scary quality of World War II. Looking at Bob's jutting chin, his face wreathed in patriotism, excited me. I hoped the war would end soon...before his graduation.

We drove from 21st and Montana through the bedroom community of Santa Monica, soon turning left on to the Pacific Coast Highway. I stole a sideways glance at him. There was something different about him since our last date, but I couldn't decide what. His slicked down brown hair shown in the sunlight, and as it dried, springy hairs lifted one by one from his temples, reminding me of Dagwood Bumstead. No, it wasn't just his looks, because despite his unruly hair, he was handsome. My attention rested on his powerful shoulders. His right hand steered, while his left arm loafed on the rolled down window. Occasionally he tapped his fingers on the necker's knob attached to the wheel.

Relaxed, that was it! On our first date his nervousness created a feeling of being locked in the car with a caged animal. I decided afterwards not to go out with him again, but darn if his face didn't radiate a hopeful grin when he asked me out again. He talked my ear off about taking me sailing, not letting me get a word in edgewise. Pretty hard for a girl who had been nick named "Gabby Clabby." He plain wore me down. His tone had implied his life would ruined if I didn't go.

I studied him again, and his brown eyes caught mine with a questioning look. I blurted, "You're different today."

He smiled, "Am I? Must be the boat. I'm excited about showing it to you."

We continued on to San Pedro, a older Portuguese fishing community, finally stopping at a run down marina. He parked the car in a weed filled lot, and before he came around to my side, I slipped out of the car, closing the varnished wood door. He grabbed my hand and led me around a scarred work shed where flaking chips of paint rested at the bottom of dry rotted boards. Carefully I side stepped over a rusted marine railway, avoiding drops of different colored paint splattered on the ground. A mixture of a foul chemicals and decay permeated the area.

"What stinks?" I asked.

"Bottom paint. It has copper arsenic in it to kill sea growth on boat bottoms. You probably smell dead barnacles too."

I wrinkled up my nose in disgust, "The smell's enough to kill." So this is what boats are like I thought. Not for me, no matter how cute he is.

I trailed after him down a row of slips, careful to avoid loose nails sticking up through the boards. He stopped. "Watch your step. There's a hole in the next board."

My eyes were glued to the rotted board, and I bumped into him when he paused in front of a twenty-three foot, buff colored sailboat. It had a loving cared for look, with high gloss varnish gleaming from the wood cabin top and sides. Freshly painted decks preened in the sunlight, an awesome contrast to the faded docks. It was obvious this man loved varnished wood.

I hung back when Bob climbed aboard, noticing an array of unfamiliar equipment. An uneasy sense of doom nagged at me. He turned and reached his hand out, holding tight to my fingers when the dock waffled climbing aboard. With a confident tone he said, "Welcome aboard the sloop *Scud*. I know you'll love sailing."

My stomach lurched when the boat rocked back and forth at the change of weight, convincing me I would probably *loath* sailing. I made a silent promise that when I turned nineteen I would have enough confidence to say no to boys who insisted on taking me sailing.

Once aboard the craft Bob's enthusiasm for sailing oozed out in all directions. His eyes twinkled as he explained the boat's virtues, giving my arm a reassuring squeeze when he explained why a boat heels when sailing, and how this boat had a keel which would keep it from turning over. "It's easy to sail. You'll catch on in no time."

I looked at his hand on my arm, then stared up into his face. "I'm not so sure....I'm afraid of the water."

A tiny frown of concern plucked at his forehead, but quickly passed when he put his arm around my shoulder, giving it a squeeze. I was surprised to feel more at ease for the moment. "If you're sure it's really safe...ah, and you promise it won't tip over ah..ah." The unfinished sentence hung in the air like a giant question mark.

"Don't worry. I won't let anything happen to you. Trust me," he said.

Marie Antoinette trusted King Louis, I thought, and look where it got her.

Bob disappeared below while I fidgeted on deck. He reappeared shortly, carrying a musty smelling sail bag. "The mainsail's made of Egyptian cotton," he announced. "A little old, but still good."

I held the bag open as he pulled out a large yellowed sail, watching him attach one end of it to a line he called a halyard. He went below again, this time lugging an even more evil smelling bag on to the deck. The aroma reminded me of an old sweat sock that had died in a forgotten gym locker.

"This is the jib. It didn't get a chance to dry out much after my last sail."

"Oh," was as much as I could muster.

He started the motor, skillfully he slipped the mooring lines off the boat and maneuvered out of the slip. The fresh air and sunshine felt good, with dazzling pin points of light winking across the waves, almost matching the gleam in Bob's eyes when he spoke about boats. The tangy sea breeze aired out the sails, driving the boat ahead through the water in an effortless manner. When we sailed out the entrance of the breakwater the bow lifted easily up over tiny ground swells, then returned to the surface, lightly bouncing and sending tiny droplets of spray into the air.

Bob looked down at my white knuckles gripping the rail. "Okay. to hold your hand?" he said.

"Sure...unless you need your hand to sail the boat."

As the day progressed I relaxed, mesmerized by the day's spell, Bob's charm, soon forgetting about my fear of water, heeling boats, or the fact there was so much to learn about sailing, even if I wanted to learn. My musings were interrupted when his hand reached out and stroked my cheek. His voice took on a husky tone when he whispered, "Someday we're going to sail across the Pacific ocean."

My half shut eyes snapped opened, "What's *this we?* I hardly know you."

He went on speaking as if I hadn't uttered a word. His voice gained excitement as words tumbled over each other. "We're going to sail all over the world... Of course we'll get married first."

"Wait just a minute," I said, pulling away. "First you talk me into going out in this boat, and now you have me married. Are you crazy?"

"Maybe. You forget I've been trying to take you out for a year."

I blushed, remembering the first time we met. I had just gotten pinned to his fraternity brother and was giving my boyfriend a more than friendly kiss. Bob had walked up and introduced himself. Shy, he wasn't.

"Slow down, I said." "I just got out of a relationship. I've no intention of getting serious now, much less sail around the world with someone I hardly know."

He shrugged his shoulders, a mischievous grin pulling at the corners of his mouth. "I'm a patient man. After meeting you at the house party a year ago I told my mother I had met the girl I was going to marry."

I drew in a breath. "You didn't... You did? What did she say?"

"She wanted to meet you, but I told her it was too soon because you didn't know about it yet."

I pushed him away, smiling in spite of myself. "Now I know you're crazy."

He rambled on about far away beaches, warm winds, radiant sunsets, new cultures, time to read books while cruising the blue waters of the Pacific. I stopped laughing when I realized how fascinating it sounded. I watched his face glow with a far away look, enjoying the tender touch of his hand on mine. Of course he left out a few little details about cruising, such as being sea sick, hauling water and fuel, watching eighteen foot waves looming at the boat's stern, winds ripping sails. I straightened up to remind myself that the whole thing sounded a mite too scary for a girl who hadn't lived much, and suspected life wasn't as simple as he made out. We both had to finish UCLA. Before I entered college I promised my mom and dad I would get my BA degree.

At the end of the day Bob walked me to the door and kissed me, then held my hands to his lips. I whispered in a tight voice, "You know I still think you're crazy, and I'm not a very brave person. I don't like the water, and I'm only eighteen."

He drew me closer, planting warm kisses on my upturned face. "And another thing," I murmured, "people don't fall in love so quickly." But I was wrong. Some do.

A year and a half later we were married. His talks of cruising were silenced because we both were too busy writing term papers, taking tests, eager to finish school. Besides carrying eighteen units of business courses, Bob worked thirty hours part time as a production control clerk, leaving little time to think, much less sail. That was okay with me, the sailing part that is, since I discovered what it felt like being sea sick. It wasn't good.

What little money we had went for school supplies, food, rent, and gas for the car. Being in love didn't prevent the arguments that exploded from time to time.

"Marlene, did you see what's in the refrigerator?"

"I would assume food Bob."

"No, you assume eatable food. What's in here died a long time ago. That's wasting money we can't afford."

"Well, it isn't just *me* you know. I told you not to buy that coconut. You paid a whole quarter for it and it was rotten. Not only that you bought tools we can't afford, and we have no place to use them."

"The lathe was a good buy. We'll use it later when we get a house. Can't you be logical and see that."

Sailing on the sea to matrimony.

I didn't feel logical. I felt mad. Here I was, twenty years old and fighting about some stupid moldy food and a sixty year old lathe. Instead I wanted him to hold me and not yell until I turned deaf. Well, he did hold me, but I suspected he was still thinking about the food in the refrigerator. Love helps, I thought, but when you're broke little things nag at you. At least we weren't stuck living on some little boat, bouncing around with moldy food sloshing in the bilge.

One day Bob decided to ask his boss for a raise. He felt confident he had performed well at his part time job, deserving the extra money. He came home that evening, chin down to his shoes, and flopped into a chair. I stood in front of him. "Didn't get the raise huh?"

"No," he said, explaining times were hard for the company right now, and that before his boss answered his request he told him a little story. "It seems once a year a farmer used to come to town in his five seat car, bringing his wife and two children. The next year the farmer brought his wife and three children, with the wife obviously pregnant. The store keeper looked at the five seat car, the farmer, wife and three kids, scratched his beard and said, 'Appears to me you've screwed yourself out of a seat.' I didn't need a ten story building to fall on me to get the picture that I better not ask for more money."

"I guess he thinks we can live on jokes instead," I grumbled.

We managed to live without the raise, and Bob graduated with a B.S. in business in 1952. I received a Kindergarten-Primary teaching degree a year later. Six months after his graduation he finally had the opportunity to go cruising in the Pacific...on a destroyer. The destroyer didn't meet his specification of a dream-boat, and the natives on the peninsula of Korea were not the friendly ones he had hoped to meet on a Pacific isle. Two years later the Navy discharged him, coming home to his new son, Bill. He proved the old navy adage that you had to be there at the laying of the keel, but not at the launching. But no sailboat waited for him. The twenty-three foot sailboat had been sold before he left for the navy, increasing our saving's account by $700.00.

But a consummate dreamer like Bob didn't give up fantasizing about boats, even when money proved tight. One day while tending babies, we had added a baby girl named Lori, I heard him talking in the living room to his best friend, Will. They traded stories about their navy days and how they missed sailing. They had been thumbing through *Yachting Magazine,* drooling over the variety of boats for sale, looking as goggle eyed as men reading *Playboy* magazine.

"I can't afford a boat," Bob said. "All our money goes into our mortgage, not to mention eating."

" I've got a little money...we can build a boat," said Will. "That way we don't have to pay for it all at once. Besides, I know where we can get a thirty-six foot navy motor launch, engine and all for $1400.00."

"How are we going to design a sailboat out of that?"

"Easy, we'll get a naval architect to help us."

Bob rubbed his forehead, "He'd have to work awful cheap."

Will grinned, "Right, we'll find a new one who's hungry for business and a challenge."

After Will left, Bob and I cleared the dinner dishes, his face wreathed in smiles. He looked like he had discovered a new cure for an old ailment. I should have known right off it had to do with the debilitating disease of *No Boatitis.* After we put the kids to bed he sat me down on our ancient couch. The look in his eye made me nervous. "Will and I have an idea," he said, "but I need your opinion since we make big decisions together."

"Especially financial. Bill needs new shoes, and Lori's last doctor bill for her congenital hip problem was a doozer. You know she has to have periodic x-rays, and they don't come cheap."

Bob looked at the floor, then at the ceiling, biting his lip. I glanced at him, noticing his discomfort, but kept quiet for a change, waiting to see if he would say something about building a boat. I counted on the overheard conversation being the usual kidding back and forth, because we were all too broke to start a project of such magnitude.

He cleared his throat with a squeak, his words running together. "You're right. It's a financial decision. Will and I want to build a boat, but he would provide the up front money. I told him we could add some of our money later."

He saw me look toward the play yard and shook his head. "I know what you're thinking. The last boat Will and I built sank in Marine Stadium, but this is different. That was a speedboat. This time we're going to build a sailboat."

I shook my head from side to side, not saying no, just in wonder. I had known how he felt about boats when we married, so it shouldn't have come as any great surprise. But it did. I felt giddy remembering how hard Will laughed when *The Damn Boat,* the speedboat named by Bob's mother and me, had sunk the second time it went into the water. "How can you laugh at a time like this," I said, hot tears rolling down my face.

Will's strained face turned to me, "You gotta laugh, or you'll cry," he choked.

I still couldn't laugh, nor did Will's brother, Jack. Just before we launched the *Damn Boat* Will borrowed Jack's new car battery. Part of the bubbles bursting like champagne up through the water belonged to the dying battery. *The Damn Boat* now lived in the children's play area where it couldn't possibly get into any more trouble.

Bob and Will found a hungry naval architect who made the conversion possible, and even he was amazed it came out so well. After years of hard weekend work in Will's back yard the boat took shape. We decided on the name.

"She's like a beautiful woman. We'll call her *Venus,* said Bob."

Will, an artist, carved a stunning Venus figure head. Her ample bosom on the bow caused an erotic stir from many a passing horny sailor. He also did the precise wood work on the interior of the boat, while Bob did all mechanical work. He rebuilt the old Buda engine and installed it, took care of all the electrical projects, water tanks, and keel pattern. I did what I could by painting, drilling holes for fasteners, helping install the teak decks, and of course, bringing beer to the thirsty workers, me included. I took a substitute teaching job to earn money to buy materials for

9

Venus under sail on Master Mariner's Race, San Francisco Bay.

the boat. Building boats didn't make me sea sick, but it sure made our pocket book sick.

By now I learned if you can't beat 'em, join 'em. But that backfired on me. I must have been brain dead not to remember the beautiful varnish on Bob's car and first boat. My second job as first mate meant keeping *Venus* varnished in the manner that Bob had been accustomed.

Three and a half years later we launched our 47 foot wooden schooner *Venus* in San Pedro harbor. I broke a bottle of champagne over the bow, "I christen thee *Venus,* mindful of your beauty and strength. May you sail on calm seas and enjoy happy times."

The next twenty four hours may have made *Venus* happy, but not the crew who manned the pumps twenty four hours straight to keep her from sinking until the wood swelled up. We didn't have an automatic bilge pump then, just weary arms. When we went to bed that night I realized this wasn't one of the happy times I had looked forward to, nor was the first sail. It is one thing to build a boat, another to sail her for the first time.

The big day arrived along with waves driven by an eighteen knot breeze. Will and Bob stood on deck taking turns at the tiller. The stiff breeze blew hair into their eyes, and a silly grin appeared permanently plastered on their face. At the first lurch and heel of the schooner Bill and Lori turned pale and grabbed their stomachs, turning green. They begged to go below and lie down, but only if mom went with them. My own stomach felt like a rock, but the kids needed me. I disappeared below. Soon Bill and Lori looked like they were turning their stomachs inside out, both weeping as I guided their heads into a big bucket. Between the noise and accompanying odors my own head took turns at the bucket. I gritted my teeth and murmured to no one in particular, "I can't believe he thinks sailing is fun. I should have remembered our second date when I thought I would *loath* sailing."

I forgot about my stomach while I rubbed Lori's back, whispering, "It'll be all right honey, daddy will take us home soon."

Just then Bob poked his head down the companion way, "How's everyone doing down there?"

I mumbled to myself, intent on keeping my mouth closed.

"Are you okay?" Bob continued, his voice taking on a concerned tone.

I heaved, happy it was only a sigh this time, "Sort of. When are we going home?"

The next four years I spent many hours trying to learn how to sail a schooner. The harder Bob tried to teach me, the worse I became. His usual easy going manner disappeared. His attempt to be a patient had a rigid, logical edge, and as I strained to listen, my emotional response echoed the uncertainty I felt. Both approaches disconcerted the other. Another time, while on a twenty- seven mile run to Catalina Island, I hung on to the large tiller, daydreaming about being home. The sails started to flap, slowing the boat down. Bob's voice rose in irritation, "Look at the wind direction. Watch your sails."

"I'm trying damn it. Don't yell at me."

Both kids jerked their heads in our direction, then turned their backs. Will looked pained, but kept his mouth shut. Bob waved his arms about, "I'm not yelling," he howled.

Gritting my teeth in embarrassment I hissed, "Excuse me. Don't scream at me then." I drew myself up to my five foot six inches, threw back my head in disdain, trying to maintain some measure of dignity, even though I felt five years old. At that moment Will looked up, "How's about me taking Marlene dinghy sailing when we reach Catalina. Okay. with you?"

"If it's okay with her, go ahead. Maybe she'll listen to *you*."

Wonder of wonders I did listen. We were not emotionally involved. His calm voice and encouraging manner rounded the edge of my nervousness. "Hold the tiller in your right hand, and the main sheet in your left," he said. "Try and figure out where the wind is coming from. Can you feel it on your cheek? If you get a gust of wind and the boat heels a lot, loosen up the sheet and turn slightly into the wind."

"When I try to sail close to the wind the boat slows down too much."

"That's because you're pinching."

"I'm what,?" I said.

"Pinching, getting too close to the wind. Fall off away from the wind and you'll go faster."

After a while I sailed the dinghy by myself, conscious of the same sailing principles between the dinghy and the schooner. The schooner had more sails to watch, running backstays to change, and heavy enough to crush another boat, or dock, into little pieces, with very little help from me. I tried to like sailing. I wanted Bob to be proud of me, but until I could be pleased with myself, the joy of sailing eluded me. And to think I used to get mad at mom for being a perfectionist.

Four years later Bob was offered a new job in San Francisco and we moved north. Will decided he wanted to build an experimental trimaran and sold his half of *Venus* to us. For the next six years we sailed as a family on *Venus,* but she wasn't the dream-boat Bob longed for.

One summer day we sailed up to Vallejo from Mill Valley, the beginning of a short vacation. I felt more sure of my sailing ability by now, but that day I must of left my brain at home. We had all three sails up, the mainsail, the gaff rigged foresail and jib. I looked up in surprise when I half jibed the foresail, swinging the boom over to the opposite side. The upper half of the foresail flew the opposite way, twisting the sail in half. Bob stared in disbelief. "How did you manage that?"

"Must be my lucky day." I mumbled. Just when I thought I had sailing down to a pattern, I broke the mold.

People say the two best days of your life is the day you buy a boat and the day you sell it, and *Venus* needed a new home. Selling our creation felt like hawking our child, but a wanton child who demanded more and more from her creators each day. We eventually sold the boat to a hippy who announced he planned to sail to Hawaii, navigating by following the exhaust trails of the airplanes. We figured when he got over the effects from what he had been smoking he might change his mind. He did.

The big day arrived when the new owner took possession. A tiny flutter rolled around in my stomach when she left the dock. First relief washed over me, replaced by a twinge of sadness. I shaded my eyes while watching her grow smaller in the distance, then lifted a hand in salute, "Goodbye dry rot and varnishing, goodbye engine that hated to start, goodbye seasick pail, goodbye to great memories of building you with friends; thank you for all the good times too, but not the fights between Bob and me because you were so damn hard to sail."

Chapter 2

TIME TO GET OFF THE POT

"Come, all you young fellows that follow the sea,
To me way, aye, blow the man down!
Now pray pay attention and listen to me.
Give me some time to blow the man down."
(Halyard Chantey, "Blow The Man Down")

With *Venus* gone Bob faced being a boatless person again. His listless attitude, heavy sighs when looking at the water, made it seem as if a living substance had been excised from his psyche, replaced by a hole, but not a hole in the water. No matter that he had a good job, nice house, kids who minded most of the time, and a wife who *almost* missed a boat. The tide had definitely gone out and left his emotions high and dry.

"It could be worse," I said one day. I could be a kleptomaniac who only stole marine supplies and filled up your work shop with things you couldn't use."

"It's not funny. I don't even have the right kind of dreams anymore."

"I know I'm going to get in trouble, but you're too old for wet dreams."

"Ha, ha.....," he growled. " I'm serious now. When we had *Venus* I

15

used to dream about using our boat as a back up in case of disaster...you know, an earthquake or fire. It's like losing a life link to my safety and future."

With all this sad talk even I started missing a boat. Some of *Venus* must have been absorbed into my bloodstream when I wasn't looking.

Five years marched by without a boat cuddling up to our dock. A common problem afflicted us, not enough money left over after paying for food and a roof over our heads. It was uncanny. Just when we thought we had saved some money for the future the car broke down, the water heater crashed, or Lori needed braces. By 1973 calm spread over the Allen house. Lori's smile showed off beautiful straight teeth. Bill's smile revealed no need of braces, just caps for the two front teeth he broke off at age eight, tripping on the cement driveway roller skating. The car chugged along contentedly. We actually put away boat money in a savings account. Lori's enthusiasm for sailing stopped at the seasick bucket, but Bill thought a new boat would be great. He loved to sail. By this time Bill attended UCLA, supposedly studying engineering while trying to stay awake in class. Lori looked forward to graduating from high school and setting the world on its ear. The world would have to wait. UCLA's girl's athletic department offered her a basketball scholarship. Joy filled our pocket book, turning into pride as we watched our daughter's clever fingers steal the ball from opposing teams. Bill's grades improved when he realized he needed glasses. The scribbles on the black board were not hieroglyphics after all, but meaningful equations.

One day Bob brought a sailing magazine into the kitchen as I cooked dinner. He waved it about under my nose and said, "We've got to find the right boat."

I looked up, still stirring the spaghetti sauce, "And what exactly do you mean by the *right boat?*"

"You know, one you and I could sail by ourselves."

I put down the dripping spoon. "You trust me? Brave man."

I felt him move behind me, nuzzling my neck, "Don't put yourself down. We'd make a great team."

I thought about the schooner, being seasick, the jibed foresail and the million fights we had, especially when I became fearful. "Well," I said, "If Mutt and Jeff, or Frick and Frack can be a team I guess Marlene and Bob could give it a try." But secretly I thought of the team of Tweedle Dee (Bob) and Tweedle *Dum*. (me). My bravery quotient and self confidence took a slide downward. I kept this news to myself, not wishing to be a wet blanket staining his dream teak deck. I would just have to deal with it later when I pulled my thoughts together.

In the first week of January 1974, Bob sat down at his desk, paid our numerous bills, then pushed the checkbook back into the drawer and slammed it shut. He flipped open our savings book, eying the final number with a satisfied look. "We have enough for a down payment on a sailboat. What do you think? It's your money too."

Looking at his joyous face, I pushed all negative thoughts out of my mind. I took the savings book away from his hand, planting myself in his lap. "When do you want to start looking?"

He squeezed so hard it left me breathless. His nose tickled as he whispered in my ear, "Would five minutes from now be all right?"

I grabbed his ears and pulled him forward so I could kiss him, then removed myself from his lap to look for the phone book. "It sounds about three years too late," I called over my shoulder," but it'll do. I'll look up boat dealers in the classified, and then we can take off."

Maybe this boat would be different, I thought, and I would be good at sailing. Miracles still happened. I had to believe that. I flipped through the pages and told myself that any boat had to be easier than our last one. This time I would stop being afraid. I had to grow up some time.

"Wait a minute," Bob said. I saw an ad in a magazine for a Morgan 41 in Alameda that looked interesting." He strode into the living room and picked up several sailing magazines from the table. He whipped through them quickly until he found what he wanted. "Here it is. Take a look. I also want to check out a Coronado."

We drove from Mill Valley to Alameda in record time, coming to the Coronado boat dealer first. We parked the car, introduced ourselves and the salesman led us aboard, leaving us alone to wander through the boat. Bob checked out the entire boat first, rigging, arrangement below, then jumped off the boat and walked up forward, pushing against the outside of the hull. The fiberglass flexed. "Hmmm," said Bob. "I don't like that. The hull looks too thin here, and it oil cans. Let's go find the Morgan."

"Good." I said. "The inside of this boat looks like an RV ready to roll down a highway,."

We found the Morgan boat dealer a block away. We parked the car in an empty lot, apparently the only people looking at boats this raw winter day. The bored looking salesman jumped up from his chair to greet us, his face bright with the hope of landing a live one. He walked us

down the dock, stopping before a 41 foot blue and white Morgan sailboat. I felt a stir of excitement inside. She looked beautiful, sturdy, but
graceful. Well, maybe a little wide in the middle, but that would make her
more steady, I thought, and Lord knows, I could always use a steady boat.
We walked forward and Bob pushed against the hull. "Good sign, no flex-
ing. It looks solid enough," he said.

The salesman motioned us aboard, waved his arms fore and aft, pointing out her good features on deck. "Built in St. Petersburg Florida. Good
old United States. See that rigging? She's got 3/8 shrouds, and the stays
are 5/16."

I watched Bob inspect the rigging, seeing elation written all over
him. He rapidly shook his hands back and forth, rubbing them on his
pants, a sure sign of his excitement. He squinted when he looked up to
the top of the fifty five foot mast, noted the self furling jib with interest,
glancing aft to see how the main was rigged.

"Big cockpit, can have an army in here," said the salesman.

Bob climbed down from the deck. "I want to look below with my
wife, you know....., take my time."

"Sure, be my guest. Any questions just give me a holler."

We climbed down the companionway steps and entered into the
main salon. I drew in my breath at the spaciousness. Bob could stand
straight up without hitting his head. I turned and looked at a table that
could fit six people, then my eyes locked on to the galley. There were
two deep sinks, lots of cupboards and a....."Oh no," I cried, "an alcohol
stove."

"That's no problem. We could always change that."

I peeked into the bathroom, better known as the head, delighted to
see all kinds of cupboard space, hand shower and stainless sink. "We
would have killed for this on the *Venus*," I said, laughing

"What's so funny," Bob said.

I just remembered your first boat *Scud,* and how there was only room
for me to back in to the head. My pants fell around my ankles as I shut
the door. It was like taking a whiz in a broom closet with only enough
room for a dust brush. What a contrast."

Bob moved in to the forepeak, "The bunk up here is pretty good size,
lots of leg room. But I wonder where you store extra sails?"

I was too excited to worry about extra sails, since the two already
bent on seemed plenty enough for me. Then I saw that there were two
hanging closets. We had one tiny closet on *Venus,* which made for imag-

inative packing. Bob poked his head around the corner and nodded in approval, went back to the main salon, pulled down a back cushion revealing three separate compartment behind the seats. He lifted the seat cushions finding more storage room under each seat. The exhilaration on Bob's face grew. "Let's go aft into the Captain's cabin," he said.

We had to bend slightly to enter the walk through aft, all worth it once we came into the cabin. The bunk could sleep three, not that I had anyone else in mind to join us, lots of cupboards for clothes, three large drawers, plus six small drawers. My heart thumped. I love it, I thought. I can't believe I am getting so worked up over a sailboat. I opened another door and found a second head, bigger than the first, also with ample storage space. I turned and clapped my hands together, exclaiming in a loud voice, "I *want* this boat."

I wasn't aware the salesman had come down the companionway steps into the main salon, and when Bob saw him, he turned to me and hissed, "Thanks, fat chance of me getting a lower price now with your big announcement."

We climbed up the companionway to the deck, and sat down in the roomy cockpit. Bob spoke first. "I know the advertised price is $55,500. but I'm sure you could do better. After all, you've been using it as a demo."

A sly smirk tugged at the salesman's face when he glanced at me and said, "It's pretty bare bones now. I had to pay shipping costs from Florida, rig the boat, pay a skipper to take people out, and....I have to make money on it."

Bob winced, wanting the boat, and afraid the feeling showed.

"If we like the test sail I guess you've sold a boat," he murmured.

"I know you won't be disappointed. Come on up to the office, give me a deposit and we'll arrange a time for the sail. If you aren't satisfied, I'll give you your money back."

We took delivery of the boat on February 2, our anniversary, naming her *Maria Elena,* a song we both loved from our younger days. Bob also pointed out that *Maria Elena* was Spanish for Marlene, a point not lost on me.

On February 2 it was colder than hell down below, but I cooked our anniversary dinner on the dreaded alcohol stove, managing not to burn the boat down, but barely. How I missed the propane stove we had on *Venus.*

At last Bob had a tangible hold on his dream, and I had a boat that didn't require paint, the Morgan 41 being constructed of Fiberglass.

Some of our traditionalists friends hinted that wooden boats were the only salty ones, calling ours a "Tupperware boat." Plastic or not, if we kept the finish waxed, the boat wouldn't require painting for many years. I still had some finishing responsibilities since there were teak grab rails, hatch covers, and about ninety four feet of teak gunnel. I put my hands on my hips, bent over and looked at the teak closely.

"I don't want to go through what I did on *VENUS*. I'll buy some teak oil. That'll be easier."

Bob bent his head to the side and shook it vigorously, "No. I want it varnished. Looks better that way."

"That means more sanding. You know how I hate to sand. Let's oil it this time."

"No let's varnish it. I'll do the sanding."

"Deal." I hoped I didn't look too triumphant because I secretly wanted him to come up with that compromise. My triumph was momentary because his expression told me he knew what I had been up to anyway.

Over the next year we added towel racks, made more shelves to hold canned goods, and generally worked to make the boat a part of us. I had left the teak down below natural, but that was unnatural for Bob. He loved varnish, whether it was on boats, or his 1947 Ford Sportsman, now long gone.

"It won't take much sanding," he said. "It's new wood. Hasn't been exposed to the sun."

"I sound like a broken record, but I hate to sand. Couldn't we please oil it?"

He put his hands on the table and stared at me. "It won't work this time. With all the traveling I have to do I don't have time to sand."

"Means a lot huh?"

"Yeah, it does."

"Damn," I grumbled to myself. "I must have been deaf, dumb or blind when I commented how nice his boat and car had looked back in 1950. The tooth fairy hadn't done the varnish. He was just waiting for me."

There were always lots of things to fight over in a marriage, and I did think long and hard on this. If I didn't want to do it I should stand my ground and say no. But he was right. He worked hard and traveled a lot. He couldn't do everything, even if it was his idea. After squashing my guilt complex I decided the only thing that could make me sand and varnish below was love. Being caught in a trap of my own making I would do it. After all he still loved me even after I had tied a bow in *VENUS's* foresail.

Two days later Bob installed a Homer Winslow print on my newly varnished bulkhead in the main salon, showing two grizzled seamen taking a noon sight with a sextant. I used the word installed because we couldn't "hang" a picture on the bulkhead, it had to be screwed to the wall. Later , during rough weather when I bounced off the bulkheads below, I would envy that picture's security.

After two years we bought a three burner propane stove in the galley, complete with oven and broiler, which made my cooking chores more like home. We had installed a Onan generator in order to run equipment requiring 110 V. After the installation I heard Bob talking to a friend at a party, "We added the generator so Marlene could run her hair dryer."

I turned around, "Hey, no fair. You wanted it to run your drills and the microwave."

"I know, but I like to tease you a little anyway."

On one of Bob's business trips to New Zealand we ordered a large sheep skin to put on top of our bunk. Later on that summer I woke up in our bunk, turned over and ran my fingers through the fluffy wool of the sheep skin. It was soft and cuddly. I reminded myself that the old sheep who "donated their all" had ground down their teeth so far that they were unable to eat and would starve. Suddenly my dentist didn't seem like such a bad guy after all. "What a difference the sheep skin makes," I purred." I used to wake up all stiff from these hard foam cushions."

"Me too. When I was a kid at YMCA camp I slept on the ground in a sleeping bag and thought nothing of it. I hate to think it's old age, but comfort means a lot more now."

Our cabin had a cozy feeling to it, a place where we could read, sleep, with all the comforts of home, just scaled down in proportion. Because of the limited space in our small aft hanging closet, the hangers managed to look pregnant. Many items had to hang on top of each other, each vying for precious space.

Gradually over the next eight years I began to fine tune my sailing skills, but full confidence stood just out of reach. One Sunday, after an all day sail, we approached our dock at home. Bob dropped his hands from the wheel and turned to me. "You bring her in."

I squirmed, flicking my hand, "I'll do it next time."

"Why not now?"

"I get nervous when you're watching."

"You did it by yourself when you brought the boat home from San Rafael."

"Yes, but you weren't watching.......oh all right. Give me the wheel." I gritted my teeth, passed our dock and prepared to turn the boat around. Our area had silted in over the years, making it difficult to back around in the mud during a low tide. I put the gear in reverse and gave it a little push, swinging the wheel the opposite way so the stern kicked around. I straightened out, put the gear in forward and slowly moved ahead toward the dock.

Bob stood behind me, "You can go a little faster."

Frowning, I retorted, "I don't want to go faster. We'll get there."

"I know honey, but the wind on the bow is keeping you from turning straight. Just give it more throttle."

I sighed and pushed the throttle a little harder than I meant. The boat leaped ahead, scaring the heck out of me. I throttled down and threw the gear into neutral , gliding along side the dock. Bob jumped off and tied the mooring lines to the dock cleats. He climbed back on board smiling, "You did fine. You just got a little excited there for a minute."

"But I wanted it to be perfect."

"Don't worry, there's always next time."

I had to smile despite my disappointment. "At least it's easier than our schooner. I probably would have taken the whole dock out."

Now that we had our dream boat I thought we should think about Bob's hopes and expectations of cruising, but retirement remained a distant dream, floating in blue water out there in the future. I realized I still referred to it as Bob's cruising dream.

Suddenly we were aware that time had marched in double time. It was the 1980's, and the future had become the present. It was "get off the pot or pee," time, but no one informed us how hard it would be to let go of those mooring lines.

Employed for nineteen years as an executive in a major semiconductor firm, Bob had commuted a 106 mile round trip from Mill Valley to the plant. He had often talked of taking early retirement at fifty five, cruising while we both still had our health and original working parts. But, that's all it was, just talk, the dreams remaining as illusive as ever.

After a particular rough day the "talk" would start, "Well, I guess I'll look into retirement next month," he'd say.

I would nod my head, having heard this many times before, knowing at the end of the month the paycheck would became a smothering security. We could always find a way to spend money it seemed. It began to look as if paychecks were going to be harder to let go of than mooring lines.

In September of 1983 Bob traveled constantly for the company. One day I dragged his suitcase out of the closet, wondering why his clothes couldn't pack themselves since they had so much practice going in and out of the case. I picked up his passport to put with his tickets and stopped, opened his passport and peered at the picture. Bob came in and threw in underwear, shirts, and his shaving kit into the suitcase while I continued to gaze at his picture. He finally looked up, "What are you staring at?"

I handed the passport back to him and said, "Hate to say this dear, but your passport picture looks better than you."

He reached out for the passport and flipped it open. He looked at his picture, then turned to the mirror to see an older, drawn face reflect back at him. "Hmmm...see what you mean."

I walked over and tucked some handkerchiefs into a side pocket of the case, turned and slipped my arms around his waist, staring up into his tired face.

"I hate this. It's like watching someone slowly fade away. I don't want to lose you."

Bob rubbed his temples, then stretched out his arms in a hopeless gesture. "I don't want to lose me either, but what about my job? what am I supposed to do?"

I took a deep breath, knowing what I was about to propose would change our lives, perhaps forever. I didn't have to be a rocket scientist to know there was more to cruising than sailing a boat. On the other hand, I couldn't stand to see Bob's health and happiness being sucked dry by the vagaries of the corporate world.

"Retire and go cruising. I'm up for it, how about you?" I gulped, thinking the cat was out of the bag now.

I glanced up at him, expecting to see a look of excitement, but instead his shoulders sagged, dragging his face along with them. "I don't know if this is the right time," he sighed.

I tried to keep my voice from taking an edge, angry to see him look defeated when he had new choices in front of him. "Well, we can wait until you drop in your tracks. Think what I could do with your life insurance check." I knew I sounded like a bitch , but I couldn't stop myself.

His eyebrows peaked at the word insurance, and the beginning of a smile tugged at his face. "Maybe you're right. I'm not accomplishing a damn thing in this job anyway."

"Good, there's no perfect time to retire, so why not now? Neither of us is getting any younger." I held my breath, watched his face relax, looking more like the young man I married. Deep etched laugh lines replaced the frown lines. "Life's too short not to take a chance. You told me that long ago on our second date, " I said.

He buried his head in my shoulder, squeezing me so tight I gasped. In one swoop he picked me up and threw me back on the bed, first laughing, then stopping to touch my face with his fingertips. "How long since I told you I loved you," he murmured.

"Too long," I whispered back. "Stop talking and being logical. Kiss me."

Bob boarded the plane to Japan, a bounce in his step exuding kinetic energy. I drove home, walked into our house and threw my purse down on the floor, lowering myself into the lounge chair in the living room. I drew in a big breath, exhaling a sigh as I shut my eyes and thought about what had happened a few months earlier.

I pushed the vacuum across the wool rug, the drone of the motor drowning out the outside noises. I stopped in the doorway, thinking I heard something, but I couldn't be sure. I turned off the switch. The insistent ring of the phone demanded an answer. I picked it up and heard Bob's anxious voice. "I thought you weren't home. I'm not feeling too good.....I've some pains in my chest."

My own heart turned over, "Where are you?"

"In the nurse's office at work."

"Do you want me to come down and get you?"

"No, but call our doctor and get the name of a cardiologist. The nurse thinks you should make an appointment for today."

My hand shook when I tried to replace the phone in the cradle, knocking it off the hook the first time. I called our doctor and he made the appointment with the cardiologist.

Head throbbing, I thought, Oh dear God,....not now. We haven't completed our dream yet. It's not fair...Lord please not now. I walked around the house, picking up objects and setting them down, wandering from room to room, seeing his picture at the tiller of VENUS in the bar, stroking the 3rd place cup we won in Master Mariner's race in 1966. I walked into the bedroom and picked up his sweater, holding it close, aware of the special scent that belong just to him. Then I heard his key in the door and I raced to the den, throwing my arms around him as he walked in. His gray face told me all I needed to know.

After the examination we sat in the Doctor's office, answering questions relating to his activities at work and home. A frowning cardiologist grilled Bob. "You're over weight which works your heart too much. You need more regular exercise, and you have to change what you eat. Do you smoke?"

"I used to, but I gave it up. But I never smoked more than a pack a day."

"One pack too many." he intoned piously.

You could tell he had never smoked, I thought.

"I'll need to run another thallium treadmill later and see if there's any improvement. You've got your work cut out for you."

Bob didn't care too much for the new doctor. "He seems to enjoy making me feel guilty."

Bob lost weight after a diet of fins and feathers. (fish and chicken) Every weekday morning at five Bob rode the exercycle for a half an hour, while I studied my Morse code in the same room. Just the presence of another person in the room helped us get through the boring parts of our work.

Six months later it was then my turn to give everyone a scare by almost dying from a ruptured appendix and peritonitis.

I opened my eyes and smiled. I *had* done the right thing by pushing his retirement, I thought. Sailing now sounded like a fantastic idea, so alive and adventuresome. With the earlier two reminders of our own mortality still vivid, I reasoned we were quite lucky. Some people never had a second chance to think life through.

A new, exciting chapter in our life had been born. When Bob returned home from his trip it was up to us to put our energies into getting the boat ready. But first we needed to figure out where in the world we wanted to go.

Chapter 3

A Boat Worth Her Weight In Gold

"You Captains bold and brave, hear our cries, hear our cries,
You Captains bold and brave, hear our cries,
You Captains brave and bold, tho' you seem uncontrolled
Don't for the sake of gold, lose you souls."

(Forecastle Chantey, Captain Kidd)

Bob returned from his trip, threw his suitcase in a corner, pulling off his tie in one swift motion. "Sure won't miss wearing these things."

I hung the offensive item on the rack. "Want to start planning our trip?" I said.

He shook his head up and down, removing his suit coat. "Why not. Let me get out of this monkey suit and I'll meet you in the living room."

Over the years we dreamed of spectacular sunsets, but choosing where to view them now became a game. We had talked about going north, bundled up in warm clothes while watching the northern lights. Or bask in the tropics with hardly any clothes, watching blood red clouds slide down the horizon and consumed by the sea. Our beautiful world offered us an embarrassment of riches.

I walked into the living room and picked up a large rust colored pillow, dropping it in front of the fireplace. I placed myself with my back toward the fire, hugging my knees to my chest. Bob strolled in sporting an old pair of stretch pants, soft shirt, and sweater. He sprawled on the couch with a sigh of satisfaction, his right arm flung across his closed his eyes.

I raised my head. "Want to go to Alaska?" I asked. "There could be a polar bear you might like to meet. I take that back, maybe a caribou would be better company."

Bob opened one eye, "Too cold and too short a season. If I want bear I would prefer your bare bottom. And speaking of cold, you look like you've got the right idea."

He got up off the couch and pulled down another pillow, moving closer to the heat. "Which reminds me," he said, "we still don't have a heater that works on our boat."

"It's good at making black smoke. It's just not any good at heating. Why don't we join the Canadian cruising boats going south to Mexico. They're trying to warm up too. We won't need a heater if we head in that direction."

Bob jumped up. "I'll get some of the cruising books we've been saving down stairs."

He returned with a big grin and an arm load of paper and books. He spread out the large area charts in front of the fire, opening the book, *World Cruising Routes.* He set aside several books on cruising Mexico. Reading intently for several minutes he looked up at me with a pleased expression. "Baja Mexico," he exclaimed. He took his finger and traced the California coast, ending up in Cabo San Lucas.

"Afterwards we can go over here," I said. I pointed to Isla Isabella and the West coast of Mexico, reading out loud the names of San Blas, Puerto Vallarta, Monzanillo, Acapulco.

Bob pursed his lips as he studied the over all chart. "And then home?"

I could feel a zing of adventure rising , and before I knew it I pointed to a group of islands in the South Pacific and said, "Marquesas." I must have a split personality, I thought, because half of me couldn't wait to retire and sail away, the other half shrank away from thinking about water, water, water everywhere.

"You're kidding," Bob said. "I've talked about cruising the south seas for years, but that's a big commitment. Suppose we don't like cruising?"

"I know we will....I can feel it."

I felt something all right, slight panic nipping at my toes as that fleeting zing of adventure flew out the window. I tried keeping my face neutral. "Besides, you promised me on our second date to take me to the south seas. What are you, an Indian giver?"

His voice squeaked in excitement. "Okay, then to Tahiti, Bora Bora, Hawaii," then trailed off as he looked at me intently. "Are you *sure* you want to do that? Most of our sailing has been up and down the coast in sight of land. You don't have to do it to please me."

"I know that. And yes, I do want to please you . The only thing you have to understand is I don't plan on having a love affair with the ocean."

He reached out. "You've never gotten over almost drowning have you, even after all these years of sailing."

"I've tried. I really *have* tried." It had been years since my last nightmare about the sea. I dropped my chin to my chest, and squeezed my eyes tight, but the images leaped out ....

I sat on a wide beach in Santa Monica in front of Cary Grant's home. Slippery baby oil covered my skin, sizzling in the hot August sun. Next to me sat my first boyfriend, Bill. I hung on every word he uttered, hoping he wouldn't noticed the new pimple on my chin. I felt so grown-up, alive, and maybe a little bit in love. A flutter tickled my stomach, and I just knew fourteen was going to be the best year in my life.

"Wow," he said, "those waves are really big today. Guess that's why everyone's sitting on the beach."

I glanced up at the water. A fifteen foot green wave stretched skyward, its crest a lighter shade, crowned with sand-filled dirty foam. With one final effort the breaker hung in mid air, curled over itself with a powerful roar, reaching out to the beach and devouring it with swift flowing suds.

"Not everyone," I said. "there's a guy going in with a surfboard. He's not afraid,"

Bill jumped up. "Me neither," he said in a voice filled with destain. He ran in long strides towards the water

"Hey, wait for me," I cried, trying to catch up. After all, I thought, nothing could hurt me. Bad things only happened to old people, or at least to other people.

I waded out ten feet behind Bill, startled when a wave formed in front of me, rising taller and taller, until there was nothing left to do but dive deep under the water. I hoped the roller would pass over me, but the powerful wave sucked me down and pounded me into the sand below. The swirling under-current took over my body, spinning me about like a pebble. I felt my first prickle of fear. I kicked my legs as hard as I could, beating my arms against the water. Gagging salt water seeped into my mouth. When my head broke to the surface I tried to call Bill, but was forced to shut my mouth when another breaker hit me, pushing me down again. Time stood still when the air escaped from my lungs, leaving me light headed. My chest cramped. When a dreamy sensation overwhelmed me I stopped fighting The stabbing hurt went away, and I half wondered why I wanted to sleep in such a strange place. Abruptly my head broke the surface again, but I couldn't make my eyes open. My mind sensed a wave when it rolled me over, then under and up again.... filling my ears, nose and swim suit with fine sand. I stopped moving. I lay in the receding water, afraid to breathe deeply because my chest hurt again.

A man's voice boomed out, "Is she breathing?"

Near my head a little girl's voice squealed , " I've never seen a dead person before daddy."

Dead? My eyes opened as I gulped a deep breath, gasping when I tried to stand. My knees buckled and I threw up. With my teeth chattering it was hard to let people know I was going to be all right. I looked around when Bill called my name. He ran toward me, his feet splashing water in all directions. He reached down and pulled me up, took a towel from one of the on-lookers, wrapping the terry cloth around my shoulders.

Bob took my hand in his, "Are you all right? You have that scared expression in your eyes when you looked up."

"I'm okay. I just remembered how stupid I was at fourteen. Almost drowning taught me a little about common sense. I just wish it hadn't spoiled enjoying the ocean. I used to have so much fun body surfing on those blown up pillows. I think having that recurring nightmare afterwards made it worse. It was so real."

"I remember a few when we first got married. You'd moan and move your arms and legs around, pulling all the covers off me."

"I know. You probably wondered what kind of a nut you married. Even though it's been years I can remember that dream like yesterday. I'd be walking on a beach and the water would come in and touch my foot.

I would try to run away, but my legs felt like they were made of rubber. Then I'd climb up a sand dune in slow motion, almost free, but the sand would shift under my feet, and I'd fall back down the hill. The water would creep toward me and barely touch my toes, then slowly drag me into the deep ocean. At that point I'd wake up."

"Once you scared the hell out of me screaming. I was so sound asleep I thought someone had come into the room and hurt you. Talk about adrenalin. My heart about jumped out of my chest." He rose up from his pillow, put his arms around me, and held me close. "I'll never let anything bad happen to you," he said softly. "I'll protect you with my life."

I felt safe next to him, and the memory faded. "I'll be fine. It really helps to talk about it. I guess I've put off consciously thinking about it for years." I snuggled up and relaxed by the fire. I wanted both of us to make this trip and have fun doing it.

While ironing the next morning I tried to reason with myself and shake off the old memory of near death. I argued with myself that I was the one who pointed to the Marquesas, so some inner part of me must believe we would be safe. I knew with my questionable swimming ability the only way for me to cope with the ocean would be to take each day one at a time. That's why we have lots of life jackets, I thought. But it would be strange to be out of sight of land for days at a time.

That night Bob brought out the Pacific Pilot Charts and spread them out on the dining room table. We arranged them in order of months to determine which particular month was the best for a long passage to the Marquesas, choosing the one with the least chance of encountering gales, and a reasonable direction of the wind in order to make good time.

Bob reached over the pile of papers to pick up a pencil and notebook. "Our marine insurance says we can't enter Mexico until November, so that's a set date."

"Why so late? I thought October weather was warm then."

"Sometimes Mexico has tropical storms coming up from the gulf in October."

"What does that mean in terms of leaving Mexico for the Marquesas?"

"Just a minute. I need to study December and January pilot charts. You take February and March."

We both were absorbed in our reading, looking for the number of cyclones that occurred (on the average) for these months. A cyclone was definitely an experience I wanted to miss if possible.

I put down my charts, "February doesn't look so hot, but March might be all right. What about December and January?"

"Cyclones. Hand me March." He studied the chart and looked up. It looks like we'll stay in Mexico from November to March, ...how far we get depends on how good a time we're having."

We went back to *World Cruising Routes* and looked at different passages. The names of islands called out to us, Tahiti, Moorea, Bora Bora, Huihine, Raiatea and Hawaii. Just reading the names sent little shocks of excitement through us.

After several months we realized planning to retire could be both thrilling and scary. The good news was we were finally going to get off the pot and sail away; the bad news being the unknown financial picture. Would we be able to afford the same pot in the future?

This dilemma created the beginning of the "Cruising List Caper." We thought we needed to jot down a few essential items, but hours later our crabbed fingers still clutched our pens, and we realize we were trapped by chains made of paper and words. I slammed my pen down in frustration. "I can't believe this. It reminds me of Mickey Mouse in the old movie *Fantasia*. Do you remember it?"

"Yes, Mickey was a sorcerer's apprentice. He cleaned up after Merlin's spells."

"The part that reminds me of us is when he goofs and tries to create some spells of his own. His broom divided, and soon there were hundreds of brooms, but he couldn't stop the spell."

"I see," said Bob "We've created a 'list spell,' and for everything we cross off two or three new items take its place."

"You got it. I just can't figure out how to stop it."

"You can't. Hand me another piece of paper, I've thought of something else we have to do."

My scream of frustration didn't seem to phase him, for he continued writing, the list growing longer than Methuselah's beard.

Our next big planning job was our getaway, figure out what to do with the house, how to pay bills, and most of all, build up a good cruising nest egg. Bob sat at his desk in the den, his head buried in another long "to do" list. I sat in a chair beside him, scribbling on a yellow legal tablet. He put his list down and swung around in the leather chair. "We won't sell the house. There's too many years of work getting it the way we want."

"I agree, we couldn't afford to buy it back anyway."

"We'll rent it. The money will pay for our cruising as well as the mortgage, taxes and keeping the house up."

I frowned, the thought of someone else living in my house made me uncomfortable. "We've never rented any house of ours. Do we have to?"

"Be practical. You can't leave a house empty for a year. Besides, we need the cash."

"I wish there was another way. Too bad Lori lives in Southern California. She could live here. Or maybe Bill would want to live here."

"There's no way he wants to do the commute I've been doing. His house is only twenty minutes from his job."

"Okay, so we'll rent the house out. But I want to make sure it's the right couple. One who will love it like we do."

Bob patted my hand. "We'll do the best we can."

I knew we didn't have a lot of choice when we added up the money it would take to buy the extra equipment needed for the boat. Our cruising nest egg began to dwindle, disappearing like a snack down a teenager's gullet.

Bob held out a long list, "Here's some of the equipment we need to buy."

I looked at the list in disbelief, "Holy cow, are you trying to buy out West Marine?"

"It may look like it, but going so far off shore changes things. We need another anchor, Satellite Navigation, ham radio.."

"Whoa," I said. "I haven't passed the test for my General license yet."

"Oh you will. It's just a matter of time."

But how much time, I thought. I had passed my theory test earlier, but failed the thirteen WPM code. A Technician's license wouldn't allow me to call the family from the boat. One more thing to deal with later. I sighed, "Okay, what else?"

"Spare parts for the main engine, generator, outboard motor, rubber dinghy that can plane, 250 feet of 3/8 anchor chain, sextant..."

"Stop, I can't stand it. At this rate we'll have to sell the house to pay for parts."

"Not to worry. If we start buying stuff a little each month it won't strap us. We have a year."

My head started to ache and I walked into the bathroom to get some aspirin. I could still hear Bob's pen scratching as he mumbled, "We'll need new rigging, our's is old, the mainsail's too light and the pocket is stretched......"

Not nearly so stretched as our pocketbook I thought. I wish someone would give us a gold mine, even a little one would do. My hand picked out two aspirin and I swallowed them quickly, trying to blot out Bob's voice, "New sheets for the jib........."

Chapter 4

WORK, WORK, WORK

"Come listen unto me a while
And I will tell you then
The hardships and the misery
Of life on a merchantman.
(Forecastle Chantey, Old Sailor's Song)

In the following days I found no amount of aspirin could cure the pain of watching our money leak out of our bank account into the "hole in the water," and flow into the coffers of every marine chandlery within driving distance from our house. Each day our carbon covered fingers clasped Visa charge slips while we worked toward being the most prepared boat to leave San Francisco harbor. One half of me respected and was thrilled by each item we added to the boat, but the opposite half felt a bit reticent about spending so much money, especially with retirement just around the corner. I didn't want to end up eating a boiled shoelace for dinner like Charlie Chaplin did in an old movie. In our case, our dinner would be a boiled jib sheet, or a roasted Sat Nav.

Winter days blended, folding themselves into warm longer days, heralding the arrival of spring. While tiny flowers pushed up the earth around them searching for the sun, new boat projects appeared like weeds, seeking our hands to complete their mutant growth.

On a rainy April night after dinner I washed off the few remaining scraps of our spicy sweet and sour chicken, scooped up the silverware and set it into the dishwasher. My wet hand grasped a wine glass. It slipped out of my fingers, crashing to the floor, and tiny shards of glass flew in all directions. I stepped back in surprise, crunching several pieces of glass into the vinyl.

"Damn," I said. "I thought I only dropped things when I was pregnant."

Bob looked up with a sardonic smile, "And we know that's not possible. But the broken glass does remind me about insurance."

"What insurance? The house? Our boat policy isn't any good once we leave California."

"I know. But I've been wondering whether we should get a cruising policy since we've added a lot of equipment to the boat. Give our agent a call tomorrow and ask him about price and availability."

The next morning I called the insurance office. The agent put me on hold while she searched for our boat policy, and I chewed my pencil top in frustration when forced to listen to canned elevator music. Mercifully in a few minutes the music stopped, an aloof voice came on the line. "Sorry to have kept you waiting Mrs. Allen, I have your policy in front of me. Now what is it you want again?"

"We're going cruising on our boat to Mexico and the south seas. My husband wants to know about off shore cruising insurance. How much is it, and what do we have to do to get it."

"Well, it's quite expensive and hard to get. Depending on the size of your boat, oh.. I see it's forty-one feet. Probably around three thousand dollars a year."

"Three thousand," I screeched. "For just a year? How come so high?"

Too many collections by owners on their policies. Many companies are dropping cruising policies entirely."

That bit of information didn't exactly make my day. A collection meant damage of some kind, or at its worst, a boat sitting on a reef being ravaged by coral, waves and wind. I cleared my throat, "What do we have to do to qualify for insurance, even if you can find a company willing to write a policy?"

"We have a particular surveyor that some companies insist on using. He'll go over your boat, and if he's satisfied with the boat's safety and you and your husband's experience level, he'll make a satisfactory report to the company. They will make the final decision. I have to warn you the surveyor is very picky."

I placed the phone back in its cradle, wondering what kind of an unholy inquisition we would be facing. I didn't have to worry about Bob's experience, but what if the surveyor didn't think I was good enough for crew? At that moment my mind went into over-drive, and a scary scenario rolled through my head.

The doorbell rings and I open the door. A grim faced man stands on the stoop holding a heavy notebook in one hand, and a sharp pick in the other, announcing he is the surveyor. I take him to the boat, and when we go aboard he reaches into his back pocket and takes out a huge magnifying glass. A wicked smile crosses his face. "Harrumph," he exclaims, as he lumbers through our boat, searching out criminal acts of irresponsibility in our preparation. He fills his notebook with scribbles, careful to keep them hidden from my sight. I try to watch him and see if he is sticking holes in our fiberglass with his sharp pick. Abruptly he turns to me and snarls, "What makes you think you can sail?"

I shrink back, my hand on my chest, "I've been doing it for years. Why I even brought the boat home by myself from San Rafael."

"So,....San Rafael isn't in the south seas. You don't look like a sailor to me."

I looked down and noticed my hand was still holding on to the phone handset. What a worry wart I am, I sighed, always looking at the worst case. My kids were right to name me Mrs. W. Wart.

The following week the surveyor arrived. I opened the door and found a grim faced man loaded down with a notebook and pick. Deja vu suddenly smacked me in the chest, my heart skipped a beat. I tried to keep from staring as I swung open the door.

"I'm Jim, the surveyor. I suppose you're Mrs. Allen"

"Yes, please come in. Bob is down on the boat waiting for you. Ah, it's in a slip behind our house."

He looked at the tall mast rising out of the backyard area and pursed his lips. "I noticed when I drove in."

His long legs carried him swiftly down the driveway, leaving me to skip to keep up with him. I watched him step aboard our boat, his steel blue eyes sweeping over the deck in a practiced motion. Bob's voice rang out in a greeting and an exchange of names took place. For the next hour the surveyor checked out ever hidey hole, through hull fitting, electrical connections, and safety equipment. When Bob went up to the boat house to get the new EPIRB (emergency automatic radio beacon), Jim motioned me to the engine room. "Do you know what model engine this is?"

"Yes, it's a Perkins 4-108. We used to have a Westerbeke 4-107, but the crank broke coming up the coast in 1982."

His eyes widened and his mouth worked back and forth as if suppressing a smile. He pointed to our generator next to the motor and looked expectantly. I found my voice squeaked when I answered. "The generator is an Onan 7.5 KW. Bob said we didn't need that much power, but a two cylinder engine wouldn't vibrate as much as the smaller one cylinder engine."

Bob returned with the EPIRB and Jim made more notes in his book, rechecked the 110 wiring panel, and sat down the main salon, spreading his fingers out on his thighs. A long silence hung in the air. I held my breath until I looked at his face and saw the beginning of a smile,...well a sort of a smile. His weathered face resembled a road map, making it hard to see which deep line went up to smile, or which furrow turned down to frown. He reached into his notebook, took out a list and handed it to Bob.

"I written down a few things that need to be changed. Over all the boat is in good shape. I'll have to see the boat out of the water, so make arrangements for a haul out. I also want you both to write out a sailing experience resume and send it to me at this address."

He reached into his back pocket and pulled out his wallet, removed a card and handed it to Bob. He put his wallet back and stood up, a broad smile creasing his face. "It's been great meeting you. I know you'll have a wonderful trip. I'll be sending in my report after the haul out and receiving your resumes."

He crossed over the main salon and started up the companionway steps, stopped and turned his head. "You're smart to go after your dream while you can. I've been planning to cruise for a long time too. Maybe next year will be my time." He let himself off the boat, his boat shoes making a soft slapping sound as he walked up the gangway.

I looked at Bob and blurted, "Did you hear him say we would have a great trip? Doesn't that mean he thinks we're going to do all right?"

"Slow down...I think so, but he has to have the sailing resumes anyway for the insurance company. We'll know for sure when the company writes us. Right now I want to see what he has on this list."

Bob read the first page, slowly turning to the next page, and then re-reading the first part.

"Well, what did he say we had to do, rebuild the boat, or spend another thousand dollars?"

Bob looked up and grinned. "It's not that bad. The obvious things were to update the fire extinguisher, getting rid of the navy one that's so old. He wants a plastic cover over the ex posed terminals in the 110 volt circuit breakers in the engine room. He also wants a separate vapor proof battery switch for the generator, extra clip on battery type running lights in case of failure of our regular ones, have our life raft certified, and install a manual bilge pump in the engine room. Those were some of the main things, but there are a few smaller items."

I took the paper from his hands and read through each item. "Do you still want to spend three thousand on a cruising policy?"

"Yes. If we lose a mast in the south seas you can kiss ten thousand dollars goodbye to get a new one."

"Ouch," I exclaimed.

"Let's do it this time. We'll know better if it was a good idea after we've cruised for awhile."

During the next few weeks Bob sent in our resumes, and completed the tasks the surveyor suggested. Two weeks later we had *Maria* hauled out at the local boat yard. Pungent smelling barnacles clung tenaciously to our keel, despite our best attempts to dislodge them with a sharp putty knife. Bob decided to get one of the yard men to help.

Later we both crawled under the hull to check on some small blisters that had formed on the hull. He took a small knife and popped one. Water ran out in a little rivulet, then stopped. I watched for a minute and said, "Reminds me of popping zits as a teenager. If you want I can take over this job and you can go on to something else."

"Good, I need to install the transducer for the Sat Nav."

I drilled out each little blister using a tiny hobby kit bit. I was so intent on my job I jumped when a voice behind me said, "Well, I see both the Allens are hard at work."

I turned to see a pair of legs belonging to the surveyor, Jim, his head bent sideways to see my work. "The blisters don't look bad, not like some of the ones I've seen. Drain 'em, then fill 'em with epoxy."

"Thank goodness they're not very big."

He laughed good naturedly, "Don't want to keep you from working, or me either. I have some surveying work of my own. After I finish looking over the hull and see the changes Bob made, I'll make my report and send the papers to you."

He's such a nice man, I thought. Can't understand why I had been so scared of him. Although seeing his stern face, a notebook and pick in his hands, had given me a start. The only thing missing from my daydream had been the magnifying glass.

A week later a letter arrived from him written in a most positive attitude. Jim spoke of the professional manner in which the work required had been done, and how he had complete confidence that the "couple" could make their trip and return safely. He felt that we would not have to have a third crew member to qualify for the insurance.

I picked up the report, reading with avid interest up to the part about returning safely and exclaimed, "What does he mean we'll return. Of course we're going to return."

But he knew better about returning than most people, because not all boats or their owners return safely. A fact which I accepted, but didn't necessarily like.

As the weeks passed quickly I began to yearn for Bob to quit work so we could both work full time getting ready for our cruise. One night after dinner I brought the subject up again.

"I'm worried about getting everything done as long you're working. I can't do it all."

"You worry too much."

My face burned as I spat out, "And you're not worried enough."

"Calm down. I don't have to worry, because you do enough for both of us."

I stomped out of the room, exasperated. With May just around the corner, the rest of the months would take wing, leaving us earth bound, not water borne. I heard the bedroom door open and Bob's voice, "Okay, I'll tell my boss I want to retire in June. Now quit fretting and come back into the living room. I hate to fight."

May arrived. Bob awoke Monday morning and hummed *What Do You Do With A Drunken Sailor* to himself while shaving. He actually smiled when he put on his shirt and tied his tie. Before leaving for work he hugged me and said gleefully, "Today's the big day. I'm going to tell my boss I'm retiring."

"What do you think he'll say?"

"Don't know. He'll probably be surprised though."

"I don't think he'll be too surprised. For the last year the only ties you've worn had sailboats on them."

Bob threw back his head and laughed, "Wish me luck. First time in a long time I'm anxious to get to work."

I couldn't wait for him to get home to hear how it went with his boss. I kept going from job to job, but I couldn't seen to complete any of them. At seven that night I heard the diesel engine of the car on the upper road and hurried to meet him in the garage. He drove in, shut off the engine and climbed out. From his expression I couldn't tell how it had gone.

"Come on," I said. "Tell me what happened."

He walked in the house, took off his tie and hung it up. "First get me a glass of wine."

Oh, oh, I thought. Is he thirsty or upset. I knew there was no point in asking him more questions because he would tell me in his own time. After he finished changing into comfortable clothes, I poured white wine into a glass and handed it to him.

"Come out on the deck and we'll sit and talk," he said.

I sat down in a chair next to him, nervously sipping my wine, trying not to scream out questions. After a few quiet moments he said, "My boss was a little surprised, but not too much. I told him I wanted to retire in June in order to get ready for our trip."

"And?" I asked.

"He wants me to finish up a few things, go to Germany and announce it at our overseas meeting in early July."

"Oh rats, we'll lose another month. We planned to leave in September sometime, and this delay may put the whole thing off."

"It's not as bad as you think. He suggested I take you along too since some of the other wives plan to be there. Actually, I've so many frequent flier miles you can fly free on an upgrade,...and...we can have a little vacation. We'll just work a little harder when we get back to make up for the delay."

I drew a deep breath, thought about not working on all our projects, and decided not only wasn't it such a bad idea, it was a great idea. "Might as well enjoy the luxury hotels. Once you retire it will be budget travel packages from then on."

Now that we had a firm date for retirement we decided it would be wise to take some educational courses, namely Advanced First Aid, and a refresher course in Celestial Navigation. Bob was not thrilled with the prospect of taking a twice a week course for six weeks in First Aid while he still worked, but he would be less than thrilled if we found out at sea the course would have saved either of us pain and sorrow.

Two weeks into the course in the middle of June Bob drove home, starved, eyes half mast, and his tail dragging. "I can't make it to First Aid tonight. I'm too bushed."

"I'll get dinner, but I still want to go to class. Sit down, have a glass of wine and relax."

Wine and food had amazing restorative powers. He pushed back his plate, finished his wine and exclaimed, "Much better. Maybe I can make it after all."

"Tonight's important because it's CPR," I said.

"That's for heart attacks isn't it? What do we do?"

"You get to kiss a dummy, hold her nose and blow into her mouth while I pound on her chest and count breaths."

"What's the dummy look like?"

"Just what you like, she's blonde."

We took the course with half a dozen firemen who had to meet a yearly requirement to keep up their CPR cards. They were much more relaxed than we were, and their humor in the class proved to be rib tickling. During the first CPR demonstration a muscular, bearded fireman joked to Bob, "Hey, watch that dummy. If you really get her to breathe she'll be drunk after inhaling your wine."

The First Aid course kept us so busy we decided to wait until after Bob retired in July to take the Celestial Navigation review. We would have changed our minds if there had been a spell that increased our days by another twelve hours, but alas, the only spell still working was the "List" spell.

We returned from Germany and attacked the house and boat with fervor, trying to get both in shape. With the job taken care of, our two kids educated, married and busy with their own lives, our only responsibility remaining was our fifteen year-old cat, Poosy Gato, who had at least four of her nine lives left. We would have to find someone who would feed and care for an aging love sponge. We hoped we could rent our cat (free) to the new lessees of our house, whoever they might be.

In early August Bob finished installing the rest of the Satellite Navigation and turned it on. I looked up at the luminous numbers in the display, remembering how different our first cruise down the coast was in *Maria*. "Hard to believe on our first trip in 1974 we only had a compass and depth sounder," I said.

"The thing that sticks in my mind about the trip was the sail back up the coast. You said you wouldn't go out the gate again until we got a dodger."

"That's because most of the waves went over the bow and landed right at the wheel where I sat. I wore my sun glasses out rinsing the salt water off them so I could see. You have to admit the dodger has made me one happy wife."

"It's been worth the expense. At least you go out willingly now."

I thought about all the equipment we had added the last ten years. Some to make the boat safer and easier, others to help us on our cruise. We now had a fathometer which could read to six hundred feet, ham radio, VHF radio, Radar, Satellite Navigation, auto pilot, self steering vane, wind direction and speed indicator, weather fax, his and her sextants, and a radar warning device to alert us to ship traffic. We now looked like the Fairsea ocean liner off on a world cruise. We had so many warning beepers; (engine oil or over heat, propane or fuel leak, bilge alarm, sat nav power failure, depth sounder) that if they all went off at the same time it would sound like a Caribbean steel drum, with each alarm fighting for the right to lead the tune.

Bob's voice broke into my reverie. He pointed to the Sat Nav. "I've got it working. See, there's the Lat and Lon of where we are."

"I could have told you that. We're home. Which reminds me... we need to talk about how we handle our home. We've been so busy worrying about the boat, and I'm getting anxious about the house."

"Wrong, not *we* worry, *you* worry."

I felt like a sadist who had just popped a kid's balloon. Why did I have to be born with a worry gene, I wondered.

Reluctantly Bob shut off the power switch on the Sat Nav and sat down. "I guess we do have some decisions to make."

Chapter 5

WHEN A HOUSE IS
NOT A HOME

"Oh, Boston's a fine town, with ships in the bay,
And I wish in my heart it was there I was today.
I wish in my heart I was far away from here,
A sitting in my parlor and talking to my dear.
Then it's home, dearie, home, it's home I want to be."

(Forecastle Chantey, "Home, Dearie, Home)

Bob leaned back into the cushions and folded his arms across his chest. "I know the house is important to you. It's just I've been caught up in boat work. It's hard for me to concentrate on two things at once."

"I know, but you know me. My mind is usually going in ten directions. Right now it's on the house."

"All right. What concerns you the most?"

"I know we have to rent the house, but what are we going to do with all the furniture?"

"We'll probably have to store it. We could use the boathouse for part of it. If we're careful we can stack most of it and protect it with a cover.

What won't fit will have to go into a storage garage."

I tried to imagine some of my favorite Chinese tables and the dining room set residing in the cold, dank boathouse. It hurt. "What about the big items that are too heavy to carry down there?" I said.

"If we find the right tenant we could trust them to take care of the big items."

But where was the right tenant, I thought, never realizing that luck would play into our hands, delivering the perfect family right into our special home. Several days after our last conversation we received a call from our neighbor, Craig, telling of a family from England who was look-ing for a house on the water.

"We've known them for several years and I would trust them implic-itly. They keep things cleaner than I do," he said.

That did it. Craig was the only person I knew whose white painted boat engine was forbidden to have an oil stain on it, and his scrubbed bilges shouted "Clean." One could eat out of them. Not that I would, but they were impressive.

We invited the English family over to see our place, and after a short visit we all agreed this was to be their home for a year. Of course, when things seemed to be going perfectly there appeared the good news-bad news-syndrome. With the family came their dog. He was a perfectly nice dog with itchy skin, his leg beating a constant Congo rhythm on the floor while spreading fur in all directions into the air. I could only hope an English family of fleas hadn't stowed way away with him. A flea was a flea, no matter how proper its British background might be. After think-ing about the dog we came to a wonderful compromise with the family. Our cat purred her way into the lease, with the family's promise to love and care for the old dear.

With the signing of legal work out of the way, I could concentrate on boxing up all our belongings. The packing dragged. Each time I started to wrap up something special, I remembered how we came by it. It start-ed with a comical statue. The arms reached out, ready to embrace the nearest being. Written across the bottom were the words, "I love you." It brought tears to my eyes when I remembered the day Lori gave it to me. Her gift pulled at my heart strings because we had reached a point in our relationship where we both suffered from the normal love/hate relation-ship between mother and a strong willed fifteen year old daughter. As long as I didn't bother her, (check up) she tolerated me. I loved her, but there were days I definitely didn't like her, or what she did. It proved a learning experience for both, because she wasn't the only one that had to grow and change, so did her mother. Lori matured and become my best friend, a treasured relationship. I hugged the statue and wrapped it in tissue paper.

I unrolled an old poster with two buzzards sitting on a branch. Underneath it said, "Patience hell, I'm going to kill something." This had been tacked up by Bill in his room during one of his most impatient moments. Inside the poster lived another one from his wall, given to him by Lori when he had been saddened by a lost love. It said, "Love is like a butterfly. Leave it alone and it will come and sit quietly on your shoulder." I think I'll give Bill these posters, I thought. They're the quintessence of his life back then.

My fingers closed on an old manila package, knowing at once what it contained. Blue stationary peeked through a hole in the envelope, revealing Bob's wide, expansive handwriting. Love letters, lots of them, poured out into my lap, written during the times he marched in drills at Reserve Officer camp, others when he plowed the seas near Korea on the destroyer *Harry E. Hubbard.* Stamp cancellations of 1954, 1955 marked the corners, making me wonder how the years slipped by so fast. I read through some of them, crazy at times, love starved, lonely for home, but excited at seeing Tokyo, Kyoto, Unzen and Nagasaki. Were we really that young once? Several "business cards" from Japanese taxi drivers dropped out, "You come to my house for girls, just like home." I remembered writing back that his business *better* be kept at his home. It had scared me to think he lived so far away, having an everyday life that didn't include me anymore, especially peppered with so many temptations. I stopped and looked at the clock, realizing two hours had flown. With a grunt of resignation I stopped reading any more letters, because dishes couldn't pack themselves, nor decisions be made about what to keep, or what went to the salvage shop for someone else to cherish.

Each day started with a half hour of Morse code practice and ended the same way. Dit, dit, da until I wanted to howl at the moon. Boring, boring, boring, but necessary. In between times more objects were packed away, with the house taking on an impersonal look. Walls wailed in mourning without pictures to brighten them, absent rugs made the floors appear faded and worn, rooms suffered in loneliness without the comfort of furniture and nick knacks. What happened to my wonderful house? Moving out had transformed our dwelling into a hollow four walled nothing, no life within to reflect that a warm, loving family had lived there. I take that back. I saw the pencil lines on one wall that showed how much each child had grown during each year. Bill's line showed he was taller than Bob, and Lori's line beat mine by an inch. That made me feel like the house belonged to us, even just a little.

Mid August arrived, carrying thick damp fog from the sea to do battle with the hot winds from the inland valley, wrapping its cold fingers around mine. After a day of organizing the canned food, writing the date on the top, and then writing down the item in a notebook, weariness set in my bones. I sat down in the barbecue area on the beach, elbows resting on my knees, and my hands on either side of my chin trying to hold up my head. I felt a kiss brush the back of my neck, and Bob appeared, a glass of wine in his hand for me, and one for himself. He sat down next to me. "Time to set a date to leave, otherwise we'll stay here and keep working on the boat forever."

"Don't even say that in jest. I'm so tired I could leave tomorrow."

"Tomorrow is a little soon. How does September 19th sound?"

"Like a million years away right now. All right, September 19th is it. But you know what?"

"What?"

I always thought being retired meant relaxing. Retired is spelled wrong. It should be spelled t i r e d. The only "re" sound in retired is in ridiculous."

The next month we worked ten to twelve hours a day, seven days a week, trying to get our house, boat and affairs in order. Bill drove up from San Jose, packed up our computer, printer, files, and checkbook, promising to keep us solvent and maintain our good credit. We had given him power of attorney to handle our affairs, and had full faith in his ability and caring. Now he was in charge of taking care of *us,* strange but comforting.

We went to dinner at his home a couple of nights later to visit, as well as go over our accounts. He sat in the middle of his living room surrounded by our files. I think for the first time he realized the enormity of what he had gotten himself into.

"Are you sure you want to take on all this?" I asked.

"Yes. You've done so much for me all these years. It's about time I can do something for you."

Bob's face softened, and I felt my jaw constrict, swallowing hard at the lump in my throat. Our son, yet not just our son anymore, but a husband and father...and now a savior of our financial world.

I smiled inside. He had always been such a serious youngster; avid science fiction reader, good at school, interested in chemistry. Of course his interest in that turned out to be making gun powder which he used in a small cannon. Thank God he didn't decide to make nitro glycerin. He had access to the formulae. An associate of Bob's, a PhD. in Chemistry, loaned Bill a book about the inventor of nitro glycerin, Nobel, complete with formulae. His only comment to Bill was that he would promise to read the beginning chapter when Nobel began his experiments. Bill read the book in awe. He declared afterwards that there was no way he would fool around with anything that volatile. He had good sense then, and good sense now. He wouldn't fool around with our volatile check book.

My musings were interrupted when I heard Bill's voice, "I don't want you to be concerned about Lori either. If she needs any help I'll be there to be back her up."

"Oh you don't have to worry about her," I laughed. "She has her husband and baby to keep her busy."

Later those words would clang like cymbals, reminding me that life always has some little surprises in store.

The days and weeks passed quickly, too quickly. Our friends dropped by to check our progress, and as the departure time came closer, our family began to openly be concerned about our safety. Roll reversal had arrived in spades. I think the kids were still unable to believe their easily accessed parents were actually going to be at sea for a year, out of reach. It is always hardest for those left at home, imagining all kinds of things from pirates to storms. Lori put her thoughts in perspective. "I've always thought parents were supposed to be home when their kids called them. It'll seem so strange."

We now lived aboard the boat because our English family moved into the house. I looked up at glass windows of the house, wondering what everyone was doing inside. The family had moved in their own furniture, strange bright pictures hung on the walls, the sound of childish laughter echoed in the rooms where our kids used to be. But a new sound could be heard, the thump of a dog leg as he scratched his fur.

I looked at the huge pile equipment on the cement driveway waiting to be put aboard *Maria*. "How can we possibly get it all in our boat. "There won't be room for us," I complained

"The spare engine and generator parts will go under the seat in the cockpit, along with another anchor chain and line. We'll find room for the rest inside the boat."

The word "osmosis" came into my mind, figuring somehow the boat would magically absorb it all. I only wished it could happen without us having to carry it all aboard.

That night Bob and I curled up close to each other in our sleeping bag, and I thought about some of the horror stories I had heard from returning cruisers. Some couples found living in confined quarters for long periods of time stretched their marriage into a hanging noose. Even couples who had been happily married for years found too much closeness brought out the destructive Mr. Hyde personality in the captain, with a Lucretia Borzia urge by the wife to get even. I can hear it now, a furious wife saying, "Poison you say? How was I to know the canned food had gone bad. It was just an unlucky trick of fate that he liked spam and I didn't."

Unfortunately, a few of the cruising marriages hit the rocks, sinking faster than a boat run down by a freighter. It made me think about our own personality differences. Our approach to life and problem solving were diametrically opposed in some ways. I walked fast, thought fast, made snap decisions, and lots of mistakes because of the above. Bob's thought process moved slowly, logically and in an ordered manner toward making decisions. Conversely in driving I always change lanes early, Bob waited much later until we had to whip into the next lane. Would that drive us crazy in such close quarters? I rolled over and whispered in Bob's ear, "You don't suppose well be like the couples who break up after cruising?"

"Are you kidding? Of course not, as long as you remember who's captain."

I punched him playfully in the ribs and moved closer. At some other time I would have to remind him that I had decided to be the Admiral. The title Admiral had such a nice ring to it.

September 18 arrived and found us packing, packing, packing. The boat fairly burst, filled to capacity with everything we could conceive of needing at some time during the year's cruise. "Here's my baritone ukulele," I said. I can't forget that. Now maybe I'll have enough time to learn the rest of the sea chanties."

"I really started something when I bought our first sea record."

"The first record was the Coast Guard Academy one wasn't it? My favorite memory was the time your mom bought "Bawdy Sea Shanties" in Sears for your birthday. We had no idea it was such a risque record."

"I know," he said. Remember when she insisted on listening to it one night? I tried to tell her it wasn't her kind of music. I think she almost dropped her drawers when they played *Three Old Whores From Winnipeg*."

"She didn't move, but her eyes bugged out when the song started." I sang a couple of lines, "Three old whores from Winnipeg were a drinking sherry wine. Said one old whore to the other old whore, none is bigger than mine. Said the whore to the other old whore, I'd laugh to be so small, many a ship that sailed right in and never came out at all."

After a few more choruses I laughed so hard my stomach hurt, finally managing a gasp, "She turned pink and looked at you with surprise, "Oh my, I hope you enjoy your record. Hmmm, and to think I bought that at Sears."

We went back to our job stowing gear, giggling to ourselves.

The last things to be stowed were the five gallon containers of diesel fuel, each tied securely to part of the rail. The outboard motor sat on its teak perch, attached to the aft rail, wearing a special cover to keep the salt water away from it. Bob brought our ten foot New Zealand dinghy along side and attached the extra halyard to a sling. He handed up the oars, climbed up on to *Maria's* deck while I stowed the them. He had made a special cradle to hold the dinghy upside down on the forward deck. The oars, and dinghy sail fit underneath the boat. We raised the dinghy up, carefully bringing her over the life lines, then gently lowered the line and turning the boat over on its cradle. The dinghy covered the main hatch, a great disadvantage because it made it dark below. No matter how we turned it there wasn't any other place to fit the dinghy. At times I wished for a Genie who could make it disappear until needed.

We went to bed that night exhausted, exhilarated, and anxious to get on with our new lives, surrounded by aching muscles and thoughts that we might have been a little naive in estimating the work involved in preparing for our long awaited dream voyage.

Bob took off his work clothes and climbed into his pajamas, groaning as he tried to lift his leg into the bottoms, "I'm so tired I don't know if I can go to sleep."

"Me too, but I guess we still have to leave tomorrow huh?"

"Oh yes, we'll go. But maybe just as far as Half Moon Bay. That's only five hours."

Sleeping fitfully that night our dreams called out to us in the dark, *just wait until tomorrow...*

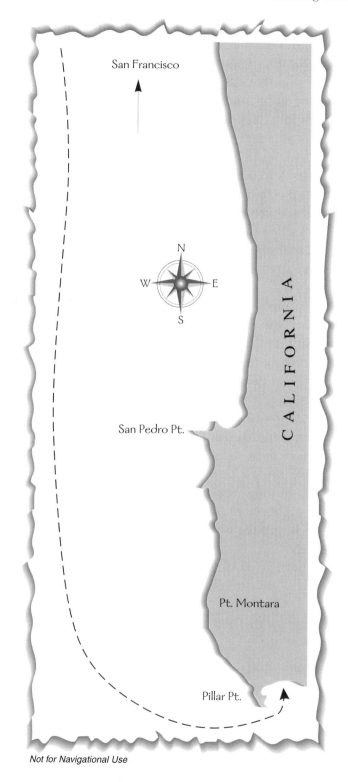

San Francisco

N
W E
S

CALIFORNIA

San Pedro Pt.

Pt. Montara

Pillar Pt.

Not for Navigational Use

Chapter 6

"D" DAY

"Our anchors we'll weigh and our sails we will set,
Good bye fare ye well, good bye fare ye well.
The friends we are leaving we leave with regret,
Good bye fare ye well, good bye fare ye well."

("Homeward Bound," Windless or Capstan Sea Chantey)

September nineteenth arrived with a bang at 6:45 am when heavy foot steps echoed above our heads from the deck. Bob sat up, quickly pulling on his pants and scrambling up the companionway steps. I dressed in my jeans, and threw on a tee shirt, padding up the steps behind him. We were surprised to find our friend Chris dressed in a suit, holding a bag of donuts in one hand, and a container of hot coffee in the other. He grinned, "With so much going on today I thought you might need these."

Bob laughed and reached eagerly for the coffee, "You're a true friend. Thanks."

"I have enough for other people too. God I wish I was going."

Chris's voice strained with emotion, his eyes darting around the boat, mentally checking out the equipment.

Impulsively Bob grasped Chris's hand, almost spilling his coffee. The touch said more than words. My attention centered on the beautiful, warm day, welcoming us with a gentle breeze that set the Monterey pine needles quivering. A little gust of wind swept over the lawn ruffling the surface like waves at sea, while white Shasta daisies in the flower beds dipped their heads in greeting, swaying back and forth like tiny ballet dancers.

Soon other friends started to arrive, each looking restrained in their working clothes, wearing an expression of wistfulness. Neighbors remained pensive. One boating friend exhibited an entirely different emotion. His hands tightly gripped the dock rail as if to keep himself from leaping on to the boat, exclaiming loud enough for all to hear, "It should be me going."

We munched on our donuts and drank coffee, trying to make it seem like an ordinary morning in order to keep us from jumping out of our skin in excitement. Chris walked over and whispered to Bob, "I thought you were going to leave at nine o'clock. I have to get to work."

Other people who needed to get to work began to shuffle from one foot to the next. We uttered a few nervous giggles. Bob looked out at the group, put down his coffee cup and started our engine.

"I guess this is it, "D" day," Bob said.

A big cheer went up from the crowd. While waiting for the engine to warm up we stepped off the boat and hugged our friends.

"I'll write when we can," I said. "But don't worry if the letters are slow. Mail is a problem outside of the US."

Bob laughed, "It's enough of a problem in the U.S."

My neighbor Miriam looked up with tears glistening in her eyes, her face such a picture of doom I felt she thought she might never see us again.

"Hey, we'll be back, don't worry," I said.

My voice sounded confident, covering up a niggling worry in the back of my mind, because who really knows for sure what life has planned for you.

We climbed back aboard our boat amidst the sound of snapping cameras, and as Chris untied our lines, a big cheer sent us off. It was "D" day all right, definitely departing, leaving both of us numb from excitement. When Bob engaged the gears the boat surged forward, pushing aside the bay water and sending it outward in little waves toward our house. I looked up at my bedroom, no longer ours for a year, wondering how I

Goodbye, have a good trip, have fun, be careful.

could leave the security of our home. Bob reached over and squeezed my hand, his eyes searching out the house too. For a single instant I felt a twinge of regret, then remembered a friend who cruised Mexico for six months and said, "When you pass under the Golden Gate bridge you won't give your house another thought." Ha, I thought, but she isn't me.

We turned our heads, waved to our friends one more time, then headed *Maria Elena* out the Strawberry channel into Richardson Bay. My ears still held the echo of voices saying "Goodbye, have a good trip, have fun, be careful, come home safe."

The Sausalito channel markers became a familiar blur, but about to be forgotten as new markers appeared in our lives. We steered past a long forgotten boat relic, half sunk, the remnant of its life's existence being devoured daily by worms and barnacles. I glanced at Clipper harbor, noting the slips which sheltered each owner's dream boat, or nightmare, as the case may be. We passed the Spinnaker restaurant, watching the busy clean up crew prepare for the noon crowd of bejeweled ladies and dark suited gentlemen who hoped to catch a glimpse of a sailboat, a seal, or just delight in the vision of the spectacular San Francisco sky line. Goodbye to the familiar Mediterranean homes hugging the Sausalito hillsides, perhaps sheltering a tired mother sitting down for her second cup of coffee after taking the kids to school. Glancing down at us in the water she may even wonder where the blue and white sailboat was headed so early in the middle of the week.

The bay water began to change when we reached Yellow Bluff buoy and passed the entrance into Presidio Yacht Club. The tidal shifts from the run-off of the Sacramento and San Joaquin rivers met the encroaching ocean, concocting water that looked like a boiling witch's cauldron. The turbulent water seized our bow in the tidal rip, jerking the boat to the right, and forcing me to spin the wheel the opposite way to correct our course.

We approached the orange Golden Gate Bridge, long a surprise for tourists who expected to see it painted gold. As we passed under the giant span a shadow of the bridge enveloped our boat in shades of gray, followed by a muffled roar of traffic above our heads. We had been out under the bridge many times, but this time we wouldn't be returning in a few hours, days, or even months. Today was special. Moving into the morning sun the shadow slowly released our boat, wrapping everything around us in bright colors. It felt like someone had waved a magic wand, knocking aside a great weight from our shoulders. Besides feeling excited we now carried the heady emotion of pure independence. I looked skyward, watching the circling red tailed hawks swoop around the north tower of the bridge, listened to their harsh, down slurred scream. I opened my arms, stretching them outward while shouting into the wind, "What house!"

Bob patted our boat and said softly, "This house."

The true meaning of home overwhelmed me. It wasn't just a dwelling we hammered and nailed, or changed to reflect our wants and needs. Our house now became the one we carried in our hearts. We could be home anywhere.

Our attention switched to high gear when we entered the shipping channel. Escalating wind grabbed our hair with a moist sea flavored breath, as masses of waves born by wind, current, tide and sea swells, folded on top of one another, thundering between the cliffs of San Francisco on one side, and the headlands of Marin on the opposite shore.

Bob cautiously went forward to raise the main sail while I concentrated on keeping the boat headed into the wind. The wave motion made footing difficult and I called to him, "You should have your safety harness on."

The wind snatched my words, carrying them away toward the brown hills. Bob turned, gave me a quizzical, uncomprehending look and shouted back, "I can't hear a word you're saying."

Little did we know that phrase was to become the war chant of our year at sea.

Bob tightened the halyard, secured the line, keeping a low profile as he scuttled crab like back into the cockpit. His hair glistened with droplets of sea spray, his face flushed from the effort of raising the sail and keeping his footing. "What were you yelling at me?" he said.

I was worried. In rough water you need a harness."

He dismissed the idea with a wag of his head, but I persisted. "I'm serious. I don't want to lose fifty percent of my crew."

"Next time I'll remember," he said.

I gritted my teeth in dismay, "I want to feel you are being careful all the time, even if you decide to take a leak over the side."

"Well, I'm sure as hell not going to put on a harness to do that!"

"Please be careful, even if it's just for my sake. Didn't you read the article in the paper that said a large percentage of the men who drowned at sea were found with their fly open? Obviously they were holding on to the wrong thing."

Maria climbed up one steep wave, standing on the wave top momentarily, then sliding swiftly down, making us think of a hobby horse. We sailed past the last high jutting cliff where Point Bonita light house clung to the barren rocky soil, watching over the green seas carrying sailors on their way. At this point the seas became mixed, coming toward us in all directions, and my stomach churned. In all the excitement I had forgotten my Merazine. Bob brought it up since going below didn't seem wise at the moment. We were approaching a rough area called Potato Patch, a shallow site that had been formed from silt being carried down the rivers, but made worse by the hydraulic mining techniques used in the gold rush era. So much silt had been deposited in this area over the years the shallowest part of the water was only twenty- three feet deep. Potato Patch's name had originated when old time schooners, en-route from Bodega Bay, lost their deck load of potatoes crossing the shoals. *Maria* had climbed these steep twenty to twenty five foot waves breaking over the bar on previous trips, and we were always happy to reach the deeper water of the shipping channel, staying alert to keep out of the way of the freighters and tankers moving sixteen to eighteen knots.

The seas calmed down a bit after we sailed further away from shore. Bob released the furling line to the Genoa jib, pulled hard on the starboard sheet, and set our course for Half Moon Bay. At the moment Half Moon sounded as good to us as some exotic tropical island, the seduction being we would arrive in only five hours sailing time before we would have the anchor down. Then we would have leisure time to sleep, read, play, make love, or just vegetate. The Marazine started working, fooling my stomach into thinking the sea ran more smoothly than it actually did.

"Hi handsome," I said, snuggling up close to him, while I placed my hand on his leg. "Want to fool around?"

He laughed, drew his arms around me and hugged me tight.

"Plenty of time for that," he said. "In fact, there's a whole new life time ahead of us. I never thought I could be this happy. I love you so much."

"I love you too. Don't stop holding me close."

The feelings of closeness helped dispel the tension of leaving, releasing an incredible high energy feeling. We had been to Half Moon Bay many times over the years, and took comfort in the familiar sight of the dark rocky promontory of Pt. San Pedro, then the glowing light of Montara that warned ships away from the rocks. Our eyes and ears picked up the lighted whistle buoy 1.5 miles off the point, its hollow tone warning sailors of the impending reef. We followed the channel markers into the bay, pleased to see the familiar fishing boats of all sizes and shapes. Gulls swooped and massed near the stern of some boats, eager to grab any scraps discarded by the fishermen. A strong aroma surrounded the boats, reminding me fish wasn't always my favorite dinner, unless of course it was so fresh it practically leaped on my plate. Fishing had been the heart of most of the Half Moon Bay community. At times we were reminded by harrowing tales that fishing is a difficult and dangerous occupation. Crews scratch out a living in lean years, while making good money in better years. Somehow our sailboat seemed frivolous here, even though pleasure boats were welcomed as long as they didn't take over a buoy belonging to a fish boat.

It was 1600 when we dropped our anchor in Pillar Point harbor, finding a quiet empty spot in an area called Princeton. We fell into our bunk with a sigh of contentment. Several minutes later Bob rolled over onto one elbow, supporting his head while he looked at me. "Guess what," he said.

"What?"

"We forgot our old back stay we planned to bring as an extra."

"We're not going back. I couldn't bare to leave twice."

"No, we won't go back. If worse comes to worse and we need it, Bill can come up and get it out of the boat house and send it to us."

Turning my head I noticed the ham radio we had installed in our cabin, feeling a thrill of accomplishment at finally passing the thirteen words a minute code test three weeks earlier. I had been gently pushed into this responsibility when Bob, the old romantic, had given me a set of

58

Heathkit Ham Radio Theory books for Mother's Day. A hint about as subtle as a freight train. I laughed to myself, "You actually did me a favor giving me the Ham books. My life wouldn't have changed as much if you had decided to give me a box of candy, or flowers. When Bill calls me "My mother the engineer" I'm so jazzed. There's a different kind of respect from him now, especially since he's a *real* engineer."

Bob took my hand, gave it a kiss." I'm proud of you. You worked your buns off." Then he cupped my buttock in his hands, "Thank God, not all of them."

"I'm being serious now," I said softly.

"So am I," said Bob, a leer making his eyes sparkle. "I'm not nearly as tired as I thought I was."

Our new life was starting out just right.

The next morning we awoke with a lazy awareness of our surroundings, knowing we didn't have to get up unless we wanted to. We snuggled down in our sleeping bags, feeling like little kids at recess, with a year ahead consisting of all weekends and no Mondays. We languished for fifteen minutes until our stomachs reminded us that food might be a good option, coffee an even better one. After breakfast we pulled out all our charts, spreading them all over the main cabin in groups. One of California coast, second Baja, Mexico, third West coast of Mexico, fourth Marquesas, fifth Tuamotus, sixth Society Islands, seventh and last, Hawaii and home. Bob had sewn a special canvas divider that fit the inside of the chart table. We folded our charts for each area, marked on a corner what number and location in order of use, while I made a separate list in a notebook for reference. We had been too busy earlier to organize the charts, but now it was fun because it represented the first time we could see progress on our trip.

After two days we were rested, anxious to sail to our next port, Monterey. Harbor hopping at a leisurely pace provided time to see and appreciate each place for its own uniqueness, something we hadn't accomplished on earlier vacation schedules.

Bob went to the fore deck and started to pull up the anchor.

"Do you want me in neutral?" I called.

He looked back in irritation, cupping his hands around his mouth and saying, "I can't hear a word you're saying."

Guess I'll just make my own decisions then, I thought. I Looked to see the way the anchor tended and followed it with the boat. My hand put the gear in forward, a little too fast, and Bob whipped around, waving his arms and shouting, "Don't do anything unless I tell you."

The tone of voice and remark whip sawed my memory banks, bringing back an unpleasant recollection.

I was in "charge" of engaging the gears on our old schooner, Venus. We had a division of duties because of the gear shift's location, too far away for the helmsman to reach from the tiller. The day loomed bad for Bob because I fit the old adage, "A little knowledge is a dangerous thing." I had convinced myself I had enough experience and knowledge to judge when it was time to put the engine in reverse, or when to put it into neutral, but Bob, who had maneuvered a destroyer in the navy, was not ready for my putting the engine in neutral. He needed the last bit of backwards thrust turning the boat around in a tight spot, and I screwed up the maneuver by slowing the momentum of the boat. Very quickly I heard Bob bellow, "Reverse,.... do what I told you, now".

"Don't scream at me Bob Allen, " I screeched back.

"I won't scream if you just do what I tell you to, " his voice seething in anger.

"Shut up, " I wailed. My face turned a deep red, and tears of humiliation and fury ran down my face.

"Shut up yourself," he screamed back. His fingers turned white as he gripped the tiller.

It was a grim, and definitely not loving time, with our children sitting rigid, looking first at dad and then at mom. I imagined other people in the harbor must have been listening to this charming exchange of words. When we arrived home Bob sat me down to explain his side of the problem. "Don't second guess me. You can't see as well from your vantage point by the gears."

"I know, but I was afraid we were getting too close to that other boat."

"Let me be the judge of that. I'm at the tiller."

After much pouting and grumbling on my part, I knew he was right, even though my bruised ego hated to admit it.

Bob held his arms out toward me. "Come over here."

I snuggled in, "Love on a boat isn't always soft and sweet is it?"

"No, " he said, "my ego got involved too."

"The poor kids probably think we're getting divorced."

"They've heard us yell before. Frankly, that's real life. We can't be adjusted all the time."

We talked quietly for an hour and I promised to listen to his orders, but he had to promise not to yell at me. A tough task for both of us.

We apologized to the kids, explaining parents were only human and hoped they would act better than we did. Bill and Lori looked relieved to see their parents talking in ordinary voices again.

The memory gave me a good idea. I put the engine in neutral and walked up on the foredeck to talk with Bob. "Communication is so important on a boat, and I think we're blowing it. When you're up here, and I'm way back at the wheel, we can't talk because of the wind," I said.

"So, what's your idea."

"Hand signals. You stretch your arm toward the direction you want, and I'll put the gear in forward and follow your arm. Do the same with reverse. On neutral drop your arm. When you want the engine stopped, make a fist and pull your arm down."

"Good idea. I think it beats screaming at each other."

For the next fifteen minutes I followed the arm signals to a "T," amused that Bob looked like a traffic cop on a street corner. He secured the anchor and joined me in the cockpit. Next stop, Monterey.

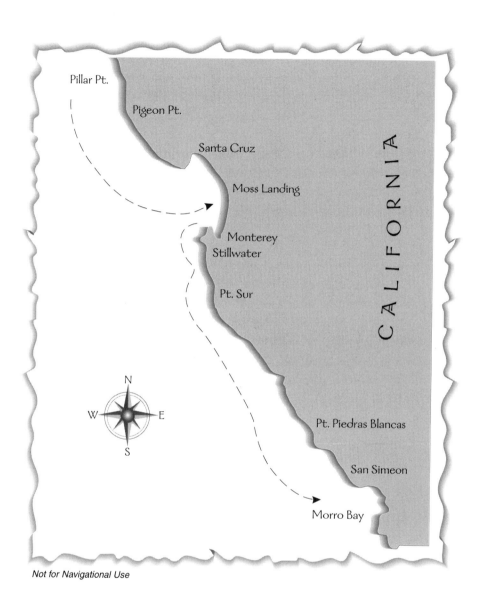

Pillar Pt.

Pigeon Pt.

Santa Cruz

Moss Landing

Monterey
Stillwater

Pt. Sur

CALIFORNIA

N
W E
S

Pt. Piedras Blancas

San Simeon

Morro Bay

Not for Navigational Use

Chapter 7

A LITTLE SEAWEED
GOES A LONG WAY

"The phosphorus shone in her seaweed hair
I looked again, but my mother wasn't there
A voice came shouting through the night,
To hell with the keeper of the Eddystone Light."

(Sea Chantey, "Eddystone Light)

Sailing through the Half Moon Bay breakwater we noticed the wind and seas building outside. Foam spewed high in the air when the rolling seas discovered the reef's hiding spot. We followed the channel markers out past the reefs and set sail for Monterey Bay. It didn't take long before the swells captured *Maria,* tossing and bouncing her as if King Neptune reached up and tickled her bottom with his trident. We shifted about trying to maintain our balance, while I prayed my stomach wouldn't notice the sharp change in motion. Hurrah, I thought, not only did I have my sea legs at last, but my sea stomach too, which in my case went together.

We looked forward to revisiting Monterey, the old capitol when California lived under Mexican rule. Inside the Custom House were antique pieces of furniture, colorful clothes worn by the ladies and gentlemen of the 1800's, pictures of wealthy landowners and governors staring stiffly from frames at scantly clad summer tourists wandering from room to room. I could envision the 1800's with beautifully dressed young ladies walking down the promenade hoping to catch the eye of a handsome caballero, followed by their chaperons dressed in black, making sure the eye was all she caught. One of those pictures might have fallen right off the wall if the person had seen the scandalous behavior of one modern female, me. Only my chaperon in Monterey wore white instead of black.

"Bob, remember your navy days at the Postgraduate school in Monterey?"

"How could I forget. It was the first time we had been separated since we got married."

"I hated it. It was worse when they put you in the hospital with mononucleosis."

"I've never been good at staying in bed, except when you're in it with me. Speaking of which," Bob laughed, "remember when you came up on the bus to see me and got in big trouble for lying down on the hospital bed next to me?"

"You can laugh, but I was so embarrassed. If I had been under the covers I would' have understood it, but that male nurse acted like I was about to commit the act right there."

"He was pretty uptight all right. Told me he came from a strict religious background. I'll never forget the shocked look on your face when he yelled at you. You even blushed. I had forgotten that I had married such a brazen woman."

"I would have understood it if you had been operated on and he thought I might tear open some stitches."

Bob put down the end of a sheet he had been whipping with marlin cord. "Come here and we'll test some pretend stitches. You can lie down with me anytime."

As I lay in his arms I thought how easily old time memories kept popping up during sailing. Without the interruption of telephones, TV, or someone knocking at the door we had more time to reflect. Many of the memories had to do with old friends, funny times, and the changes that had taken place over the years. As always, some of the changes had been good, like learning to talk things over before getting furious. Or bad, losing our parents.

The day wore on, seemingly endless as one wave after another shoved us all over the ocean. Toward late afternoon we neared Monterey and I stood up to give some life back to my buns and legs. "Want me to radio the harbormaster and see if there's a slip available?"

"Sure, but I don't hold much hope. The harbor seems to be full most of the time."

He was right, goodbye restaurant. The harbormaster advised us to forget coming in as all slips were occupied, and worse, the heavy surf conditions that had built up all day made the outside harbor dangerous. "Go to Moss Landing," he said, "I'll call on land line and arrange a slip for you there."

"Nice guy," I said. "At least I don't have to look for navigational entrance lights like the last time I almost ran us up on the beach."

"Yep, you were positive you'd found the red entrance buoy and headed straight for it."

"I felt like a damn fool when the light turned green and I realized it was a traffic light on shore. I spun that wheel so fast I almost lost my balance. My great night vision did me in again."

Bob chuckled. "We make a great pair. I can't hear, and you can't see."

We headed toward Moss Landing with *Maria* leaping like a demented ballet dancer as the short waves smacked her stern. The fishing fleet chugged along behind us in a long line, the ocean too rough for catching anything except a cold. As we neared Moss Landing I opened up the cockpit compartment and took out our mooring lines. I started up, one foot on deck and the other in the air. I received my first knuckle rap for doing something stupid. Rule number one, always have one hand for the boat. Just as I moved to grab a rail a large swell caught *Maria,* giving her a thump on her stern quarter. I flew through the air like a missile, fortunately landing on something soft, Bob. The whip lash I nursed for the next week reminded me of my error in judgement, pain being an exacting teacher.

We searched for the lighted bell buoy near the harbor entrance, staying away from the south side where most of the shoaling had taken place. Once again *Maria* docked in a fishing community, looking a trifle out of place with her tall mast rising high above the commercial boats.

We secured our bow and stern lines, then ran a bow and stern spring. Wiping my hands on my jeans I turned to Bob, "I'm glad it's afternoon and not night. I get nervous coming in a new harbor."

"Not to worry, we could have followed the fishing boats in. Being able to see made it was easier that's all. I'm going to look around the harbor for the head. See you in a minute."

I snickered to myself as I watched him walk away. His soiled, rumpled tee shirt covered his broad shoulders, but his jeans had dropped just low enough to show the top of his underwear. I was always reminding him to pull up his pants, but two seconds later, they usually snuck down again. I heard the dock squeak under his determined rolling gait. He turned to smile, and I realized he looked every bit like the fisherman around us, three days growth of beard and all.

We stayed a couple of days to wait out the bad weather, then headed next for Stillwater Cove in Carmel, only a few hours away. The crisp morning air woke up my face. I moved forward and stood on the foredeck, watching a fast darting fish trying to escape from something bigger. When we passed the rocks by Monterey harbor a strong fishy odor wafted outward. Ah, I thought, you can't miss the seals. They must all be exhaling at once.

An hour and a half later we found the cove entrance to Stillwater, tucked way to one side. Bob steered toward the opening and found a picturesque bay surrounded by golf courses and stately homes. At that moment *Maria* began to move like a slug through the water, acting as if she had a tether attached to her keel. "What's going on?" I asked Bob.

"Looks like we're surround by kelp. The prop is probably loaded with it."

I looked down into the water and saw it alive with long strands of pungent yellow-brown kelp. It lay waiting on the surface like a spider who had spent all night spinning his web.

"Well, time for my hand signals. Anchoring in this mess may be a problem," Bob said.

Down went the chain, bump, slide went *Maria's* anchor as it skipped over the slippery kelp. Down went the anchor again, more bump and slide, until I heard him shout in frustration, "Ah come on now, bite damn it."

The anchor must have been listening because the flukes caught the bottom. Our motion stopped, and the boat settled down with the bow slowly turning into the wind.

"Well now," Bob grinned. "The sun's over the yardarm. How about a glass of wine to toast the sunset."

"Aye, Captain, great idea. Give me a minute and I'll get some munchies to go with it."

I came back carefully holding two stainless steel wine glasses, trying not to crush the bag of chips I held under my left arm. "I know chips are bad for us, but sometimes being bad feels good."

The next morning we reversed our anchor drill. Bob slowly raised the chain and found the rubbery kelp embedded in each link. Trying to dislodge the kelp with a brush proved futile, so I put the engine in neutral and went forward, armed with a serrated knife. A half an hour later I had cut and slashed enough seaweed from the anchor to supply every sushi bar in the world. With the anchor secured I put the engine in gear, but the boat crept ahead like a stalking cat. Bob walked back to the stern. "Still must be kelp wrapped around the prop.. Put it in reverse and goose it a little."

I revved up the engine, sending the seaweed flying. We thought that would be the end of our problem, but a new weed predicament would present itself much later....at the wrong time.

We raised the sail and set our course for San Simeon Bay, a well sheltered area unless a south wind blew. Both of us settled into a nice relaxed mode when the irritating buzz of the bilge alarm jolted us.

"What the hell?" Bob said.

He jumped up and disappeared down below. I could hear him pulling up floor boats, trying to find out what had triggered the alarm At last he reappeared. "I turned off the alarm."

"What set it off?"

"I only know one part of it. When I opened the bilge I stuck my finger in the water to see if it was salty or fresh."

"And?"

"Fresh. Stay here while I find out what caused it."

Fifteen minutes passed before he popped his head out of the cabin, holding a hose clamp that had given away. Disgustedly he said, "Can you believe we lost fifty gallons of fresh water into the bilge?"

"What if this happened in the middle of the Pacific?"

"We'd be mighty thirsty, not a pleasant thought."

A chilling image on a sunny day. No matter how hard one works at preventative maintenance on a boat something happens, and usually at the worst possible moment. Salt water atmosphere played havoc with parts, constant movement loosened fittings, wearing holes in plastic bottles and cans, the sun ate away at plastic, the sheets frayed with constant use, and sails wear when in contact with stays and shrouds. I decided when you own and maintain a house you expect problems from time to time, but on a boat things happen faster. Maybe the anonymous person who said, "Happiness is often the result of being too busy to be miserable" owned a boat.

By the time we reached San Simeon Bay the sun had gone down, making land and sea blend together into a solid mass. We had been into this harbor several times, but the absence of the moon turned everything around us to ebony. I felt like a mole burrowing through a black hole. Oh hell, I thought, how am I going to keep my mouth shut. Robert Louis Stevenson said "Keep your fears to yourself, but show your courage." How could I show my courage? I didn't have any at that moment. But if he wanted to see my fears I could have handed him a whole box of them, the dark being one of the worst. I held the wheel tightly while Bob stood on the foredeck with a search light, using it sparingly to keep us from being blinded by the glare.

"That's just great honey, you're doing just what I want. Go to your starboard a little."

"Are you sure you can see, or are you just trying to impress me." My heart pounded in my chest as we inched along, skirting sleeping fishing boats and pleasure craft.

"Not to worry. We're almost there. You're doing fine. Slow the engine and cut a little to port. I'm going to get the anchor ready and you prepare to back down."

I knew I trusted Bob, even if I had to repeat it to myself several times. It was me I didn't trust. I cupped my hands around my mouth and yelled. "When you're on the foredeck I won't be able to see you for our hand signals. Please turn your face toward me when you give an order."

We ghosted past several more boats until Bob turned and yelled, "Neutral...back her down a bit...neutral...now back a little faster to set the anchor,...neutral....shut her down."

A short time later he joined me in the cockpit. We sat for twenty minutes until we were satisfied the anchor was holding, then retreated below for dinner and a good night's rest. Thank you Lord, I thought. I didn't blow it by yelling, so Bob didn't blow it by yelling back at me. Good. In the daylight my courage sits on my shoulder, but sometimes in the night it hides in my box of fears. I've got to bury that box some day. The ocean seemed a likely spot, it's deep.

The next morning we quietly sipped our coffee in the cockpit when we heard a gentle splash along side the boat. Bob cocked his head, raised up and looked into the water, "Come look, it's an otter. He's on his back with a shell on his chest."

I jumped up. I had see otters in the zoo, but seeing one in his own environment was too good to miss. "It looks like he has a sea urchin. Or at least a part of one."

The purple color of the sea urchin contrasted with the black fur. I wondered why the spines of the urchin didn't infect the otter like they did people. Bob pointed to the otter "See the rock by the urchin? They use that to crack open the shell. Surprise. I got so smart because I read about it in the Sea Frontier's magazine before we left."

"And to think I thought you only read the jokes in Reader's Digest. Wonders never cease."

"Smart ass. I like you better when you're not sarcastic."

I mouthed a sorry. For the next half hour we watched the languid motion of the otter swimming on his back, lazily peeking at us with his round dark eyes, then moving away to take inventory of the rest of the boats at anchor. We were glad to see the little guy, because his ancestors had almost been hunted to extinction for their fur.

"You know when we took our dive lessons twenty years ago no one gave the sea urchin much thought as a major seafood industry," I said.

Bob wrinkled up his nose, "It wouldn't be my choice of food, but the Japanese consider the roe a delicacy. Fish eggs aren't for me. Ill stick to the good old hen, God bless her cholesterol soul."

He turned and picked up his jacket. "Time to get ready for our next landfall. Morro Bay is only a few hours away."

We skirted the kelp beds, but were close enough to see a couple of otters floating in the seaweed. The Sea Frontier article had mentioned that otters liked to twist around in the kelp at night, tangling themselves up in the strands so they didn't drift away from each other. That thought appealed to my romantic nature because I didn't want to drift away from my mate either. I promised myself I would try not to be sarcastic.

We approached the harbor in good spirits, happy to be back in one of our favorite places, good food, good people and wonderful art work.

"I feel like I'm returning home after my last trip here," I said.

"Well, it was your home away from home. I sure missed you."

"I'm glad the terminal heart attack turned out to be our engine instead of you. What an awful day that was......

Summer 1982, a wild kind of day, flags shredded in the wind, and the seas rolled in deep trenches as we made our way up the coast from Morro Bay. After the engine breakdown Bob seemed determined to sail into Monterey, no matter how long it took. After five hours of fighting each mountainous wave, retreating two feet for any one foot of progress, I tapped Bob's shoulder. "I wasn't born a masochist. How long are we going to keep trying to get around Pt. Sur?"

"*I just checked our position and we haven't made a mile forward in five hours. I hate to give up, but I guess we have to. We'll head back to Morro Bay. What a bitch.*"

The afternoon wore on and the wind proceeded to fade away to nothing, leaving us filled with a different frustration as we watched the limp sails slat back and forth, nudging us toward Morro Bay. We were convinced we could walk faster, but learning to walk on water had not been part of our sea training. Disgusted Bob grumbled, "I never thought I'd be measuring our progress in feet instead of miles."

I turned and watched the swell lift the boat, inching it forward as if she had been stuck in a sticky web of foam. Bob had to be back at work in thirty six hours. It should be quite an interesting commute, I thought.

0200 found us drifting around the outside or Morro Bay harbor. We were at Mother Nature's mercy when the tide turned, leaving us to battle a five knot current without an engine, or wind to fill the sails. I felt very uneasy watching the boat drift closer to shore. The moonlight revealed swirling foam bubbling around chunks of concrete and sharp rocks.

"*I know you don't want to call for help, but I'm getting scared. What are we going to do?*"

"*I'll call. We don't have a choice with the current running us aground. I could put out an anchor, but we'd block the entrance.*"

The Coast Guard arrived fifteen minutes later. They pulled along side, hoisting a breast line that looked big enough to haul a super tanker. We have fairly large cleats, but they were dwarfed next to the humongous manila lines. I had an uncontrollable desire to laugh, but I was too busy doing my job of worrying. We secured the lines and they towed us side by side toward the Morro Bay Yacht Club. We passed the club on our port, then the Coast Guard seaman gunned his engine to turn us both around in a circle in order to drop us starboard side to the club. At that point the swift current grabbed a hold on both boats, and we found ourselves going five knots sideways down the middle of the channel, headed for a long string of docks. I gulped when I heard the seaman rev up the engine until it whined in a scream of rpms, trying to turn the two joined boats around against the current. For an instant I closed my eyes and wished we were still floundering around outside the harbor dodging rocks, instead of heading pell mell toward a dock full of fishing boats. The engine shrieked at the added revolution, expelling black unburned fuel out the exhaust. Gradually the movement of our boats changed. We swung around and headed back up the channel again toward the Yacht Club, thanking the Coasties once we secured to the dock.

"That's as close to wetting my pants as I want to come," I said.

Bob pulled off his clothes and fell into the bunk. "What's important is we're here safe. Tomorrow I'll call Bill and see if I can get a ride home. I may have to take the bus if he can't make it down here."

"You're leaving me, just like that?"

"I trust you. You can find a mechanic and see about getting a new engine installed. I have to get back to work to pay for all of this."

"You're not worried about leaving me all alone?"

"Whether you believe it or not, you're very resourceful. I think you'll have a better chance talking a diesel mechanic into a new engine faster than I will. Just give him that smile and he's a goner."

Bob guessed right again. After a lot of smiling and a couple of glasses of red wine with the owner/mechanic, we motor sailed Maria home two weeks later, the new engine purring contentedly.

Bob's voice woke me from my reverie. "Here we are. We'd have to be blind to miss that huge cone shaped rock."

We passed the three 450 foot power plant stacks, standing like watch dogs by the shore. Two brown pelicans flew toward the boat, alternately flapping and gliding. One peeled off from the other, swooping closer to *Maria* and plunging awkwardly into the water, packing a big fish into his beak. I couldn't help but think of part of the poem, "A pelican can hold more than his belly can, and I don't know how the hell he can."

We tied up at the Morro Bay Yacht Club and introduced ourselves to several other people on their way to Mexico. We would be know as the Class of 1984.

I had been having trouble with my new ham radio. I noticed the boat directly in front of us had a ham antenna. I decided to introduce myself and see if he had any brilliant ideas.

"Hi, I'm Marlene, from the boat behind you. I'm a ham too, but I'm having trouble with my new radio."

He brightened up, smiled and said, "Name's Jack. Let me grab some test equipment and have a look at your rig."

He checked the radio fittings, antenna, and ground plane, finally shaking his head. "Everything looks okay. You're sending CW at 80 watts, but you're only getting 10 watts with voice. I'm afraid I can't help you. Better find a technician who can open up the radio. I wouldn't want to fool around with it."

I thanked him and decided to wait until we reached Marina Del Rey in southern California. We would have a larger choice of technicians.

Bob and I walked up to the showers, anxious to clean up and relax. I reveled in the warm shower, but not too long. Having been through a severe drought at home I couldn't bear to waste water. After the final rinse of my hair I stepped out of the shower and heard someone call my name. Winding a towel around my head I looked to see where the voice came from. I saw an older, slightly plump wife if another cruiser standing by the door. Her accusing voice startled me when she barked, "Do you really like to sail?"

I was a bit taken back. "Ah..yes..most of the time. Why?"

Her skin flushed and little spots of color stood out on her cheeks. "I do it because my husband says our religion says I have to be with him." Her voice dropped down. "I'm so afraid all the time."

I pulled on my tee shirt, reaching for my shorts and shoes while thinking how to answer. "I've been afraid lots of time, but mostly when I first started to sail. Back then I didn't trust Bob, the boat, or me."

"How did you stop being afraid?" she whined.

Oh brother, I thought, how do I answer that one. "Being afraid isn't all bad because it makes you cautious. That's different from being terrorized. At first I was terrorized. Then I learned to sail and understand the boat myself. Of course I still get concerned when things go wrong. The last time I remember being afraid was four years ago when we lost our engine and were about to go on the rocks at the Morro Bay entrance."

"I would be terrified if that happened to me. My husband does everything on our boat. I don't know anything about boats, except that I hate them."

"Then why do you stay on one. If I hated it that much I wouldn't set foot on it."

She picked up a hair brush, running it absent mindedly through her greying hair. "My husband sold our house and bought the boat. Said it would be the great adventure of our life. All I ever wanted to do was work in my rose garden and see my grandchildren."

By now I felt very uncomfortable. How could a man sell a house and force his wife to do what he wanted? He treated her more like a possession than a wife. Captain Bly lives. Now wait a minute Marlene, I thought. He couldn't have done it all by himself. Maybe she played the marriage game the only way she knew how, complete capitulation. My being bitchy at times didn't seem so bad. At least Bob knew where he stood when I objected, and nobody pushed me into anything unless I really wanted it. The same went for him. Of course that meant fighting, never much fun, but making up was worth the effort. More importantly we each had to compromise to get through the big problems. I had an inkling how this reluctant cruising wife thought, but felt non pluss how to answer her. Our coping mechanism were different. I finally spoke up, "You mean you don't know how to run the boat at all by yourself? You can start the engine can't you?"

She looked away, acting as if I hadn't said anything. She folded her towel, tucked it into a bag and then picked up her dirty clothes, folding those neatly, placing them in the bag on top of her wet towel. Finally she turned with anguished expression, tears welling up in her pale blue eyes, "I just wish he didn't want to go to Mexico."

I felt my arms wanting to reach out to comfort her, but she seemed to shrink backward, blinking away tears in embarrassment. "Is it because you're afraid something night happen to him along the way ?"

"Oh yes," she gasped. "I wouldn't know what to do at all. He gives me orders and expects me to follow them. But when I get confused he yells at me and I go below and cry. But what if he fell overboard and I couldn't get him out? I don't even know how to start the engine," she said.

Now the tables were turned. I felt helpless. Nothing I could say would change their situation, but I tried anyway. "You're welcome to try my engine anytime. Yours can't be that different. Might even surprise your husband that you wanted to learn."

She shook her head and thanked me for listening. I turned away, torn with various emotions. One side of me hoped her grandchildren would know how much she wanted to be with them in her long-lost rose garden. The other side remembered a remark by James Cabell, "An optimist is one who makes the best of it when he gets the worst of it." At least it's a step forward, I thought.

I walked out into the bright sun and saw Bob's smile of greeting, his hand outstretched to hold mine.

"What would you have done if I refused to go cruising?" I asked.

"Nothing, we wouldn't have cruised. I admit I would have been disappointed, but without you wanting it...it wouldn't have been the same."

Peeking over his shoulder was our dreamboat, waiting for us to come aboard. The flags fluttered grandly, and her varnish gleamed in the sun. People certainly cared about her, ...yes, we did.

Two days later we planned our next stop, Cojo bay, located around the southern side of Point Conception. We went to bed and set our alarm for six the next morning

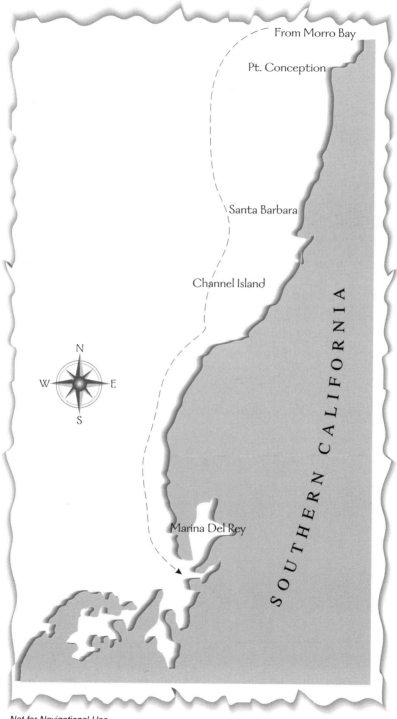

From Morro Bay

Pt. Conception

Santa Barbara

Channel Island

N
W E
S

Marina Del Rey

SOUTHERN CALIFORNIA

Not for Navigational Use

Chapter 8

WHALE WATCH

"The lookout in the crosstree stood,
With his spyglass in his hand.
There's a whale, there's a whale, there's a whale
fish he cried,
And she blows at every span, brave boys,
And she blows at every span."

(Forecastle Sea Chantey, British)

We were not surprised the next morning to see swirling clouds of fog embrace the harbor, first revealing bits of the shore, then like a modest lady, pulled down her misty skirt to hide everything from sight. Morro Bay, and nearby Estero Bay, have the reputation of being the foggiest areas along the Pacific Coast. We picked our way carefully through the harbor, searching for the red and green markers in the narrow channel. Once through the harbor entrance we followed the course to Point Conception Bob had laid out the night before. He turned on the radar to check for other boats on our course, finding none, put the radar back to standby to minimize our power drain. Stagnant air hung suspended in the flapping sails, the water disturbed only by the boat as it ghosted through the moist veil. I strained my eyes peering ahead, trying to will myself to see what was in front of us. I laughed when I realized I was trying to do the job of the radar.

Several hours later the sun burned off the fog, leaving the reflection of clouds swimming in the glassy blue-green water. First we took off our jackets, then our sweaters, shoes, socks, long pants and turtle neck shirts. A half an hour passed as the sun radiated down, leaving pink spots on each uncovered part of my body. I brushed damp bangs away from my forehead and called below, "Can we put up the new sailing awning? I don't want to get sunstroke on our first hot day."

"Oh boy, I have to remember where we packed it. Do you remember?"

I groaned as I thought of "our garage" in the forepeak. At the last minute before departing we had thrown loose gear up in the peak until we could find a permanent place for it. I scanned my memory banks, but with age creeping up, withdrawals from the bank sometimes got misplaced. After a minute it came to me.

"I've got it. I think I remember stuffing it up on the port side shelf toward the back. If it's not there look under one of the sail bags. It might have fallen down."

He returned several minutes later carrying the rolled up acrylic sun shield under his arm. We zipped the front part to our dodger, stretching it to fit, then attached it to the gallows. Even with the sun shield the warm weather caused us to think about changing into our "cruising" clothes. I quickly looked around in a 360 degree arc to check for other boats in our area. Not seeing any, I started by taking off my shorts, shirt, panties, and bra. I noticed I had Bob's full attention by this time. There is nothing quite like a Bob grin, especially as he started removing his clothes, some with a flourish as they flew through the air and landed on the cushions. I glanced down, feeling self conscious about the angry dark rose scar stretching the full length of my tummy, a result of exploratory surgery the year before. Instinctively my hand partially covered it. Bob studied me, shaking his head. "Don't cover it, it's a battle scar."

"What do you mean battle scar? It's ugly."

"Not ugly at all, it was a battle for your life. I honestly don't know what I would have done if anything had happened to you."

His eyebrows arched upward, and his eyes glistened. He covered the distance between us in a millisecond, drawing me into his arms, almost crushing me in the intensity of his feelings. Oh how I love this man, I thought, and thank you God for not taking me away from him. I playfully pinched his bottom. "You handsome devil, that's some sexy suit of clothes you're wearing. How do you keep it from getting wrinkled?"

"Genetics. And I might add I've never seen your buns look better. I don't see any wrinkles there either, only a dimple."

Making sure the boat was operating well on automatic pilot, Bob signaled me with his brown eyes, then caressed my dimple, leading me down to our cozy aft cabin. Afterwards, laying in his arms contentedly, I thought cruising had some powerful effects on our love life, as well as life in general. I should have insisted we cruise earlier!

A quick study of the time meant we should be on deck to check for hazards. I picked up my baritone ukulele and songbook. I looked around to see if we were near any other boats, then settled in the cockpit to pick out a song. The engine propelled the boat effortlessly through the glassy seas. I loved a placid ocean, so calm any ripple on the water attracted our attention, treating us to a sighting of a seal, porpoise, a large sun fish resting on top of the water, or even a long string of jelly fish. This time a new surprise awaited us. As I sang about the different fish in the sea my voice rose, "Next came the whale which was biggest of all, he climbed up aloft and he let each sail fall."

As I finished the last line I heard a loud splash, followed by a "whoosh" sound. I looked up to see a vision of a black and white Orca whale fifty feet from us. Grabbing Bob's arm I pointed, "Look over the starboard side at about 1100 o'clock. I think it's a killer whale."

Bob stood up and turned. We both drew in a quick breath watching his glistening body leap out of the ocean, a plume of water escaping from his blow hole. His two toned body arched, then sliced downward through the water, sending a wave skyward, distributing millions of droplets of water into the air in a fan shape. He reappeared a few minutes later, but further away, leaving us relieved there had not been whale and fiberglass in deadly contact. We witnessed nature at its best, but from a safe distance.

Reading about whale's evolvement was a fascinating subject. They were the first to invade the sea about sixty-five million years ago, with some species hunted to extinction. This was our second whale sighting of the year. Earlier in the year we spied a gray whale feeding around the Farallon Islands when we delivered several marine biologist from Point Reyes Bird Observatory to the main island. Besides the biologists we brought boxes of food, two propane bottles, and some scientific supplies to carry them through their two weeks stay.

"Remember the sixty foot gray whale we saw on our last Farallon run? " I said.

"Sure. He was only thirty feet away from us. I was surprised he was splotchy, sort of pink -grey with the barnacles on his body. In all the pictures we see of whales they're one color."

"That particular run was interesting in more ways. It was the first time we've ever seen krill. We've heard about them for years, but finally seeing a ribbon of tiny shrimp in the ocean was a thrilling. Hard to imagine that krill is the main food of a creature so large. You'd think they would be just a little hors d'oeuvre served before the main course."

The awning did its job and kept us from getting fried while we kept an eye out for other boats. Our real clothes went back on later in the afternoon when a breeze piped up, guiding *Maria* in a smooth rhythm through the waves. The engine proved unnecessary now, alleviating the noisy drone of the motor. We reveled in the exquisite silence, broken only by a slight hiss of water caressing the hull.

After an easy rounding of Point Conception, normally one of the roughest, we searched for the small anchorage called Cojo. We had anchored there the last time we traveled north, using it as an escape hole while waiting out bad weather. We wanted to get settled and get a good night's sleep before heading south to the Channel Island Marina near Oxnard.

"It's only 1700 but I'm tired. Amazing since we haven't been doing much all day but motoring," I said.

Bob winked and said, "Maybe a little more than motoring."

After getting our anchor down, several more boats motored in, each looking for an area close to shore. One young couple on a twenty -five foot boat appeared to be new in the anchoring game. A young woman stood on the bow of the boat. She stared nervously at the other boats, and suddenly threw the anchor into the water before her boat slowed down. When the bow crossed over the line and anchor a bearded young man at the tiller screamed a few choice expletives deleted at her. The wind snatched away some of the words, but when she saw his angry red face, words wouldn't have mattered anyway. He waved her back to the cockpit. She looked bewildered as he spat out rapid fire directions while waving his arms, finishing with a loud, "God damn it Maggie, listen to me this time, and don't drop the anchor while we are still moving forward."

Whirling on him she pointed her finger and waggled it under his nose screeching, "How *dare* you scream at me that way. I'm not your damn servant." Tears sparkled in her eyes.

While the couple continued to argue their boat drifted dangerously close to other anchored boats in the area. A grizzled, old skipper came on deck shaking his head. In his hand he held up a small air horn, giving it one loud blast. The fighting couple nearly jumped out of their socks. The embarrassed young man grabbed the tiller, gunned his engine, dragging his anchor along with the boat. He anchored far away from the group, and we decided despite the balmy weather outside, it was probably going to be very chilly inside his boat.

"Were we that bad?" I asked.

"Honey, a few of our fights would have made that couple look mute."

All I could think of to say was, "Hmmmm," but I had to admit I tended to forget the bad times and remember the good.

I awoke the next morning, stretching lazily in my sleeping bag, then rolled over to give Bob a big good morning squeeze. He mumbled sleepily and reached his arms out to me.

"No more getting up at five in the morning to go to work. I love it. I could stay in the sack all day if I wanted to."

"True, but knowing you it wouldn't last long. You're too hyper."

Me too, I thought as I crawled out of the sack, grabbing my clothes in order to get to the galley to start the coffee. Both our brains seemed to hang in limbo until the caffeine could jump started our bio motors. While making coffee I wondered what Bob's retirement would have been like if we had stayed at home. Both of us had been so busy he hadn't had time to miss his past working life. The truth was he might have driven me crazy. It had been bad enough when I turned on a soap opera one day. He looked at me incredulously and exclaimed, "You don't watch television in the daytime do you?"

My answer had been, "You have no idea all the things I used to do. But I guarantee I didn't sit in bed and eat chocolates."

At least I had it better than my mother. Dad retired and followed her all over the house, even standing outside the bathroom door talking. At times she prayed he would find another job, or hobby that took him away, just so she could have some time to herself.

We went on deck to take up the anchor, and I noticed the red sky. They were small puffy clouds we called a mackerel sky. A little rhyme bounced into my head, "Red at night, sailor's delight. Red in the morning, sailor's take warning." I also thought of a second old rhyme dating from clipper ship days, "Mackerel skies and mares' tails, make tall ships carry low sails." There wasn't much sign of wind yet, but I knew by afternoon we might be in for it.

The moderate morning wind moved abaft the beam. We polled the Genoa jib out to keep it from moving side to side, sailing a respectable six or seven knots through the water. I sat at the helm, filled with the joy of independence, loving life and breathing in the cool sea air. The past months of hard work and preparation were truly worth the strain, and the tiring memories started to fade away like yesterdays flowers. Even the ocean looked less threatening, with rolling waves glistening in the sunlight, filled with all types of living creatures below. I felt secure and safe as long as I stayed on top of the water, interesting sea life or not.

The afternoon arrived, carrying with it the expected weather change of a thirty-five knot frisky wind. Down came the pole, next the Genoa, and in went the first reef in the main, the boat now riding more under control. Our VHF radio traffic increased noticeably, with one distress boat call after another. The first cry for help came from Anacapa, one of the islands in the Santa Barbara channel, telling of two boats who managed to wrap their anchors together and were now drifting toward the rocky shore. A passing boat played good Samaritan, tying a line to a boat and his boat, keeping the vessels from shore until professional help could get there. A good diver would make a lot of money untangling situations like this one.

The saddest call came next. An older man's voice shouted on Channel 16 to the Coast Guard. "My engine on our sailboat conked out. With these high winds I don't have enough crew to sail into the harbor."

"Are you in any immediate danger?" asked the Coast Guard.

"No, I'll just drop my anchor over for now. I belong to a Triple A towing service. Can you call them for me?"

"What's your location skipper?"

"I'm just off Point Hueneme breakwater."

"Have all people aboard put on life jackets. We'll call the towing company for you."

"Thanks Coast Guard, we'll do that."

The tow boat must have been inundated with calls, because the waiting skipper of the sailboat called two hours later, his voice shaking with emotion. "Coast Guard..... Ah....the wind's gotten so strong my anchor pulled out. The Triple A towing boat never came. Oh no...no...Help me, I'm being set on the breakwater. There's three people aboard. Oh God....oh my God, we're going to have to jump in." Silence.

The Coast Guard called back saying they would come right out, but no one was left on board to answer them. We heard later the people were picked up safely, but when we approached Point Hueneme, we saw little bits of flotsam and jetsam floating by, all that was left of someone's dream boat. It was hard to imagine the shredded pieces of fiberglass and wood we saw once had shape and form. I looked at Bob, "We'd be devastated if this had happened to us. Imagine life without *Maria*". Tears filled my eyes as I deliberately turned my head away from the floating debris.

The day was not through with us yet either, proving if anything can go wrong, it will go wrong. As we were making our approach to the Channel Island breakwater a large rolling swell pushed the boat ahead of us sideways, rapidly carrying it toward the rocks. Their rudder made a crunching sound as it hit a rock and splintered, leaving them without anyway to steer. Their anxious call to the Coast Guard produced fast results. The rescue boat arriving within a minute from their station just inside the harbor, towing the crippled boat to safety.

Knowing the wind and swells would try their worst on us too, we took a heading to the far left of the entrance. We increased our engine speed to give us more headway and control. At that precise moment the engine over-heat alarm went off and I yelled quite needlessly, "The alarm went off."

"To hell with the alarm, we have to keep going or we'll hit the rocks too. Rev up the engine some more."

"Won't that hurt it?"

"Do what I said. We don't have a choice."

Amid the roaring engine, punctuated by a screaming alarm, we inched our way through the entrance into calmer water. I heard Bob's breath come out in a hiss as he instructed me to throttle down the engine, only relaxing when the alarm quit ringing when the engine cooled down.

"There must have been some eel grass stuck in the intake," he said.

"I don't get it. You cleaned out the filter after we left Morro Bay."

"I'll find out once we're tied up. Get the mooring lines ready so we can check into the harbormaster's office."

Once secured in our newly rented slip Bob went below to see what had caused the boat to overheat. He appeared a few minutes later and announced wad of grass was stuck in the raw water engine intake.

"Turn on the engine, I want to see what else happens."

I started the engine, revved it up a little in neutral until I heard Bob shout for me to shut her down. He reappeared with a short piece of hose, holding it up like a trophy, "The hose flattened out as soon as you revved up the motor. Let's find a store and hope we find a better quality hose to replace this."

Boats breed problems like rabbits, I thought.

On the way to the boat store I discovered a treasure, a small room with a washer and dryer used by people who rented the slips. I grabbed Bob's arm. "When we're done at the store I want to bring our clothes back to wash. I don't think I'll ever take a washer or dryer for granted again."

"There's a lot I won't take for granted. At home I had a place for all my tools. On the boat I can't remember where I put them because there's not enough space in one central area. I should write down where everything is located. I'll drive myself nuts looking for stuff."

I thought about what I had left at home; one heavy vacuum in the hall closet, compared to the tiny vacuum on the boat. No more hours of cleaning and moving furniture, since ours was built in. No telephone ringing at all hours. We had a radio to take it's place which we could turn off. I missed the tub, but showers cleaned me just as well. Someday I longed for the ease of going to the grocery store, and switching on TV. But as I thought of those mundane things I realized they were not that important. Yes, I missed my washer and dryer the most, the rest depended on reprogramming my thinking. Water on a boat became too precious to waste, by night-fall I was too tired to stay up and use lights, Bob turned into a part time dishwasher, also as a wringer for the wash, TV was boring compared to the real life happenings, and best of all, the depth of my feelings for Bob reached greater proportions every day. We met new people which helped keep us from missing our friends too much, the added excitement refurbished the old brains, and best of all, we were having fun. One thing we couldn't replace, missing our family.

"What time is it?" said Bob. He had just returned from the shower at the marina. His hair stuck up at angles, his face rosy and sweet smelling from shaving soap. I rubbed my cheek against his saying, "Who knows and who cares. I made a significant decision by taking off my watch and I don't plan to put it on again. Those little hands aren't going to run my life anymore."

"You're a little crazy, but I love you anyway. You may not wear your watch, but I still have mine; which reminds me, where did I leave it?"

"With your change and wallet, extra screws, pencils and pieces of paper. The only messy part of the boat."

"I hear you. While I do that, turn in the key to the harbor office and we'll get going to Marina Del Rey."

It was now October 2, another warm southern California day begging to be enjoyed, as long as the boat behaved itself and didn't create new projects. I wondered what we would do if we had a friend who created as many little problems everyday as *Maria?* I decided if the friend gave as much as he took, then it would be acceptable, and *Maria* being our best friend, now gave us joy most everyday.

I couldn't wait to get to Marina del Rey, for two reasons. The first and most important, seeing our daughter, grandson, and son-in-law. The second was finding a technician to fix my ham radio so the voice output worked correctly.

About thirty minutes into the trip I wondered what happened to Bob. He had gone below leaving me on watch, and I couldn't believe his morning constitutional took *that* long. I stuck my head down into the companionway and heard a small voice calling, "Marlene, Marlene, come down here." I couldn't imagine why his voice sounded so faint until I discovered my brave captain securely locked in the forward head. The head has two doors, but one was blocked off with the sewing machine on the outside, and the other faced two hanging lockers. One locker door had opened and jammed itself against the head door, trapping my stalwart mate. "What am I bid and what am I offered," I teased.

"Get me out of here and we'll discuss it later," said captain grump."

With that kind of answer I decided not to press my luck and I let him out of his self made prison. If he had been single handling the boat he would have had to break down the door.

It wasn't long before the large man-made harbor of Marina del Rey appeared on the horizon. The rock breakwater rose parallel to the shore, seaward of the jetties protecting the entrance. This entrance took us into the true meaning of "La La Land," meaning the crazy Hollywood type of atmosphere which permeated everything it touched. As we started down the traffic separation lanes we saw boats fighting their way through the crowd like spawning salmons. Further into the harbor area, boats of all sizes (mostly huge) rested in their docks, some being washed by boat girls, others with grime streaked faces forlornly waiting for absent owners to pay attention to them. We wondered how so many people could own million dollar boats, row after row, each bigger, grander, trying to out-do the following row of humongous yachts, many who probably never left the dock.

"Don't worry *Maria*, not only are you beautiful, but paid for, not like these other Taj Mahals," I said.

"Sounds like sour grapes to me dear," Bob intoned.

"Maybe. I just didn't want anyone looking down on our boat."

We called ahead and reserved a slip at the California Yacht club, finally finding it and squeezing in the narrow channel between the rows of slips. *Maria's* forty -one foot length and thirteen feet six inches breadth got us in trouble when a stiff breeze blew her sideways, necessitating some quick maneuvering on Bob's part, and fending off other boats on my part. Once tied up we went into the club to find a phone.

Disappointment reigned when Lori failed to answer the phone. I slumped disconsolately into a chair while Bob checked the advertisements for a radio technician. He had better luck, and got a technician named Randy to meet us at our boat in a half an hour.

Randy arrived, checked our radio ground plane system, ran some tests on the radio, finally announcing, "Your problem is in the mike gain. I'll open up the radio and make an adjustment inside, then you check into a net."

My face turned hot. Stuttering I said, "Bu..t I've nnn..never checked into one before. I've only used the radio for my code work."

He adjusted the radio, found the Manana Net, then turned to me with a smirk. With a slight tremor in my hand I picked up the mike, blurting out, "Um. um. uh, this is N6 LDM." I jumped when a voice answered back.

"YL trying to check into the net. (young lady) Please give me your call signs phonetically, the noise level's high today."

Oh God, I thought. I can't remember my phonics. An agonized silence followed until my brain unraveled, a wavering voice which hardly sounded like me said, "This is November 6 Lima, Delta, Mike."

"Hello N6, LDM. What's your handle?"

"Marlene, I repeat, Marlene." I prayed he wouldn't ask for my long name in phonics.

"Hello Marlene, where you located?"

"Marina Del Rey. We're on our way to Mexico on our boat."

"Great Marlene. Call in again and let us know how you're doing. We give great weather reports for the Mexico area."

"Thanks net, I'll call again. This is N6 LDM clear."

I turned to Randy, "I can't believe how my voice shook. I think my brain died and my tongue grew three sizes."

Randy slapped his knee and let out a huge good natured guffaw. "You've experienced the supreme in mike fright It's all down hill from here."

I climbed out of the boat and ran up to the club house, hoping Lori would answer the phone this time. Digging deep in my blue jeans I found my change. I placed the money in the coin slot, thinking how much alike we were, dishwater blonde hair, long legs, and an athlete's body like mine used to be. Lori's face was longer, and she had brown eyes like her dad's, but like me, filled with the devil as we teased each other and others. We were both so sentimental we cried at every little tugged heart string. Please, please be there, I thought, squirming in place as the telephone rang. I heard her voice answer "Hello," and tears pricked at my eyes. I cleared my throat," Hi honey, we're at the California Yacht Club harbor. When can you come down."

"Soon as I change Brad's diapers and grab my purse. I can't wait to see you and dad."

Lori and two year old Brad arrived at the boat a half an hour later, climbing aboard and giving us hugs while shrieking little squeals of joy. Lori sat down asking all kinds of questions about the trip when we all realized it was too quiet. Where was Brad? Worse, what was he into? We found a little trail of crackers crumbs following him as he investigated each area of the boat, ending up with a sizable amount in a pile in front of him on the cushions in our aft cabin.

Lori picked him up, bringing him into the main salon and sat him in her lap. She looked anxiously at us as she delivered her bomb of an announcement. "Mom, dad, I'm leaving Mike."

I nearly choked on my words. "You're kidding. I knew you were having some problems but...I didn't expect you to say this."

A frown of concern passed over Bob's face, his eyes searched her face. "Honey, what are you going to do? There's no home for you to come home to, it's rented."

"I don't want you to worry about me dad. I don't know what I'm going to do yet, but it won't interfere with your trip."

"It's not the trip I'm worried about. It's you."

He went over to Lori, putting his arms around both she and Brad, while I held on to Lori's hand. Silent tears flowed down her face, wetting the top of Brad's head and spotting her red blouse. Brad looked up at all of us, his lip puckering as he reached up and touched Lori's face. "Mama," he whimpered.

"It's okay Brad. Mommy's fine, and we all love you. How 'bout another cracker for my big boy."

Brad's eager hand sought out the cracker, grasping it and taking a generous bite. He slid off Lori's lap to do some more exploring. While he rummaged around in our things we talked quietly with Lori about what brought about the separation, how to handle the coming year, trying to give her all our support and love in a concentrated form, but frustrated with not being able to help her more later. She smiled, "Remember how Bill looked after me when we were both at UCLA? I know I can count on him to give me advice and help. He's a wonderful brother. I'm a big girl now. I'll take care of myself and Brad."

Bob took her hand. "You'll always be my little girl, no matter how old you get, and don't you forget it."

After she left the atmosphere became subdued and gloomy as we both delved privately into our thoughts. How, I thought, would she get along alone? Obviously she's a grown up woman, but Bob's right, she's my little girl too. Oh, Lori, I wish I could be here to lend you my shoulder to cry on, or listen to you when you need to talk. Maybe it won't end in divorce. Thank God Bill will be around, but still he's 500 miles away. Bob's voice interrupted my thoughts,

"Your face looks like it's fighting four battles at once."

"I just need you to hold me, then I can deal with my thoughts."

He wrapped me in his arms and stroked the back of my head. "We'll keep contact by radio and the phone. I know you're worried, so am I, but we have to live our lives too."

"You're right. It might even be for the better, not depending on us I mean. In the final analysis, she is the only one who can make decisions."

"True, but we can talk later. I want to take you out to a nice dinner. It's you and me time now. Okay?"

"Okay, you're on. I'll go change my clothes and comb my hair."

While I changed Bob pulled out a chart marked "Catalina," making notes on a pad beside him.

Not for Navigational Use

Chapter 9

CAPTAIN BOB VERSES ADMIRAL MARLENE

"Essequibo Capten is the King o' Captens all!
Buddy tanna na we are somebody O!
Essequibo Capten is the King o' Captens all
Buddy tanna na we are somebody O.
Somebody O, Johnny, somebody O!
Buddy tann na we are somebody O!

(Sea Chantey, "Essequibo River")

Before setting sail to Catalina island in hazy weather we stood on the dock hugging Lori and Brad one more time, our ragged emotions surrounding them like a blanket. It felt as if we were trying to will immediate happy changes in their lives through this moment in time. I knew we had to go on with our planned trip, but my heart ached for Lori and her uncertain future. We watched her smile and wave, looking gutsy and vulnerable at the same time.

Bob maneuvered the boat out of the slip, but when the lines dropped, so did our spirits. Letting go of our youngest suddenly seemed a desertion. But deep inside we knew the ultimate truth we hadn't wanted to admit, the knowledge our little girl had grown up and left us years ago. Now would be a time for her to mature in a different way, hopefully to gain new insights. Oh Lori, I thought. I wish you love and strength, for I know you will be in need of both in the days ahead.

We adjusted our sails to fit our course to Catalina. Unfortunately the course proved to be hard on the wind in a light breeze, not our best point of sail. Wanting to get my mind off leaving my hand sought out the Spanish language tapes from College of Marin. The conversational Spanish class last spring hadn't lasted long enough, which left little to talk about unless people wanted to know our names, our children, or grandchildren's names. I made sure if people asked me where my house was I could tell them I lived on a "barca de vella," which I hoped meant sailboat. If all else failed I planned to carry my Spanish-English dictionary around in Mexico and let my fingers do the walking.

After playing the tape for a half an hour Bob looked over at me with a frown, finally reaching up and scratching his head in an irritated gesture.

"I'm tired of listening to that lesson," he said.

"I know, but it's better than worrying about Lori and Brad."

His eyebrows raised in a half circle, accentuating the wide eyes below. "How did you know I was thinking of that?"

"Because we're so much alike, and I was thinking about them too through Spanish words."

I shut off the tape recorder, and put it below, grabbing the binoculars out of the rack to see if I could pick out some landmarks on Catalina. Even through the haze I could see the "N" cut designating the Isthmus, often called two harbors, Isthmus harbor on the lee side, Cat harbor on windward side. A few head of cattle lazily munched on dried up plants growing along the rugged, arid mountains. We stayed clear from the kelp line where the prop would tangle itself in the seaweed.

Catalina had a special meaning to both of us; mine brought out feelings of pleasure because my mom and dad honeymooned there, but Bob's feelings were somewhat bittersweet. His eyes had a soft, far away look, remembering the circumstances that brought him to live on this island. I put down the glasses and stood next to him, reaching around his waist with my arm.

"The island has a wild sort of beauty doesn't it? Must have been interesting to live there after your father died," I said.

"Sort of. It was more important to my mom because she met dad in Avalon. She was working as a secretary in a real estate office. Neither of them were spring chickens when they fell in love." He looked at me with sorrowful eyes, "I wish my dad could have known you; he would have loved you, and you would have loved him too."

"It must have been hard to lose your dad at nine. And your poor mom. There weren't a lot of single parent support groups in that day."

"It was hard on her. She waited a long time for the right man, then to lose him after ten years was tough. I think she wanted to come back to Catalina for awhile to feel close to him again."

"Did it work?"

"Not really, at least, not like you think. She had memories all right, but she looked sad lots of times. She tried to hide it from me. I helped by being the "nine year old man" of the house, and mom let me help make simple decisions. I think she needed me as much as I needed her. She never found another man like my dad."

We sailed on, each in our own emotional world. Bob's mind appeared to be in the past, while mine dwelled in the present, thinking how awful it would be to lose a husband, especially mine.

We had visited Catalina many times when we lived in southern California, but it had been years, and growing older somehow had a way of making our memories and moments more poignant.

We sailed by Fourth of July Cove, one of the areas we had anchored during our skin diving lessons years ago. I groaned inwardly to myself, remembering how startled I was when Bob decided to take scuba diving lessons, and wanted me to try too. He must have read my mind because he said, "Remember when we took our scuba test here?"

"How could I forget." Boy, that was the understatement of the year, I thought, my mind reaching back..............

"I want to get my scuba certificate," Bob announced. "It sounds fun, and we could dive for abalone at Catalina."

"You've got to be kidding. You know how I feel about the ocean. Scuba diving means going under the water. I don't like being under water. How could you even suggest I do it."

He leaned over and grasped my hand. "I would be with you every minute. I wouldn't let you out of my sight," he said softly. "You know I would never let anything happen to you."

I refused to discuss it, or make up my mind right away. I felt clammy thinking about the walk in the surf with Bob a couple of months after we married. There had been a storm the week before, and waves had eaten away at the beach in big bites. When I waded out into the water I stepped in a hole and the water closed over my head. I panicked and couldn't take a breath., What ever made him think I would take diving lessons?

The night of the first class I consented to go with him to see what it was all about.

"Does this mean you're going to take the class?" Bob said excitedly.

"Don't make me answer now please. Let me think about it."

I really had no intention of joining the class; I was just curious what was required, and why anyone would want to take the dumb course anyway. I looked around at the other students, all much younger and eager to get going. I looked at Bob, just as eager as the rest, but wearing a hopeful expression in his eyes. I stared at the pool, almost gagging at the over whelming odor of chlorine. I vacillated, finally deciding to give it a chance, praying it was worth it to be Bob's partner in the water as well as life.....if I lived that long. The swimming test left me exhausted, barely passing before my endurance ran out.

"Don't think about being under the water," I said to myself. I closed my eyes.

Pretty soon I joined the rest of the class, spitting into my mask to keep it from fogging, buckling on my weight belt which would keep me under water, and getting a dry throat from breathing compressed air.

Toward the end of the our six lessons, I realized how far I had come. I felt proud of myself for not going ape when the instructor came up behind me and turned off the air to my tank. Without thinking I reached around and turned on my valve....No panic attack. But I was in a pool, not the ocean.

I found the worst thing that happened to me during the whole time in class was my blond hair turning a ghastly green from the heavy chlorine treatment in the pool.

Things were a bit different when I took my ocean test. I picked up abalone, stuck to Bob's side like glue, and felt only partial happiness being in the ocean. I always hoped in time I would enjoy it as much as he did, but my past invaded my diving experience like a silky shadow, reminding me of the ocean's powerful potential. I did pass the course which gave me some measure of comfort.

It was close to six in the evening and the October sun sagged, then disappeared. The lights illuminated the large Casino nearby, and warm yellow shadows cast window pane patterns across the water. I used to hear mom and dad talk about the big name bands that thrilled dancers of the 1930's. Now the bands were replaced by movies in the Casino. Not very glamorous, but it paid the rent.

We were delighted to see so few boats moored, unheard of during the busy summer season. A harbor patrol boat met us, issued a mooring assignment, giving us the good news that it was half price to stay in the off season.

The next morning we rowed into Avalon in our dinghy, tied up at the small dock and walked into the main part of town. Bob chattered away. "There's the Busy Bee Cafe," he said, "my uncle used to own it. Mom and I ate there lots of times. Uncle Phil invented the machine that took your picture in a little booth? He made quite a bit of money from his invention. Dad invented things too, only his patents were on steam equipment. He never got much money from them though because the patents stayed with the company he worked for."

"It must run in your family. You had several patents too, but the only money you made was a bonus and a plaque to hang on the wall."

Bob smiled. "Don't knock it. The company owned the patents because I worked there. Those were the days when I really loved work. I could build and design things at home, just mess around the work shop, trying out ideas without being pressured."

We walked the streets, ate ice cream and decided to rent an open air gas cart to see the house where Bob lived. We rode to the top of the mountain and looked down at the spectacular view of the harbor. From our vantage point the tiny boats bobbing at their moorings looked like miniature toys, placed in a sparkling blue bathtub. I tried to imagine what it would be like to be a child living on the island.

"Was it fun living here?"

Bob nodded his head, a half smile on his face. "I loved roaming the hills and playing on the beach. Of course I learned to row a boat, and wanted to own a sailboat even then."

"It must have been hard to move back to the mainland with your mom and live with your grandmother."

"Mom felt bad that I didn't like my grandmother, but for a kid she was a real pain. She had a hearing problem and thought people were talking about her behind her back."

"Did people talk about her?"

"Mostly me. She was very crabby and demanding. She wanted the lawn mowed so that there wouldn't be any lines showing. I had to mow it in one direction, and then mow it all over again in the opposite direction. It took so much time when I wanted to play. I got mad."

"You weren't the only one with grandmother problems. Mine made me chew my food twenty seven times with each bite,.... and she counted. When she wasn't looking I swallowed my peas whole like pills."

We both looked at each other and laughed, especially since we were grandparents too. "I wonder what weird things our grandchildren will say about us?" I said.

"No, telling, but I'm sure they'll think of something."

As we rowed back to our boat I teased Bob, "For years you've told me you wanted to be King, not President of the United States. Kings aren't very popular you know."

"Being King is easier; that way I could cure the world's problems without bureaucratic crap. No long meetings that waste time. But I'd be a benevolent king."

"All right, I'll go along with your being King as long as I get to be the queen. After all, a queen has a lot of influence as long as she is subtle about it."

"Subtlety has never been your strong point. Sometimes when you have an idea you're like a bull dog hanging on to a bone for dear life, and you won't let it go."

My face flushed. "Oh, you're just prickly because your grandmother bossed you around so much. You never have liked women telling you what to do PERIOD. When we were first married you used to huff and puff about not letting any woman run your life."

Bob glowered over the oars, increasing his speed with long strong pulls. "I admit I used to be chauvinistic, but I don't think I am now. I'm not confusing you with my grandmother, only when you act like her,...which is now. Crabby." He bent his head and back, pulling harder, propelling our dinghy through the water at a mad pace.

Conversation ended for awhile until I could organize my thoughts. No point in getting into a big fight over a dead grandmother whom I'd never met, but I bristled just thinking he had compared her to me in that tone of voice. He hardly liked her at all.

We sailed away from Catalina the next morning, spending the next three days in Newport Beach visiting friends, then continued on toward San Diego. Newport had huge yachts like Marina del Rey, and many women wore expensive clothes and jewelry. "How come I don't look like that?" I commented.

Bob laughed. "Now you know why I've always kept you on a budget."

"How come your budgets didn't apply to you buying tools?"

"Because I'm king." Bob put his hands up as I rushed over to find his tickle spot.

The day turned cloudy, but the temperature remained a comfortable 75 degrees, little one foot waves gently helping push us ahead. As we came abeam of Dana Point buoy we saw seals all over the place, crawling up on each other on the buoy, pushing and shoving smaller seals into the water, all discussing in loud snorts the state of the day's affairs.

"They remind me of fifteen circus clowns all trying to get in or out of a small Volkswagen," I said.

Bob went below and picked up the chart for the area, folded it up and placed it near the wheel for quick viewing. He remembered reading about a submerged reef about 500 yards north-west of the pleasure pier at San Clemente, and reef translates into grief if we sailed too close. We contacted the harbor master's office, paid slip rental for two nights, settling down for a good night's rest.

The next morning Bob bounded out of the sleeping bag, pulled down my coverings and said, "Get cracking, I want to look for an electrical part to install in our new amp meter."

Bob was anxious to find out how much power we were using, and what equipment gobbled up the most amps. We returned from a two mile hike into town after finding the part. After working diligently for five or ten minutes the unit was installed, and the needle quickly peaked upwards. He shook his head, "Turn off the radio."

I reached over and flipped off the radio switch, but the needle barely moved downward.

"Turn off the wind machine."

I switched off our wind speed and direction finder, still the needle barely moved downward.

"Turn off the depth sounder."

The needle made a dramatic downward thrust with Bob exclaiming, "I'll be damned. We're so used to leaving the depth sounder on at home I never thought about it being such a amp hog."

No excuse for being power wasteful any more; one quick check of the meter made us true believers. We knew the ham radio drew the most power when transmitting, making it important to keep one battery fully charged to start the main engine. There was no way we could hand crank our diesel engine.

We were antsy to get started for San Diego, leaving at eight in the morning in moderate winds. Maria hummed through the water at a super pace of seven knots, tossing aside frothy water from her bow. The sound of the water had a hypnotic affect, and I found myself in a meditation mode of complete relaxation. Several hours later something large and white abruptly registered in my consciousness, along with a call on the radio.

"This is the Coast Guard cutter Pt. Hobart on channel 16, calling to the vessel off my port. Come in please."

I looked up to see an eighty foot vessel standing off in the distance. Bob picked up the mike.

"This is Maria Elena, Whiskey Yankee Whiskey, 3036 back to the vessel calling."

The Coast Guard voice answered, "Thank you Maria Elena. We wish to come aboard and give you a safety check. We won't interfere with your progress, or reduce your speed. Several men in an Avon will come over, match your speed, and come aboard. Do I have an affirmative?"

"Affirmative. This is *Maria Elena* WYW 3036 clear."

Bob turned to me with a wry look, "Looks like we have company."

"It's no wonder. *Maria* is so low in the water from all our supplies they probably think we're transporting bales of pot."

Bob rubbed his face, forcing his three day growth of beard to move back and forth, "They'll probably think I'm a pirate."

The black Avon, filled with three young men carrying side arms, drew along side. Bob took their lines, secured them to cleats while I stayed at the wheel and continued our course. Two men came aboard, the third man stayed in the Avon looking very serious. I felt a laugh pull at me when the two officious boys, much younger than my son, came aboard. The laugh soon evaporated when they patted their pistols. One petty officer stayed with me while Bob took the second one below for the "safety check." I chatted with the officer until Bob and the second man came up the companion way. He turned to Bob, "Everything is in order here sir. Thank you for your cooperation. Please keep this report and if you are asked to be boarded again give them this number at the top of the page."

Bob reached out, taking the paper in his hand, and trying to keep the wind from snatching it away. The young man shuffled his feet momentarily, then said, "Excuse me skipper. You don't have to answer this question, but do you carry any weapons?"

With a half smile Bob replied, "Yes, a Walther P38 and a stainless steel Winchester shot gun. We were concerned about foreign waters because our boat fits the profile of ones stolen to transport dope."

The man pulled at his sun reddened nose. "Unfortunately, you're right. There have been over 150 boats that have disappeared in Mexico. Be especially careful in the small, deserted anchorages on the West Coast. I hear from some of the big sport fishers that there's been some trouble in that area. Have a good sail sir, and you too mam."

By the time we reached San Diego we made some important decisions. The shake down cruise along the coast had shown us some of our weaknesses which would interfere with our comfort factor level on the high seas. Bob kept worrying about the small amount of fuel we carried, fifty gallons in one tank, twenty gallons in jerry jugs. He paced up and down the deck until I accused him of wearing a hole in it.

"I think the safety margin is too small, considering the long distances we have to travel," he said.

"Lots of boats travel with less, " I mused. "But I know how you like back ups for back ups. You should change your name from Bob Allen to Bob Redundancy."

"I've been looking at the charts and the Marquesas are 2700 miles from Mexico, Hilo is 2400 miles from Bora Bora and Hawaii is anywhere from 2500 to 3000 miles, depending on how far north we have to travel to get around the high."

"You're the captain. Figure out what you want."

Bob contacted a man who would build us a new fuel tank, taking out a fifty gallon water tank and replacing it with an eighty gallon fuel tank. I wondered how fuel would taste if we lost our water into the bilge again. The queen used her influence, none too subtly, talking Bob into buying a rubber bladder bag to fit under the seat in the main saloon that would hold twenty-five gallons of water. This would be in addition to the seventy gallon water tank in the bow.

In order to get all our errands done we rented a car from Rent A Wreck, the price being in our range. The car had been recycled from the wrecking yard and fixed up, the motor chugging comfortably as we drove to the Mexican Consulate to get our paper work out of the way. We arranged for our visas and boat permit, struggling over whether to try and get a gun permit too. We finally arranged for a quasi gun permit for hunting, but in retrospect, would not do that again. There didn't seem to be a good way to get a permit easily, or legally. I felt uncomfortable and told Bob.

He replied, "You never know what can happen in another country. It's a chance you have to take. If we're boarded by the Federalies it's possible we might lose our guns, or even spend some time in a Mexican jail."

"Prison pallor is not on my color list, and I hate fleas and rats. But I guess I'll have to trust your judgment."

I still felt uneasy, but I reminded myself that life's a risk anyway. We busily looked over the many forms and questions we had to answer at the Consulate, filling them out in triplicate. I tugged at Bob's sleeve, "What are you going to put down for crew?"

Straightening his shoulders he stared back replying, " You are crew. And I know what I'm putting down for captain, me."

"Wait a minute," I countered. "What if something happened to you? They wouldn't let me bring the boat back unless I was a co-captain. Can I be co-captain?"

I looked at his face and saw a look in his eye, not necessarily the one I had hoped for. "I don't think they would allow a co-captain. Just put yourself down as crew."

Drawing myself up to my five foot six inches, I looked directly into his brown, somewhat defiant eyes. Finally, at the risk of making a scene I asked, "If we are going to spend twenty-four hours a day, no further than forty one feet for a year, there has to be some great compromising going on."

"A boat can only have one captain and I intend to be it."

"Fine," I said. "But do I get some input, or do I just take care of your breadfruit plant Captain Bligh?"

Squirming slightly Bob said, "Look honey, there's times when decisions have to be made immediately without discussion. I promise we'll talk afterwards."

"So, you get to make all the decisions and I get to make dinner," I wailed.

He laughed, breaking the tension, kissed my nose and hugged me tight. "You have great ideas, and you know we will make decisions together. What's the big deal?"

"I just want to make sure my captain will be loving, not just an inflated male ego running amuck. Besides, I've made my own decision. Being captain is old hat. I have decided what I really want is to be the admiral."

After a surprised look Bob howled. "I remember my navy days when the Admiral was around our squadron. I don't think you have anything to worry about, because I learned an important lesson. Woe be unto any captain who did not listen to the words of the admiral."

It didn't answer my question about Mexican law, but I guess if something did happen to Bob I decided I would be game enough to steal away in the night and get home somehow. Wow, I thought, have I changed. I used to be afraid to drive to a new place because I might get lost. I had good reason to worry because I *did* get lost, but that was a long time ago.

At least I knew we were starting off with a good compromise and open communication. It's not often you could get a captain and an admiral aboard a forty-one foot boat who could kiss and make up.

With the visas out of the way we prepared to leave for Mexico, shopped for supplies, using the Laundromat one last time, checked for mail, trying not to get too excited so we could sleep that night. We settled our bill (five dollars a night) with the San Diego Police dock, thanking them for their good wishes of fair seas and a good trip. Twenty four hours from now we would be in sunny Mexico, trying our best to make our Spanish believable, and hopefully, understandable.

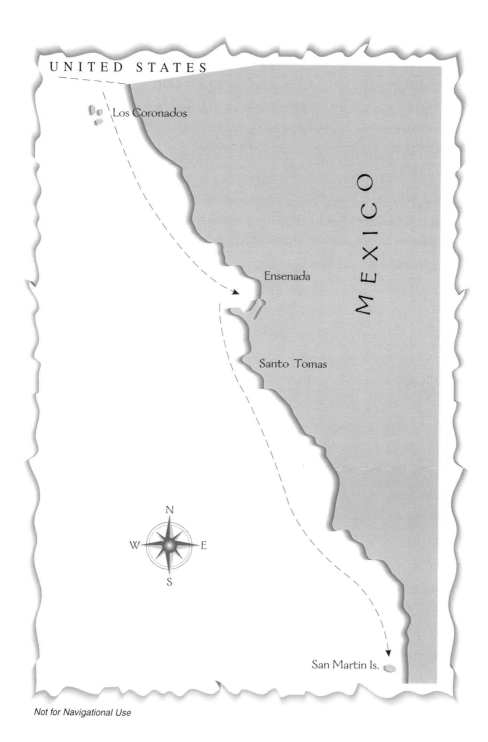

UNITED STATES

Los Coronados

MEXICO

Ensenada

Santo Tomas

N
W E
S

San Martin Is.

Not for Navigational Use

Chapter 10

GOODBYE CALIFORNIA, BUENAS DIAS MEXICO

"O Santy Anna gained the day, hooray Santy Anna.
He lost it once, but gained it twice,
All on the plains of Mexico."
(*"Santa Anna" Windless, or Capstan Chantey*)

At 0430 the next morning, (not my finest hour) we slipped off our mooring lines from the Police dock, elated to be on our way at last to Mexico. Our first stop, Ensenada. We whispered quiet instructions to each other, stepping carefully in the dark to avoid tripping over lines and jerry jugs. The blackness of night clung to our boat as we passed the shadowy forms of nearby vessels, only the growl of our engine and the bubbling discharge water disrupted the surrounding envelop of silence. We were momentarily startled when we crossed between the last ship channel markers, #5 and #6, finding an enormous shape loom ahead of us. When we drew nearer we recognized the contours of a small aircraft carrier. Bob quickly altered our course ten degrees, letting the ship pass our bow within a safe distance.

Soon dawn robbed the day of darkness and we settled into our morning routine of coffee. We sipped the hot coffee, wondering what we would find over the horizon. The first surprise: the quick demise of our Loran signals when we reached the Mexican Coronado Islands. It signaled the end of the Loran stations, and our "Sleeping Beauty" Loran would stay comatose for almost a year, not awakening until the first kiss of a signal when we approached Hawaii.

Bob went below to program a group of way points to Ensenada in the Sat Nav. I gave a quick 360 degree look for other boats and settled down in the cockpit. How many years had it been since I last saw Ensenada? I had been thirteen, I thought. It was hard to believe it had been forty years ago....yet the memory felt vivid and alive...

Mom, dad and I left San Diego early one August morning and crossed the border into Mexico. We were in a joyous holiday mood, bumping down the uneven road in our oil guzzling 1939 blue Pontiac. Dad had finished up his teaching duties for a summer English high school class, and we had been eager to pack the car with food and blankets and get away. It was the summer of 1940. We arrived in Ensenada, a dusty, sleepy town where life moved in slow motion. We couldn't wait to drive to the beaches and leap into the warm, blue water. I never got enough of beaches, even though I had grown up living near one. But this beach proved different. Vacant hot sands stretched for miles around......or so I thought.

After our picnic dinner we rolled ourselves up in blankets, and by early morning I found a disturbing event. I shared my bedding with a million sand fleas, no longer homeless. I discovered the fleas had the upper hand..the upper leg.....and anything else they could feast on.

I wondered what Ensenada would be like now. Would the beaches have the same fleas with a voracious appetite? Was the water as blue? The beaches empty and pristine clean? Bob came back on deck.

"How long will it take us to get to Ensenada?" I said.

"I figure about eleven hours if we get a reasonable wind."

"Good, I want to take a shower in the cockpit. The shower at the Police dock didn't work."

"I'm not sure the water in the wine box bladders has had time to warm up yet in the sun."

I smiled at the sight of seven silver wine box bladders lined up on the foredeck. We had been saving them over the months to be used for a variety of reasons. Not only were they good for shower water storage, but they made great pillows when you blew them up, as well as anchor markers. Bob also discovered they made a perfect non leak container to store used engine oil. And heck, we had a great time emptying the wine bladders earlier, glass by glass by glass, by glass.

After showering a strong afternoon wind arrived, forcing *Maria* into a gallop through the water. I picked up our Mexican cruising guide, settled down in the cockpit and read avidly about Ensenada. The Guide mentioned that some cruisers skipped Ensenada because of the dirty harbor and crowded tourists attractions. Well, I thought, Ensenada just might have changed more than I thought. I put a marker in the book and called Bob, "Here's something we should think about."

Bob looked up from his book. "What?"

"It says to be careful picking up moorings inside Ensenada harbor. There's not much weight holding them. Also it's pretty dirty there."

"I still want to go. It's an easy check in port and I want to see it. We've got plenty of time."

"Okay...just wanted to warn you."

Late in the afternoon we caught sight of the harbor. We took down the sails, secured them and motored through the entrance. A big cruise ship lay along side one section of the harbor, flags flying while waiting for returning passengers. We were so busy looking at the ship we jumped when a voice boomed out next to us.

"Buenas Tardes Senor. I have a good mooring for you."

The voice belonged to a friendly man in a small boat off our starboard. His dark brown eyes were framed by deep sun lines, his head shaded by a broad brimmed hat. His clean clothes were carefully patched, showing neat small hand stitching around the former rents. Seeing us hesitate after his offer he spoke up again. "It's a safe mooring senor. I take good care of you."

"Now what," I whispered to Bob. "We don't want to insult the first person we meet."

Bob smiled back and waved his hand toward the harbor area. "We just got here, and want to take a little harbor tour first."

We needed time to see how many yachts hung on moorings, and how many had elected to anchor. As we toured the harbor our would be guide followed us around, making sure he didn't lose us to some other enterprising Ensenada native. We were surprised to find most boats were moored. So much for the book. Since the news reports indicated continuing mild weather we told our new-found friend we would accept the mooring. His face glowed with happiness. He bent over the side of his boat, picked up a line attached to the mooring, and handed it up to me before we could change our mind. When I leaned down and accepted the slimy manila line I could almost feel *Maria* shudder. Bits of fish guts hung from the oily, ragged line, the smell of it creeping into my nose while I reluctantly secured the line to our cleat. Obviously, this was not the beautiful, clear blue water I remembered forty years ago. The word progress and civilization suddenly took on an ugly, new meaning.

"My name is Villa, Senor and Senora. It's too late to see Capitan del Puerto, and Migracion. They go home. I pick you up at eight oclock tomorrow morning with my boat. Very safe. I only charge you one dollar American."

"Okay," Bob said. "I'll be ready, but don't forget about me."

"I no forget Senor. You see. You tell many friends about Villa and how he care for you. Adios."

A few minutes later our friend Peter arrived in his boat, *Wild Spirit.* He noticed we had tied up to a mooring, shook his head deprecatingly at us, and proceeded to drop his hook. He must have read the same cruising guide. We sat in the cockpit drinking a glass of wine while watching Peter try to get his hook to take a bite, intrigued as it slid over the slimy bottom, refusing to dig in. Swearing under his breath he made several more unsuccessful attempts, then disgustedly hauled the anchor up. Black, smelly, ooze caught on the anchor and chain, running in inky rivulets down the topside of his once white boat. More muffled epithets fell from his lips. Swinging a bucket by its line into the water he sluiced his topside with some relatively clean water and then looked around for an empty mooring. At precisely the same moment a smiling, but patient Villa, motored over, talked for a few minutes and offered Peter a line from another mooring. Scowling slightly, Peter accepted it and paid him for the night. When Villa went by our boat he turned and gave us a conspiratorial wink. Villa knew what the slimy stuff was on the bottom of the harbor, but I decided that ignorance was bliss.

The next morning Villa arrived on time at our boat. He hung on to our topside with both hands while Bob climbed down into his boat. The Captain had decided he should be the one to clear customs, and the "Admiral" had been left as crew. The little boat returned almost immediately since my presence and signature were needed for immigration, true for each port from there on. That will teach the Captain to leave the Admiral behind.

We wanted to do some sightseeing later on in the afternoon so Villa promised he would bring the boat back and take us back to *Maria* We changed money for pesos, walked the streets until we found the infamous Cantina called Hussongs. The Cantina had a reputation for wild night parties, people crawling in and out of the windows, beer and wine flowing down throats as well as shirt fronts.

We went inside and sat down, but before we could order, three Mariachi singers came over to serenade us. My eyes bugged out at the ample figures, stuffed like a sausage into their tight charro pants. I wondered how they could breathe, much less sing. I tried to push the saying out of my mind about ten pounds of potatoes stuffed in a five pound bag, but it kept haunting me. I concentrated on their joyful singing and knew we would enjoy Mexico.

"Why don't you ask the waitress were the tortilla factory is," Bob said.

I summed up my courage and signaled a passing waitress, "Donde esta tortilla factoria?"

She gave me a puzzled look. "Huh? or sure lady, two blocks over and down the right side of the street."

So much for my Spanish in a foreign country. I might as well have been in Brooklyn. We finished our beer and took off to find tortillas for breakfast. I noticed that Ensenada had changed in every way since my last trip. The streets were paved, the stores displayed native Mexican merchandise, grocery stores were filled with recognizable items found in the United States, but forget the paper products. Scratchy. Every time I tried to look at an embroidered blouse Bob gently steered me away.

We found the tortilla factory and joined the line of waiting people. The Mexicans had brought a towel, or bowl, to carry the hot tortillas home, something I had not thought about. When our turn came a man behind the counter piled a huge amount of corn tortillas (100), wrapped them in paper and held out his hand for money. I didn't know how to ask for just a few, so I paid him the going price of about forty cents, wondering how in the heck we were going to eat that many tortillas in a year. We would end up weighing 400 pounds each.

"Well Bob. Put your brain to work. We figured out how to use the wine bladders for different jobs. What can you do with tortillas?"

"We could make tortilla chips out of the older ones later."

"We'll have enough chips to fill the forward cabin. Next?"

"Ah...., use them instead of toast, make sandwiches, feed the birds, make clothes out them, I don't know."

"One thing for sure. We won't go hungry."

The day grew hotter, and Bob's thirst grew larger, prompting him to look for a place to have a beer. I saw a nice looking bar with red lights around the windows. "Look, there's a bar. It looks clean."

Bob threw his head back and laughed. "Didn't you read the sign, Ladies Bar?"

I frowned. "What's wrong with a ladies bar? You could come in too."

"Did you think the red lights were Christmas decorations left over from the holidays? Of course I can go in, but they wouldn't want you there. Competition to the other ladies waiting for my business."

Thud. Each time I thought I was a woman of the world I found I hadn't been around the block enough times. Later I learned Ladies Bar meant it *was* okay for women. Even a captain can be wrong.

We walked to the harbor and stopped for beer and dinner at a local cafe. The waiter looked strangely at the huge pile of tortillas we set down on the table, probably wondering how hungry we were.

We found Villa asleep in his car, his round brown wife cuddled up close to him with her head resting on his shoulder. We saw the remains of their dinner next to glowing coals of a barbecue. Bob whispered, "I hate to wake them up."

"Me too, but we have to get back to the boat. The tortillas are going to be worn out from carrying them around."

Villa's eyes opened wide when he heard our soft voices next to his car. He sat up, waking his wife when he opened the car door and slammed it shut. She opened her eyes, snorted and went back to sleep. Villa took us back to our boat and we paid him $5.00 a day for the mooring, and the rest of the $20.00 bill paid for the numerous trips back and forth from our boat to shore.

Once settled I repacked the tired tortillas into zip lock bags while Bob opened the top to the nav station and and took out the next chart showing Puerto Santa Tomas, our next anchorage. He placed it on the table to study in the morning. "Looks like a good anchorage. The chart says there is protection from the wind and swells."

A bright sun greeted us the next morning and after a breakfast of.... surprise..tortillas.... we slipped off the smelly mooring line from our cleat and dropped it back into the black waters of the harbor. So much for memories of pristine blue water and beaches.

We put up the sails, and *Maria* raced through the waters like a thoroughbred. Just as quickly as the wind came up, it quit, the seas flattened out, reflecting the boat and clouds in the still water. Bob started the engine, "Looks are deceiving. The weather report earlier said we would get twelve food seas by nightfall. I want to be well anchored by then."

I looked at the placid sea. "Do they have the same kind of weather reports we do at home? I remember the Coast Guard small craft warning telling of thirty knot winds while we drifted around Point Conception."

"I don't want to take a chance in case they're right. You won't mind getting to the anchorage early anyhow."

We arrived by three fifteen, picking our way around the many lobster pens which filled the cove, finally dropping our anchor in six fathoms of water. We glanced toward the shore and saw stone steps leading up from the beach to a small village. According to the chart this was part of a large ranch where cabins and boats could be rented for fishing vacations. We didn't see anyone and it seemed deserted on this particular day. Suddenly the sky clouded over, and freshening winds from the east picked up, rolling us about so that we danced around the anchor. This was just the beginning of a very long night. We went to bed early, wanting a good start on the next day's run. In the middle of the night a large waved slapped so sharply against the hull our bodies lifted several inches off our sleeping bags, almost dumping us on the cabin sole. Unfortunately this wasn't a rogue wave, but the beginning of many slaps to come which made sleeping impossible. I heard Bob sigh and desert his sleeping bag. As soon as his feet hit the companionway steps I called out, "Do you have your safety harness on?"

There was a slight pause before his foot steps returned down the companionway. A drawer opened and closed, and I heard him go up on deck. Good, I thought, it would be easy to get knocked overboard. He returned to bed later, groaning with fatigue. "I put a bridal on the anchor because the wind was setting us broadside to the swell. I also put out the flopper stoppers to slow down the roll. Move over. I'm pooped."

With that last pronouncement he fell asleep. No rest for the wicked, we woke up at 0300 to start the process of taking up the anchor and extra lines. A full moon made it easier to see while we worked. The silvery path of light captured our boat in elongated patterns of the mast and rigging, resembling a loose web built by a lazy spider. I took care of pulling up and stowing the flopper stoppers, and making coffee, while Bob argued with the seaweed stuck to the anchor and chain. It was cut and slash time again.

We finally shipped anchor an hour later, skirting a tug and barge traveling down the coast. The cool night air made us snuggle down in our warm jackets, while yawns reproduced themselves as each of us tried to recover from our restless, short night. Despite the trouble with the anchor it felt good to be on our way again, destination San Martin Island. We hoped the wind would blow strongly during the day so we wouldn't have to listen to our motor every time the wind died. Sailing tried to teach patience, but students like myself have a hard time learning. My personality was more like the poster that hung in my son's room, "Patience hell, I'm going to kill something."

Bob looked up at the cool glow of the full moon. "With the moon waning it is a perfect time to take a moon sight with my new sextant. Want to try yours?"

"Sure. I've only done sun shots. The water's so calm I'll have a better shot at the horizon. Stay there. I'll get our sextants and stop watch."

I returned with a light weight Davis sextant for myself, and handed Bob the heavier, and more accurate, Tamaya Jupiter. We spent a half an hour trying out different sights, writing down our times and readings on our moon and planet form. After a while the lack of rest made my head feel fuzzy, and I decided to put my sextant back in its protective case.

"I don't know about you," I said, "but I'm too tired to do the calculations. Let's number crunch later. I'll just end up with nothing but mistakes."

Bob placed his sextant in its case, stood up and rotated his head around in a circle, and stretched his arms out to the sky, shaking out his cramped shoulders. "Good idea. My numbers probably wouldn't make sense to me either."

When the sun finally peeked its rosy cheeks above the horizon I went below to try my ham radio. Nothing but static. I tried the Baja net later and talked to an American insurance adjuster living in Ensenada. He gave me a run down on some stolen boats to look for as we pulled in and out of small harbors. "Don't approach them," he warned. "Just call on the ham net and I'll notify the authorities."

I hung up my mike and went back up on deck., pleased to see the wind had come up. *Maria* skimmed over the ruffled water, gently pushing aside little wavelets in her path. Contentment. The night's tensions drained away and were replaced by a connection and oneness with the world and nature. I couldn't tell if I was so darn relaxed I couldn't stand up, or whether I was just tired out of my skull. It didn't really matter. I was happy.

I returned with the Davies and handed Bob the heavier more accurate Tamaya Jupiter.

My reverie shattered when several squawking gulls flew over, swooping down to see if we wanted to share any food. They inspected the fishing line we trailed behind us for anything edible, and found only a small piece of seaweed. They dropped a reminder of their disgust on the fantail.

As the day progressed the winds lightened slightly and my usual worry wart feelings appeared. "What happens if the sun sets before we get to San Martin?" I asked.

"We go on. I won't enter a strange harbor at night."

I yawned, praying we would get there on time so we could get a quiet night's sleep, not the rolly coaster ride we had the night before.

Later that afternoon we saw the outline of an island in the distance. I wondered it we would win the race to the harbor before the sun bid us adios for the night. The fifteen knot northwest wind filled the sails, humming a tune on the rigging. The ground swells swept us into their rolling grasp, lifting us up amid bubbling foam, and sending us closer to San Martin. I took out the binoculars and stared at the small island, watching it grow larger in the lens as we drew closer.

"That's it," I cried. "It's shape is a circle, and there's two high peaks near the center. Where's the anchorage?"

"The best one for small craft is off the east side of the island. I think we can tuck in down inside there and get good shelter from this wind. Take the wheel while I get the sails read to drop."

"I see fishing boats, but I think there's room for us too," I said, crossing my fingers for good luck.

Bob wound up the self furling genoa. I turned into the wind while he dropped the main, tugging at the 9 and 3/4 ounce heavy Dacron cruising sail to make it drop faster. Once the big sail was secured he went forward to drop the anchor. Waving his arms he pointed to the spot he wanted, directing me into the wind and to slow down, ...neutral, splash went the anchor, then slowly backing down to set it,...just as the sun set.

"Now that's calling it close," he laughed. "Let's eat, I'm starved."

I held up a zip lock bag of tortillas. "You can have anything you want as long as I can wrap it in one of these."

"How about some tortillas and peanut butter to start."

"Unusual appetizer, but healthy. I'll put on a sea chantey tape and get the rest of dinner started."

Around eight-thirty our eyes drooped with fatigue. Bob dried the last dish, then went on deck to check our anchor and position of the other boats. Gratefully we fell into bed and prayed for a quiet night. Two hours later I awoke, listened to the wind in the rigging and dragged myself out of bed to check the anchor. Two hours later another pair of eyes went on deck to check our position. Once convinced we were there to stay we both slept like babes.

We awoke the next morning feeling rested, and cozily nestled in each other's arms. We could hear Spanish chatter from the surrounding fish boats, but the words exploded so rapidly I could only pick out a few I knew. Once on deck I could see the fisherman attaching hooks to lines. We also saw two other boats that had arrived during the night. One was a sailboat called Moonstone, and the other was a power boat from Tacoma called Art's Toy. Evidently he had engine problems because we could hear banging, and the sound of a coughing motor. Once the engine started to purr the boat quickly left the anchorage.

The sun beamed down on the sparkling blue water and I decided this would be a good time for a shower. I called to Bob below, "Honey, could you hang up some towels around the cockpit. I want to take a sun shower, but the boat keeps swinging around toward the fishing boats. If I start taking off my clothes there are going to be more eyes in this cockpit than I can handle."

112

"You should be used to bathing with company after all these years," Bob said.

"Just because we take baths together doesn't mean I want to put this show on the road."

Taking baths together started in our first home. We had a twenty gallon water heater which was enough heat for one good bath. We either bathed together, or one person froze. Being newly married bathing sounded like fun, but it got us into trouble when too much fun made us late for work, or a party. Ah well, it appears that the couple who bathes together, stays together in our case. But unless they build bigger tubs we can't gain any more weight.

Bob hung up the towels and that's when the invasion started. First one kelp fly flew in. Then he, or she, sounded the alarm, and before we knew it, thousands of flies followed, landing on the deck cushions, towels, bodies..biting, tickling, buzzing in our ears, testing what little patience we had. This called for action by Superman Bob, The Giant Fly Killer. Faster than a speeding bullet he pulled the fly swatter from below, and thus began the carnage of black flies filling our boat like a run by Lemmings. Just when I thought he was through I bent down to get a better look at an usually large fly. I saw slight movement. There were two or three flies on top of one engaged in vigorous activity. I wondered if any of the female flies ever had a headache and said, "no." Maybe they just bathed together, I thought.

After our shower I returned from below carrying moon sight papers, books, plotting paper and a calculator, plus cortisone creme for itching fly bites. I settled down on our cockpit cushion, twisting the pencil in my mouth as I tried to remember instructions from our celestial navigation course. Bob picked up his pencil and furrowed his brow, deep in thought. He thumbed through the Nautical Almanac until he found the right page giving the moon GHA and declination, handing me the book when he was through. He looked up the correct page in the H.O. 249 sight reduction book. With this information gathered he wrote down calculations on our moon sight work paper, then grabbed a piece of plotting paper where he drew the longitude and latitude of our area, placing an X assumed position. After a half an hour he grunted in a satisfactory way, pleased with his results. I was much slower, going back over my work for errors, placing my memory banks into a flurry of activity. I peeked at Bob's plotting paper, then took one of my own, taking a slightly different assumed position. When I finally finished I felt exhausted, but triumphant.

I wasn't as close as Bob, but at least I was in the right hemisphere.

While I had been intently working on my moon sight, Bob had been deeply engrossed in charts, planning our next landfall in Turtle Bay. I leaned over his shoulder and nibbled his ear. He smelled good, mostly like Bob, and some like Zest soap from his shower. "You sure are taking a long time plotting our course to Turtle Bay, " I said.

"It's a tough section of cruising. Lots of hazards, including Sacramento reef, and very strong currents that can put you on land fast."

He pointed to the chart, his finger resting on Sacramento reef. "Here's where the old schooner *Goodwill* went down, grinding into pieces on the reef one night. Such a shame. She was a beautiful old yacht."

"You're right, not only would *Maria* not like hitting a reef, but it wouldn't do a lot for me either."

"I'll need to set a course to compensate for the swift current, keeping us well out to sea." He drew several lines on the chart.

"Great. Wouldn't you know this section would come at the beginning of our first real three on, three off night watch schedule."

Hardly aware what I was doing, I rubbed my hands together in the warm air. Well, I thought, tomorrow may turn out to be very interesting. I hope we'll be able to get a good night's sleep. I shivered with excitement.

The next morning I got up early, cooking a big Sunday breakfast of bacon, eggs, and of course, tortillas. After breakfast we cleaned up, then checked all areas of the boat to make sure we were ready for sea duty. Everything needed to be put away, cabinets secured, gear tied in, nothing left loose that could break, or fly around the cabin and trip us. Once on deck looked at the beauty of the cirrus and stratus clouds streaming across the sky. A cooling breeze piped up and caressed my face. The barometer read 30.20, so it looked like fair weather for the day. The anchor came up easily and we were on our way by 0900 in a four knot breeze. By early afternoon we had eighteen to twenty knots of wind, bringing our speed up to seven to seven and a half knots as we sailed wing and wing. Unfortunately the boat rolled from side to side in the trough of the swells. We felt the rolls more after the wind dropped later in the afternoon.

By eight that night Bob started the first watch, putting on his safety harness, and promising me he would hook it on to the steering pedestal. I looked at him sitting by the wheel, arms crossed in front of his chest while watching the auto pilot take over his job.

"I'm not tired yet," I said.

"Go below and try to sleep. Otherwise you'll hate me when I boot you out of your bunk at eleven."

I crawled into my bunk and closed my eyes. Sleep eluded me and I tossed and turned, listening to the noise of the rigging, and the groan of the boat as waves slapped the sides. I opened my eyes, but it was only nine. Rats. True to his word Bob came down at eleven, took off his harness and jacket, and climbed into the still warm covers. Blissfully he closed his eyes. I put on my jacket and harness and wished I had learned to sleep when I could.

I checked the sails to see if they needed an adjustment, but all was well. I looked twice all around the boat to check for freighters, tugs and barges, or other pleasure craft, then set our kitchen timer for twenty minutes. When it rang I would repeat the same procedure. I pulled up my collar when the breeze snuck down my neck and realized how tired, and bored I felt. Not a great beginning of a watch. About midnight our radar detector starting beeping signals and I saw the lights of a freighter bering down the coast behind me. I went below and took a reading of our latitude and longitude from the Sat Nav, then picked up the radio mike.

"This is the yacht Maria Elena on channel 16 calling the freighter off my stern" I gave him my latitude and longitude readings. "I am steering a course of 152 Magnetic and I'm wondering if you have me on your radar."

A gruff foreign voice answered, "One moment please." A few minutes later he came back, "Maria Elena, I see you. Have a good evening."

I watched him carefully, knowing that some foreign freighters do not always keep a radar watch. This would be the procedure we would use each time we made a contact with a vessel. Not everyone answered, thereby making us more careful as we sailed in busy waterways. Many times a started man's voice answered my obviously feminine voice, pausing when I asked what his intentions was. True to life some men wouldn't commit, and others pretended not to hear me.

At 0200 I was more than ready to end my watch, almost yanking Bob out of the sleeping bag. He rubbed his eyes, unstuck his tongue and opened his mouth in a loud yawn. "Night," I mumbled.

The next day the wind dropped dramatically, and glassy seas reflected blinding sunlight back at us. We retreated under the sun shield to our books. I cuddled up close to Bob and said, "I want to hold your hand."

"How can I turn the pages without a hand?" he smiled.

"Forget the book silly, you can read anytime."

We lay contentedly on the cushions for some time in quiet contemplation. I opened my eyes and looked sideways at Bob, liking what I saw. He still looked as good to me as the day I married him. Age had created a few more lines, which he called character lines. How come, I thought, men have character lines and women have wrinkles? The gray hair had softened from its wiry beginnings, but there was still enough to frame his handsome face. The physical changes that had taken place since he retired made him younger. No more pasty, gray facial color, worry lines, or frustrated hard mouth. These were removed by an operation called, "Realizing Our Dream," a non surgical procedure guaranteed to lengthen both our lives.

"I love you Bob Allen," I said softly. "I don't know how it's possible, but I love you more every day."

He sat up, leaning on his elbow and stared into my eyes. "I love you too. I've loved you from the first day I met you. You didn't believe me when I told you."

"I couldn't decide it you meant it, or were just putting the moves on me like other college guys. Persistence won out. Lord knows you were persistent."

I wondered what my life would have been like if I hadn't listened to this sailor. Probably pretty dull. I never considered myself an adventuresome person growing up, so this new life was quite a contrast compared to the hum drum suburban housewife routine I had imagined. What, I thought, if I hadn't allowed myself to grow and change? It would have been so easy not to take scuba lessons, or learn to sail, but Bob would have done both without me. I guess when it came right down to it I couldn't stand to be left behind, even if it scared the "bejasus" out of me at times.

That night on watch I looked up into the incredibly beautiful night sky gleaming back at me, like the biggest neon sign in the world saying, "Welcome travelers." The countless stars that filled the sky looked like a million diamonds spilling into a thirsty sea, sliding down on the silken path of the milky way. I was surprised to find myself humming, "Twinkle, twinkle little star," wondering if the composer had been a sailor and couldn't contain his joy.

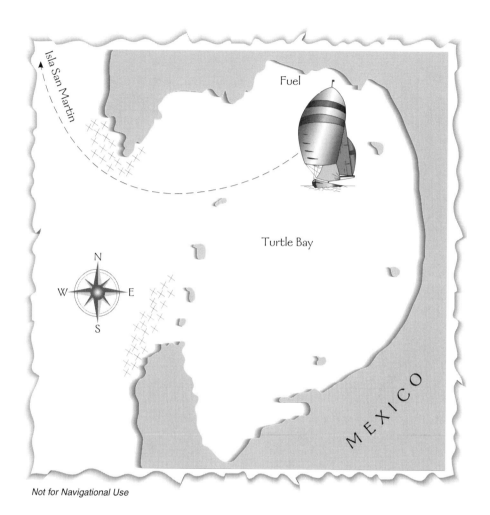

Isla San Martin

Fuel

Turtle Bay

N
W   E
S

MEXICO

Not for Navigational Use

Chapter 11

A FISHY TALE

My dad was a fisherman bold and he lived til he grew old
Til he opened the pane and popped out the flame
Just to see how the wind do blow.
He often said to me: "You'll be wise before you go
Do you open the pane and pop out the flame
Just to see how the wind do blow.
(English Sea Chantey, referring to a candle blown
out by too much wind, which was bad for fishing)

After viewing the wondrous heavens I chose a group of stars I could call mine, one that would keep me company on watch. I chose the constellation Orion. Orion's belt consisted of three major navigational stars, Alnilam, Bellatrix and Betelgeuse, lined up in a row. I found viewing something familiar each night seemed to pick up my spirits, or maybe it was just a thread of continuity weaving a path of orderliness through my new life.

I jumped when the bell on the timer reminded me it was time to take two 360 degree checks for ship traffic, look at the sails, make sure our auto pilot kept us on the right course, and write down the last satellite position from the Sat Nav. I envied Bob asleep in our bunk.

Returning to my seat cushion I ploughed through thoughts, feelings, and events running circles around in my mind, bringing back memories of my early sailing efforts. Bob tried to be a patient husband, God love him, because he didn't always succeed..

When I first sailed with Bob in a medium wind I was terrified. In a little breeze my teeth would grind, even though he tried to explain boats were supposed to heel in the wind. Heel hell, I thought, I was sure the boat was going over, throwing me into the cold, dark water. Patiently he drew a picture on a piece of paper for me. "See," he said, "this is a keel attached to the bottom of the boat. When the wind fills the sails it causes the boat to lean to one side, or heel. The weight of the keel on the bottom of the boat brings it back into an upright position again, keeping it from tipping all the way over."

"Promises, promises," I moaned, my teeth chattering.

In heavier breezes I kept trying to picture Bob's drawing, but it was hard to concentrate when I couldn't stand up straight. In a very strong breeze, my white knuckles, ashen face and urgent bladder caused me no end of trouble. If I went below to the head I knew I would get seasick, but if I stayed on deck it left me with the real possibility of peeing in my pants. I had to keep reminding myself of Bob's comment after we got married, "I hope you like sailing, or I'm going to miss you." His encouragement won out. I gradually condescended to take the wheel, sometimes pointing and shouting, " Bob, there's another boat over there. Are we going to hit it? What do you want me to do?"

Shading his eyes he peered in the distance for several seconds, finally picking out a tiny speck on the horizon. "Good God Marlene, that boat is so far away you couldn't hit it if you tried."

I remembered one special "Opening Day Of The Yachting Season." Each year Pacific Interclub Yacht Association put on an opening day parade the last Sunday of April, drawing thousands of boats of all kinds and sizes, each trying not to occupy the same space in the bay. Sailing through the fleet of yachts was something like commuting on a grid locked freeway full of drunk drivers, all squeezing their horns and shouting at each other.

Bob looked at the wall to wall boats, smiled and said, "What a great opportunity for you to sail."

Oh well, I thought, as long as he is right next to me, nothing terrible can happen. It was then he announced that nature had called and he had to go below to the head. Glancing wildly at the madhouse of boats, I cried, "Tie a knot in it. Don't you dare leave me."

But leave me he did, scuttling below decks like the rat I called him. After a few minutes I found I could steer by myself, making reasonable decisions, like not slicing another boat in half, or changing course in order to give sea room to other boats. By the time he came back on deck I wasn't willing to relinquish the wheel, electrified by a satisfying sense of power and accomplishment of handling a 28,000 pound boat. The old joke about "what does a two ton elephant do?" came to my mind. The answer being, "anything he wants." I felt as if I was in command of a 28,000 pound elephant of a boat, telling it what to do. I imagined race drivers experienced the same feelings, taking up the challenge of winning at all costs. For me, it was winning over my fear, making the boat a part of me instead of assigning the whole responsibility to Bob. Before that memorable day I had talked about "Bob's boat," now it was "our" boat. How sweet it was for me to understand that at last true enjoyment of sailing was possible for me... without peeing in my pants.

Dawn painted the sky, sweeping delicate, rosy brush strokes across the heavens. My watch ended, and despite the beauty of the day, my body cried out for sleep. I gleefully climbed below to move Bob out of my place in the warm bedding. Two hours later I heard my name from on deck,...no I thought, it couldn't be time for my watch. I dragged myself out of the covers and sleepily shlumped up the steps, wishing I could brush my teeth first and remove the fur. Once on deck Bob told me the auto pilot had committed mutiny.

"All of a sudden the boat turned in a tight arc, going round and round with the sails whipping all over the place," he said.

I rubbed sleep out of my eyes and asked, "Didn't you turn off the switch on the unit?"

"It didn't do any good. I don't understand why, but I had to turn the whole thing off at the main switch panel. I felt like the astronaut in the movie, Two Thousand One, when the computer took over control of the space station. Otto took over our boat until I pulled his plug."

I hand steered while Bob removed the relays from the auto pilot, found them pitted and welded together after arcing. Otto had really blown his top, and two fuses besides. Bob applied fine sand paper to the relays, taking away all signs of pitting, and placed the repaired relays back into the unit. Soon a healthy auto pilot was hard at work again. Now, time to pull myself together and get breakfast.

Afterwards I saw Bob pouring over the charts, his posture tense and rigid. That surprised me "What now?" I asked.

"I'm trying to gauge our speed so we won't reach Turtle Bay in the dark. I want to make an early morning landfall. It's hard to tell what our progress will be when the wind comes up like gang busters for a while, and then drops away to nothing."

"I worry more about the lack of navigational lights in Mexico. You can't count on them."

"That's why we have to be so careful. Everything looks the same at night, and daytime isn't much better. I've never sailed a coast where the countryside is so similar. If we weren't paying close attention it would easy to mistake one point of land for another."

I went below to try and get a weather fax picture. I hadn't had much luck earlier, the maps came out looking like gray paper that had been rained on. We were using my ham radio as a receiver for the Alden weather fax, which may not have been cost effective after all. I was pleased to see paper being spit out by the fax, but disappointed to see I had been too late to get the regular forecast, receiving only wind, wave or currents information. At least it was readable. I gently took a damp sheet depicting the wave patterns from the fax to show Bob. I found him staring at the water with the binoculars, intent upon an object floating in the water. Without taking the binoculars from his eyes he told me to come up next to him. "Come look at this floating tank. It's about thirty feet long and fifteen feet wide. What scares the hell out of me is it's floating so low in the water."

I could feel the hair prickle at the back of my neck, knowing in the fading light of the afternoon sun we could have easily run into the tank. "Let me look," I said. "Gosh, it's really a rusted hulk of steel. It would tear the hell out of poor Maria, maybe even sink us."

Bob got up and headed toward the companionway. "I'm going below to get our latitude and longitude reading. Then I'll call on channel 16 and put out a navigational hazard message. If there's any ham nets working at this time you can put out a QST on the net."

I went below and tried to call Peter, hoping he would be listening. "N6 DQN, this is N6 LDM. Are you there Peter?" I tried several more times, finally receiving an answer back. I explained the tank situation, giving him the navigational coordinates, and asked him to warn other boats in the area. Peter wanted to talk to Bob, so I banged on the hatch, yelling Bob's name. I knew he was on deck because I could hear the thumping noise of his feet jumping around. Strange, I thought, it sounds like he's doing a dance up there. I banged on the hatch again, receiving back a furious pounding from Bob. I signed off with Peter, feeling somewhat annoyed by Bob's break dancing on the hatch above my head. My annoyance turned to laughter when I came topside. I found him struggling to hang on to his fishing pole as an enraged fish at the end of his line thrashed and danced, jerking Bob's arms up and down.

"Thank God you finally came up." said Bob. "I was pulling in the fishing line for the night when this critter hooked on. I couldn't put the pole down and put the boat in neutral too."

I walked forward to the cockpit, disengaged the gear and went below to look for the gaff and a little league baseball bat. Bob and I knew almost nothing about fishing when we bought our equipment in San Diego, but the clerk assured us he knew everything about fishing and we should trust him. When he brought out the baseball bat I was sure he thought he had a couple of suckers on his line, but he was insistent the bat was necessary if we caught a Wahoo. "Wahoos," he said, "are real fighters with very sharp teeth. If they get near you they'll slice you up. Great eating fish though."

I thought of this conversation with the clerk as I returned to help Bob. "Do you suppose it's a Wahoo?" I said.

Sweating and hanging on for dear life to the pole, he turned to me. "Just get the gaff and hook the damn thing up here."

Bob started to pull in the two foot twisting fish, making me jump into action. I leaned over the stern as far as I could, swinging the gaff at the silvery body, surprising all by connecting the steel point to tough gill flesh. "Look at those mean looking teeth," I gasped.

"I am, I am," he said. He held the pole away from his body, keeping the thrashing fish's teeth from tattooing his legs.

"You have to use the little league bat on him, stun him," I said.

Bob picked up the silver bat, rolling his eyes in despair. He didn't have a killing instinct when it came to nature, and his first whack was somewhat half hearted, only grazing the fish slightly. He couldn't get close enough with a knife to slice his head and I called out, "Hit him harder."

"All right, give me a chance."

After the second hard hit, blood squirted out, painting the deck in streaks of red. The third and final hit resulted in more blood, spraying Bob's legs and swim suit, until he looked as if he had been in a fight for his life. He completed his task and threw the once proud fish into our igloo cooler. I looked around at the bloody scene in dismay, "This looks like something out of the Chain Saw Massacre. No wonder I buy all my fish at the market."

Bob sat down on the deck exhausted, but starved. "Now you get to fillet it while I clean up."

It reminded me of an old movie where the hunter brought in an animal, dumped it on the steps in a "Me Tarzan, you Jane mode." I made a face at the blood and put on my foul weather pants, then grabbed my fillet knife and cutting board and went to work on my first fish. I prayed I wouldn't ruin the fish or me. I neatly removed the skin from the meat and set down my knife. "You know you're a big softie when it comes to killing animals, or fish."

Bob paused, leaning on the deck brush. "I remember when I killed a rabbit with my first gun. I felt so bad,....and there was no way I would eat it. Little defenseless animals are different, but let a man try to break into my house and I'll blast him to hell."

It was a long night, no wind, but a beautiful moon to light our way. I saluted my three stars, seeing them reflected in the quiet, luminous water, then broken into pieces by little waves from the wake of our boat. The hypnotic drone of the engine made me sleepy, and I had to make a conscious effort to stay alert for coastal traffic. At this point I must make a confession. I was ruining Bob's sleep for the damndest reason, one which was common to other beginning cruisers. When a star either rose from the horizon, or was just setting, it looked exactly like a ship's light. Even the color had an incandescent yellow glow in the sky. On the first night watches I worried about other ship and yacht traffic so much I would go down and ask, "Bob, I'm not sure, but I think there's a boat coming toward us and I'm concerned."

"Ok, I'll take a look."

He padded up the companionway steps, poked his head outside, "It's just a star rising, don't worry. Can I go back to bed now?"

"How can you tell so quickly?"

"Did you ever see a mast light on a boat getting taller?"

"That's embarrassing. I'm sorry, go back to bed," I said.

At 0700 we spotted Turtle Bay. Bob went below to double check our charts, making sure we stayed clear of the rocks and reef extending from Cabo Tortola. We felt a little anxious about Turtle Bay, remembering four months earlier two yacht skippers had been murdered there. The wife of one murdered man was almost raped. The married couple's name was

Bob and Marlene, with the horrible coincidence of being the same age as we were. We hated starting out on a trip feeling uneasy about our safety. We hoped Turtle Bay would be a positive experience for this *other* Bob and Marlene.

Turtle Bay had always been a close knit community. Most of the men worked for the government as lobster fisherman, therefore the town's people were devastated to find that two of the local boys were responsible for the killings. The two young men, along with a case of beer, had been brought out to one yacht owned by a single handed American skipper. The three of them got roaring drunk, argued over something, ending up with the boys knifing the skipper. They took the dead man's dinghy, rowed over to the boat anchored close by, and confronted the skipper, Bob. They forced their way into the boat looking for more beer and money, ending up shooting the skipper with his own gun, then attempting to rape his wife. She managed to jump naked overboard, swimming to another yacht for help. The owners alerted the authorities on the radio of the tragic happenings. The killers realized they were in deep trouble, pulled up the anchor and attempted to steal the boat, but managed to only get as far as one of the large rocks at the entrance. They left the boat and swam away to safety. The authorities came out to the boat and rescued the injured husband, taking him to the local hospital where he died. When the wife finally related her story to the town interpreter she described her assailants in great detail. The interpreter turned chalk white. She didn't know she had just described the interpreter's son, complete with the special tattoo on his arm. The town people suffered along with the widow since something special in many lives had been taken away forever.

The loud moaning blast on a conch shell banished our heavy thoughts. Peter waved his arms from his boat, welcoming us into the anchorage. He blew again into his conch shell while the rest of the crew played a kazoo and a flute. Bob bragged about catching his Wahoo. The length he described kept getting bigger by the minute. He had already mastered the art of telling a fish story, or should I say, fishy story.

It was a relief to anchor in one of the best all-weather anchorages between San Diego and Magdalena Bay. One hundred and fifty feet off the fish cannery pier, our forty-five pound CQR anchor dropped through three to four fathoms of water, settling nicely into the sand. Before we changed our clothes we launched the dinghy, filling it with empty diesel jerry jugs, and empty water containers to replace our dwindling supply in our tanks. There was hardly room for us as we climbed down into the dinghy and headed for the pier.

We tied up the dinghy and climbed up the steep ladder to the pier, greeted by two young men wearing levi pants and colorful shirts. With big smiles, and bowing slightly, they called to us in Spanish, cocking their heads to one side in puzzlement when I tried to answer back in my fractured Spanish. I tried to explain I wanted to buy chicken, but I obviously didn't know the correct word. Finally the older of the two boys said, "pollo," and the word clicked in my mind. I nodded my head, answering "Si senor, es correcto." I smiled in satisfaction, while the boys giggled and whispered to each other. The older boy gestured with his hand to follow him, so like the Pied Piper we set off single file. Our young man stopped in front of an old wooden building where white, blistered paint ravaged the outside walls. On entering we found a man selling chicken. The room contained an untold numbers of flies, their insistent buzzing distracted Bob as he picked out pesos to pay for our chicken in the hot, stuffy room. Our guide pointed to his chest, then to an apple and soft drink, his face reflecting a questioning look.

"Si," I said, indicating we would pay for apples and soft drinks for both boys. "Senors, tortillas?" I asked.

He and his friend smiled again, indicating he wanted us to follow him. He took us to a private home, knocked on the door, where we were invited in by a middle aged woman covered with a light covering of corn dust. She motioned for us to sit down on an old flowered couch. She nodded and went to work, her hands making a soft slapping sound as she formed the shape of the tortilla. Her smooth brown face had a far-away look, as if she was thinking about some special place she wished to be. Repetitive jobs had the same effect on me.

Looking around I knew we had reached rural Mexico, just as I remembered it at thirteen. The unpaved roads spread out ahead of us, and little dust swirls followed our feet, settling down inside our shoes. We walked all over town, passing broken-down cars rusting in quiet disrepair. They looked as tired as we were. We decided it was time to cool down with a cold one, Carta Blanca beer. We thanked our guides, giving them some extra money as well as our thanks for their help.

Back at the pier we started to look for Gordo, the man we needed to sell us our diesel fuel. He spoke English and told us we could get good water from the desalinization plant near by. We took turns carrying our water jugs back and forth to the plant, while Gordo filled our fuel jerry jugs from rusting barrels. Thank God for fuel filters.

The hard job came next, transferring the heavy jerry jugs of water and fuel down the steep ladder and into our dinghy. Bob climbed into our dinghy and retrieved a line, then scrambled back up on the pier. "You get back into the dinghy," he said, "and I'll lower the jerry jugs."

I balanced myself in the boat, grabbed the jugs as they came down and placed them in the bottom of the boat, untying the line and sending it up to Bob again. I could feel the strain of lifting the jugs in my arms, and was glad I had been athletic as a youngster, and fairly active as an oldster. I looked down, noticing the biceps in my arms were becoming more defined and making the arm holes of my blouses fit more tightly.

When Bob climbed into the boat I pointed to my bulging biceps. He squeezed the hardened muscle and said, "I think I've created a monster, but I did a better job than Frankenstein."

"You better watch out. When we get home I'll go to Petaluma and enter the arm-wrestling contest and embarrass the hell out of you." With a flourish of my hand I sat down hard, almost rocking the dinghy over.

Once back on board our boat, I brought out two buckets, soap and our dirty clothes. I thought of my mother who had moaned and groaned about how hard it was to scrub clothes in the bath tub. In the 1930's not everyone owned a washer, and even though we were in the 1980's, I felt a time warp take place as I washed our clothes in a old bucket. My agitator was a sheet metal hand-held device which worked like a plumber's helper, sold to yachties like ourselves, as well as to people living in the Appalachian mountains. Two quite diverse consumers. I did have one luxury, a built in wringer named Bob.

After three days we needed to get going. We awoke very early, the clock showed four in the morning, and I wrote that down next to the date, November 15, in my ship's log. We quietly weighed anchor, and Bob, armed with his search light, remained up on the fore deck to watch for floating lobster traps. Unwary cruisers found the traps also caught props. After we had cleared the rocks at the entrance, he settled down in the cockpit, ready for a rest and relaxation. It was not to be. About an hour later, good old Murphy moved aboard the boat with his saying, *"anything bad that can happen, will happen."* I wondered why Mrs. Murphy put up with such a loser all those years. First, the topping lift wrapped itself around the back stay, while the engine alarm light blinked on and off. Third and worst, the Sat Nav started acting up by not updating information. I could hear Bob mumbling and grumbling by the navigation table, "Damn, it looks like the distance log isn't working. It's not updating our position at all."

My agitator was a sheet metal device....

I put my arm on his shoulder, "Calm down. I know how much you hate things not working. Why don't you wait until it's light and can check things then."

"Because I don't want to wait." He frowned, stomped around the cabin, while trying to reason out what could have gone wrong.

"I give up then," I said. "Why don't you go on watch for a minute and think, while I check into the Sonrisa ham net."

Grumbling some more, he went on deck, while I discovered Murphy had entered the Sonrisa net, making it impossible to hear anything because of a very high noise level. Now it was my time to grump.

The day got better, with Murphy retiring to some other boat, and Bob finally fixed the log. He pulled out the knot log sending unit, quickly replacing it with a plug as sea water poured in the through hull fitting. He looked at the unit, "Can you believe this," he said, "there's a whole generation of worms living in here. Their bodies are hard as rock, keeping the paddles of the log from moving."

"I'm glad you can scrape them out. I'd better get some more towels ready to soak up the water when you put the unit back in."

Later that day the noise level on the ham radio diminished, making it possible for me to place our first call to the United States. We reached our daughter-in-law, Katie, letting her know we were alive and well and missing the family. I signed off, thanking the other ham operator for his help in patching my phone call through. With tears rolling down my face I turned to Bob, "I knew we might miss the family, but it's awful when you can't reach out and touch them."

Bob bent his tear streaked face down to mine, whispering in my ear he said, "I hope the grand kids remember us?"

What a couple of old softies, I thought, but I was glad we both were sentimental.

I turned the ham radio on again to listen to the weather report on the Baja net. The meteorologist reported that a big storm was headed our way, packing heavy winds and lots of rain. The sky turned a slate gray and chased the sun into the overcast, and in no time we were experiencing winds up to thirty knots, with angry green seas spitting foam and wind waves at us. Our foul weather gear kept us relatively warm as we took down the genoa jib and put in the first reef in the main sail. Just flying one sail still gave us a speed of seven to eight knots. The winds continued to blow throughout the night, and while on mid watch, I counted four beautiful lit-up cruise ships, looking festive wearing a cloak of lights. It was comforting to have neighbors as long as they didn't get too close.

The next day the winds blew harder, necessitating a second reef in the main. I pulled down my watch cap over my ears, surprised how cold my nose felt. "Are we still headed for Magdalena Bay?" I asked.

"No, I've changed my mind. I think we'll go into Santa Maria Bay. It'll be too dark to make it into Mag Bay. I'm even worried about making it into Santa Maria on time."

Come on *Maria,* I thought. We have to make it into Santa Maria before dark. I don't want to spend another couple of nights at sea if we don't have to.

The sun slid lazily down toward the horizon when I called Peter on Channel 16. *"Wild Spirit,* this *Maria Elena.* Come in Peter."

"Maria Elena, this is *Wild Spirit.* Where are you guys?" said Peter.

"We're not too far, but it's starting to get dark. I don't know if we can make it while it's still light."

"Hey, I'll turn on my spreader lights and you can follow the light to where we're anchored. Just let me know when you round the corner of Point Huches. Be careful of the rocks there.

"What's the weather like?"

"It's blowing, but we're well protected and the seas aren't bad at all. Give me a call when you're closer."

We rounded Point Huches, giving it lots of room, and called Peter. In a short time we could pick out a pin prick of light in the distance, turning the boat into the bay and heading toward it. There wasn't a moon to help us locate other boats anchored in the bay, so we proceeded very slowly, changing course when we discovered a boat swinging on its anchor. We finally found a good spot to spend the night, dropping the hook in four to six fathoms into the sand. Peter turned off the lights on his boat, and we went below, tired, hungry and very glad to be staying in one place for awhile. We listened to several people anchored in Magdalena Bay talk about wind waves of two to three feet rocking their boats, making it difficult to sleep. As we snuggled down inside out sleeping bag we knew we had picked the right place. The wind whistled through the rigging, sometimes making moaning sounds, but the water stood fairly quiet, gently rocking us into a deep sleep.

The next day Bob got out the charts to see about our trip to Cabo San Lucas. I left him drawing lines while I checked into the Sonrisa net, returning fifteen minutes later with some boat news. "The control operator told us to be on the look out for a stolen boat. It's a Canadian boat, but it was stolen in San Diego by the owner's crew member. He lost the boat, his passport and all his money."

Bob looked up and shook his head, "What a bummer. The crewman is probably already in Mexico somewhere."

I made a big breakfast of ham, eggs, toast, coffee and juice, feeling satisfied and ready to just hang out with my book today. I picked up my book, "Poland," while Bob read "Space." Mitchner was really getting a work out today.

Sunday, November 18th, we upped anchor and set sail for Cabo San Lucas, hoping for nice winds for the day and a half trip. As the day progressed the wind came up, allowing us to try our trailing wind generator. Bob threw out the eighty feet of line, one end attached the generator, the other end to a stainless steel rod with a propeller on the end. I went below to check the amp meter to see if it the generator worked, if so, how well. Excitedly I called out to Bob, "It's putting out ten amps in a fifteen knot wind according to our meter."

"Fantastic," said Bob. "Now I won't worry about the drain on the batteries when we run *Otto.*"

The warm wind blew Bob's hair, highlighting his dancing eyes, filled with contentment and anticipation of the next landfall. I sighed, feeling elated too, and more than ready to spend five weeks in a resort area where food and drink were easy to get. We both looked forward to meeting new people and just kick back. Now that's what cruising was all about.

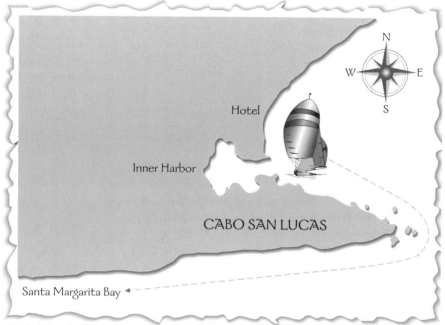

Not for Navigational Use

Chapter 12

CAPTURED BY THE TROPIC OF CANCER

"To Tiffany's I took her;
I did not mind expense.
I bought her two gold earrings,
They cost me fifteen cents.
Then away you Santy, my dear Annie,
Oh you New York gals, can you dance the polka."

("Can't She Dance The Polka," Windless Shanty)

We noticed a significant change in the weather along the coast of Baja. A swelling tropical breeze swept over the boat, breathing life into our sails. The sun's hot rays filtered through the sun shield's protective covering, toasting our bodies light brown. We passed desert like landscapes dressed in warm earth colors of ocher and brown, then woven together and pierced with speckled gray-green plants. We drew near Cabo Falso, the southern most point of Baja, California, guarded by an abandoned light house wearing a working light to warn mariners away from the rocks. I say, working, because many of the navigational lights in Mexico had low candle power, or none. It made an excellent radar target, giving us one more cross check on our navigation. Continuing toward Cabo San Lucas we were struck by the spiked angular rocks that reached high into the sky, giving the country side a surrealistic feeling. We knew we were close to Cabo when we spied the famous two high detached rocks, one shaped like a sugar loaf with a hole piercing the middle. Several large hotels rested nearby on burning white sands. They existed as an oasis for stressed out tourists in search of a tan, and if not careful, a start on skin cancer. Our bow wake elbowed aside clear blue water, a tantalizing sight which promised good snorkeling in the coming weeks.

"It feels like I'm finally in a tropical climate," I said. "I can't wait to live in a bathing suit, or shorts."

We rounded the rocks and turned toward the harbor area, wondering where we could anchor safely. The harbor entrance sprang into view, it's inner harbor beckoning to us to rest awhile. Over the starboard rail we saw the newly installed moorings that mushroomed after a devastating storm hit Cabo San Lucas in 1982. The wind and waves beached some twenty-seven vessels, littering the area with broken parts, sand filled hulls, and crushed dreams. A few uninsured cruisers ended up with humbled pocket books. The moorings were primarily being used by large sport fishers, plus several lonely looking sailboats. Bob noticed my head turning in one direction, then another, "Stop worrying about anchoring," he said.

I laughed because he knew me so well. We motored into the inner harbor, circled around, dropping our hook in a nice open area. Our enthusiasm waned when we learned the ferry from Puerto Vallarta arrived the next day, necessitating our move to a new spot. The ferry ran twice a week, turning in the nice open area we had considered our own.

"What now?" I said. "Shall we pay for a mooring, or anchor in front of the beach across the bay?"

Bob craned his neck toward the remote beach and anchorage.

"I commuted so many years, I don't want to do it anymore, even in a boat. Since we plan to stay here for five weeks let's pay for a mooring and enjoy ourselves. We'll save money later."

We picked up a mooring three rows out in front of the beautiful Hacienda hotel, happy to find the monthly rate saved us quite a bit of money. And a special bonus was added. Mariachi bands played at the hotel each evening during our cocktail hour, sending lively music across the blue water.

The second evening we sat in the cockpit, sipping our wine with contentment. Bob looked over at the hotel with a slightly wistful glance. "What do you suppose they're having for dinner tonight?"

"Hey, is that slam at my cooking?"

"Why do women always think men are being critical when they ask a question."

"I notice you didn't answer my question."

"For crying out loud your cooking is great. Satisfied? I really was thinking about the difference between the hotel life and our life."

"Well, I wouldn't mind an air conditioned room, a maid cleaning up the boat, making my bed, and someone else doing the cooking for a change."

Bob chuckled, "Of course. But what about the tourist? I'll bet one of them is wondering what it would be like to not go to work everyday and just hang out on boats and have fun."

"What a shock it would be to a wife or girlfriend when she had to carry her own water and wash clothes in a bucket."

"Do you mind it all that much?"

My jaw dropped in surprise. "Are you kidding? I wouldn't trade my place with anybody. I'm doing what I want to do. It's just different that's all. Of course I wouldn't want to wash clothes in a bucket for the rest of my life, but for now it will do quite nicely."

Bob's arm fell softly across my shoulder as he snuggled closer. "I'm glad to hear it. I guess I wouldn't want to trade our new found freedom."

"Before you get too maudlin there is something I really miss."

"What's that?"

"Taking a long, hot shower, or sitting in a nice bathtub."

"Touche, I miss that too. You can have a hot shower on a sailboat, and maybe a bath in a power boat. The last tub I remember seeing was on a sailboat, and it was used to store sails."

Most cruisers we met budgeted their money closely, preferring to anchor for free rather than using capital funds for mooring fees. They saved their cash for the fun times, balanced against the inevitable problems of paying for boat break downs. Of course that assumed you could find the parts to buy.

A large group of anchored sailboats crowded the inner harbor, situated far away from the car ferry area. When the owners checked in with the Port Captain they were told the harbor was reserved for the sport fishing fleet, a big income producing industry for Mexico. Thus far, the

Port Captain had not been enforcing this rule, so the sailboat skippers decided to take a chance and anchor there anyway.

One day a *mucho problema* arrived in the form of a one hundred foot sport fishing boat registered out of San Diego. The impressive boat chugged down the channel, careful to avoid the many bow anchors set by the row of sailboats, then swung his one hundred feet around and backed towards the sea wall to refuel from a tanker truck. After several hours of refueling the sport fisher captain started the engines, moving the boat out into the channel again. At that time he appeared to experience an engine failure. The freshening afternoon breeze roared down the channel and caught the high topside of the boat, moving the vessel sideways. With only one operational engine the boat reacted like a bird with a broken wing, unable to straighten itself out, or fly away. One hundred feet of steel headed straight for the row of anchored sailboats, a veritable King Kong ready to destroy everything in sight. A startled sailboat skipper looked up and screamed,

"Hey, look out what you're doing, God damn it. You're going to hit us... back off!"

The sailboat skipper's scream was augmented by a chorus of other skippers, which only confused the worried man running the out of control sport fisher. The episode ended with the sickening crunch of wood breaking into splinters as the sport fisher hit the first boat in line. The sound hammered us like a hundred foot finger nail scraping down a blackboard, sending icy shivers down our spine. Immediately the captain of the sport fisher backed down the engine, snagging the first sailboat's anchor chain in his prop, whirling the links tightly around the shaft and imprisoning his boat. The sport fisher shuddered, stopping dead in the water, then floated sideways in the current toward the remaining sailboats.

"My God, here he comes again," shouted the skipper of the first damaged sailboat. "Lets do something. Get in your dinghies and see if we can fend him off, or push him somewhere else."

"How about pushing him to hell," grumbled another cruiser. "His boat just ate up my anchor."

In no time there were ten small dinghies with outboards rushing over to the side of the sport fisher, gently pushing the big boat sideways in the water, away from the remaining sailboats. With further help of the dinghies the sport fisher managed to get back to land and tie up to safety, proving that many boats make light work.

Not long afterwards we saw a diver leap into the water and start bringing up pieces of chain from the fouled screw. The skippers of the damaged sailboats rowed over to talk with the captain of the sport fisher, but they might as well have talked to the steel hull. The captain refused to speak to anyone, or make a report. Even the Port Captain seemed unenthusiastic. The affair climaxed sadly, no compensation for any damage to the sailboats. We realized we were not dealing with the same rules as the United States, especially with the complete absence of circling lawyers. We learned to be careful in foreign ports, because the laws that apply in the states may not exist outside its boundaries.

Sad at heart for those unlucky skippers, we returned to our boat to make Thanksgiving plans for the following day. I sat in our main saloon, pen poised in the air, "This will be a different Thanksgiving for us. It's the first time in thirty-three years we haven't been with some part of our family." Saying it out loud made me feel more lonely.

Hey," said Bob, "we're family now, even if it's just the two of us. If it's going to be different, let's make it fun."

Hearing his enthusiastic voice pushed some of the sadness aside, "Okay, you're on," I agreed. "The only turkey I've seen around this town was driving the sport fisher. Now we have to track down the biggest chicken we can find."

Unfortunately most of the chickens in Mexico grew about the size of a turkey drumstick. The biggest chicken I could find at the local Mercado looked like the runt of the flock, stuffed with his own feet to make him weigh heavier. I looked at the pitiful apparition, scrawny toes peeking out from the body cavity, looking as if someone had crawled inside to take a look and gotten stuck. I picked it up and pulled out a foot. "I found our chicken. Take a look at the feet. I swear they're big enough to support Wilt Chamberlain, or Kareem Abdul Jabbar. All they lack are the sneakers."

We met other cruisers shopping in town, and thinking a party would cure our homesick blues, we invited four other boat crews over for Thanksgiving dessert and a party. I had packed canned cherry pie filling for the trip, so when we returned to the boat I made pie crusts, added the cherries, and popped them into the oven before cooking our dinner. It didn't take long to cook, or eat our little *turkey*, dinner. We anxiously awaited the rest of our guests for the party.

The crew from *Wild Spirit*, *Prima Donna*, *Taleisin*, and *Southbound* arrived, carrying their plates and eating utensils, ready to eat and party.

The cherry pies disappeared in a matter of minutes, but the wine and beer took a little longer. Bob put a blank cassette tape in our recorder to make a record of our first big party. Lynn brought her guitar and started the evening by singing folk songs. As the evening progressed the lyrics, and the jokes got wilder, dirtier, and funnier. Or was it the wine and beer? Cherry pie alone never brought on this reaction.

Bob started out with his old joke about the three nuns. Waving his glass he said, "Three nuns were on a train going to Florida. One of them was deaf. The first nun was describing the grapefruits grown in Texas. She held her hands in a round shape and exclaimed that they were that big. The second nun told about the bananas grown in Costa Rica which were that long, holding her hands about twelve inches apart. The deaf nun cupped her ear with her hand and said, "Father who?"

I laughed heartily with the others, even though I had heard the joke the umteenth time during our marriage. I decided that laughing at old jokes had to be a sign of true love.

Annie clapped her hands, saying "I've got one since we started on nun jokes. There were three nuns killed in a traffic accident. They were all a little scared when they got to heaven and Saint Peter was waiting for them. Saint Peter told them they just had to answer a simple question. He turned to the first nun and asked, "Where was the first place on earth?"

The first nun said, "Oh, that's easy. The Garden of Eden."

Well the bells rang, the trumpets blared and the gates flew open. Saint Peter told her to go in.

Saint Peter told the second nun she needed only to answer one question. "Who were the first people on earth?"

"Oh, that's an easy one," said the second nun. "Adam and Eve."

Well the bells rang, the trumpets blared and the gates flew open. Saint Peter told her to go in.

The third nun was shaking as she stood before Saint Peter. "Just one more question," said Saint Peter. "What were Eve's first words to Adam?"

"Oh," said the nun, "That's a hard one."

Well the bells rang, the trumpets blared, and the gates flew open."

We laughed till tears ran down our faces, while the heat and laughter of thirteen people increased the temperature inside the boat. Soon the jokes became more bawdy, the camp songs and sea chanties a little louder, our sides aching from the merriment.

About midnight Peter stood up, "God, great party but I'm bushed. See you guys tomorrow."

A few more yawns from the rest of the group reminded us how tired we all were. Lynn picked up her guitar and guided it lovingly through the hatch way, humming a sea chantey as she stepped off of the boat into her dinghy. Soon all the guest dinghies had departed, leaving our boat filled with a quiet hush.

Bob laughed as he picked up empty glasses, "Can you believe some of those jokes? I hope the recorder picked them up because I couldn't remember them all." He reached over and flicked off the switch to the small tape recorder, then gave it a pat to say good night.

Staying in Cabo for five weeks gave us lots of time for exploration, as well as catching up on some much needed maintenance. Boats, like houses, cry out for tender loving care. The zincs we used to protect our prop from electrolysis disappeared in the warm waters, and we could practically hear the grass growing on our hull, along with the tenacious barnacles that glued themselves to the water line. It's one thing to ignore house maintenance, it won't sink under you. But if you ignore your boat it's like ignoring your wife for your girlfriend. The harmony aboard goes to hell, your money flies out the window in greater amounts, and your life may be in jeopardy as the whole thing comes apart at the seams. Besides, the reward after all the hard work repairing the boat was drinking the wonderful Mexican beer.

One lazy afternoon I reached for my canvas carrying bag, filled it will empty beer bottles, holding one bottle under Bob's nose. "Time to make the daily run into town for ice, and exchange the empty bottles at the Deposito."

Bob put a marker in his book and laid it down. He stood up, stretched his arms high in the air, grunting with pleasure. "One of my favorite jobs," he retorted, then patted his tummy.

"Hmmm, me thinks I see a little bulge. Too much beer husband dear? I teased.

"I'll work if off walking around town. Of course we might have to stop and have a beer on the way."

We made our beer and ice run that day, and the days following blended into new days, while we shopped for food, returned empty bottles, lugged ice to the boat before it melted in the bottom of the dinghy, shopped for tee shirts which didn't take up space on the boat, read books, checked into the ham nets, went snorkeling, sailed races in the dinghy, traded books, and attended GREAT PARTIES. Cruisers in Cabo seemed to make more of an effort to be together.

The following week the cruisers agreed to meet on Love beach for some serious business, book trading. We arrived by dinghy, jumping into the water near shore and dragging our 145 pound boat up on the beach. I stood behind Bob and pulled on the dinghy painter, cheeks puffed out on my red face, my breath exhaling in ragged tones.

"I swear we have the heaviest boat here. It's times like this when I wish we had the light Avon."

"I know, but most of the Avons around here have been eaten up by the rocks. We're still better off with the hard dinghy for now."

"Speak for yourself Tarzan. Jane isn't getting any younger."

We collapsed on the sand and spread out our lunch, tossing the trading books down on another towel. After lunch and a cool beer we picked up the books and carried them down to the trading area, hoping for some good exchanges. Bob had just finished his latest Alistair Mc Lean mystery and placed it in the trade pile. We were becoming less picky about books these days, and read anything, be it informative, science fiction, love stories, or plain trashy stuff. A lanky, sunburned cruiser shuffled through the sand toward Bob, holding several books in his hand. "Can I exchange my Danielle Steel books for your Alistair McLean book?" said Jim.

Bob scratched his head, not really thrilled with a romance novel. "I don't know, that's not my type. What else do you have?

"I have a Robert Ludlum. That should keep you busy trying to out-guess the author."

The exchanges were made while I checked out some new books for myself, finding "Clan of The Cave Bear." The size of that book should keep me busy for a long time. It pleased me no end to see Bob reading a large variety of books. He had done little pleasure reading over the years because of work, technical articles taking precedent over fun material.

The loud clank of chain from the harbor interrupted our trading. We looked up to see an anchor from a big cruise ship splash into the water, its chain lumped up on the sand below. In a matter of minutes shore boats dangled from cables, filled with a swarm of buzzing tourists. We groaned as the shore boats sped by our beach, leaving large wakes which splashed up on the dinghies. The shore boats continued to race full blast past the moorings in front of the Hacienda Hotel, setting our boat and others, to rock violently from side to side like toys in a bath tub.

"Thanks a lot turkeys," we yelled to the departing sterns.

We shook our heads in disgust, but we couldn't blame the tourists for wanting to get to shore the quickest way possible. Usually the time allotted them in town was a couple of hours, leaving them breathless running up one street, then down another, hurrying to buy a souvenir, or I should say, bargain for a souvenir. Little did they know the merchants raised their prices the minute the ship dropped anchor. Excitement still reined for the tourist, whose snapping cameras caught the colorful Mariachi bands, dusty streets, or a gigantic sailfish brought in by one of the sport fishers. Too bad the cameras captured only a tiny moment of time in Cabo, the interval too short to embrace the spirit that glowed within the Mexican people.

Once the cruise ship left, the town returned to the quiet ambiance we loved, the slow pace resumed when we shopped at the mercados and small frutas (fruit, vegetable stores) in leisure. We walked down a side street and glanced up at an old building, taking note of a small beauty shop. I know I must have passed it a dozen times in the last week, but now my hand reached up to my head, feeling the unruly hair that had been growing for two months. I decided to take a chance and see if I could get my hair cut, having no idea if the lady could speak English. With some trepidation I stepped inside the old building and looked around, noticing old, faded black and white pictures of young women on the wall, each wearing a hair style from some other era. Well, I thought, here goes. If I could take a chance sailing a boat to the Pacific, surely I could be brave enough to let someone new cut my hair. Inhaling deeply I called out, a little too brightly, to the possible owner of the shop, "Buenos dias, could you cut my hair?"

The woman gave me a shy glance, looked down at the floor and mumbled, "No habla anglaise senora."

I held up my fingers in a cutting motion. Snip, snip, said my fingers.

"Si senora," then motioned me into an old chair, dusting the seat with her hands. She arranged a clean towel around my shoulders while I held my breath in anticipation. She looked at my reflection in the old mirror, cocking her head to one side in serious contemplation. She pursed her lips, picked up a comb and scissors, snipping away in a most professional manner. She was probably glad I didn't speak Spanish because I couldn't tell her what to do. When she finished she stepped back, her eyes holding mine in the mirror. A broad smile lit up my face, matching the smile on her lips, with my tip reflecting my thanks better than my fractured Spanish. As I paid her I pointed to my hair and said, "Gracias senora, que bella." I hummed to myself all the way back to the boat.

One glorious day we went to the liquor store to buy some ice, but the owner wagged his head from side to side, indicating a big no. He shook his shoulders and then directed us down the road a half a block to an unpainted house. We walked down the dusty street and stopped before the house, reaching out to open an old wooden gate. A grizzled old man sat at an outside table wiping up the last of his lunch with a tortilla, smacking his lips as he swallowed the last bite. Bob started to speak, but the man waved a wrinkled hand and pointed to the back door. Bob stepped up to the door and knocked. A young girl, maybe seven or eight, opened the door a crack. She had a slight build, wearing long black braids decorated with red bows. "Ice," said Bob in a hopeful tone.

The girl's eyes opened wide and a frown appeared between them. Bob continued, "Hielo por favor senorita."

She brightened up, giggle, giggle, opening the door further. "Ah hielo, si senor, uno momento," giggle, giggle. She walked over to an old refrigerator and pulled out a soggy bag of ice, dripping a lacy pattern of water into the dust. She said the price so fast in Spanish we couldn't figure it out, so Bob put some coins in his hand and let her pick out the amount. Even though the ice wasn't that wonderful we decided to buy from her each day, waiting some days for her to return from school to count out money in Bob's hand. Her ready smile warmed our hearts, even if her ice did the same.

Three weeks went by, highlighted by our usual routine of shopping for food. Just before Christmas we stood in the Corona deposito exchanging bottles when we heard loud honking from car horns, accompanied by the shrieks of childish laughter.

"What in the world?" said Bob. We left the deposito and hopped up on the curb of the street to get out of the way of a most unusual parade. A police car led a pickup truck towing a whaler, while a "Ho, ho" Santa, wearing his heavy regulation red suit, and the largest over-sized sun glasses we've ever seen, sat grandly inside. This was one "kool" Santa. Dozens of happy, screeching children followed the whaler like a stream of lemmings headed for the sea.

The cruisers helped make Christmas happier for an orphanage in La Paz by donating money for a party, clothing, as well as presents, proving they did know how to spend money at the proper time.

One lazy day we arrived back at our boat after shopping and found a little note stuck on our deck. I stepped out of the dinghy, leaned down and picked up the piece of paper, emitting a squeal when I read the con-

What in the world?

tents. The note said, "Your daughter left a message on the mañana net. She arrives today at one p.m. by plane. "Do you think she meant Pacific standard time or Cabo time," I said.

"I don't know honey. But we barely have time to get back in the dinghy, go to the hotel and find a cab. It's a long way to the airport."

We took off, hair flying in the breeze as we flew across the water toward the Hacienda Hotel. We found a willing cab driver, and no wonder, it cost $30.00 American round trip. Once there Bob and I ran into the terminal, looking all around customs, immigration and the main area, but no sign of Lori.

"I'm so disappointed I could cry," I moaned.

"Well, she isn't here, that's for sure. Let's go back and see if we some how missed her."

The cab driver must have thought he really had a couple of gloomy tourists, not hearing any happy vacation conversation in the back seat, only big sighs. We returned to the Hacienda Hotel, paid the taxi bill, and dinghied back to the boat. As we neared our mooring I looked up to see Lori sitting in the cockpit reading a book. She smiled when she saw us, "Hi mom and dad. I was getting worried about you. When I didn't see you at the airport I shared a ride with a couple I met on the plane. Would you believe they live in San Rafael, not far from where you live."

"How did you get out to the boat?" Bob asked.

"I walked over to the small boats tied to the quay and asked a guy if he had seen a boat named *Maria Elena*. He said he would take me out for a dollar. He even asked me for a date. I let him know I was married and he looked kind of disappointed."

"You're pretty resourceful. I'm proud of you," I said. "But why am I sitting here in the dinghy talking when I could be hugging you."

I crawled up our boat topside, lifting my leg over the rail. Once aboard I ran and threw my arms around her, her beautiful face tearing at my heart strings. Our grandson Brad was staying with his dad, giving Lori time to visit us. We had two fun filled, but too short days with her. We didn't have to quiz her about her leaving her husband. She assured us all was going well, and that she could handle her affairs without us. What a burn. Our daughter had grown up and didn't need us.

After she left we felt happy and sad at the same time. Sitting down in the cockpit I drew my knees up to my chin. "I hated to see her go, didn't you?"

"Oh sure, but she has her own life that she's anxious to get back to."

"Oh, I know that. It does help to see family when you've been gone a long time. Now I know what "cruising blues" means. At least the cure was fun and easy to take."

Another way to cure the blues is to have a Christmas party. A group of cruisers got together and organized a big potluck party to be held on a deserted beach, well away from the hotels and restaurants. By the time we arrived the beach had seventy dinghies pulled up, resembling "D" day and the Normandy invasion. I think the Port Captain thought so too. He arrived with his little daughter by car soon afterwards, and cast a jaundiced eye up and down the beach, taking in all the people, boats, and food. He put his hands on his hips and swung his head around as he spoke, "Senors and senoras, where is your permit?"

My friend Lura blinked, thoughts running quickly through her mind until she came up with, "Let's all give a cheer for our great Port Captain and his beautiful daughter." A resounding "Yea" filled the air, along with vigorous clapping. When the din ceased Lura called out, "Please stay for dinner and be our guests. We have lots of food."

The Port Captain's face beamed, then a slight frown, "Gracias Senors and senoras y senoritas. We happy to stay, but you must clean beach, si?" he said. "If beach no clean, mucho problema."

Once again a big cheer rose in the air from 140 cruisers and Lura said, "We'll clean the beach, no problema. Now let's get on with the food."

We overturned several dinghies to use as tables, placing a variety of food dreamed up by enterprising cruising cooks. Some dishes were made from rice and the usual scrawny chickens, bean salad made from canned beans, pasta and canned corn beef, sliced Mexican cheese and crackers, deserts such as home made brownies and cakes. We noticed the Port Captain and his daughter had no trouble putting away the feast, licking their fingers after eating a scrumptious chocolate cake.

Afterwards, each boat crew helped clean up the beach. Bob placed our bags of garbage in the dinghy and headed toward town. Over the roar of the outboard he hollered, "I hope all cruisers leave a clean wake. Nothing worse than when the locals cheer as you leave because you've been a lousy guest."

Later in the afternoon we heard our names being called from shore. Bob took out the binoculars and trained it on two figures waving from the beach in front of the Hacienda Hotel. "It's Chris and Nedra. I was wondering when they would get here," Bob said.

We jumped in the dinghy and raced to shore to pick up our friends from home who were sharing Christmas with us. As we neared I saw Chris's tall figure and ruddy complexion, a big smile covering most of his face. His graying hair looked longer than when we last saw him. Nedra's petite stature stood next to him, her newly permed curls shining in the sun. They both were loaded down with duffel bags. They dropped the bags and ran to help us pull up the boat on the sand. "My God, you're so brown," said Chris. "And I don't think we've ever seen you looking so relaxed."

"Hi Marlene," Nedra said. How's the ham stuff going?"

"Great. If you ever decide to go cruising you should get your license too. It really helps." They stowed their gear in our boat, presenting us with cheddar cheese, summer sausage, and newly taken pictures of our grand-daughter, Kara, as a surprise. Chris leaned back in the cushions and folded his arms, a big smile spread across his face, "You haven't seen Kara for three months, so I drove down to Cupertino and took some pictures of her, and Bill and Katie."

He knew he hit the right button when tears filled my eyes. Bob turned his face away momentarily. I wiped my face, and hugged Chris, "Thanks so much. That's the best Christmas present ever."

After dinner we sat down to discuss our future plans. Bob spread open the Mexican charts, smoothed them out and turned to Chris and Nedra. "You didn't say exactly where you wanted to sail, but I thought you might want to go to the west coast of Mexico."

"Great. Nedra and I haven't done any real blue water sailing. Sounds like a good start, not too far."

"Okay, I think we'll start by going to Isla Isabella, then over to Chacala and down to Puerto Vallarta."

"How about Mazatlan?"

"No, that's mostly a shipping port, and people get their dinghies and motors stolen all the time."

Chris sat down. "You're the skipper. We'll go where you want."

December 27th we did our last minute grocery shopping, planning to leave by seven thirty the next morning. While Chris and Nedra shopped I put on my ear phones and turned on the ham radio, tuning to the Sonrisa net to check in and give the net manager our sailing plans. After the weather report I pulled off my headset and hung it up on a hook. I called to Bob.

"The weather report said there's a frontal system due to pass through here tonight. It's packing some heavy winds with a possibility of rain. Still want to go?"

"Sure, the weather map didn't look too bad. There's two highs and two lows in this part of the world. I'm supposed to get a new one weather fax map at ten today."

The next morning we awoke to muggy weather with a high overcast. Bob turned on the weather fax to get the latest map, and soon the black dots were arranging themselves in a pattern revealing the latest prediction. He gently tore off the map and walked into the main salon. "I think it's a go today. There is some unsettled weather with possible rain, but I think we can handle that."

Chris pointed to the hanging closet, "We brought our foul weather clothes, so no problem. Any time you're ready to drop the mooring lines, I'm ready."

Once the lines were undone we pointed *Maria 's* bow out of the harbor. Rats, I thought, the darn knot meter isn't working. "I thought you dove on the log yesterday Bob."

"I did. Guess I missed something. Maybe it'll loosen up a little later."

After motoring out of the outer harbor protection I looked at the beginning rolling seas, feeling the change of motion. Despite the confused seas the winds seemed to have disappeared, leaving us the choice to sit in the same spot, or use our noisy motor.

Chris staked out a comfortable spot in the cockpit, threw back his head and enjoyed the warmth of the sun. Nedra found another cozy corner and curled up with her book. Bob went below to check our position while I stayed at the wheel and headed out to sea.

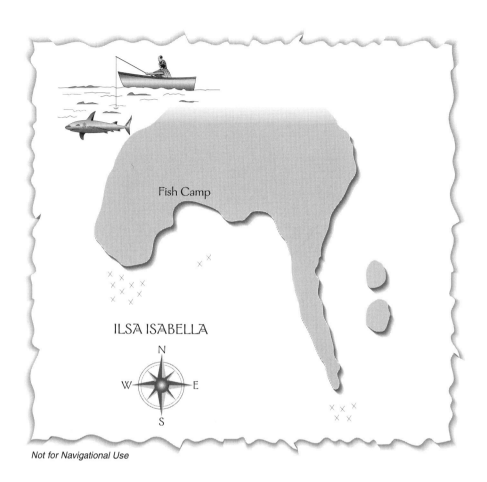

Fish Camp

ILSA ISABELLA

N
W — E
S

Not for Navigational Use

Chapter 13

AN ALMOST
PERMANENT SIESTA

"The boy swam back first upon the starboard side,
Crying "Captain, pick me up, for I'm wearied with the tide,
Oh Captain, pick me up, for I'm wearied with the tide,
And I'm sinking in the lowlands low,
I'm sinking in the lowlands sea."

("The Golden Vanity," Forecastle Chantey)

The first day out on glassy seas from Cabo we all grew weary of listening to the injectors on our iron genoa (engine), missing the tantalizing wind buffeting the sails. Even though we ran the engine at 1500 rpm to conserve fuel, the constant drone became an irritating nuisance. Where did the wind hide for crying out loud, I thought? And worse, in the dead air I inhaled whiffs of noxious engine fumes instead of crisp salty air. Despite the extra company on hand the day dragged by, time seemingly held in suspension.

After dinner Bob and Chris cleaned up the dishes and put away the food. "The cook doesn't clean," explained Chris.

"Marvelous," I said, looking pointedly at Bob.

"I think we had better talk about the watch schedule tonight," Bob said, turning to Chris. "Safer subject. You and Marlene can share a four hour watch, and Nedra and I'll share a watch. Sound okay to you two?"

They nodded their head in agreement, and it was decided that Chris and I would take the first watch at 8:00 p.m.

We said good night to Bob and Nedra, both settling down in the cockpit area, me at the wheel. I looked over at Chris, "This will be a different night for me. I'm usually all by myself on watch. First let me show you my three stars, Orion's belt. Look over to your right...tilt your head up a little more, there that's it."

"Oh I see it now..." He craned his neck around searching the sky. "I can't get over how many stars you can see. Fantastic.... By the way, do you want me to take over now?"

"No, just relax. You forget I've been doing this for months. You're just not used to seeing me in charge. Are you worried?"

Chris tried to look nonchalant and unconcerned, failing miserably. "Err,....of course not."

I immediately experienced a prickle of anger, followed by a feeling of foolishness. Both Bob and Chris had exhibited male chauvinistic tendencies in the past, but Bob had put his under wraps since we had left home. I knew I had his confidence and respect, but it looked like I would have to earn mine with others. Our conversation turned into exchanging news about each other's "doings" and I soon forgot my earlier mood.

The next day Bob spread out his charts and doubled checked his navigational calculations, abruptly frowning at the reading. He put down his pencil, shook his head in wonder. "You won't believe the current here. We literally have been going sideways toward another group of islands the past twelve hours. They're pulling us over there like a magnet."

"Is it the Tres Marias?" I asked.

Bob nodded his head as he plotted a new course. "I'll adjust our compass reading to make sure we compensate enough for the current."

"I asked about the Tres Marias because I heard on the ham net about problems in that area. The Mexican federalies rammed an American boat near there."

"Why?" asked Nedra, her head swinging in a wide arc toward the charts.

"One of the islands is a prison, and the government gets pretty nervous whenever a boat gets any where near there. So nervous in fact the rammed cruising boat was at least twenty miles away from the prison, or so they claim."

"I can't imagine a local prisoner being able to swim that far," said Nedra.

"Me either. Anyway the Federalies boarded the boat and searched through everything, taking the skipper's guns away. They escorted him and his wife back to the mainland. Right now the skipper is in jail."

Chris fanned his face, "God, a Mexican jail. I wonder if he'll ever get out."

"I imagine he'll get out all right, but it'll cost him some hard cash. Not only to get out of jail, but to fix the hole in the hull."

"Do you know if he had Sat Nav? asked Bob.

"I don't know for sure, but without Sat Nav he probably didn't have any idea the drift from the current was so bad in this area."

Our whole crew sobered at the idea of being boarded and taken off to jail. Bob sat down and re-calculated his navigation so there would be no boarding aboard this boat..

The next evening the weather began to change, definitely not for the comfort of people aboard our boat. During the second hour of our watch the absent wind returned with dramatic intensity. Chris hurried back to the stern to retrieve his fishing line before the heavy seas knotted it into a permanent filament puzzle. I heard the wheel moan and looked up at the jib, realizing the large sail area created a strain on the steering gear. We were over driving the boat. The wind escalated quickly, and I decided I couldn't wait for Chris to finish with his fishing pole. The genoa definitely needed to come down.

"Bob, up on the deck." I banged on the aft hatch where he slept below. "Now...., we have to get the jib down."

Chris yelled back from the stern, "Give me a minute, I'll stow this as fast as I can."

"I can't wait Chris," I said.

Bob arrived on deck still buttoning his pants; handed me the jib sheet to hold while he prepared to roller furl it in. I let out the jib sheet slowly while Bob quickly rolled up the genoa. Chris secured the last of the fishing line, taking the pole down for safe keeping below decks. Bob climbed up on the upper deck to reef the main, the wind whipping hair into his eyes.

"Head up into the wind," he yelled. I turned the wheel until we faced the wind, feeling the cool air tear at my clothes. Waves whacked the boat until she bucked like a wild horse. Water spewed into the air, carried away by the wind and sprayed over the deck and everyone on it. Bob held fast to the mast with one arm, trying to let the main halyard down enough to drop the boom into the gallows. Chris appeared, and in record time his long legs covered the distance to help on the upper deck. Bob gingerly let the mainsail down. Chris grabbed the winch handle and plugged it into the winch on the main boom, winding in the jiffy reefing line. Suddenly the Lewmar winch snapped off, falling with a clatter to the deck, while three pairs of eyes stared at it in disbelief.

"Son of a bitch," Bob screamed.

With outstretched hands Chris rushed toward the winch as a wave hit the stern, knocking him off balance. The next sound was the tearing of the dodger as he fell hard against it, the aging material no match for a flying body. Bob reached out his hand to help Chris, and managed to fall into the same place, ripping open the dodger further. I gazed in utter fascination at Murhpy's law working in third gear, wondering if the next moment Murphy would decree the complete demise of the dodger, or worse, deposit someone unceremoniously overboard. I looked at the wind machine reading thirty knots, with gusts peaking at thirty-five. Dark ugly seas raked our beam, making the boat rock from gunnel to gunnel.

Chris crawled back into the cockpit. One quick look at him and we knew this wasn't his finest hour. A hollow, green face stared out of his jacket, his hand grabbing at his stomach while a roar from the ocean drowned out a similar roar and heave from Chris. I steeled myself not to listen to the retching since my stomach tried to play copy cat. As usual, Bob showed no sign of sea sickness and was able to finish coiling the lines and clearing the deck.

I heard footsteps and Nedra come up on deck, wearing the same familiar shade of green belonging to Chris. She carefully set her small frame down in a corner, almost disappearing into the fiberglass as she tried to keep a horizon in view to reduce her vertigo. The waves continued to break midships making Otto work too hard to correct the course. While trying to maintain our position I gripped the wheel tightly, acutely conscious that my hands ached from the effort of straightening the boat out after each wave slapped our beam. We flew only the reefed main, but the boat galloped ahead at seven and a half knots as if running a race against time. It was going to be a long night, I thought. I had to forget my Orion's belt, no time left to star gaze.

With bloodshot eyes Chris looked up at me and sighed, "Lady, you're one tough hombre." Respect at last.

"Why don't you and Bob go below and rest. Nedra and I can hold down the fort," I said to Chris.

"Maybe you're right. If I go to sleep I think I'll feel better. I sure couldn't feel any worse."

He picked up his heavy frame and descended down the steps. I glanced at Nedra. "How are you doing?"

"Fine as long as I don't move my head. I'm not much help, but I'm not sure I'm strong enough to handle the wheel. Sorry."

After another hour the wind began to die down, the waves flatten out and the fierce rocking back and forth motion became more gentle. Our speed dropped to four and a half knots and steering became easier, but I decided to wait until the change of watch to shake out the reef in the main. With quieter waters I could see Nedra relax her stiff stance. I too sat back against the cushion, gazing at the bubbling ebony water.

"I wish we had a moon tonight. I don't like it so dark when I'm in a strange place," I said.

Nedra turned around to look out of the battered dodger. Raising up slightly she squinted into the blackness. "I think I see something."

I stood up, trying to peer over the top of the dodger. "I'm not sure..ah, I think I see something but I don't know...did you see a light?"

"Yeah, little lights. I definitely see little lights."

"Do you suppose they're fish traps? We're at least thirty miles from land."

The hair on my neck prickled as the blackness closed around me. I immediately felt claustrophobic, and my heart did a tap dance under my jacket. I hit the wheel with my the palm of my hand, "Damn, I wish my night vision was better. I hate it when I'm unsure. I'm better off changing my course right now and steering well away from the lights."

I swung the wheel away from my original course and watched the little lights dim in the distance. My jaw unclench when I relaxed a little, then a blur ahead caught my eye. "Do you see something white up ahead? I can't tell if it's solid, or phosphorescent foam rolling off a wave."

"I don't know either..it's too far away."

I strained my eyes and willed them to see something.... anything. Some sort of instinct made me spin the wheel hard to port as fast as I could. A thud sound boomed out of the darkness as our bow struck an object. The boat rose up slightly, then rolled a little from side to side. I let go of the wheel and rushed to the starboard to look over the rail, "Oh my God Nedra, it's a panga with two men inside." I flung my arms out straight in fright, "No lights," I shouted down at them in a futile gesture. Not one word of Spanish came to my mind. I returned to the wheel because *Maria* had started to round up. I changed the course to fill the sails.

Nedra turned and looked at me in incredulity. "You won't believe it, but when the panga went by us and I saw two fisherman sit up and rub their eyes. They must have been sound asleep. Even their outboard was pulled up. They didn't have any lights on, so it's no wonder you didn't see anything."

I turned my head in all directions, glimpsing only the few tiny lights we had noticed earlier. I looked at our stern, and in the dimness saw the two men in the twenty foot Mexican fishing boat gesturing toward our boat, a frightened look barely visible upon their faces. They hurriedly put their outboard motor down, pulled on the starter cord several times until the motor sputtered, then chugged away into the darkness, a ghostly apparition ready to surprise another unsuspecting mariner.

Seeing the boat leave activated me into action. "Nedra, I need some help. Can you release the preventer on the main for me."

Nedra crawled out of her comfortable spot and reached up to the preventer line, giving it a jerk to release it from the cam cleat holding it. The block swung down gently as she stepped back, but before she could secure it, Chris clambered up the companionway, huffing and puffing. Without a second look he walked head first into the block, banging his forehead hard. His eyes bugged out at the same time a squeal of pain left his lips. He staggered and asked, "Am I bleeding?"

Nedra and I both could see Chris had a small bruise and a several drops of blood, so I threw him a towel, "Here Chris, I don't have time to do anything right now. Just press the towel against your forehead. I'll look at you later." He opened his mouth to say something more, but Bob interrupted, "What did you do? I felt us hit something and saw a boat with two men go by."

I rose up off my seat in astonishment, "What do you mean what did I do? That's a hell of an accusation. I did what I was supposed to do, try to avoid an accident," I replied angrily. I quickly explained what happened. "Why should you assume that I had done something terrible and that it was all my fault. What kind of a crummy attitude is that?"

Somewhat taken back at my tirade, Chris sat down and moaned, still holding the towel to his head, while Bob said quietly, "You did just fine. Sorry. I guess I was just surprised. I'll go up on the fore deck and watch for more stray boats."

Nedra went over to Chris, took away the towel to check his forehead. "Don't worry about him, he's not bleeding now. He gets a little dramatic about cuts."

The memory of the thud came back as I sat down on the cushion. I thought I knew at last what having a heart attack must feel like. Under my breath I groaned, "If we had been going seven and a half knots, like we were earlier, there would have been even less chance seeing them in time to turn the wheel. Our twenty eight thousand pound boat would have climbed up on their boat and rolled them over. Oh Lord, I would have killed them for sure." My hands shook.

After fifteen minutes Bob decided we were clear of any boat traffic and came down to the steering station. "You might as well go back to bed, my watch isn't over," I said. My icicle voice must have had an effect because, like the rat I called him under my breath, he and Chris scuttled down below.

As the enormity of the near sinking of the panga began to lapse, adrenalin raced through me, making it easier to stay awake. I felt angry, hurt and betrayed, and by my best friend besides. Damn you Bob, I thought. You reverted back to the old chauvinistic role. Did he feel peer pressure from Chris? How dare he forget I was his partner. The one he supposedly trusted. All my newly found confidence eroded, slipping down a wave and flowing behind. "Damn you Bob Allen," I hissed to myself again. "We'll have a long talk about this when our company is gone."

"Did you say something?" said Nedra, her voice soft and sleepy.

"Not nearly enough," I said, my confidence returning like a boomerang.

Not for Navigational Use

Chapter 14

DON'T GET CHUMMY WITH A SHARK

"In came the herring, the king of the sea
I think it high time our anchor to weigh.
For it's hazy weather, blowing weather.
When the wind blows it's stormy weather.
Then in came the shark with his sharp teeth:
let to the clew-gallans, haul in the main sheet.
For it's hazy weather, blowing weather.
When the wind blows it's stormy weather."

("The Fishes' Lamentation," Sea Chantey)

God, I thought, I'm so tired it hurts. I glanced at Nedra and imagined seeing a mirror image of myself. Dark circles encroached toward her eyes, accentuating a hollow, detached look. If someone had said, "are we having fun yet" I would have choked them. I checked our position and compass reading twice. After last night's episode I wanted everything on my watch to be taken care of properly.

The clock on the Sat Nav looked blurred, but my eyes finally adjusted and I read, 0500. What an ungodly hour, I mused. I looked up at the sky and turned to Nedra, "I can't tell if there are really streaks of pink across the sky, or if I am going to look at life through permanently blood shot eyes."

She laughed and adjusted her pillow so she could lie down.

The half light revealed a small gray silhouette of an island on the horizon, Isle Isabella, a sanctuary and home to a million Boobie and Frigate birds. As dawn continued to glow and mature, my fatigue gradually faded away with the blackness of the night. The warm morning sea breeze had a revitalizing effect. I drank in the salty air, filling my lungs with it until I felt more alive. Of course alive was a relative word at this point. Dawn, with its peacefulness and renewal, instilled a hope for better times. I looked forward to finding a safe harbor, time to read, or swim lazily in the blue water. But one vital image kept coming back, and that was the sight of my bunk,....with me in it.

"Come on Nedra, our watch is over. It's been some weird night."

"That's for sure."

I walked over to the companion way and called down, "Bob and Chris, up and "attem" for watch."

Two sleepy-eyed souls emerged on deck, their faces crying out for coffee, especially Bob. He took the wheel, yawned and squeezed his eyes open and shut a few times, while small tears formed at the edges. The last sound I heard before my body dissolved into the sleeping bag was Chris filling the tea kettle for coffee. The gurgling water had a comforting sound, reminding me of familiar tasks. Home seemed light years away, but strangely enough, even that felt just right.

At 1100 we arrived at the island, somewhat buoyed by a substantial breakfast. The three hours of rest only teased our sleep starved minds. Bob entered the sanctuary harbor, turning his head from side to side. "The harbor's pretty small. We need to get in close to the rocks for protection from the wind," he said.

He turned the boat in a circle, viewing all of the area until satisfied he had found as safe a place as possible to drop anchor. Eying the rocks close proximity made me a little uneasy. The memory of what happened to a friend's boat in Mexico last year didn't seem too comforting. While our friend Don was ashore a fifty knot wind suddenly appeared out of nowhere. Within five minutes the heavy wind buffeted the topside of his boat, rocking it violently until the anchor jerked upwards and pulled out of the sand. Within minutes the wind had driven the sloop hard on the nearby rocks. Green water sloshed through the gaping holes torn in the hull, the boat hungrily gulped ocean water until it could hold no more. In slow motion the sloop settled to the bottom beginning a new life as a fish hiding place. I muttered aloud to Bob in my best worry wart voice, praying it wouldn't sound whiny. "I'd hate to be stuck in here during a fifty knot Chubasco."

Bob nodded his head, "Me too, but we could get out of here fast enough if necessary. Take the wheel Marlene...Chris and I'll drop the hook."

Once anchored and settled, I surveyed the area with binoculars, especially the beach. Through the glasses I could see six men milling around four dilapidated shacks, cooking fires and some sort of drying racks. I swung the glasses away and trained them on another part of the beach, seeing five twenty foot pangas resting well above the high water mark.

I handed the binoculars to Nedra. "I thought this was a bird sanctuary. Who do you suppose those people are? They kinda look like fishermen."

Nedra held the binoculars, changing the focus to fit her eyes. "I think you're right, they do look like fishermen. They're putting something up on those racks to dry. From the smell it must have something to do with fish."

Curiosity proved to be no match for our fatigue, and we all decided to take a long nap, eat dinner and go to bed. The mystery of the people and boats would have to wait until the next day.

Early the next morning Bob and Chris swung the dinghy off *Maria* and lowered it into the water, rowing quickly the short distance to the beach. They returned a half an hour later, all smiles. Bob pulled himself aboard. "We ran into a biologist from the University of Mexico. Nice guy. He said to come back around one this afternoon and he'll give us a tour of the island."

Chris piped up, "He hasn't told you the most interesting part yet."

"What's that?" said Nedra.

"The island is used three or four months out of the year by shark fishermen, which explains the shacks and drying racks."

My head jerked up as a bell went off in my head, " The smell,.....AND BOATS, boats working thirty miles from land." I interjected. "So that's what I hit. A shark boat."

"Right," Chris said. "When we were rowing back I saw a panga with two men come over to the boat and look at our bow. They reached up and ran their fingers over the gouge on the bow, then stared at your big Bruce anchor."

"Did they say anything to you?"

"Nope, when they saw us they turned and motored away."

I shook my head in awe."Maybe they realized how close they came to being breakfast for the sharks. That would have been a real turn around."

Suddenly my light hearted comment seemed flippant. Ever since I almost drowned life had been too precious to take for granted, yet the other night I had almost condemned two men to the same fate. I wondered if their feelings about life had changed after their close call. Maybe fisherman viewed near death as part of the job, but I hoped they were sufficiently scared to carry lights on their boat at night.

Large drops of rain interrupted all thoughts as we leaped into action, quickly shutting the open hatches. It didn't take long for the air inside the cabin to heat up and feel oppressive. We wiped the sweat from our eyes and turned our attention to the loud clanking of anchor chain announcing a new neighbor. Bob bounded up the steps to get a look.

"It's a boat from Alaska named *Abundance,*" he called down.

An hour later the rain lightened up. The four of us retreated to our cabins and pulled off our sticky clothes, changing into swim suits. Bob stood poised by the swim ladder, soap in his right hand and a wash rag in the other, momentarily startled when a man from the boat *Abundance* called out in a warning tone, "Don't go swimming here."

Bob stepped back from the ladder. "Why, is it polluted?"

"Not the way you think. I was here last week when the fishermen chummed the harbor with buckets of shark guts. They're trying to attract sharks closer to shore."

As if on cue a panga motored over near by us, and two fishermen hoisted several pails of shark innards, tossing the tangled gore into the water. Immediately the bay around us changed into a turgid, bloody scene.

"Great," I said, looking at my thighs. "Liposuction done shark style."

The words were hardly out of my mouth when hundreds of large, blue web-footed Boobies plummeted from the sky, wings folded back as they lunged into the bay in a feeding frenzy. Upon capturing pieces of shark the Boobies rose high into the air, immediately intercepted by the larger Frigate birds. The Frigates, superb aerial pirates, swooped in to harass the boobies, their long, sharply hooked bill menacing their prey, hoping to make the Boobie drop the food. The hum of wings beating the air felt like a physical force. We stood at the rail transfixed by the scene of aerial combat, and awed by the outraged squawking between the Boobies and Frigates. The harassment worked, because time after time Boobies dropped shark bits, which were quickly snatched in mid air by the bullying Frigates.

160

Bob let out a low whistle. "The Navy's fighter planes have nothing on these guys. What magnificent moves."

We stayed several days and caught up on rest and reading. Once the rains stopped we took an arranged trip to shore with the local marine biologist who promised to astound us with facts about birds and the island. He explained the island was of volcanic origin, and the bay its crater. "We figure there are about a million birds on this sanctuary," he said. "The two main species being the blue footed boobies and the larger frigates."

He went on to comment that the frigates had to live in trees because they were not strong enough to lift their bodies from the ground. The red wattle under the beak inflated during their mating courtship. This excites the lady frigate into thinking she had found a cool dude with a great outfit. If a baby bird fell from its nest it was eaten by feral cats, or rats. The rats originally stowed away on boats, jumping ship when they arrived at the island. To counter the problem of proliferating rats the cats were introduced, but then they became part solution as well as part of the problem later. No matter what, the birds were the losers.

"We also have marine iguanas living here. I'm sure you've seen them on the rocks ," he continued. "The shark fisherman you have seen on the beach are only allowed on the island three or four months out of the year. They make most of their money drying and selling the shark fins to the orient for shark fin soup."

We enjoyed our stay, but time became the enemy of progress. We needed to head toward the west coast of Mexico. We awoke to warm weather at 0530, dressed and had the anchor up in thirty five minutes. Our new destination, San Blas. We lucked out with good winds of ten to fifteen knots, pushing *Maria* along at seven to seven and a half knots through a fairly calm ocean. Bob found the knot meter log didn't register, and after grumping around, he discovered the connection had been pinched by empty beer bottles stored on the floor in the hanging closet. Imagine, done in by an empty bottle. We reached the newly dredged harbor at San Blas by two in the afternoon, finding out the area had been sprayed recently for "noseum" bugs. They were a tiny black fly with a bite like a tiger. Cruisers anchored around the corner from the harbor in Mantachen Bay were assaulted by waves of these pesky insects.

After anchoring we went below to tidy up and get ready to go into town. At that moment we heard a noise.

"Was that a knock on the hull?" Nedra said.

"I think so. Check topsides and see what's going on," I said, tying up garbage bags to go ashore.

She poked her head down the companionway and laughed. "We're surrounded by children in little boats."

I stopped what I was doing and grabbed a box of hard candies, bounding up the ladder topside.

"Hola ninos," I said, holding up the candy for all to see. Screams of delight, pushing, rocking boats didn't deter the kids. Their outstretched hands greedily snatched the sweets, and soon all the candy disappeared into little mouths.

"Gracias, gracias," they cheered, waving their arms as they rowed back to shore.

We organized ourselves for a trip to town. We had three large sacks of garbage and two containers of empty beer bottles, barely leaving enough room for passengers in the dinghy. We walked all over town looking for trash containers, dutifully carrying the aromatic garbage as far away from our nose as possible. I went into a hotel and asked what to do with the bags of refuse. "Pardone me Senorita,... Basura?" I said, holding up the smelly bag.

She drew back her head and waved her arm toward the front of the hotel, indicating I should leave it there in the street. In quiet desperation we set the bags down next to other rotting sacks of garbage awaiting pickup. It still didn't seem right to leave it, and as we left guilt stuck to us like gum on a sneaker

The next important job was turning in empty beer bottles for full ones at the deposito, a job as necessary in hot weather as washing one's clothes. It would have been easier on our livers if the Mexican beer had been lousy, but the different beers in each Province proved fabulous. We rationalized that drinking beer prevented dehydration. Well, after a couple of beers it sounded reasonable at the time.

We celebrated New Year's Eve at La Familia restaurant, but try at we might, we couldn't stay up until midnight. Sailing had a way of exhilarating you to the point of exhaustion. The next morning we made up for it. Chris fixed a wonderful fruit plate for breakfast, accompanied by a bottle of French Champagne. The champagne must have pickled my good sense because Bob talked me into sanding and varnishing the rails, plus some other horizontal surfaces that had frizzled in the sun. As I worked away the image of his varnished Ford Sportsman doors and sailboat waltzed through my mind, playing tunes that did not include, "Happy Days Are Here Again."

After work, fun begins. We had been told about a junket called the Jungle Trip, sort of a Disneyland boat trip, Mexican style. We walked to the river the other side of town and hired a panga, the sight of it giving me a slight pain of anguish. The peeling paint gave it a care worn look, but the outboard engine looked new enough. We paid the guide and seated ourselves in the boat. We passed by dense green mangrove trees, sprouting stilt like roots which rose in the air like an impenetrable wall. My worry wart mind flipped into gear, wondering how a person could penetrate the land if the boat broke down and someone had to go for help. How silly, I thought, why do I do that? Within a minute the shear pin broke on the outboard motor. Clunk. The guide made a face and pulled a new pin from his pocket, making his repairs in record time. Obviously he had plenty of practice with shear pins on this motor. I eyed the engine with a jaundiced look. A half hour later the engine stopped again, this time due to a broken spark plug. Once the plug was replaced I stifled my instinct to say, "nice motor." and pat it confidently.

All negative thoughts dissolved as the boat roared up river. We slowed down in a narrow section where we watched colorful small birds flitting in and out of trees, and a stately egret with a veil of white plumes stared at us impassively. Abruptly, an alarmed blue heron took flight, whipping his blue-grey wings, and extending his long neck, calling out in a hoarse voice, "grak." We saw turtles of all sizes sunning on branches and rocks, uncaring about the boat wake as waves lapped at their shells. Soon the river narrowed down to its beginning where a waterfall cascaded over rocks, emptying into a clear pool. Bob and Chris soon joined the dozen or so people that swam in the tepid water, transformed from sailors into two carefree kids. After two hours we returned.

Once back in town Chris, the salesman of the year, found a kilo of shrimp for our dinner. The cost? $6.50. That kilo of shrimp tasted a lot better than my kilo of tortillas!

The next morning Nedra went shopping for food and I tuned up the ham radio. I listened for twenty minutes and then sought out Bob. "I heard W5 IVI on the radio. You remember the boat *Esperanza Viva?*"

Sure, that's a 58 foot power boat. I think the skipper's name is Dick."

"Right. Well he heard a call for help from a thirty-two foot sailboat called *Three Passions* outside of Cabo. Evidently the sailboat had lost its engine. They had been trying to sail into Cabo, but were not making very good headway. The crew reported only five gallons of drinking water remained. Dick took his boat out and tried to rescue them."

"When you say try that sounds like he didn't make it."

"You're right. It was pretty rough out there, with winds up to 60 knots, and seas of six to eight feet. In trying to get a tow line to *Three Passions* he got a line wrapped around his prop."

"What did he do?"

"He called to another ham on the radio who agreed to come out and help. I'm glad because Dick is no spring chicken. He must be in his seventies, but maybe his voice just sounds older."

Ah, the joys of cruising, I thought. I remembered earlier in our cruise when we lost fifty gallons of fresh water from a broken hose. Deja vu. I felt thirsty again.

By now it was almost eleven. We needed to get going to our next destination, a small harbor named Chacala. When everyone had returned from town we brought up the anchor, motoring out into smooth seas and two knots of wind. Bob went below, and from the tone of his voice, he was not pleased.

"I can't believe it. Our second log stopped working."

"Maybe there's a log strike and no one told us," I ventured.

"Very funny. I think I'll wait until we are in the next anchorage to look at it. No telling what hard shelled bugs have set up housekeeping in there."

Later in the afternoon I heard good news on the ham radio net. Dick had freed his prop, and the sailboat was being towed into Cabo by another boat. I felt proud of the helpful cruising sailors. It reminded me of frontier days when people depended upon each other for survival. The saying, "Lord thy sea is so big and my boat is so small," brings out compassion from the cruising community, acting as an extension of a family unit. We shared concerns, bitches, spare parts, labor, and a shoulder to cry on it needed. It was old fashion and wonderful.

We motored into the bay of Ensenada de Chacala, good anchorage as long as the wind didn't blow from the SSW. Palm trees lined the tropical white beach, and campers nestled into the sand in bright colored tents. We dropped our anchor in three fathoms of water, and settled down to see how the boat rode. The anchor held fine, but the merry-go-round ride left comfort sadly lacking. The swells hit us from the side. Bob and Chris lowered the dinghy into the water, and Chris rowed out with the stern anchor, setting it so the bow faced into the swell. Much better. Now that the duties had been taken care the fun began, swimming in the blue clear water. We didn't have to worry this time about fishermen chumming the water for sharks. I swam over and hung on the bow anchor chain, looking up at the blue paint gouge carved out from the panga I had hit. Sigh..I had thought about that night often, yet, given the circumstances, I didn't see what I could have done to prevent it, I resolved to try and rub out the paint marks, the gouge would have to wait for the boat yard. I wished the memory could be rubbed out as easily.

Bob put on his snorkeling gear and checked out the long distance log. He stayed down a minute, and then splashed up on the surface. "You should have seen the calcified worm in the log. It's like the body turns into a piece of coral. I got it loose with a screw driver."

The next day we roamed the shore, talking with some Canadian campers who revisit this area each year. They showed us another beach where the bushes were covered with bright orange and yellow butterflies. After beach combing we were starved and ate a fish lunch of Corvino at a little palapa called El Amigo.

We motored back to the boat and picked up several buckets. The Canadians told us we could find water for washing clothes at the small pier, and hot weather really soaked up clothes with sweat. When I reached the pier I turned on the spigot. I jumped when a voice behind me said, "Senora, I would not use that water. Do not drink it. I'm from Mexico City, and there's no place in Mexico where water is fit to drink."

I smiled and said, "Thank you, Senor. I'm just going to wash some clothes. I promise not to drink the water."

The water pouring into the bucket looked like brown dye, and I wondered if I would be washing the dirt in, or washing it out. The clothes cleaned up pretty well, and as they hung to dry on the life lines, *Maria* resembled a mini Chinese laundry. The amazing part to me was it didn't matter about the water, or difficult clothes line. When cruising you take the good, the bad, and the dirty. One finds life too short to worry about details like that, for it is better to save the stress for important things, like saving yourself, or the boat.

At six the next morning I realized we had overslept. With amazing speed we all dressed, had both anchors up in thirty-five minutes, and were on our way to Puerto Vallarta. The air felt lifeless, the seas glassy, only the motor made a statement to the world around it.

Isla Isabela

WEST COAST OF MEXICO

San Blas

N
W E
S

Chacala

Puerto Vallarta

Not for Navigational Use

Chapter 15

Puerto Vallarta, Paradise Lost

"As I was a walking down Paradise Street
To my way-aye, blow the man down.
A pretty young damsel I chanced for to meet.
Give me some time to blow the man down."

(Sea Shanty, Blow The Man Down)

Frustration! No wind to fill the sails that could drive us quickly toward Puerta Vallarta harbor. The noisy motor roared as the sun blazed down without mercy, leaching out the little moisture left in our bodies. I felt like a grape that had been sucked into a raison.

Come on wind, I thought. At least blow enough to carry the diesel exhaust away from the cockpit. Even the sea gulls were avoiding us.

Chris brought up his plane tickets from the states, looking them over carefully. "I thought we might get as far as Manzanillo, so I ticketed us out of there. I hope there's room on a flight out of Puerta Vallarta."

"I hope so too. You didn't tell us you had planned to leave from Manzanillo. We would have had to travel night and day to make it in time."

He sighed and folded his hands across his stomach, a frown pinching the space between his eyes. "After two weeks of cruising I understand distances better."

"You don't look like you feel well Chris. Are you all right?"

"Not really. At first I thought I was sea sick because of the swells, but now I think the fish I ate yesterday didn't agree with me."

We all ate the same kind of fish, but each of us had his own whole fish for lunch. I felt fine, Nedra looked okay, and Bob hadn't mentioned anything. But Chris began to turn an unflattering shade of green, and soon the head below became his home away from home.

We all looked forward to Puerta Vallarta, a well advertised tropical paradise, white sands, palm trees, cobblestone street lined with red tiled roofed buildings, and of course, good restaurants. The movie, *Night Of the Iguana,* with Elizabeth Taylor and Richard Burton, had driven tourists by the hordes to see the beautiful scenery. The harbor was also known as a safe haven for boats during hurricane season, mid May through mid November.

Before arriving we reset our clocks to Central time. Forgetting little things like that play havoc in navigation and airplane departures, and we didn't want to be one of the sailors caught with our minute hands down.

We approached the harbor carefully, watching our depth sounder to avoid the shoals on both sides of the entrance. The mangrove surrounded marina nearest the main harbor had a reputation for being hot and a haven for bugs, neither which made us anxious to find a slip there. We took a quick look around the main harbor, noting the ferry terminal and cruise ship piers, and the need to stay far away from the turning basin of the large boats. We discovered an area just big enough for us to drop *Maria's* anchor in front of the Mexican Naval base. We put down a stern anchor also to keep us in line with other boats around us.

"At least there are guards here at the base," I said. "This may turn out to be a good spot." I would eat those words early the next day.

The first clue to trouble in paradise made itself known right away, in sight, odor, and sound. The dark and uninviting harbor water smelled. We had read about the non poisonous sea snakes around the area, and decided it would be bad enough to see one, but here it would be impossible to detect them in this water. Our crew looked about with a glazed expression. We had been used to clean ocean air, azure blue water, and small quiet villages. We shrank back from the noise level of buses and cars roaring back and forth, belching exhaust from engines that sounded like jack hammers, people yelling to each other, crowds of tourists departing from cruise ships, construction workers tearing up buildings and replacing them with new work, plus the loud American rock music that didn't sound any better in Mexico.

"I'm not sure I'm going to like this place," Bob said. The noise level is awful."

"Maybe it's like this in all big cities and we've just forgotten how bad it is," I said.

We shook our heads in dismay.

"I've got to go into town and change our airline tickets," Chris said. "Let's launch the dinghy."

He started to step on deck and stopped, his face the color of unripe fruit. "In a minute," he said, "got to see a man about a horse."

Poor Chris. Montezuma seemed to be playing horse shoes with his digestive track. While Chris crossed his legs we crossed our fingers. So far, we were in Montezuma's good graces and planned to stay that way.

We all checked into the Port Captain's office, a white circular building next to the ferry building, and then while Chris and Nedra rode the 20 peso bus into town to check into immigration and the airline, we found a place to get good bottled water. Immigration would have to wait several hours. We learned earlier Puerta Vallarta had a bad reputation for hepatitis and amoeba flare-up. Bob and I had taken gamma globulin shots in San Diego just in case of such an outbreak. Looking at the harbor water I believed it was one of our better ideas.

Later that day Chris and Nedra returned with good and bad news. The good news was they found some beautiful hotels and good beaches with clean water, so only part of paradise had been lost. But the bad news turned out to be the planes were full for two weeks. The only way home would be a ride on a bus a hundred and fifty miles south to Manzanillo, and then a flight to the United States. It's not that a bus was a horrible way to travel, but it lacked a necessary item, a porta potty for Chris. The next day I feared the worst for Chris and Nedra as they left loaded down with luggage and souvenirs, waving goodbye somewhat bravely, considering. I hoped when the Mexican bus riders saw Chris they wouldn't think all Americans walked with their buns held that tight.

Being alone again on the boat felt good. Privacy felt even better. Two weeks of company, no matter how nice, meant a lot of planning, entertaining and work. The up side meant help in the watch schedule, sail changes, dinghy launching, and enjoying our friend's stories and jokes.

But I realized I hadn't had company for so a long period, nor in such a confined quarters. Even a tiny fart sounded like a cannon.

"I never thought I would be tired of talking," I exclaimed.

"That's the last thing I thought I would ever hear from you."

"Thanks a lot! But seriously, since we've cruised I feel like a new person, more unique, not just an extension of you."

"I didn't know you felt like an extension of me. I've always thought of you as being your own person, a little stubborn maybe, but then who am I to talk."

"Right. But you knocked a heck of a hole in my new unique persona a while back."

"I think I know what's coming. I've been surprised it hasn't come up before this."

"Why did you assume it was bad seamanship when I hit the boat?"

"I plead guilty. Guess I was sleepy and disorientated when I came up on deck."

I gave him my fish eye. 'You hurt my feelings, and really embarrassed me. You didn't just ask what happened. You yelled and said, 'what did you do?' I thought you trusted me more than that."

"I do trust you. It wasn't intentional, because I wouldn't hurt you on purpose for the world." He looked at me seriously and opened up his arms. " I'm really sorry I hurt your feelings. I love you very much."

"I love you too. Now I feel better."

I laughed and fell into his arms, glad to have the conversation over. I hated having bad feelings hang around for so long, but it wouldn't have been fair to spoil the fun for our guests just because my pride got crushed in the wringer.

That night I couldn't go to sleep right away. While the boat rocked gently from side to side from an outboard boat, I listened to Bob's gentle snoring. I thought how much easier it had been to talk with him since he had retired. When he commuted 110 miles a day, plus working long hours, he would come home frustrated, and it was very difficult to discuss the problems that bedeviled the rest of the family during the day. In his mind his plate was already full, but I still needed help solving problems too. Sometimes I felt I had to walk on egg shells. But this panga incident did remind me of one particular crummy night in our relationship.

It was summer, and I was very upset when I discovered dry rot in our schooner, Venus. Despite my best sanding and painting along the cockpit edge, rot appeared, spreading like a case of poison oak. It made

170

crumbs out of two planks. When Bob came home from work I practically jumped on him as he sat down outside with a glass of wine.

"Bob, there's dry rot in the planking on the starboard cabin side. We've got to get at it right away."

He rolled his eyes and narrowed his lips. "Don't bring up more problems now. Can't I at least relax a minute when I get home? Besides, I can't work on the boat until I finish up some of the house projects."

It was all downhill from there. I insisted the rot must be looked at, and he insisted it could wait. Good sense dictated I shouldn't keep at him, but some days I didn't listen to my intuition. We screamed a few, "damn," "hell," and an occasional "shit." I slammed the door and heard another expletive deleted from Bob. I stalked out into the garden and attacked every weed I could find. The green clods flew in all directions as my anger flamed inside.

All this had not gone unnoticed by Bill and Lori, thirteen and eleven at the time. Bill decided to take action. Unbeknownst to either Bob or myself, he ran down to the boat with a chisel and hammer. He tore out all the dry rot and returned to the house. He stood defiantly in front of his dad. " I cut out all the dry rot in the planks, but you're going to have to fix it."

He left Bob slack jawed, a look of surprise stuck on his face.

Next Bill went outside to the garden and confronted me. "Mom, I tore out all the dry rot in the plank and Dad will fix it. Now...you don't have anything to be mad at."

It was my turn to look surprised. Bill turned on his heels and went back into the house. I surveyed the now weeded plant bed, deciding anger had quite a positive effect on the garden, but a hell of an effect on my broken finger nails. I went inside and washed my hands. Bob still sat on the deck chair looking down at Venus, and when he saw me, he waved to come outside. "It looks like I've some work to do on the boat," he said with a sheepish grin.

"Bill sure took things into his own hands, " I said. "I guess he thought we were pretty dumb to fight like that. What a neat kid he is. I wonder who he takes after?"

Bob grabbed me and sat me on his lap. "Maybe he's taken the best from both of us."

I stretched and rolled over to my other side. Dry rot happened in marriages too, I thought. First it starts out as a little problem, just a soft spot, hardly noticeable, like hanging up clothes without checking to see if they had spots on them, or leaving the dirty clothes next to the chair in the bedroom. Then the rot begins to grow on itself when not exposed. Communication, never a simple answer, because much of my communication was talking to my self with Bob the disinterested listener. Early in our marriage getting Bob to talk about problems was like preforming surgery without anesthetic. And I was just as bad. After an annoying problem had finally been resolved I kept reminding him how hard it had been for him to change. I called the word nagging. Bob had a more precise "B" word expression for me, and it wasn't brat. I snuggled up close and promised to do even better about putting a zipper on any nagging.

At six the next morning we were awaken by a loud shriek of an off key bugle playing something close to a Mexican reveille. The annoying sound bled through the fiberglass decks and bulkheads, reminding us we had indeed anchored in front of the naval base.

"My God," Bob cried, "That guy has to be the worst player ever inducted into the navy." He pulled the pillow over his head.

"It sounds more like the music the Kindergarten kids played when I taught school."

Sitting up Bob said, "Do you suppose it's a record? If it is maybe there is some way to break it."

But there wasn't, and we didn't. The bugle playing never got better during the ensuing weeks, but it still beat being devoured by the mosquitos in the inner harbor... I think.

We had an opportunity to take an inexpensive three day packaged trip to Mexico City to see the Pyramides, and other historical points of interests in the city. We would spend two nights in a hotel. A hotel with a bath! We asked the Canadian cruisers next to us if they would watch our boat for a couple of days, and they were happy to help us out.

When we arrived at the hotel we threw off our sticky clothes, drew the bath water and both climbed in. Heavenly.......

"Together again at last," Bob laughed. "It feels so good to soak in fresh water."

"You bet. Sun showers on the boat are more like spit baths, because we are always worrying about using too much water. Swimming in the ocean with soap isn't too satisfying either. We get salt all over us, and it takes forever to get out of your hair."

Later after a good scrub Bob watched the water drain out of the tub. "Look at the ring around the tub. You'd think we hadn't bathed in years. I hope it's just dead skin."

172

"Whatever it is there's enough dirt in the tub to grow crops. How embarrassing," I said. We both scrubbed the stubborn ring so the maid wouldn't see it.

After two exciting days of visiting the pyramids, historical building in Mexico City, plus Guadalupe, we were ready to return our life aboard *Maria*. I have always been a white knuckle flyer and our plane trip back turned into something terrorizing. By the time we reached Puerta Vallarta the skies were alive with black, angry clouds. A driving rain scrubbed the sides of the plane, beating out a staccato rhythm. Great streaks of lighting arced across the sky, and thunder rumbled and grumbled around us, as if to ask why we would choose to occupy the same space. But it was the pilot that got our attention. He made three attempts to land, over running the landing field twice, and pulling up at the last possible minute. On the last attempt we saw most of the passenger put their heads in their laps, and many were praying out loud. Bob watched my lips move too. We finally touched down on the tarmac, bounced hard up and back down, the whining tires eating up the runway as the pilot applied the breaks and reversed the engines.

"I'm really going to appreciate my bunk," I whispered, " especially since we're in one piece instead of many little ones.".

We untied our dinghy from the pier, and by the time we reached the boat, we were soaked to the skin. We learned later that the stern anchor had pulled loose. Our friends thought it was caused by a navy launch churning too fast through the water and running into our chain. It made me wonder if the bugle boy ran a launch like he played reveille. Fortunately our friends re-anchored our boat and all went well.

By now *Maria* and crew wanted to get going, but we were stuck waiting for our new dodger and water maker to arrive from the states. We made sure that the packages were labeled, *"Maria Elena,* Yacht in Transit" so that we would not be required to pay duty. When our packages finally arrived by plane the custom official said he was very sorry, but there would be a slight fee.

"What slight fee, and why," Bob asked in a guarded tone.

"Senor, we must make sure that you do not sell your packages. I have to send a man with you to see that the packages go on your own boat. I need $10.00 American please."

Needless to say we never saw him again, the ten dollars, or his "man" who was to escort us back to the boat. I believe the term is "Mordida." Bob labeled it blackmail.

We found wonderful cruising friends, not only around us, but more arriving day after day. Later in the week an affable, well built fellow named, Dick, arrived by dinghy as we sat reading in the cockpit. He looked to be in his late forties, with a winning smile of mischief creasing his bearded face.

"Hi there," he said. "I saw your boat and decided to come and say hello. I'm Dick and my wife is Denise. She's busy canning meat for our crossing to the Marquesas. I thought this was a perfect time to get out of her way."

"Glad to meet you. I'm Bob and this is my wife Marlene. Come on aboard and have a beer. Where are you from, and which is your boat?" Bob said.

"My boat's the seventy foot ferro cement boat, *California* you see over there. We built most of it ourselves in Ventura. We're on our way to New Zealand."

"New Zealand," I cried. "I love that country. I went there with Bob on a business trip."

"My wife's from New Zealand, and we're emigrating with my sixteen year old daughter Ginger. I've had it with the United States for now. I'm going to try my luck in New Zealand. Los Angeles county isn't a great place to raise kids, so here we are."

We talked more, and learned he had been traveling with another boat from Ventura, *Starlight. Dick had come to Puerta Vallarta to get parts for an ailing generator and wait for a crew member to fly in from the States. We were surprised to find the crew member, Tom, was in his seventies, recovering from heart bypass surgery.

"He really gave us a scare when it happened. The doctor says he all right now, but Denise worries a lot."

"Is he a long time friend?" Bob asked.

"No, not really. I met him when he was a bartender in Ventura. He listened to all my sea stories of when I sailed in Hawaii, Raiatea, and Australia. He begged us to let him come on the trip. He offered to pay his way out of his social security check. Since we were a little short on funds we finally agreed. He's a nice old guy. He intends to stand watch. We'll see if he's up to it."

Here's another senior citizen grabbing on to life and taking a chance, I thought. It took courage to follow his dream after heart surgery, but it didn't stop him. Dick returned to his boat, but during the next few weeks

* *fictious name*

we would share cocktail hours with his family, and the crew of *Starlight* many times.

Before leaving for points south we explored Puerta Vallarta, finding many good shops for food, but never good wine we could afford. What we drank, Padre Kino, would have turned most cruisers into teetotalers. I guess we kept thinking we might find one good bottle someday, which was about as probable as Captain Ahab kissing Moby Dick. I don't think the wine did Bob in, but a shrimp cocktail did. I could count on one hand the number of times Bob had thrown up in all the years we had been married, so when he became deathly ill, I listened to the sounds in perfect dread. We had already learned via ham radio that good health care appeared lacking in Puerta Vallarta, but respectable in Guadalajara where there was a medical school. But we reasoned if we had to fly somewhere it might as well be the United States where we could be understood and trusted the doctors. This was not as easy as it sounded because it was against Mexican law to leave your boat without first putting it in bond. Knowing that it would take a lot of bureaucratic time, something Bob's insides didn't have, we talked to the neighboring cruisers who again promised to watch our boat. We flew Aero Mexico to Tiajuana, cheap, crossed the border to San Diego, and flew to Long Beach via free tickets because Lori worked part time for PSA. Lori met us at the airport and drove us to Long Beach Hospital's emergency room.

"Dad, you're growing a beard and mustache. When did that happen?"

"It just seem the thing to do. Lots of cruisers hate shaving."

"I can tell by mom's face she's not really thrilled."

"If you like being kissed by a stiff hair brush it's okay," I said.

"Oh, it's not that bad. It'll get softer over time."

The doctor walked in and shook Bob's hand. "Good afternoon," he said. "What brings you here to our busy establishment?"

Bob related the annoying symptoms he had been living with the past several weeks.

"I know just the tests you need. If I'm right, you'll be fine in about two weeks. You can't have alcohol with the medicine, but the way you look I don't think you'll care."

Afterwards we learned that if a cruiser had a problem while a sea he could call collect by radio to Long Beach Memorial Hospital. The number was 213-595-2133.

While in the states we touched base with Bill and family in northern California, kissed our granddaughter, and told them we would be on our way back to Mexico. Bill frowned and shook his head. "Are you sure continuing on is the right thing to do?" Bill said.

"Yes," said Katie. "Have you considered all the consequences of you're being sick at sea?"

Bob and I looked at each other, realizing the shoe was now on the other foot. We were the children, and they were the parents. Very strange.

"I promise not head out to sea until I feel well enough. Don't you trust me to drive the boat safely?" Bob said with a wink in my direction.

We finally convinced them we were responsible enough to make decisions at our tender age, and would not take any chances that would deprive our grandchild of her grandparents.

After we flew back to Mexico and returned to our boat, I sat down beside my gray looking husband.

"All kidding aside Bob, there's no way I am going to sea until you're in good shape. When I volunteered at the hospital I saw people in intensive care that looked better than you do right now."

He moaned as he lay back down on our bunk. "All right. I'll take it easy for at least a week. Then we can decide if I'm alive, or just putting on a good act."

He stayed in bed and rested that week. I rode the 20 peso bus into town and bought provisions for the next harbor hopping trip down the coast. I filled my back pack with can foods, stuffed fresh vegetables, fruits and chicken into carrying bags, waddling back to the bus. I had to admit this was not much fun. I realized how much I depended on Bob to carry the heavy items, something I had taken for granted. I kept reminding myself that this was part of the experience of cruising, but when I passed by a window I looked like an old homeless bag lady carrying all her worldly possessions. I would have killed for a Safeway food cart at that moment.

By February 8th Bob looked pretty good, but still had a temperature of 101.

"You're running a temp," I said. " We should wait until you're normal for at least twenty-four hours."

"Don't be a worry wart. We need to leave, or we'll be behind schedule for the Marquesas."

"I thought we were through with schedules, so to speak."

"Ocean crossings need time frames, temperatures don't."

There was no stopping him when he makes up his mind. He decided it was time to up anchor. Well, at least that was what we thought he were doing. The stern anchor had such a good set, combined with the suction of gooey mud, that we ended up having to run the line to our big genoa winch to break the suction. I watched Bob carefully to see how he reacted to working with a fever. Other than sweat running into his eyes he smiled and said he felt fine. Once the anchor broke loose we found the line and anchor foul smelling and filthy, reminiscent of our first Mexican port. We motored out to sea and I retrieved our bucket and boat soap, scrubbing down the decks. A freshening breeze dried everything, and we set sail for Ipala, glad to be on our way again after so many weeks of being a prisoner of the navy bugle.

"I'm starved," announced the Captain. "What's for breakfast"

"Bacon, eggs and fresh baked bread. Also fruit."

I went below and found I had left my sea legs back in Banderas Bay. The beam seas slapped our hull in a sickening rhythm, and soon turned my stomach into a knot. Bob got his breakfast, but I had to close my eyes while he ate it.

The wind died down and Bob decided to change sails. "Honey, go below, open the hatch and hand up the MPS."

"Oh no, not that multi problem sail," I said. "I've never been so humbled by a piece of dacron equipment in my life. I swear it's evil."

"That's a multi purpose sail, not multi problem sail, and don't look for trouble. Today we'll be its master instead of the other way around."

Soon the huge white sail puffed out with powder blue and red stripes reaching toward the sun, guiding us in effortlessly through blue water. We had kept the main up, and rolled in the genoa. The salt air smelled clean, with just a hint of vegetation from the land masses we passed by. I'm one of those strange people who believes that every thing has a life, including this sail. I talk to boats, cars, food I'm cooking, in hopes of building a relationship with my environment. It usually worked.

Bob and I had now been lulled into letting our guard down with the MPS. If a sail could smirk, ours would win first prize in a smirk contest, especially as it lay in wait for us to take it down. Just as I uncleated the tack sheet a gust of wind whipped the line through my hands, leaving large red welts on my palms. I caught the end before it went over.

"Oh, sorry. The sheet pulled through my hand," I said.

"Damn it. The line is caught underneath the boat." Swinging his head up to look at the mast he saw a new calamity. "Jeeze, now the dowser line got away. We have to be more careful."

The air became blue to match the skies as we tried to undo our mistakes. Much grimacing and orders given through clenched teeth continued until an exhausting thirty minutes went by. At last all the lines were captured and stuffed into the sail bag.

"I swear that sail is laughing at us inside that bag," I exclaimed.

Bob scratched his head and looked at the mainsail. "Have you noticed that this sail gets out of hand every time we have the main up too? Since I have a dowser I really don't need the main to blanket the MPS when we take it down. Maybe that's our problem."

"At least it's our problem. After all the gnashing of teeth we really did cooperate pretty well together. Teamwork, working together instead of against each other. Wish the sail would learn that."

By late afternoon we arrived at Ipala. We were delighted to find *Starlight,* and *California,* already anchored. After a drink and dinner we fell into our bunks, dreaming of our next port, Chamela.

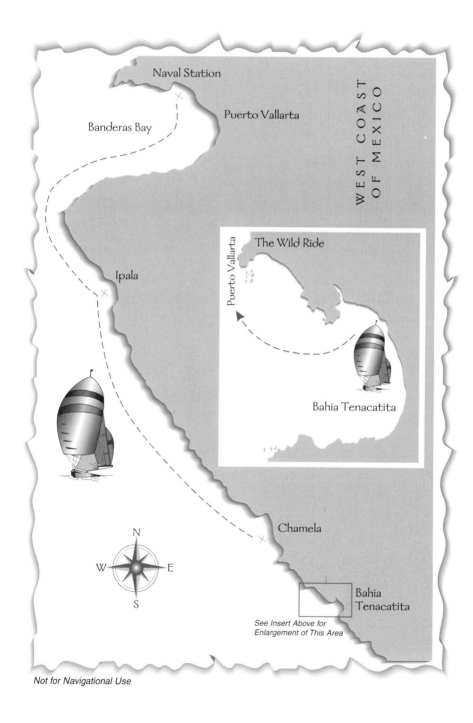

Not for Navigational Use

Chapter 16

MR. TOAD'S WILD RIDE

"There was once a Blackball ship
That fourteen knots an hour could slip
To my way, hay, hoo, ro, yah.
They'll carry you along through ice and snow
They'll take ye where the winds don't blow
To my way, hay, hoo, ro, yah.

(Sea Chantey, The Blackball Line)

I open my eyes and stared at the clock. The hands pointed to 0540, and when I peeked out of the port hole I saw rosy clouds strung in careless fashion across the sky. Dare I wake Bob so early? Slipping out of the sheets I climbed up the companionway, surprised to see the rest of the fleet had quietly taken up their anchors and sailed away.

"Wake up sleepy head. Everyone else is gone," I whispered in Bob's ear.

Bob rolled over and glared. "Not everybody. Besides, it's looks too early."

"It's a beautiful day, and you told me last night we have a lot of miles to cover."

Bob slowly smiled and raised himself up on one elbow. "With you yakking I can't sleep anyway. I give up."

All was forgiven once I handed Bob his big cup of coffee, followed by breakfast. Soon we were under way steering a course of 185 Magnetic along the coastline, a cool two knot shore breeze barely pushing us along.

"You look like you feel lots better," I said. "I think you are finally getting over the Vallarta shrimp cocktail blues."

"I hope so. I don't get sick often, but when I do I seem to make up for it." Bob cocked his head to the side, "Get the radio please. I think I heard *Starlight's* calling us."

I jumped up and went below, returning in a short time. "*Jim said they've noticed a current set of 1.5 knots in the opposite direction. That'll slow us down in this light breeze."

"Good time to get the MPS up again."

I groaned outwardly, but I knew he was right. It seemed so ridiculous to hate an inanimate object like a piece of cloth, but it did seem to have a life of its own.

"Last time the sail heard my derogatory remarks. I'll try to say only good things about it today," I said.

Bob pulled down the main and set the MPS. Once the sail was in position our boat moved gracefully forward, and even I was impressed by the extra knots the sail gave us. The weather warmed up and we took off most of our clothes, totally relaxing in the sun and moist sea breeze. By 1530 the wind piped up to fifteen knots and it was time to drop the MPS.

"Well, here we go again," I said, my voice guarded.

"Just hang on to the lines this time," Bob said.

"I noticed last time you let a line go too."

"Touche. You didn't do it on purpose anymore than I did. We'll make it work this time."

I couldn't cross my fingers and hold on to the lines at the same time, but all went well. It was the only sail up and came down perfectly like an obedient child, if there ever was such a thing. It has forgiven me, I thought. We stowed the sail and raised the main, steaming along at a good clip toward our destination, Chamela. We looked for two peaks at Punta Rivas, the yellow bluffs make a good landmark, then passed Punta Perula and headed toward a sandy beach to drop anchor nearby. At 1915 we had our hook down near *California* and *Starlight*. We could see *Johnny, the slim blonde twelve year old off of Starlight, rowing around the harbor. His parents waved at us and then disappeared below. No schmoozing and boozing tonight. It was time for all tired cruisers to eat and go to bed.

*fictious name

The next morning we awoke to dense fog, and I wondered how the San Francisco weather had tracked us down this far. I was secretly delighted, because this meant we would stay on the boat with time to play, relax, read, or get on the ham radio.

"Good," I said to Bob. After we clean up from breakfast I'll beat you at dominos."

"Fat chance, you just got lucky in the last game. Prepare to lose."

After losing miserably I put away the dominos. "You're as bad as Lori."

"Why, what did I do?"

"It's what I let you do. Remember when Lori swam in the Marin County League championships?

"I think so. She won first place and set a record."

"When she was on the block ready to dive she told the girl next to her that she would beat her. It really psyched her out I guess, because afterwards the girl cried and told Lori it wasn't fair. But the girl allowed it to happen because Lori sounded convincing.

"You mean I can't psych you out anymore in dominos?"

"Nope, not anymore."

The next day after the fog lifted we headed to Bahia Tenacatita under power, chugging away in windless sea. A little later a southerly breeze picked up, blowing right on our nose. Bob checked the course and speed and decided we were stuck in the north current again. I glanced up at the sky, noticing narrow bands of thin white fleecy clouds. Above them were more thin clouds, creating a hazy look.

"Look at the cirrus and cirrostratus clouds. I think we have an occluded front today. That might account for the unusual south wind at this time of year," I said.

"Sounds impressive. You've been reading the weather book I bought."

"Yep, it's pretty interesting, but it won't take the place of my novels. Too big a cast of characters that play the same role.

At mid afternoon we passed Los Frailes, and the weather turned muggy and oppressive. Bob went below to study his charts, checking to see what, if any, problems lay ahead of us. He discovered one, a sneaky rock four feet under water. The rock lay about six hundred yards west of Roca Centro, but at that time we couldn't see any difference in the wave pattern. We had heard earlier that another boat, called *Stone Witch*, miscalculated the distance entering Tenacatita Bay, hitting another rock not listed on the chart, and sinking within two or three minutes. Now the unknown rock took on the persona of a shark waiting to attack its prey. We were unsure enough of its location, so we gave the whole point wide berth. We found out later that a publication called Charlie's Charts had listed the rock. I don't know why the Mexican charts didn't show the danger spot .

We anchored later in four meters of water within a short dinghy ride of a large hotel, staying out far enough from land to discourage any nose-ums from eating us alive. Bob got out the binoculars and steadied his arms, directing his gaze toward the beach..

"You know what I see?"

"Something good I hope."

"I see four outdoor showers quite a ways from the hotel, just waiting for someone to use them."

"I know just the someone. I'll get our towels and soap. You start get-ting the dinghy ready to launch."

We were not the only ones to see the showers, the crew from *California* and *Starlight* were blowing up their rubber dinghies on deck. Fortunately the surf remained calm so we wouldn't get pooped in the wavelets traveling toward shore. We pulled up our boats on the sand near the showers. We sashayed slowly toward the showers, hopefully looking like guests from a distance, then whipped out our shampoo and soap, murmuring sounds of joy and contentment. Denise's Kiwi accent intermingled with the rest of our American twang.

Denise, *Jan and I all had short hair, the only way to go when sailing and living on a boat. Ginger, almost sixteen, had long brown hair, but then she was young and didn't mind fussing with it. Denise was the youngest married lady, in her thirties, long legged and slim, with an infectious laugh, and light hearted attitude toward life. I figured Jan to be in her for-ties, slightly plump with a sharp mind, and fun loving also. Needless to say I was the oldest of the gals, but I didn't feel it. Before I left on this cruise I had taken aerobic jazzersize five days a week, feeling more fit than when I was much younger. We had fun together, giggling, telling stories about our husbands and families, trading books and recipes. Our husbands were always off to one side, talking about boats, engines, and how to fix things. That made sense since Dick had been an airplane mechanic in the navy, and Jim a retired aircraft mechanic from one of the domestic airlines. They probably talked about pretty girls too, and from the sound of their dirty laughs, they told some raunchy jokes.

The next day Denise, Jan and I all agreed we needed to replenish our food supply.

*fictious name

184

"I talked to another cruiser who said there was a little town over there," Denise said, pointing her finger at a distant shore. "He said we could buy chicken and some vegetables."

Bob looked at the distance to the opposite shore. "I better blow up the rubber boat if we all want to go that far. Our hard dinghy won't be fast enough."

By the time we reached the shore an hour later we had about given up. We beached the boat and found a foot path leading to a dusty dirt road, expecting to find the small town a short distance away. No town. The sun beat down on our heads, and soon stinging sweat gushed from every pore. After a half an hour of trudging along the road the subject of chickens was the furthest thing from our minds. We could only visualize a frosty cold beer with little chips of ice dripping down the sides of the bottle, and lifting up the amber liquid, pouring it down our parched throats. Denise stopped at the side of the road. "I'm going to stick out my thumb and see if anyone will pick us up."

We stood there for several minutes until a dust cloud whirled toward us, followed by an old yellow pickup truck. The driver squealed to a stop when Denise held up her thumb and pulled her shorts up further on her thigh. I hope he wasn't too disappointed when we all jumped into in the truck bed. Once in town I used my survival Spanish and found we could buy chicken at a house about a block away. When we opened the door we were inundated by a dense cloud of buzzing flies, tiny chicks, and small children running in and around each other. The first thing that came to my mind was the thought of the little chicks looking up and seeing their parents hanging high on a hook, all dressed up in a black formal coat of flies. I guess I must have looked incredulous because Jan and Denise abruptly howled with laughter, held their sides and leaned helplessly against the door. Finally Denise caught her breath and sputtered, "You should have seen your face. It was priceless. Why don't I ever have a camera when I need it."

We all agreed to cook our chickens to death to get rid of any lingering fly germs. After finding the veggies we looked around for some sort of transportation to get us back to our dinghy. An ancient flatbed truck with a faded Corona beer sign on the side stopped in front of a the vegetable store. He opened the back of the flat bed and pulled out a hunk of ice, carrying it on his shoulders into the building. We waited until he came out and asked if we could ride in the back of the truck to our dinghy. Luckily he spoke English and told us to hop in.

We pulled ourselves up into the back and grabbed the sides just as the driver tore out. He must have been a frustrated Indy driver in another life, because we had to grab the rails, hang on with a death grip when the tires hit huge pot holes, sending us high in the air as if we had been jumping on a trampoline. We were airborne more than landborn. We made quite a spectacle, white knuckles gripping the wood, hair flying, jaws snapping, followed by whoops of "ohmigosh, oops, aaakkk."

"Does this remind you of a ride at Disneyland?" I asked Bob.

"I know the one you mean. Mr. Toad's Wild Ride."

Suddenly my long lecture to the kids about choosing responsible drivers sounded hollow.

A couple of days later we pulled up anchor to head for Bahia Navidad, no wind, blue skies, but eager anticipation of a bigger town, and better sources of food, water, and beer. As we passed the area of the hidden rock we were surprised to see spume rise up from the waves. Now you see it, now you don't. I figure it must have something to do with the difference in height from tide, or possible tidal action.

We dropped anchor in Bahia Navidad three hours later in front of the beach hotels, very anxious to get ashore to eat lunch. The town of Melaque by the bay proved to be good size. We heard on the marine radio about a palapa called Los Pelicanos, run by an by an American named Philomena, married to a Mexican. She helped the visiting cruisers buy meat and fish, and sold bottled water. She also had someone who took care of laundry.

"Get all your dirty clothes together," I yelled to Bob. "We're going to have someone else do the laundry for us."

I pulled dirty clothes, sheets, towels and pillowcases into two bags, setting them in the front seat of the dinghy as we motored ashore. We were followed by a parade of dinghies, each loaded with bags of laundry. We were the first in which proved to be more important than I thought.

"Here you are Phil," I said, "handing her my bundles. "When can I have it back?"

"Tomorrow. I will make sure it will be done tomorrow. Good price too."

The next day I picked up my laundry and a pillow slip was missing. I talked with Phil and said we really had to have it back. It was King size and hard to find a replacement. The older women who worked for Phil, and who had taken care of my laundry, gave me a black, malicious look. I gave her one back. She shrugged and said she would look for it. The next day she handed it to me, but she was far from pleased. The laundry from *California* and *Starlight* looked as if someone had gone on a shopping spree, missing tee shirts, regular shirts, pants and skirts. Denise and Jan confronted Phil, who in turn interrogated the old woman. The woman finally admitted she had sold the other items, and there was no way she could get them back. Phil fired her on the spot, and Denise rolled her eyes and said, "To think my favorite skirt is going to the fiesta tonight and I'm not in it."

Trash presented many problems on boats. We tried to not throw anything overboard that wasn't biodegradable, thus ending up with lots of junk that threatened to take over the galley area. We filled up a big plastic bag, praying it would hold together long enough to get it into a can. Phil took the bag and added to others in back of her place, placing them by her automatic garbage disposal unit, five or six goats. Those were the healthiest, happiest goats I have ever seen.

Before we left we heard Phil had a birthday coming up, and the six cruisers in the harbor decided to give her a party as thanks for all her help. The decorations in the palapa looked pretty bare boned, so we decided to make it into a type of yacht club.

"We're going to give her a trailboard with *California's* name engraved. We saved it after it got torn off during a storm in La Paz," Denise said

"I've got a club burgee. Maybe that will do," Bob said .

Jim and Jan gave her life ring with their name on it, others donated shirts with their boat name, a chart and a bottle of wine. One cruiser had a good sense of humor and gave her one of their dog's bones for the wall.

The party went on long after midnight, but we couldn't last that long. Fortified with good Mexican beer, we rowed back to *Maria*. We decided to let the younger cruisers shut down the place. Bob and I didn't even think about our next port, Bahia Santiago, sleep became the dominant goal. Besides, we had hours of sailing ahead of us tomorrow, and we could do all the planning we wanted then.

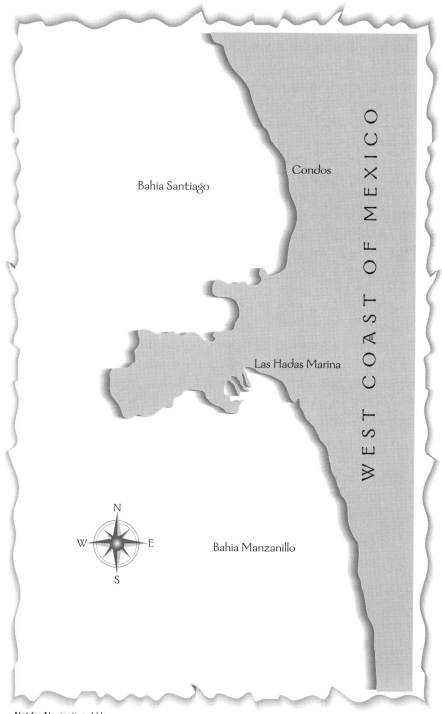

Not for Navigational Use

Chapter 17

A ROWING, A ROWING, A ROWING TO SHORE

"Here's health to our captain where'er he may be;
He's a friend to the sailor on land or on sea'
But as for our chief mate, that dirty old brute,
I hope when he dies straight to hell he'll skyhoot!
Singing, row, row bullies row
Those Liverpool gals they have got us in tow.
(Sea Chantey, Row Bullies Row, a Forecastle Chantey)

I looked at the calendar, surprised to see it was already February 23. Our planned departure to the Marquesas loomed in the very near future. So many tasks lay ahead of us before we could leave, but first things first. Depart Melaque and head for Santiago Bay. By eight in the morning we were on our way toward our last contact in Mexican waters. The excitement, anticipation, plus a little concern of the unknown long crossing, assailed us, leaving all kinds of prickly feelings. Bob went below to figure out the way points to Santiago Bay and enter them the Sat Nav.

The occluded front has gone the way of all fronts, leaving us with high clouds and blue skies. We hauled up the main and genoa jib, moving ahead through the ground swells that undulated rhythmically down the coast.

"When do you think we'll drop anchor In Santiago Bay?" I ask Bob

"Around two o'clock if the winds hold."

"We'll be a long way from the port captain's office won't we?"

"Yes, but I don't want to anchor in Manzanillo. It's strictly a commercial port with the usual dirty water. We can take a bus from Santiago to check in."

I returned to my novel, "Clan Of The Cave Bears," soon lost in prehistoric civilization. With a minor in anthropology at UCLA, this kind of book satisfied my deep craving for knowledge of ancient cultures. It made me even happier that the book had over a thousand pages. My mind buzzed with millions of little details that would bore Bob out of his skull. He chose lean books. He claimed that long novels had too many unnecessary words which dragged out the story. One of the many differences between the Captain and the Admiral.

By afternoon the air had lost its crispness, replaced by a sultry hot blanket. The further south we traveled the hotter the weather, making me glad we decided to leave from Manzanillo instead of Acapulco.

In the early afternoon we reached Santiago Bay, dropping anchor in four fathoms of sparkling blue water. Once changed into our swim suits we leaped into the water to cool off. Swimming around *Maria* we found signs of grass attached to her water line, and algae turning the blue bottom paint into an unhealthy brown. The ugly gouge on the bow stared at me. Unsettled I grabbed the anchor chain and turned to look toward shore. We planned to land our dinghy tomorrow in front of a huge modern condo complex that lined the bay. The gentle surf looked docile enough, but a surprise awaited us in the near future.

Within the hour three more anchors splashed to the bottom of the bay. *California* and *Starlight* arrived, followed by a new, smaller boat, *Smiling Jack*. Bob and I climbed back on board. The air quickly dried the salt on our skin, the white crystals sticking to us like bubble gum to a shoe.

"Go below and hand me the Avon please," Bob said. "I think it will be easier to maneuver in the surf than *Nina Maria*."

I opened the hanging locker, lifting out the clothing on hangers first, then the small vacuum, dinghy anchor and chain, dinghy seats, floor boards, oars, and at last,....the rubber boat bag. The main saloon now looked like a bomb had gone off in the locker, scattering equipment on every surface. I dragged out the boat and pushed it upwards through the companionway into Bob's eager hands. Panting from the effort I gasped, "This boat's heavier than it looks."

"Just keep shoving," Bob retorted, his face red from leaning down and pulling the boat up.

"Ah, just another joy of boating," I mumbled through tense lips.

By the time the boat had been pumped up the sun slipped down, swallowed by the horizon. In its place were wispy, burnished-red clouds strewn across the sky like a long silk scarf. We stood transfixed as the night slowly gathered up the clouds and smothered them in darkness. Bob broke the moment. "We'll see the Port Captain and Immigration tomorrow. I want to find out if we can check in and out at the same time by giving them a specific date of departure."

"Good, it's a long way in there."

"I want to go early because I'm thinking of buying another battery to have on line."

"We already have two, why more?"

"We're using lots battery power with the ham radio, and I have to be sure we can start the main engine at all times."

"You are the most redundant man I know. I'm glad you're not planning to have another wife on line in case the old one wears out."

"Say, I never thought of that. What a great idea."

"Best you don't, or the Admiral will keel haul you, you old buzzard."

The following morning I composed a poem for Ginger's sixteenth birthday, wrapping up a blue stone necklace I had purchased the year before in Tahiti.

"Hurry up and finish," Bob called from the deck. "Dick and Denise have already started rowing to the beach."

"Do you have all the document papers?"

"Yes, but I'm wondering how to make sure they'll stay dry."

"I'll get the water tight bag we use for the camera. I wish my purse would fit there too, but it won't."

When I stepped into the dinghy I noticed the surf looked heavier than when we anchored yesterday. The light breeze ruffled Bob's hair, blowing some of the longer strands into his eyes. Palm trees on shore shook their fronds back and forth like hula dancers .

"I decided against the motor in case we dump the boat," Bob said.

"What a pleasant thought," I said, wrapping my purse strap securely around my arm.

We watched Dick steer the boat to the surf line, waiting until the waves quieted down. At that point Dick rowed as fast as a galley slave who had been given orders that the Captain wanted to water ski. Unfortunately he wasn't fast enough, and a rising wave caught his stern and curled over it, pouring gallons of sea water in his lap. The boat settled lower in the water and headed sluggishly toward shore. Two very wet people got out of the boat.

"Oh boy," I said. "What now."

"We go in," said my Captain. "I think I've learned now by watching Dick."

The question in my mind was did he learn how to do it, or how not to do it? The residents from the Condos now lined up on shore watching us. Several carried chairs and sat down. It appeared we would be the free entertainment for the day. Bob surveyed several sets of waves, trying to figure out the pattern. There were five waves fairly close together, then a break.

"I'll try for the break after the next group," he said.

I dipped my hand into the warm water. It felt cool and refreshing.

"Now," shouted Bob, dipping in his oars and pulling as hard as possible. Beads of sweat rolled down his forehead into his prickly salt and pepper beard, and slowly the boat pulled ahead, staying just behind the wave pattern.

"I think you've done it," I shouted as we neared the shore. The words had hardly left my mouth when a surprise wave rose up, curled, spanking our stern and spinning us around broadside to the surf. Foam topped water poured into the dinghy in prodigious amounts. Bob pulled as hard as he could on the oars to straighten us out, while I held my purse up above my head. I felt a giggle starting as I looked at our predicament. We were dead in the water, figuratively speaking. The sand filled water continued to pour into the dinghy, and when we were close enough to shore, we climbed out. We put our soggy belongings on the beach. We went back to the dinghy and tried to lift it on its side to spill out the water, but it was too heavy for me. A soaking wet Dick and Denise walked up laughing. "You're as bad as we were," Dick said, reaching down and helping Bob turn over the boat.

"There's a fresh water shower up by the wall. We took a shower with all our clothes on to get the salt out," Denise said.

"How are we going to get to Manzanillo in these wet clothes," I said with a frown.

"No problem mate," laughed Denise. "We'll be dry in no time in this weather."

192

Nearby stood a silver haired woman with heavy gold jewelry, bright red nails flashing as she waved. In a soft southern voice she asked, "Do you'all do this for fun? I wouldn't do it if someone paid me a million dollars."

She dismissed us with a wag of her head left, walking swiftly to the outdoor bar on the beach.

"She thinks we're crazy," I said. "Maybe we are, because it was kind of fun. Not that I would do it every day."

Bob and I stood under the shower until we were sure the salt had been washed from our clothes. "Where's Jim and Jan?" Bob asked Dick.

"They were smart and came in early this morning before the surf got heavy. They plan to leave a few days before we do to practice their navigation."

"That's interesting, and probably a good idea for them. Now for new business. How do we get out of this Condo complex to catch the bus?"

"It's a pretty long walk, maybe a mile or more up to the road. We should be dry by then."

But we were not dry. All the water drained downward to our shorts as we walked, and when we boarded the bus for the half hour ride to Manzanillo, the thirsty seats sucked the water from our shorts. I hoped it would be a refreshing experience for the next rider.

We arrived near the dock area and found a large cement government building where we started our check in process. We visited immigration first; they sent us to the Port Captain. We went to the Port Captain, and they wanted to send us back to immigration. We now knew what a yo yo felt like, except most yo yos didn't have to go up two flights of stairs, down two flights of stairs. One clerk insisted we needed a special paper issued by an agent.

"We don't need an agent," said Bob. "That is for big ships, not yachts."

"Oh, but I think you do," said the clerk with a smirk. " I think I can work something out for you since the Port Captain is out of the office for now." He waited, staring into Bob's eyes with a knowing look.

Bob kept his face impassive, knowing full well what the clerk wanted. "I'm sorry, I just don't know what you mean. Immigration told us we didn't need an agent, and we don't need a special clearance."

"But I must insist on this clearance. You will not be able to enter the Marquesas without this special paper."

"I'll take my chances. Now please issue the paper, or I'll have to sit here until you do. I appreciate your wanting to make sure we can enter French Polynesia. You're a good man."

The clerk looked disconcerted and guilty at the same time. He hemmed and hawed, chewed his lip, finally taking our papers and stamping them in a proper form. We then went down two flights of stairs to immigration and settled our business. We met Dick and asked how things were going for him.

"This guy in the Port Captain's office insisted we had to have an agent. We walked into town and finally found one, and it cost twenty dollars. I'll bet that clerk gets a kick back."

"I pretended not to understand and sat there. He finally backed down and stamped our papers," Bob said.

"Damn," Dick said. "I knew we were getting jerked around, but I didn't want to waste a whole day here. It sure cost me."

"Are you all done for now?"

"No, not at immigration. Denise met this gal from New Zealand, *Adrianna, who begged us to take her with us. She promised to cook, and do the watches. I wasn't too sure about the whole thing, but Denise said we can always use an extra hand. Jim and Jan are lining up an extra crew member too. Someone they met in the bar at the Condos. He's supposed to be a gourmet cook and they're all excited."

"Well, I hope it works out," Bob said. "We're going to look for a store that sells batteries. See you for cocktails on our boat tonight."

We trudged all over town, finally locating a store that sold 8 D bus batteries. Between my Spanish dictionary and gestures we bought the battery. We made arrangements to have it delivered to us at Las Hadas harbor the next day. There was no way we could carry a 150 pound battery out of the store. I started laughing as we walked to the bus stop. "Can you imagine us trying to load the battery in the dinghy, rowing it through the surf, and then lifting it up into the boat? It would make a great slap stick movie for the three stooges, or better yet, Laurel and Hardy."

At cocktails that night we told Dick of our plans to move the boat into Las Hadas harbor. "I want to get water, fuel, and pump up our batteries before we leave for the Marquesas," Bob said. "Also you can use the phones in the hotel to call home instead of going into the telephone office in the city and waiting in line."

Dick decided the idea had merit and called the Harbor Master on his radio, making arrangements to stay for two days. *Starlight* decided to remain in Santiago Bay.

---

* *name change*

194

The next day we entered a beautiful inner harbor next to the impressive, and expensive, Las Hadas hotel. Brilliant white moorish style buildings greeted us once we rounded a rocky point jutting out of Santiago Bay. By paying a modest fee we had full use of the hotel facilities. There were restaurants, huge swimming pools with waterfalls, marine iguanas on little islands, bridges, fantastic bathrooms with lots of hot water, power, diesel fuel, and telephones. The harbor had one drawback. A storm generated ocean surge caused all the boats in the harbor to act like they had the St. Vitus Dance. We had to tie up Mediterranean style, bow out, stern in. We put out a stern fender so we wouldn't bang against the dock. We could hear the groan of lines cinching up, rigging whining, and Dick's boomkin chain riding up and down on the end of the dock. But what really rocked me was the sight of his new crew, Adrianna, bringing her things aboard *California*.

"Bob," I said in a hoarse whisper, "isn't that the girl we saw in Cabo San Lucas giving haircuts on the beach?"

Bob squinted in the sunlight and nodded his head. "Yeah, she was living with a fellow from Sweden on a boat. I think he threw her out."

"I know she went to another boat, but didn't stay too long. Do you think we should say anything to Dick?"

"I don't know. She's already moved aboard. Denise seems determined to take her because she's a Kiwi too."

"I'm glad it's just the two of us. I may change my mind in a storm, but for now I don't want anyone else on our boat."

We stayed several days, and then motored back to Santiago Bay. *California* left also. The bay looked empty now that *Starlight* had already left for the Marquesas. *Smiling Jack* returned and anchored near by. The sea calmed down, which was in our favor since we had to take our dinghies and go to town to stock up on food for the crossing. We deflated the Avon and put it away, using *Nina Maria,* plus engine, to land on the beach. On our trip to the beach I had all my fingers crossed. It worked.

The town of Santiago felt like the inside of a blast furnace. Not a whisper of air, just crowds of people shopping in the open market. We bought another case of beer, a ham, wine, bacon, eggs, and lots of vegetables, especially cabbage. Cabbage was the one vegetable that lasted a long time. I wasn't too thrilled with the eggs. They were covered with chicken excrement.

"They look awful," I said. "I guess they'll be all right if I scrub the shells well, and cover them with Vaseline." I was wrong, big time.

We dug down into our pockets and paid for a taxi to drop us off in front of the Condos. The heat was almost too much for us, especially with all the food and heavy beer we had to carry. Some residents shook their heads and fanned themselves as we walked back and forth with all of our packages. I think a few were disappointed not to have the excitement they experienced last time. Not me. We made a dry, safe trip back to *Maria Elena,* and by time we had stowed all the supplies we were absolutely pooped. I did feel my age.

That night we were invited to *California* for cocktails, and to meet a fishing Captain from a ten million dollar vessel, the *Gloria H.* The fishing boat had a private helicopter. Before long Bob and I started to droop like day old roses. We made our excuses and motored back to our boat. Tomorrow....the big day...still so much to do. First sleep.

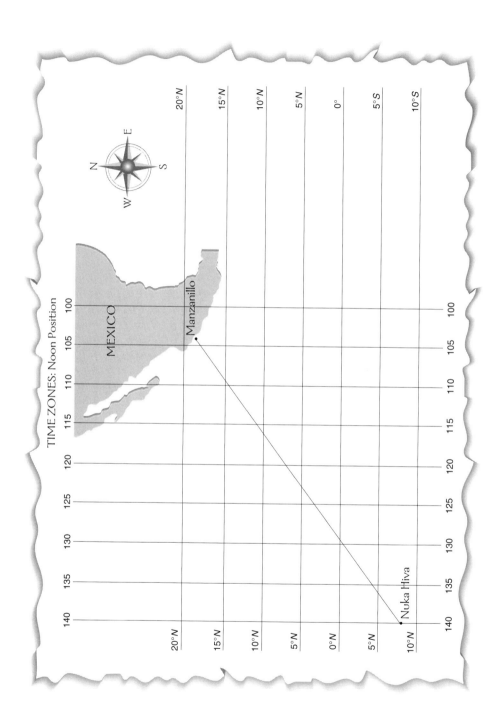

TIME ZONES: Noon Position

MEXICO

Manzanillo

Nuka Hiva

20°N 15°N 10°N 5°N 0° 5°S 10°S

140 135 130 125 120 115 110 105 100

Chapter 18

THY OCEAN IS SO BIG, MY BOAT IS SO SMALL

"Only one more day me Johnny, one more day.
Oh come rock'n roll me over, one more day.
Don't ye hear the Old Man growlin'? one more day!
Don't ye hear the Mate a-howlin'? one more day!

(Sea Chantey, One More Day)

Both of us woke up early, tense with excitement. This could be a day that would change our lives forever, for the longest we had been offshore was three days. Twenty seven hundred miles of sailing lay head of us before our first landfall. At five knots an hour, unpredictable winds and possible gear problems, it was anybody's guess how long it would take us.

Up and at 'em," Bob said. "I need to do some more bottom scrubbing. *Maria* needs to sail as fast as she can go."

"How much air do you have left in your tank?"

"Enough for today, plus some. I'm sure we can refill it in Tahiti."

"Be careful. You can't clear your ears like you used to."

While Bob scrubbed I started tying down loose gear, getting out the harnesses we would wear at night, and generally checking each cabin to make sure *Maria* was ready to go to sea. As I worked I wondered about *Starlight*. Dick had talked to Jim several times, and we all planned to rendezvous at some point out in the "great pond." I hadn't figured out how that would work since he started three days ahead of us.

At noon we ate a quick lunch. Mine sort of stuck in my throat, but Bob never let anything interfere with his appetite.

At 1325, we pulled up anchor, the wind blowing gently out of the south-west. The afternoon sparkled in a cloudless sky, warmed by an air temperature of 75 degrees

As we left the anchorage in Santiago Bay several sea gulls rose swiftly into the air, squawked in raucous tones, then used their wings like elbows, rudely pushing each other out of the way.

"No food this time gulls," I shouted. "You'll have to wait for the next gringo."

I felt a shiver of anticipation. I headed into the wind as Bob hauled on the main halyard, bringing the large sail slowly up the mast. He secured the main, then freed the self furling genoa line and pulled the sheet in tight. He wrapped the line around the port winch. The 130% genoa flapped, then swelled with the warm Mexican air, gracefully lifting up our bow. Moving about in a purposeful manner helped to calm our excitement, and we focused attention on getting lines secured, stowing the winch handle and carrying the bumpers down below. Bob looked at the mainsail and genoa. Frowning he said,. "On this close hauled tack we might get more out of the boat if I put up the new staysail."

We were pleased to see it boosted our speed considerably. The boat sliced through the waves, bouncing slightly as the sea swells swept under us. Bob turned and gave me a thumbs up signal, his eyes showing the same thrill I felt. He jumped down from the upper deck into the cockpit, letting out a whoop as he landed. "I can't believe the big day finally arrived. I had a hard time going to sleep last night."

"Me too, you probably noticed because I kept bumping into you when I turned over."

His expression abruptly changed from joy to concern. "I need to check a few things below. I want to see when the next satellite update is."

He went below to check our course, punching a button on the Sat Nav to check the next scheduled position reading and its expected accuracy. Some readings were rejected by Sat Nav because of a low pass by the satellite. We knew with so many miles ahead of us precision navigation counted. Nuku Hiva may loom massive when seen up close, but it was merely an insignificant blip in the immense Pacific. We mentally prepared ourselves for possible electronic equipment failure due to the damp marine atmosphere. Bob and I planned to use our sextants, each taking numerous sun shots and practicing some of our navigational skills. It had been months since our last shot in Mexico. We knew when it came to complicated celestial navigation skills, what you don't use, you soon lose.

Up on deck I could see *California* and *Smiling Jack,* putting up their sails.

"Where do you suppose *Starlight* is by now?" I asked, staring at the empty water ahead.

Bob waved his hand, "Out there somewhere. I hope their practice navigation is going as planned since all they have is a sextant. We'll hope the skies are clear. We've had a lot of cloud cover."

I wondered if the crew on the other boats were thinking about the days ahead, traveling so many miles at five knots an hour for days on end, seeing nothing but sea, sky and each other, especially the new pick up crew members on *California* and *Starlight.* Concerns about spending twenty or more days at sea, cabin fever, lack of exercise, or whether Bob and I would still be friends when we arrived in Nuku Hiva passed through my mind. Being married for thirty seven years didn't guarantee anything.

Bob poked his head up out of the companionway, giving me a funny look, "What in the world are you thinking about. You look so serious."

"I know I'm the one who suggested coming this far, but I hope you won't get sick of me and think you've made a big a mistake."

He came up the steps, and as he took me in his arms, he leaned down and gave me a warm kiss. "That would be impossible," he said, "besides, you may be the one who gets sick of me."

He sat down next to me at the wheel, leaving his right arm draped around my shoulders, then closed his eyes as he leaned back in the cushion. As we sat there I could feel a rush of love for this man, and my worry melted away. The warm breeze brushed my face, making me realize the unhurried speed of five knots was precisely what we loved about sailing. Mesmerized by the sensation of moving along a floating highway, gently rocked by the boat's motion, and hearing the hypnotic song of hissing water brushing past the hull, acted like the hum of a mother's lullaby in my ears. Staying awake became difficult. Both mind and body unwound, and a feeling contentment overtook us. Bob had experienced this many times over the years. Knowing I could feel the same filled me with plea-sure, and I wished all sailing could be this heavenly. But a shadow of real-ity pressured my consciousness. Sailing, like life, had two sides, and one could be hell.

An hour later Bob awoke when he heard the beep of the Sat Nav. "A new satellite's been logged on," he said. I'll see if I can get position fix. I still can't figure out how we misplaced that large area chart of Mexico to the Marquesas."

He grumbled to himself some more going down the ladder. It didn't matter at this point who lost the chart, the Captain or the Admiral. I was proud of him because he turned the frustrating disaster into a more posi-tive experience. He created his own chart the next day . He took plotting paper, drew lines of Latitude and Longitude which matched the scale appropriate to our Latitude, then marked our position. Future positions would be taken from Sat Nav information, or celestial sights, then plotted on our newly created chart. Our heading would then be based on our pre-sent position. Later when we reached a new Latitude line he would draw a new chart. It should work as well as an expensive chart,...we hoped.

Bob was a man who liked organization, me too, but not so much that a little chaos ruined my day. Raising kids cured me of thinking organiza-tion would assure a plan would work. That's because I learned early in planning that chaos and kids were linked together like super glue. Mom told me when I was growing up that I had to learn to roll with the punch-es. I didn't know then that raising a family meant rock and roll until you're punchy.

Even though he hadn't said anything more after discovering the miss-ing chart, the crossing, and what lay ahead of us, filled his mind with ques-tions. Being close to land along the coast we could obtain help, but once the boat sailed deep into the Pacific, the captain and crew were on their own, especially in this lightly traveled part of the ocean.

Bob came back on deck with his book and settled down on a cushion.

"I'm thankful we've had all these months of Mexican coastal sailing experience behind us" I said. "Except for bare boat chartering in the Caribbean and South Pacific, most of our other sailing has been up and down the California coast."

"I had plenty experience in the navy. Of course the ship I was on was quite a bit bigger."

"I love our ship. *Maria* is the right size. She's become my friend, and not just a hunk of fiberglass." I stared out at the deep blue water. What about you ocean I said silently to the restless sea that surrounded me. Will you be my friend too?

Bob stood up. "I'm not in the mood to read. I'm going below to check on the weather fax. I thought by now we'd have had a new map."

The machine had stopped making maps two days ago, but being an optimist, he thought it might stop being perverse and start up again. It only seemed to print weather when we didn't need it.

Several hours later the warm wind began to bluster, and evening found *Maria Elena* charging through the waves at 8 1/2 knots. The old saying, "Wind down at sun down," didn't seem to apply in this part of the world. Bob and I settled ourselves in the cockpit, ready to begin our first night watch on our crossing.

"I'm not going to relax unless you promise to wear your harness and attach it to the steering ring." I said.

"Don't worry, I won't let a rogue wave carry me off."

Teasingly I grabbed his ears, putting my nose up to his nose, staring into his eyes so closely it made him look cross eyed. "The only rogue around here is you. What if you were washed over the side like the story in *Overboard.*

"Great, you would have to think about that book now, just as we take off in the black of night."

"I did it on purpose so you would think about it."

"All right. I'm thinking. Now go to bed."

"I'm too excited to sleep this early."

"You'll be sorry in three hours if you don't," countered Bob. "The weather's picking up. Could be a rough night ahead, and I want you rested and ready to go."

Despite his warning I found it very hard to go to sleep, creating a feeling of deja vu of my first night watch in Mexico. My excitement, coupled with my unbalanced internal clock, still kept me tossing and turning on our bunk until 2300. Whether I was rested or not, it was now time for my watch, and as I buckled on my harness I watched a sleepy Bob take his off, lightly snoring before I left the cabin. At 0200 am I was more than ready to take his place, falling asleep immediately. No wonder people called this the hot bunk system. At 0500 am we traded places again, but before I went on deck I fixed myself some hot chocolate as a special treat. Daylight arrived, and while my spirits rose, my eyelids drooped like a dying Boston fern.

Around eight o'clock I heard the radio squawk, *"Maria Elena,* this is *California."*

Dick's deeply depressed voice caught Bob's ear, and his brows knotted together in worry as he reached for the microphone. *"California,* this is *Maria Elena,* what's up Dick?"

"Last night the chain on the boomkin parted, leaving the main mast unsupported. I'm sailing under the genoa alone."

Bob thought about Dick's seventy foot main mast mounted on the deck, shivered at the thought of it dropping like a stone and crashing into everything. "That's bad, do you know what caused the break?"

"Yeah, remember the big surge we had the first day in Las Hadas Harbor? I think that caused the chain to ride up and down on the edge of the dock. I didn't see any damage at the time, but it obviously weaken it."

"Are you going to head back to Mexico?"

"No, I don't want to turn back, we'll keep going. I think we can make it if we take it real easy."

Bob shook his head disconsolately, "We'll slow down too Dick. We won't leave you."

"Thanks buddy. Talk to you later."

Afterwards Bob and I looked at each other, both calculating what we would do under similar circumstances. "If it was me I'd turn back. We're only twenty four hours out of Mexico," said Bob. "I'll bet Dick doesn't want the hassle of going through Mexican check out again."

"The difference between you and Dick is you're extra cautious. You're still adventurous, but you don't like leaving obvious problems to chance. That's okay. with me."

I thought how each captain had to make up his own mind to fit the situation, his crew, and his boat. Tough decision to make sometimes. Cruising provided many opportunities to encounter the unknown and meet new situations which challenged the captain's ingenuity. Weather could be unpredictable and wrathful, other important equipment might break down, or a crew member injured, or taken seriously ill. The lives and well being of everybody aboard was the captain's responsibility, a role that could prove to be a heavy burden at times. Suddenly, I was quite happy not to be captain, Admiral would still do for me.

We shortened sail, knowing *California* would have a better chance catching up to us. In case of any new emergency, we wanted to be closer in order to help. The combined problem of shortened sails and beam seas triggered waves of nausea through me. I couldn't believe after all these months I would be bothered by King Neptune's revenge. I went down below to look for my ginger pills. I wanted to try something different that wouldn't make me sleepy, and was surprised the pills worked so well. But there's nothing quite like a pungent ginger burp later. It made my eyes water.

We continued to have mixed, sloppy seas, light air and a beam swell during the day. As the full force of a wave struck our boat's side, the wind spilled out of the sail, causing the boat to rock violently in the opposite direction. The taunt cloth on the main sail snapped with a loud whack. We attached the preventer to the main boom to keep the sail from being knocked constantly from side to side, but it was only a partial solution, not *the* solution. Between hearing "smack" on the hull, and "whack" of the sail, my temper rose in irritation. This wasn't the mellow feeling I had experienced the day before, and I bared my teeth as I spoke to Bob, "Are we having fun yet?"

He shook his head no. As he stood up, the boat started to go around in a circle. *Otto* was sick of the whole thing too, arcing his relays. Bob sanded the pitted areas of the relays, and replaced them in the unit, but the directions of the seas made it too hard on *Otto* to use without causing a repeat of the same problem. It was back to hand steering for the next eight hours. We both suffered bone breaking exhaustion by morning, knowing for sure we weren't having fun, but enduring our predicament because there wasn't anything else we could do. The winds continued to blow fifteen to eighteen knots, but our speed forward remained minimal.

When we made our crossing plans earlier, we intellectually understood there would be good days and bad days. Good days would stand out like a brass band, bad days were......bad days. At this point, intellect was not in control, crabby emotions had taken over, making me feel as humorous as a cat in a bath tub. Bob sighed, stood up and stretched, then patted his stomach. "I'm hungry. How 'bout lunch."

I could feel my fingers curl and my teeth clamp down on my jaw. With great effort I said, "Why don't you get some peanut butter and crackers. I'm not hungry. Besides, I'm too tired to eat."

He looked sideways at me, opening his mouth to say something, then closed it, retreating down below to the galley. A few minutes later he returned, holding out a plate full of crackers topped with peanut butter. "Thought you could use this," he said.

I felt down-right mean and foolish, plus a little hungry.

"I'm sorry I snapped at you," I said. "It's not your fault you get hungry. Thank you for the crackers."

Bob chewed on his cracker, looked up at the sails and said, "There were plenty of times when I was working that you've gotten me out of a blue funk. I figured it was my turn this time."

When I finished eating, I brushed the crumbs from my legs, suddenly laughing at the situation, because both of us were in our cruising clothes, stark naked. Being naked, even after all these years of marriage, made me feel a trifle vulnerable, as if clothes somehow could protect me, from *what* I didn't know. Maybe in this outfit I could truthfully say I had nothing to hide, but what about my emotions, did I hide those? Maybe with some people. But not when it came to Bob, I trusted him with all my secrets, warts and all. I went over and took the plate from his hand, placed it on the deck, giving him a hug. "Omigosh," I said. It's so hot we're sticking together like fly paper." That took care of a romantic possibility....What a shame.

As the day progressed, the tropical heat began to tell on us. Our sun shield and dodger kept our bodies from turning into blackened beef jerky, but the trapped humid air inside the area made us breathless. Even a light piece of clothing seemed confining and oppressive, except at night when we wore a tee shirt to keep the harness from digging in to our shoulders. We unzipped the front of the dodger, allowing hot, but somewhat cooler air to flow into the cockpit, drying the sweat on our bodies into salty white lines. The blazing sun leached moisture from our pores, making us eternally thirsty. For years my family has teased me about my complete disinterest in drinking water, giving me the title of, "The Camel". Bob disappeared down below to get himself a glass of water when I called out, "Get me one too please, Gunga Din."

He came up with two glasses, holding one out to me, "Do my ears deceive me, or did you really ask for water?"

"That shows you how desperate I am. I wonder how we could make it taste like wine?"

"As I remember, only one man did that, I don't think I could repeat it. Aren't you glad we installed our water maker in Mexico?"

"That goes without saying. You're usually right in making decisions on equipment. Who would have dreamt that I would actually crave water to drink. I thought water was only good to bathe in. The kids won't believe it."

Our water maker could desalinate sea water at four gallons an hour, either electrically or manually. We filled the Soda King we had brought from home with water, carbonating it with the CO_2 chargers, then cooling it down in the refrigerator. It was much more refreshing than sweet soft drinks, or plain water. We had a limited the amount of beer we consumed, compromising by rationing one beer per person per day. If I wanted to win a heart I would give Bob my beer.

We had several long discussions before leaving on our crossing, deciding to drink only the one beer, and no wine. We felt we would be tired enough from sailing, and alcohol might interfere with our judgment and navigation. It proved the right decision for us.

We had been at sea for two days and decided it was time to try and reach *Starlight* by radio and effect a rendezvous. No joy.

I hung up the microphone on its hook, pacing around the cabin sole, "I'm getting worried. They expected us to catch up with them by now."

"I know," said Bob. "Jim wanted three days to practice navigation, but I think we should have been in VHF radio range by now, they're not that fast a boat."

"I'm sure *California* would have told us if they'd heard from them."

"The last time I talked with Dick, he said that *Smiling Jack* had broken a shroud during the night, nothing about Jim."

"The sick boat list is growing. I hope its not contagious," I sighed.

Healthy *Maria* had never been noted for her speed, quite the opposite in fact, since she hardly moved in a light breezes. She weighed 28,000 pounds plus, loaded with extra gear, spare parts and supplies, now, due to the break down of the other boats, we were suddenly considered the fastest craft. *Maria Elena* was fairly dancing to get away, but we felt honor bound to wait until we got the group closer together. Not an easy matter. This kind of antsy waiting reminded me of the day my parents said I could have a horse when I turned 18. Unfortunately, I was nine at the time. My parents were pretty smart, because at eighteen I was too busy horsing around with boyfriends.

Traveling as a group with other boats worked on short coastal cruises, but on a long crossing the differences in sailing capabilities made it too difficult to remain together. It was wonderful to have companionship in a big Pacific pond, but it not practical, only working for the tuna and porpoises who swam together in schools.

That night before the first watch Bob and I scanned the starry skies, quickly finding my special constellation, Orion's belt. My voice sounded husky when I spoke, "I feel like they're watching over us, leading us across the Pacific to safety."

"Many a sailor has followed a star across the ocean. I don't know if they felt like you, most were hoping it would lead them to new continents, becoming rich and powerful."

"All you wanted to do was follow your dream."

"I wouldn't have gone without you."

"Are you sure? Other men go without their wives."

Bob picked up my hand, turned it over, caressing the palm with the tip of his fingers. "You forget that you are part of that life, very much a part of my dream. The dream would have been worthless without you."

Tears pricked at my eyes as I wrapped my two hands around his, holding him in a tight grip. It was hard to speak over the lump in my throat, barely able to say, "Thank you. That means everything to me."

On my 0200 watch I sipped hot chocolate, put it down to re-adjust my harness, enlarging it slightly. Hmmm, I thought, am I gaining weight? I really must do some kind of exercise, one that didn't include jogging or jumping jacks, impractical on a moving boat. The whole idea made me tired thinking about it, so I switched mental gears, contemplating the concerns that had been worrying me about the crossing. Besides the obvious problem of exercise, I had worried about needing distance and space to be alone. I was pleasantly surprised to find our boat was large enough, our personalities weren't at war, and we had become immersed in our books, or busy with maintenance work. Instead of having dead time on our hands, I found we had wonderful opportunities to talk about anything and everything, different from the coastal sailing where we stopped and socialized a lot. I definitely didn't marry a boring person.

The next morning we finally reached *Starlight* by ham radio. We were out of VHF range. A sense relief flowed through us, hearing his voice after the many days of silence. Bob was excited, "Where have you been? We've been so worried when we couldn't get in contact with you."

"Well, you weren't the only one worried," Jim said.

"What happened, did you have a problem with the boat?"

"No, the problem was in my navigation. I can get a super LAN (latitude at noon), but I'm having trouble with longitude."

"Tell me where you think you are and I'll head for the Latitude and Longitude you give me."

Jim gave him a probable Lat and Lon, and Bob plotted a converging course, hoping to meet up by afternoon. Dick on *California*, and *Smiling Jack* heard the radio transmission and changed their course too. We arrived at the position Jim gave us and found an empty ocean. All we could see was our two companion boats on the horizon. Bob picked up the mike and called Jim. *"Starlight,* this is *Maria Elena.* I'm at the Lat and Lon you gave me. I've looked around, and even turned on the radar to the 25 mile range. No sign of you anywhere."

"Maria Elena, this is *Starlight."* "I don't know what's wrong. Damn big ocean." His voice sounded very discouraged, plus a little scared.

I could understand his feeling like an insignificant star in what appeared to be a galaxy of water. Before I left home I thought of the Pacific ocean as being well traveled, criss- crossed with freighter traffic following the great circle routes. But I realized now that the great circle routes covered only a small portion of the ocean. Unless a cruiser sailed in an area of a known ocean route, he was on his own in case of trouble, and it seemed Jim was in trouble.

By the end of the radio transmission *California* and *Smiling Jack* were in closer visual contact with us, only several miles away. *Starlight* remained missing.

Later in the day Dick made contact with Jim by ham radio. "Listen to me Jim. I'm going to shoot off a parachute flare at 2100 pm. tonight. If you're close enough you should be able to see a red light. When you see it, call me back right away on the radio."

Several minutes before 2100 Dick turned on the VHF to channel 16, announcing his intention to shoot off flares. We were near the Panama to Hawaii shipping lanes, and Dick didn't want to alarm any ships that might be in the area. At exactly 2100 pm Dick shot off the first flare. The sharp noise of the twelve gage shot gun shell seemed louder than normal, especially when contrasted to the dark, still night. A warm, rosy glow filled the sky, then gently swaying like a pendulum, the parachute flare floated down until it was swallowed by the black sea.

"The radio crackled and Jim said, "Dick, did you fire the flare yet?"

"Yes, guess you didn't see it. I'll try a couple more."

Two more loud retorts of the gun boomed, sending shock waves across the sky, followed by two red lights, beaming brightly as they appeared in the heavens. These too were captured by the sea. Crew members on each boat waited anxiously, each praying in their own way, that Jim would see the lights. Jim called again, "No luck. I'll contact you tomorrow and see what we come up with."

We could hear the keen disappointment in his voice. It was a scary situation not knowing where you were, or if anyone would be able to find you. As captain, Jim's responsibility for his crew must have felt like a sack of lead hanging from his neck. I'm sure the others were thinking along the same lines.

Our mood matched the failure of the flare sightings. The weather changed, becoming so fluky each boat was forced to change sails frequently. It frustrated us to put effort and energy into a job, only to start over again. When Bob went on the fore deck, he spent an inordinate amount of time hooking and unhooking his safety line as he made the changes. It was a tiresome bitch. An Irish crew member on *Smiling Jack* gave us our first good laugh when she said, "How did you all like the sail changes today? It reminded me of a whore's knickers, up and down, up and down."

The next day Bob made VHF radio contact with *Starlight*. "Jim, I've got an idea. I'm gonna use the squelch on the VHF as a measure of signal strength."

"I'm ready for any idea," sighed Jim.

"Your voice is getting weaker Jim. I'm going to turn the boat around until you come in stronger. Aha! I've got you now. Just keep coming. I'll head toward your voice."

Bob turned our boat until Jim's voice sounded very strong. We knew we were at least within twenty-five miles, which was better than one hundred miles and lost. We sailed, staring hard at the at the horizon. Where were they, we wondered? The tension fed on us like a parasite, making the hours seem like days, dragging on and on. Later in the afternoon Bob scanned the horizon with the binoculars, suddenly letting out a whoop of joy. "I think I see them. There's something blue out there, yes...good, it's their blue genoa."

Finally, after six days of being apart, the lost was found. Within an hour we saw Jim standing high in the rat lines, waving his arms back and forth, with Jan standing by the steering wheel wearing a beautiful smile. Her first look showed relief, then sheer happiness as she let go of the wheel, waving both arms and shouting. I had gone below earlier and taken out my ukulele. Bob grabbed the harmonica, and when they were along side we sang, "Happy days are here again." No one cared that Bob didn't have the slightest idea how to play the harmonica, as long as he made noise, we were happy.

We contacted *California* and agreed to try and rendezvous the next day. We arranged our course to intersect with theirs, with Dick letting *Smiling Jack* know what the new plans were.

Finally, after six days the lost was found.

The wind came up, and *Maria* started moving ahead of *Starlight*. We tried to de-tune our sails in order to slow down, giving the other boat a chance to keep up. It was my watch, and as the winds escalated further I knew the MPS (the only sail up) had to come down. Time to wake up Bob. He came up wearing only his safety harness, rubbing the sleep from his eyes. We worked like demons trying to get the sail down, but with little results. Bob went forward to see if he could find the problem. He found it. "Damnit, you've got the head of the sail wrapped around the halyard," he shouted, totally disgusted.

"Well double damn," I shouted back. I'm not an owl with a swivel neck who can keep track of everything."

I was not pleased. He was not pleased. We worked as fast and efficiently as possible, untangling the mess while grumbling and mumbling all the way. My night vision had done me in again, and short of getting a seeing eye dog, I would have to do the best I could. Bob understood my problem, but understanding a problem didn't necessarily solve it.

The next day all the boats rendezvoused. Jan came on the radio, "Okay guys. This is a QST (ham talk for important message). The game of hide and seek is over. *Maria Elena* won the game. The first boat to make it to Nuka Hiva buys beer for everyone."

"Great," said Bob. "It'll be us, if we're lucky. Will the three of you be all right without us?"

"Get going Bob. With the three boats together, we'll be just fine," said Jan.

I grabbed the mike from Bob. "Good bye from Ma and Pa Kettle. (We were the oldest couple) We'll see you in Taiohae Bay with cold beer and munchies for every one. We'll miss you."

My throat ached with the strain of trying not to cry, even though I knew we were best off alone.

Up went our sails, out came the reef, and I swear we could hear *Maria* breath a sigh of relief. Her bow created a frothy wake, and soon we were flying down wind with the MPS. (I can't seem to get away from that sail) Since it was night time, and my watch, I could imagine the sail chuckling as it planned a new game for me. One minute I was looking at the sail, and the next minute it disappeared from sight. How can that be, I thought? "I hate to do this again Bob," I yelled. I banged on the cabin top over his head.

He came up, giving me a patient, but rueful smile. Buckling up his safety harness he said,

"What's up now?"

"The sail just disappeared."

"It can't disappear. There's three lines attached to it, the halyard, tack and clew. Let's look and see what we've got."

Muttering under my breath, "Why always my watch. Did the tack or the clew wear through?"

"Hold your horses. I can't see that well in the dark."

Welcome to the club, I thought. Carefully stepping up to the bow he found the clew line hanging straight down, the sail still attached. "The sail's in the water. Help me pull it in. We're lucky we didn't run over it."

Our former light air sail, now felt like it weighed a thousand pounds. Inch by inch we carefully, slowly hauled the sail up over the side, finally bringing it into the cockpit, panting from the effort. We sat down, completely surrounded by a voluminous mountain of wet multi colored cloth. "I feel like I've been swallowed by a sail," I said, trying to make room for my feet. "It must be my karma. Somehow it seems fitting I would be done in by our MPS."

We were lucky the sail had been taken down, because within minutes we encountered a quick moving squall with winds up to twenty-five knots. What had seemed a disaster turned out to be a blessing.

The next day we discovered the pin on our swivel block had parted on the halyard, dropping the large sail like a stone in the water. "Much too light weight a swivel," Bob said. "We'll buy a new one once we reach Tahiti."

Ten days had passed when we saw our first ship. We were quite surprised by the sighting because we had left the shipping lanes several days before. As we began to close the distance between the two boats, it became obvious we were on a collision course. We found it hard to believe that with all the water around in the Pacific ocean, these two boats wanted to occupy the same space. We could have altered our course easily as a sailing vessel, but our curiosity got the best of us when we caught sight of the ship's unusual profile. We wanted to find out what the ship was doing out here, and if someone was on watch. We had been privy to some horror stories concerning collisions at sea between sailboats and Korean fishing boats. The fishing boats were known to motor full bore by their auto pilot, but without anyone on deck keeping watch. This caused a bang, bump...resulting in one dream boat down the Pacific drain. Bob grabbed the mike and called channel 16. After identifying himself he gave our position and asked the ship what their intentions were. The ship's radio officer answered. Speaking in a thick accent, he identified his ship's name, which we couldn't understand, and asked Bob if he spoke Russian. Bob blinked in surprise, answering, "No."

The radio operator said, "Von momet plis. I get Kaptin." A minute passed while Bob fidgeted, shifting his weight back and forth as he rocked on his heels. The radio crackled as the Russian captain spoke, "Do you need help?"

"No". We're fine, except for the fact we're on a collision course."

"Ah, so I see," said the Captain. "First how many people aboard, where have you been, where are you going? Do you need a Latitude or Longitude reading?"

"Don't tell him there are only two people," I hissed.

Bob eyed me with his patient look, "There are two of us. We left Manzanillo ten days ago. We're on our way to Nuka Hiva in the French Marquesas. Thank you, we know where we are."

The captain replied in a polite tone, "I and my crew wish for you a good journey. Please clear my stern by two and a half miles because I am Russian research vessel, and I am dragging a cable behind two miles."

We changed course, following the captain's instructions to the letter. As we cleared his stern, we noted a large number of electronic antennas, and hoped the Russian ship wasn't researching us.

The three days following were broken only by swiftly moving tropical squalls. We followed our three on and three off watch schedule, with the squalls appearing on my watch, not Bob's. The ten minute squalls swept in with great force, squeezing stinging rain from the blackened clouds, and sending it horizontally toward me as I hid on the companionway steps. There was no way to avoid getting soaked except to retreat below, but I needed to be where I could see what was happening to the boat. The thermometer registered a comfortable 72 degrees, warm until the rain hit, making my tee shirt feel like a soggy wet sock. It was the only time I felt cold.

The next night, after I had retired below to sleep, I heard Bob yell, "Damnit to hell."

I ran up to the deck panting, worried that he had hurt himself. "What happened. Are you all right?"

"My watch band popped and the watch fell overboard."

"Don't worry, you've another one in the chart table."

"I know, but that watch was special. It's the one I won in high school." He stared into the black water as if he could see his watch spiraling down, alerting the fish to the correct time.

I realized I had made a mistake. This was much more important than just losing a forty year old watch. It had been a pivotal point in his life. I remember his mom telling me how his physic teacher had failed him for not working up to his potential. Even though he did "C" work she said he could be an "A" student. Bob had been outraged at the time, and just to show her he repeated the course and got an "A." All the rest of his grades improved too, and the school saw fit to award him a watch for the most improved grades.

"When my watch fell off I had a strange thought," Bob said. If I hadn't gone to college I wouldn't have found a job that paid as much as it did. I wouldn't have had the money I used to buy this boat, and you and I wouldn't be sitting here in the middle of the Pacific ocean achieving a life long dream."

"That's a lot of wouldn'ts."

"I wish I had thanked Mrs. Davis. It's probably too late now because she was pretty old when I was in High School."

"I guess she got her thanks when she saw you being presented with the watch. Any how I'm sorry the watch is gone, but not forgotten. I'm off back to bed."

Two nights later Bob's glasses were knocked off into the water by a loose line. "If the fish with my watch swims fast enough it can use my glasses to read the time," he said in a disgusted voice. "Lucky I have a spare."

It was now March 19, and we had been at sea for fourteen days. Bob decided to try and reach Dick and find out how the rest of the group were progressing behind us, but they were way out of VHF range. Dick and I had set up a ham schedule before we left, but often the bands were noisy and I couldn't hear.

In the next few days we realized the continued fluky weather was due to our arrival into the intertropical convergent zone, (Known as the ITCZ) an area of low barometric pressure which lay between the two trade wind regions. The ITCZ delineated an equatorial trough in which the dreaded doldrums occurred. The doldrums, noted for dead calms and light fluctuating air, have plagued sailing ships since man first tried to further his horizons. Doldrums were also known as the horse latitudes. This referred back to times when Spain and others brought horses by ship to the New World. Delayed by lack of wind and progress on the old sailing ships the horses died of starvation, and rotted carcasses filled the seas as they were thrown overboard.

We drifted in the ITCZ, wondering how long it would be before the wind would materialize and push us on our way. I began to think I knew how the horses felt. Slap, slap, went the sails, down, down went our spirits. We had been at sea sixteen days, and I started day dreaming about arriving in Nuka Hiva. "You know the first thing I'm going to do when I jump on dry land?" I said.

"I even know what you are going to do before you jump on dry land. Put on your clothes."

"All right smarty, I'll put on clothes. Then I'll find a cold beer and eat someone else's cooking for a change. I plan to sleep the whole night through without waiting for the timer to buzz every twenty minutes. Some nights I feel like a boxer leaping into the ring as the next round is announced."

"Sounds reasonable, but it won't happen if we don't start moving. I'll turn on the engine for a couple of hours, you pray for wind. See you at two in the morning."

Three days drifted by as we made sail changes, cleaned the boat, read, sang songs, fished, calculated our navigation, made ham schedules and talked with Bill and Lori, contacted Dick and wished him Happy Birthday, cooked the tuna we caught, and lastly, had great conversations. We found sitting for long periods of time became impossible for our behinds, our buns dying faster than the victims in our mystery novels. Our day was

215

broken up occasionally by the sound of "zinnnnnng" when the fishing line became taut, whipping around the stern with a furious fish attached. The last blue tuna we caught weighed twenty-five pounds, and by the time we finished it, I was sure we were growing gills, never wanting to eat or see a tuna again.

Bob came up the companionway steps with a latitude and longitude reading in his notebook. "We are getting close to the equator. When I was in the navy the chief with the biggest stomach was chosen to dress up and be King Neptune. The first time I crossed the equator I had to crawl up to King Neptune and kiss his huge belly."

"Gross," I groaned. "Since there are only two of us aboard I guess you're King Neptune, but I'll be damned if I'll crawl."

"You can still kiss my belly," he said with a twinkle.

Before I did anything I stepped down below and checked the Latitude, making sure he wasn't kidding me. Up on deck again I went over to Bob and buried my face in his tummy. I planted a big smooch on his warm belly button, deciding to take a nibble.

"Hey, no fair," he giggled. "That tickles."

I nibbled all the way up from his belly to his chest, his neck and looked into those brown eyes. "I love you King Neptune," I whispered, gently kissing his ear.

"I love you too, crazy woman." He smiled and held me close. Our mouths found each other, and I felt his tender loving kiss brush my lips. The kisses became longer as he stroked my bare bottom, pulling me closer. I reached out to touch and stroke him, becoming as one, we celebrated our love and joy. King Neptune had never been better!

Afterwards we lay in each other's arms. The sensation of physical joy, intimacy and oneness wrapped us in a blanket of contentment. Later Bob rose from the cushion, "When you were reading earlier I put a bottle of champagne in the refrigerator to get cold. It's to celebrate crossing the equator."

"I thought that was what we just did," I said.

"True, but the champagne is a little extra bonus. Since it's daytime we'll drink very slowly and it shouldn't interfere with our night watch. You might think about what kind of message you want to send to King Neptune in the bottle."

I closed my eyes and thought seriously, but nothing earth shaking came to my mind. After so many days at sea I couldn't think creatively. It was an effort just to think. I went below, found a pencil and paper and wrote,

Dear King Neptune,
Today, March 21, 1985, I crossed the equator
and raised a glass of champagne in your honor.
Please keep us safe and watch over us in this
big ocean.

Marlene Allen

An hour later I rolled up the letter and put it inside the champagne bottle. We found another cork, making sure the bottle was air tight. "Here's to you King Neptune," I shouted as I tossed the bottle into the water. It bounced and bobbled, then tipped upright, the green glass sparkling in the sunlight. We watched in silence as the boat sailed slowly away, leaving the bottle to cruise by itself.

The long awaited wind picked up. King Neptune must have gotten my message early as *Maria Elena* appeared to come to life. Even the wind couldn't cool us down, and we poured buckets of sea water over our sizzling bodies. The indigo ocean shimmered in the heat, dotted here and there with white foam curls when a wave passed by. The water appeared pristine clean, unspoiled as yet by man, which made me wonder why humans at home were so prone to fouling their own nests.

Before the next night watch schedule started Bob and I talked about old times and when he quit work. "What's the first thing you remember when you retired?"

He threw back his head laughing, "I remember the first day I got hungry and asked about lunch. You gave me a surprised look and told me you only ate an apple."

"I remember that too. I think a lot of wives like me cut back on lunches. Could be they worry about getting fat too, or just hate getting big meals in the middle of the day. I know that's the way my mom felt. She said she married dad for life, not for lunch."

Bob rubbed his chin. "I wonder what it will be like when we get home? Will we be very different?"

"Probably, but you'll still want lunch. Some things never change."

Bob laughed and went back to reading his Alastair McLean boat mystery, but I didn't pick up my book right away. I've been pretty lucky so far with retirement problems, I thought. Bob and I were so busy getting ready for this trip that he didn't miss his job, or have time to become bored. Mom and dad had a much harder time. Watching them trying to resolve their differences helped me to be more aware of what to watch out for when Bob retired. I learned a very important lesson. Number one, dreams were hard work and didn't necessarily happen. And two, if you couldn't follow your dream you needed something else, hobbies, getting involved with community interests, fun or busy things that could take its place. Dad didn't start off very well.

Dad took early retirement at 62 as a high school English teacher. I was married by then, and mom kept busy with several volunteer organizations, as well as keeping up with her friends. She never had a specific dream of what she wanted to do at retirement, but dad did. He wanted to be a famous short story writer. He thought all he needed was time to write, but when he finally had the opportunity, the stories didn't send the publishers knocking down his front door. Then an old enemy, discouragement, sat down beside him when he wrote. The words on the paper sounded trite, the plots rambled, the characters appeared contrived, and soon the old portable Royal typewriter grew silent, gathering dust instead of words. Dad kind of crumbled along with the dream. He never had any other hobbies, and even though the house was slowly disintegrating around his ears, he wasn't capable of fixing things, being about as handy as a four year old with a broken screw driver. He started following Mom around from room to room, not wanting to leave her side for a minute. She finally looked him in the eye and said, "You're driving me crazy Jim. I don't need a shadow, just a husband. Try writing again. You're good at it. Don't let a few rejections drive you away."

He did try for a short time, but soon the typewriter became mute again. It seemed if he didn't write, then he couldn't fail.

Life had some ironic twists for both of them. Mom's heart mitral valve began to give out, and soon dad had his hands full taking care of her all the time. He had found the ultimate excuse and way out of writer's block.

Little things started breaking down after being a sea for a long time. We couldn't get the mainsail down because it got stuck under the genoa halyard pulley. Bob terrorized both of us by going aloft the fifty foot mast to free it. Then the weatherfax turned up its nose at us by not feeding the paper properly, allowing the stylus to go back and forth in the same place, shredding the paper. Besides the usual wear and tear on the halyards, sheets, and winches, the sump pump decided to give up. All the gray water from the heads, galley sink, and showers went through the sump. I guess I shouldn't blame the pump for feeling over worked, but the noxious odor of standing bilge water was getting to us. Bob had just finished using the hand bilge pump to clear out the sump area, his body covered with sweat and smelling of rotted bacteria. He tossed the dirty water overboard, "I don't think we will be able to buy a new pump until we reach Papeete."

"At this moment Tahiti seems light years away. Do you suppose Bill and family can bring one from the states when they visit us there?"

"Great idea. We'll have to call them by land line when we reach Taihoae Bay. We can't order parts by ham radio."

Several days later rain squalls rolled across the skies, bringing heavy black clouds and replacing the sun. The air around us felt pressing and uncomfortable. It even smelled heavy. We wore our foul weather jackets to keep the stinging rain from our bodies, the insides had the sensation of sitting in a sauna. My sweaty skin stuck to the jacket, making it difficult to move about. Despite the weather, the anticipation of our first landfall in the early daylight hours started to create new excitement. Night loomed inky black, broken only by the sharp stabs of lightening, followed by the deep rumble of thunder.

"I want good visibility when we approach land tomorrow," Bob said. I better go down and check our progress."

He returned a few minutes later, an exasperated look over powering his face. "I can't believe it. I checked and we're going too fast."

My eyebrows became one single line of concern. "Incredible, first no wind, now too much."

"I know. We've been trying to eat up the miles to Nuka Hiva, now we have to drag our feet. I'll go up and take down some sail."

"You mean drag our keel," I said disconsolately. "I feel like a rabbit that's been chasing a carrot, only to have it nibbled away before my eyes. I'll come help you pull down the big sail."

As daylight dawned we could see and feel the set of the seas pushing us to land, and a sweet plant odor from land swept over us. Looking through our binoculars we glimpsed large fluffy clouds surrounding the mountain peaks, announcing land in the midst of the Pacific ocean. We had been warned about a dangerous outcrop of rocks when approaching Taiohae Bay, and as we neared we turned on the engine to keep us from being set too close to the rocks. Suddenly we heard the shrill buzzing of our engine alarm.

"Oh shit. I can't believe it," said Bob. "The engine over-heat light is on." He quickly went below into the engine room. After several minutes he yelled, "The sea water pump isn't working. Turn off the engine and sail away from the island."

"Damn, damn, damn," I muttered. So near and yet so far." Disappointment fueled my anger as I tried to keep the tears from falling. The beauty of the lush green islands had been calling to me, and now I had to tell the islands they had the wrong number.

Bob located air in the sea water system and proceeded to bleed the air out. It wasn't too long before he called to me from the engine room, "Turn the engine back on, I'm coming up." He reappeared with a grin on his sweat covered face, a smudge of grease highlighting the tip of his nose.

The sound of the diesel engine played like a symphony of hope as we now turned toward Taiohae Bay. I looked up to see wild, rugged mountains and high ridges disappearing into the clouds, feeling like we were the first people to discover this lonely, stark place. We didn't have to worry about looking for a pass through a reef, because the Marquesas islands were relatively new, geologically speaking, and were not surrounded by coral reefs. My heart skipped a beat as we rounded the point and entered the grand bay. Twelve boats peacefully swung on their bow anchors, flanked in the distance by lush greenery with flecks of colorful flowers. It was a feast for the eyes as well as the soul. A powerful emotion welled up inside me and I threw my arms toward the sky, emitting loud cries of, "We did it. We really did it."

Bob's grinning face turned toward me, and with outstretched arms he grabbed me around the waist, planting a big kiss on my lips. Then a primordial scream left his lips, echoing across the bay as he whooped with joy. After 26 days at sea we had arrived.

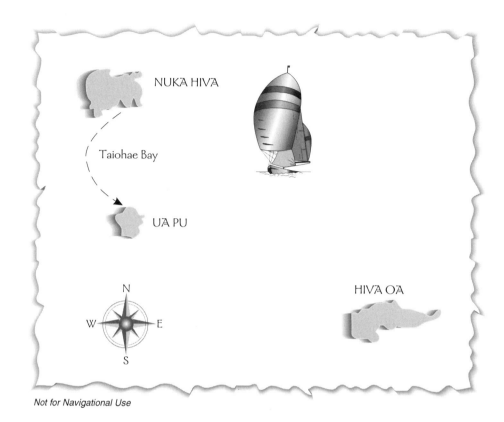

Not for Navigational Use

Chapter 19

THE MARQUESAS, WHERE THE FLY IS KING

"We laid old master down to rest,
And on a stone this last request.
Beneath the earth, I'm forced to lie
A victim of the blue-tail fly."
(Camp Song, Sung By Sailors too, Blue Tail Fly)

After passing through the rocky entrance of Taiohae Bay, we entered a large harbor, perplexed to find transient boats anchored in one corner, and the distant town in the opposite direction. As we circled the area the image of an ancient mariner rowed toward us. His weather beaten dinghy and unmatched oars emerged as the perfect counterpart to his clothes; a sun bleached blue shirt, shorts ripped at the pocket, and a yellowed straw hat shading a weathered face. The warm smile on his face made us feel we had been expected.

"Welcome to Taiohac Bay," he said. "Looks like you been to sea a long time. Best you anchor near my boat. If you try to anchor over by town you'll be run down by the inter-island ferry. Oh, the name's John."

"Thanks John. I'm Bob, and this is my wife, Marlene. I wondered why all the boats were anchored here instead of near town. It's taken us twenty-six days to sail from Monzanillo." Bob swung his head around and pointed to a classic narrow-beamed thirty foot yawl. "Is that your boat ?"

"Nope, mine's the one anchored to your starboard. It needs a bit of paint, but I'll get around to around to it someday. I'll leave you to your anchoring now, but if you need anything, give me a holler. Don't worry if I don't answer right off. My hearing isn't what it used to be."

He turned the dinghy around and rowed back to his sailboat, each of them showing the years of wear. We noticed that his main boom hung off to one side with a woebegone ripped mainsail. It reminded me of the ragged bed sheet I used at home to catch paint drops. Looking at the dilapidated scene made me tired, but maybe after a good sleep I would join the old man's casual attitude toward our own chores.

Bob judged the distances between boats, took out the pin securing our anchor and watched two hundred and fifty feet of 3/8 chain chase after our forty-five pound CQR. It snaked its way down through clear-blue water, landing on the sand eighty feet below. The sun's refraction through the water made the anchor appear much closer. Despite the disadvantages of the heavy weight of the chain on the bow, we dared not use a nylon line in the tropics. The coral heads on the ocean bottom functioned like a razor, slicing through regular nylon anchor line as if it were kite string. That could mean goodbye anchor, and hello rocks.

I shaded my eyes against the sun and looked toward town. Yep, we were back to commuting. Even traveling in a fast dinghy the settlement appeared fifteen or twenty minutes away. Bob went below and returned with our yellow "Q" flag, hoisting it up the flag halyard. We were now officially outsiders until we checked into the proper authorities, the French Gendarmerie.

We kept the engine running for another five minutes. Once satisfied the anchor had a good grip in the sand, we turned to other duties. The next job was emptying everything out our of the hanging closet to extract the Avon dinghy from the back, not unlike yanking a wisdom tooth from a crowded jaw.

"Here we go again," I whined, trying to get at our plump sausage of a boat squashed in its closet skin. I tugged, but the boat wouldn't move. Bob came below as I complained, "My arms don't have the oomph to pull this thing out."

"Let me help. Move over, you're in the way. We can't both fit in the same space."

I stepped back, "Okay crabby," I whispered, as he grabbed the rubber boat, huffing and puffing until it slid from out of its prison cell. We both hefted it up the companion way steps, plopping down its lifeless form on the deck. Bob sat down on deck to catch his breath, and then handed me the foot pump to administer some life-giving air to the dinghy. Up and down, up and down, went my foot; hiss, thud, whoosh went the air. Even though my foot did an entire Charleston dance number the dinghy slumped over like a rag doll. Bob shook his head and motioned me aside. Soon the rubber boat began to swell like a puffer fish, ready for the floorboards that looked like they were three sizes too big for the remaining space. Stinging sweat, mixed with sun lotion, ran into our eyes, then poured off our face down to our chest, and dripped into the dinghy. We pulled, stuffed, shoved, and swore like longshoremen. We let out some air and finally got the boards in place, then pumped more air back in, collapsing on deck in exhausted. I looked over at Bob, "I wish there was an easier way."

"There isn't. At least we don't have to deflate it until we leave for the Tuamotus. The hard dinghy can't plane with the two of us, and this one can. We need the speed.

No rest for the wicked. Bob got up and unlocked the outboard from the railing, tying a safety line to the motor, and lifted it over the rail for me to hold.. He stepped gingerly into the rocking dinghy. I held the eight horse, fifty-four pound Evinrude motor over the rail, hanging on tight so I wouldn't drop it and pin Bob to the floorboards like a butterfly specimen. When I glanced at my arms I wondered it they had actually stretched over the months. At this rate, I thought, my knuckles will be dragging on the ground before we reach Tahiti.

After securing the motor Bob climbed back aboard, "Got to dress up before going into town. I hope my clean pants aren't moldy."

I grabbed a clean blouse, dressed and glanced into the mirror in the head. "Oomigosh," I screeched, "I just looked at myself in the mirror, and my hair's a grease pit. I can't go like this. I have to wash it."

"Forget it. We don't know what time the Gendarmerie closes. I'm sure they've seen worse sights. You look okay to me."

"You've just gotten used to looking at it after all these weeks. When I looked in the mirror I couldn't tell if the white stuff was salt, or more grey hair."

He gave me a "stop talking" look, and we climbed into our dinghy. We both looked forward to dry, firm land, as well as fresh food to eat.

The cabbage, potatoes, tomatoes, lettuce had been consumed weeks ago, while the supposedly fresh eggs we bought in Mexico had died a smelly, tropical death. I had scrubbed and given them a coat of petroleum jelly, but to no avail. When I traced down the rotten smell I peeked through a crack in the egg and saw feathers. *Maria* must have turned into a perfect incubator. I dumped the eggs overboard, knowing something in the food chain would think they had been served a gourmet meal.

As we departed I glanced back at the boat, dismayed to see a green stain stretching the full length of the port side. "Wait a minute. I want to see what that is," I said. I reached over and touched it. A strong sea odor emanated from my finger. "Slimy algae." I grimaced as I thought of my hair matching the side of the boat. A wharf rat had more glamor.

Bob grunted, "Must come from being on a port tack twenty-six days. Amazing."

We circled the boat to look at the other side. The white starboard hull gleamed in the sunlight, but as we peered down in the water Bob's eyes widened in disbelief. "What in hell is on the bottom of our boat," he exclaimed. "There's tube like barnacles stuck over everything."

"I don't get it. I always thought as long as a boat moved nothing attached itself to the hull. Look, the steering vane is covered with tubes too." I muttered to myself about more work, when all I dreamed of was eating, reading and sleeping.

Shaking our heads we turned the dinghy toward town. There was no sense worrying about the bottom now. Neither the spirit, nor the flesh were up to it. We stepped ashore and felt the rocking motion from the boat staying with us. We looked like two tipsy vagabonds as we weaved along the shore giggling and humming, What Do We Do With A Drunken Sailor. We looked for the Gendarmerie. Deep puddles left over from the last rain shower stood in our way, but after surveying the beach we found a worn rock path leading to a white-washed cement building. A large French flag stood at attention, snapping in the breeze. Branches of red flowers created a bold picture on the white wall. We pushed open a rusted iron gate and walked into a small garden, entering an open door. We were greeted by an older Frenchman dressed in a crisp white uniform. With a trace of a smile he ushered us into an adjoining room, quickly seating himself behind a cluttered desk. A ceiling fan swept wisps of cigarette smoke from his hand. "Bonjour," he said, waving nicotine stained fingers toward a chair facing his desk. "Passports, s'il vous plait."

While I searched my purse for our passports, Bob found another chair for me, and we sat down. I retrieved the boat documents, and Bob pushed them across the desk, smiled and said, "Si."

I whispered, "It's oui now, not si." Language was not his strong suit.

Speaking out of the side of his mouth he muttered, "I barely learned si and now it's oui?"

The policeman looked momentarily distracted, then studied our documents, pulling a folder from his desk. We had given him our boat documentation papers, proof of money sent to Tahiti to cover airfare in case we lost the boat, French visas, and US passports, plus the infamous departure paper the Mexican clerk insisted we had to have. He looked disdainfully at the Mexican paper and threw it in the trash. "Garbage," he said. "That is for freighters." He gave us back our papers, plus the new official boat passage document. We would need to present this in each French Polynesian port where a Gendarmerie was located. He looked directly into our eyes as he asked the next question. "Carry fire arms?"

"Yes," Bob said. If Bob lied, and been caught, we would have been thrown out of French Polynesia. Others cruisers told us they lied, and had no problems. But it wasn't worth the risk for us. Besides, we never had enough practice lying. I learned early in life that all my mother had to do was look at me with suspicion and I sang like a canary, my petty lies covering my face with a guilty blush.

"What kind?" he asked, his eyes glinting with interest.

"A nine millimeter Walther pistol and a Winchester 12 gage shot gun."

The policeman's eyebrows rose in little peaks over his glasses. "Hmmm," he murmured. He wrote the information down on a paper and added it to his file. "How long to you intend to stay here?"

"About ten days here, maybe a day or two in other ports."

"If you stay more than two weeks in one port you must turn the guns in to the Gendarmerie for safe keeping. We don't want the natives to have access to guns. We return the firearms when you leave." He tapped his pencil a couple of times on the desk and stood up, reaching his hand out to shake our hand. "Welcome, and enjoy your stay."

As we left I was impressed how easily our business had been accomplished. No hints of needing extra money to take care of our papers, and only one agency to deal with the boat, Captain and crew. How refreshingly simple after Mexico.

"Dick and Jim will be pleased to see how easy it is to check in," I said." I'm sure they have the right papers for their pick up crew members."

Bob frowned. "I'm more curious to know how the crew turned out. Especially Adrianna. I never met the one on Jim's boat."

Now that the check-in ended we were free to go where we pleased. Clutching our special boat passport and other documents we walked into town with high hopes. We saw a group of building ahead which looked promising. We entered the first small shop. "Bob, do you see what I see?"

"You bet, ice cream. That's almost as good as a beer."

"Darn, we have to find a bank first. We have the wrong kind of money." I looked balefully at the ice cream. I could almost taste it.

We found a small bank and cashed a traveler's check, then hurried back to the store. We ordered the biggest chocolate ice cream cone available, eating it so fast we got an instant headache between our eyes. Bob wiped his face, "Well, that's a good start. Now it's time to get serious and find a beer."

In the next block we found two more small stores selling canned goods, household items, and some frozen food. Our guide book told us to look for Maurice MacKitrick's Magasin (store). Maurice's store was the largest; selling wine, beer, frozen lamb, chicken and ground beef from New Zealand, canned goods, household items, diesel fuel and propane. We found it and noticed a small lumber yard in back of the store. That would be good for Dick since he had to replace his boomkin. Maurice also had the only special fitting which could fill an American built propane tank. Bob's day was made when he ordered a Beck beer and found it ice cold.

After looking at food I was going wild with the thought of eating out. Maurice spoke English so I asked him about restaurants. "Is there a nice restaurant close by?"

Maurice frowned and shrugged his shoulders. "The only one is a block away, but it's been closed a long time. I don't know when it will open."

"You mean there's only one?" After dreaming of eating out I wasn't going to be put off so easily.

"Yes, one. But there's a small hotel run by an American couple. Sometimes they cook for outside guests," Maurice said.

I turned to Bob excitedly, "After we shop we'll go over there and make reservations." Spoken by a true San Franciscan who still thought in big town terms.

We filled up our carrying bag , no paper bags or plastic here, with wine, beer, lamb chops, and white potatoes so small they looked like mothballs. I caught sight of a sign over a big sack of golden onions, "From Gilroy, California." I couldn't believe I had traveled twenty seven hundred miles from Mexico to buy onions from Gilroy, a town only sixty miles from our home. We didn't find any fresh vegetables or fruit in the stores, and were told we would have to find a local who grew his own vegetables and had fruit trees on his property.

"First things first, I said. "Let's find the hotel and see about dinner. We can buy fresh food later."

My tongue hung out in anticipation. We found the hotel consisted of three rooms. Rose and Frank Corser owned and operated the hotel, delighted to see fellow Americans. "We haven't had many American sailors here since the bad weather hit last year. Guess the cyclones scared everybody off," Frank said. "Tahiti was hit hard."

After small talk I got right to the point, asking about dinner reservations, my face beaming like a lantern. Frank chuckled, shaking his head from side to side, and I tried not to believe he was saying no. "Sorry Marlene, but we only serve dinner when we have guests staying in the hotel. And then outside guests only on Friday night. This is Sunday."

I looked around the room, hoping to see someone sitting at a table, or at least walking around the garden. "Do you have any guests?"

"We hope to, but I never know for sure. The plane comes once a week; it's due Friday."

We talked for a while, bought two tee shirts with an emblem of a Marquesan warrior with the words underneath, "Nuku Hiva Yacht Club," and promised to return on Friday, hopefully to eat. I looked sorrowfully at Bob, "I'm going to pray for guests as much as I'll pray for Friday."

Bob put his arm around me, "It's only six days away."

But six days seemed longer than twenty-six days at sea.

Frank and Rose explained that the French government workers, teachers, and other technical staff received premium pay for working in the Marquesas. In order to save the maximum amount of money to take home to France, they ate at home. The natives had very little money, so they ate at home. Now Marlene and Bob would eat at home.

Sweating with the heat we shouldered our purchases and walked back to our dinghy. As I stepped in and put down our bag, an onion rolled out. I laughed, "Gilroy, California. It's incredible. I always thought the world was big."

"Not big enough for a restaurant," he replied.

We returned to the boat and stowed our purchases. Later I found Bob staring at the tube creatures glued to our hull. He uttered a deep sigh, "I guess I'd better start scrubbing the bottom. You take the dinghy and scrub off the scum."

I turned around to say I didn't want to scrub the boat. The words almost escaped, but the look on his face told me it wasn't going to be any fun for him either. I clamped my jaw shut and searched out my nylon pot scrubber. "Misery loves company," I said, and boy was I miserable. No matter how hard I scrubbed the slime, it looked back at me. Gradually the green color turned lighter, but it still showed. My scrubbing arm ached like a cracked tooth.

Meanwhile Bob scraped the hull until his strength and interest gave out at the same time. He finished a third of the boat, figuring he could do a better job after a good nights sleep. Taking off his diving gear he called out, "How 'bout some wine. It's been a long time."

I brought up the corkscrew and glasses. "I can't wait," I said, opening up a can of nuts.

We should have waited. Our first taste matched the sour look on our face, a disappointment since the high price of wine didn't mean quality, and we were spoiled by the cheap wine prices in Mexico. Polynesia was going to be a real eye opener, and a wallet depleater. Even though paradise didn't come cheap, it remained paradise. On that thought we ate our dinner of lamb chops, potatoes and delicious fresh bread, retiring to bed happy, and looking forward to our first night without watches. Just like the preceding twenty-six nights both of us woke up every three hours. It seemed our internal clocks had not gotten the message to reset.

The next morning a hot tropical sun made a sizzling appearance, bestowing negative feelings of ambition. Bob reluctantly put on his tank, mask, fins, and jumped over the side of the boat. I heard a maniacal laugh coming from the water, and thought island fever had hit him rather early in the day.

I looked over the side of the boat for the bubbles coming from his tank. "You all right?"

His head appeared, and his free hand grabbed a line hanging over the side to keep himself in place. He kept shaking his head.

"You're in awfully shallow water to suffer raptures of the deep," I said.

"They're gone. Every friggin' one is gone. Those tubes dropped off during the night. All that work yesterday was for nothing."

He took off his flippers and threw them on deck. He climbed up the ladder and removed his mask, a puzzled look on his face.

John rowed by later and solved the mystery. "Same thing happened to me. Those things are goose neck barnacles." He explained that the larvae live in mid ocean and attach themselves to a boat, log, fishing floats, or even turtles. They grow up and form large colonies. Hundreds of them hang like stalks from the boat. As the boat moves the through the ocean food filters out and is carried to the barnacles. "Damndest thing I ever saw. I had to stop along the way and scrub some of them off. They slowed the boat down too much."

"Weren't you scared to go in the water since you were by yourself," I asked.

"Careful, not scared. Tied a rope to myself."

"I wonder why they fall off?" Bob asked.

"I dunno. Maybe the change of temperature in a harbor, or no forward movement to bring food."

Bob laughed, "The drag of all those barnacles on *Maria* would be like me swimming fully clothed and wearing rain boots."

The next day I made ham radio contact with Dick on *California*. "How's the weather Dick? Is it treating your rigging all right?"

"Yeah, the rigging is holding up, but it's raining like hell now. Sure will be glad to get there and get things repaired."

"How many more days do you think if will be?"

"I figure we're about five days out."

"We'll have a party with lots of cold beer when you get here, that's for sure. I'll talk to you in a couple of days. This is N6LDM clear." We missed our friends, and were excited about the prospect of seeing them again.

Later that day a weather front moved in, dumping huge amounts of rain. It washed the boat clean, but it reminded me that it was time to do some serious clothes washing. It had been six weeks. We caught enough water to rinse dishes, but not clothes. Frank told us about an outdoor shower near the hotel used by cruisers, but not to expect a grand edifice with a lot of privacy.

I grabbed two buckets, an armful of clothes, and joined Bob for a dinghy ride in search of the shower. We found an open stall shower with a pipe, shower head, and a valve to turn on the water. It's utilitarian look stuck out like a thorn amongst the beautiful, wild vegetation. It was also occupied,..... not by a cruiser,...... but an over friendly horse. Somewhat bewildered we put down our sacks of clothing and sct up the buckets. The horse eyed us, swishing his tail across his sway back, sending flies in all directions. We waved our arms and told him to leave. He remained ensconced in the shower, showing us that possession was nine tenths the law, and that we could do what ever we wanted as long as it didn't include him. With baleful eyes the horse carefully watched Bob walk toward the shower. Bob tried to gage his disposition, finally reaching up and scratching the horse's ears, nose and back. The horse nuzzled his head against Bob's chest, gently pushing him out of the area and into the bushes, all the while trying to nibble his tee shirt.

"Isn't he cute? He likes you. Either you have horse appeal, or you smell like one."

"Thanks a lot."

Under the watchful eye of the horse Bob turned on the valve next to the animal. He filled two buckets, one with soap, and one with rinse water. He dropped our white clothes into the suds to soak, and started to move the buckets out of the way the horse, hoping he would take the hint. He didn't. "Hey, stop it horse...Don't drink the soapy water, come on now, move.... don't eat the clothes, we need those," Bob yelled, extracting a shirt away from the animal's yellow teeth.

The sight of Bob, the horse and our wash proved too much for me. I started laughing. I doubled up in half as I held my sides, and tears rolled down my face as I choked, "He may turn out... to be a clothes horse."

"That's bad." Bob picked up the buckets, but when he turned, the horse again reached with his mouth for our wash, stepping on Bob's toe. The mighty howl from the captain, and soapy water sloshing every-where, didn't faze the horse. But he must have thought the situation was funny. He threw his head back and whinnied, followed by a snort and stamping hoofs. Not to be undone Bob clapped his hands howling, "Shoo, go away now," in a most authoritative captain voice. The startled horse gave us one last look, flicked his tail at Bob and walked off into the brush. Alone at last with a shower. While the dirty clothes soaked we took off all our clothes and luxuriated under the stream of water until...we discovered we were not really alone after all.

"Ouch, what stung me," said Bob. He reached down and rubbed sev-eral red swelling mounds on his legs. "Damn, that's a mean bite, and do they itch."

We had been discovered by the Marquesan black fly. Soon a cloud of them appeared and we quickly dressed, trying to cover as much of the fly target area as possible.

"I think the beautiful vegetation was a lure to get us into their terri-tory," I said.

"Either that or the horse tipped them off. What sweet revenge. No wonder he flicked his tail when he left."

I found the flies lived better than we did because they dined out every night.... on us. The bites itched for weeks. The flies were not particular, liking the natives just as well as visiting cruisers. At night I could almost imagine furious scratching echoing all over the island. We had been told not to scratch the bites because of staph germs. Bacteria grew very fast in the tropics, and no one in their right mind would want to end up in the local hospital, even if it meant sitting on your hands. A quick look at the hospital could make anyone a believer. The small tin-roofed building looked more like a maintenance shack than an oasis of antiseptic excellence.

The next few days were spent investigating the town and making sure we got our daily ration of ice cream. In our wanderings we found the Marquesan people curious, friendly and wanting to talk to us. They spoke Marquesan and French, then looked inquiringly at our face. We spoke English and Spanish, resulting in little conversation, but lots of gestures, smiles and pointing.

Not being able to converse in French proved to be a definite drawback. With good intentions I had purchased French Berliz tapes before we left, hoping to listen to them on watch. But cruising fatigue won out. When my mind buzzed with tiredness I couldn't concentrate. The only thing I remembered in French was how to say hello, and how to order a draft beer, in that order.

We found a local family who grew vegetables and had grapefruit trees. They called the grapefruit pamplemousse. My taste buds hadn't adjusted to grapefruit over the years, but then I had never tasted the pamplemousse grown on the island. They were marvelous, juicy and sweet. We bargained for papayas so big they looked like a watermelon, but tasted much better. The hot weather and rain produced fruits that begged to be eaten.

The big day arrived, April 4. We expected our friends to arrive, but by afternoon we gave up watching for them. We were down below reading books when we heard a voice calling our name. Once on deck we saw Joe on *Smiling Jack* circling our boat. Both Joe and his Irish girlfriend looked bushed. Bob called back to them, "Welcome to Taiohae Bay guys. Do you need some help?"

Joe nodded. "Can you set our stern anchor for us?"

"No problem," Bob said. "I'll even bring over a cold beer."

The anchoring proceeded well at first. Bob dropped the stern anchor and got a good bite on the bottom. Joe decided to put down a second stern anchor, which shouldn't have been a problem, except he had forgotten to tie the bitter end to the boat. We all watched the anchor and line fall into the water, burying itself into the sand eighty feet below. It looked kind of lonesome down there. Bob couldn't dive that deep because of his ears, and Joe announced he was too tired. "I'll get it later," he said.

Bob gave him a cold beer. After a healthy pull on the can, Joe shrugged his shoulders and begged us for a cigarette. He took one, lit up, and put several more in his pocket before handing back the pack. Although we didn't smoke he knew we carried trading cigarettes. The cigarette burned to an ash and he finished his beer. Next he asked us for some peanut butter. We pulled out our last jar of Skippy from our stores, and to our surprise he vanished back to his boat, with the whole jar. Bob glowered. "I believe in sharing the wealth, but not *all* my peanut butter too."

A couple of hours later we saw *Starlight* making her way into the anchorage. We were shocked when they pulled alongside. Jim's emaciated body stuck out of his loose clothes. "After you clean up come on over. We want to hear about the trip," Bob said."Where's *California?*"

"She's not too far behind us. I'll just get ourselves anchored here before they arrive."

A few minutes later we caught sight of *California,* her mast reaching into the sky like a beacon. The cruising family was back together again.

After Dick had anchored next to us, we called him on the radio and announced that ice cold beer and munchies awaited his crew at 1700. "Be sure and tell the rest of the boats to come also," Bob said.

From our deck we saw everyone wore the same haggard looks and greasy hair, knowing we looked the same five days earlier. Cruising wasn't all roses. There were always enough thorns to keep things in perspective.

Later, after a shower and change to clean clothes, the crews arrived in three dinghies, tying up to our stern. They settled down in our cockpit looking rested and ready to trade sea stories, especially anxious to find out what to expect from the Gendarmerie.

But Bob couldn't wait any longer. "What happened to you Jim? You must have lost at least twenty-five pounds since we last saw you."

"I have. I have to use a rope to hold up my pants because my belt's too big. I decided to sell my boat here if I can find someone to buy it."

He noted the surprised look on our face. " The stress just got to me I guess, and you'll notice I didn't bring my new crew member with me either."

"What happened. I thought he was a gourmet cook. Did he poison you?"

"No. He was a gourmet pain in the ass. After getting sea sick for a couple of days he finally cooked a meal. Then he wanted us to wait on him. He sulked, read books and complained about everything. As soon as we can work it out he's off our boat and on the inter-island ferry."

"What about you Jan, do you want to sell the boat?" Bob asked

She looked uncomfortable, but she remained a straight shooter. "Tim and I told him we would be furious. We want to continue the trip. It's his call now."

Breaking the mood Bob passed out the drinks while I distributed the munchies. He touched Dick's shoulder and pointed to *California*. "I don't see your new crew member either."

"Ah, Adrianna. I'm lucky she owned her own airline ticket. That was the worst mistake Denise ever made. She wanted to do something nice for a fellow Kiwi, but it didn't work out at all. She played people against each other, accusing Tom of going to sleep on watch, and then telling us how she saved the boat. Tom said he wasn't asleep, and that she only stayed a short time on her watch and went to bed."

"That's not all," Denise said. "She stole my cosmetics, ate up all our chocolate, and took my favorite tapes. We couldn't get her off the boat fast enough."

"My happiest day will be seeing her bony butt going up the gangway on the ferry to Tahiti," Dick said, slapping his knee. "God what a bitch."

"Well," Bob said, "at least I have some better news. "Have you seen the goose necked barnacles on your boat bottom?"

"What's that?"

Bob pointed to *California*. Dick turned to look at his boat, and saw the tubes sticking out like a fur rug on the bottom. "Huh," he gasped. "You call that good news?"

The whole group turned to look at the sight.

"I'll tell you a secret," said Bob. "Go to bed, sleep real well, and when you wake up tomorrow, they'll be gone. Damndest thing you've ever seen."

A sigh of relief, along with nervous laughter, followed Bob's pronouncement, and the crew proceeded to wolf down the beer and food as if they had been away at sea for a year. We traded experiences about the crossing, but before too long the drooping eyes of the many crew members said it was time for sleep. We were ready to bag it too.

The following morning we met with Dick and the others to go over the procedures for check in, stores, lumber, fuel, and of course, the ice cream cones. Since Friday had finally arrived we all decided to see about dinner at the little hotel. There were guests, and this time we could make reservations. That evening we dressed up in long pants, sitting in the little dining room with our mouths ready and waiting. Frank came over to see what we wanted to drink. "We have most things, but we're a little short on white wine. It seems someone came in and bought a lot of the new shipment."

Bob looked guilty and made a confession. "Sorry Frank, it was us. It may not be great wine, but it was all we could afford."

"You know I'll have to charge you more for the wine tonight than you paid at Maurice's."

"Not to worry, we understand. Sorry we bought so much."

The visiting German hotel guests joined us at dinner. I imagine they were surprised how engrossed we were with eating, conversation lapsing to nothing as we chewed, wearing looks of utter contentment. Their puzzled expression seemed to say, "Americans were really quite an odd lot."

The next morning Dick returned from town and rowed by in his dinghy telling us about a special program that night in the Catholic church annex. "Maurice said it was to be a big affair, with the Bishop from Hiva Oa, and natives from all the surrounding islands coming to celebrate. "Dick was quite excited about it. "Easter is tomorrow, so tonight's play is a bunch of bible stories acted out by the locals. It's one big party. We won't know what they're saying 'cause it's in Marquesan. But it should be fun anyway."

"Oh, you mean like a Passion play?" I asked.

"Yeah, I guess you'd call it that. It starts around 1830. We'll meet you there because we're going to in town earlier."

We wore shorts, traveling by dinghy as fast as possible because of the rain. We pulled the dinghy up on the beach to keep the tide from stealing it away, and quickly sought shelter under a big tree. We heard a car driving up the road, and waved our arms back and forth. The Marquesan driver spoke English, saying he was on the way to the Catholic church too. We jumped in the car, glad to be out of the pounding rain. When we reached the church annex we followed him in, where it appeared the whole island had congregated in one room. At first all we could see was a sea of people and color. Then we caught sight of Dick, Denise and the rest of our crew family. They motioned us over, making a space near the back of the room. The Marquesan people wore brightly colored shirts, skirts and topped with flower crowns on their heads. Family groups of mother, father, three or four children, plus assorted relations, crowded the audience. They were going to be as interesting as the people on stage. We were impressed how well behaved the children were; no loud screaming or running about. Many babies were held by fathers, while mothers watched the other children. Each family brought baskets filled with delicious looking food, and the aroma of chicken mixed with onions, coconut cream and bacon drifted about the room, making our mouths water. We had not thought about bringing food, or something to sit on. The islanders brought a blankets, but all we had were our bony buns, which flattened out like underdone pancakes before long.

The play started with a tall man dressed like Joseph, wearing a cloak of many colors. Speaking in Marquesan, he called to an other man dressed as a Pharaoh guard. On cue we heard the deep clear voices of the men's chorus, followed by beautiful multi part soprano of the women's chorus. A handsome bare chest Marquesan, wearing a lava lava and a pharaoh's headdress, spoke to Joseph in a resonate voice. When he appeared on stage the audience clapped and yelled wildly for several minutes. He stopped, turned around and faced the audience, smiling, bowing and greeting everyone, thoroughly enjoying the adulation. The room hummed with good feelings. The curtain moved and a group of girl dancers came on stage, some smiling and giggling, but moving their hips and arms in time with the music. Their hip movements were between the slow dance of Hawaiians and the fast action of the Tahitian. As the evening wore on there were so many singers and dancers it would have made Cecil B. De Mille proud. After five hours sitting on a cement floor the situation became painful for our whole group. The parish priest noticed my squirming and motioned for me, and some of the other ladies, to sit on the wooden bench next to him. After another half hour I whispered to Bob. "How are you doing?"

"Tired, let's wait for a break in the rain and go home."

Before long we made our way out, turning back to a short cut and the beach. It poured so hard on the way back I wondered if Noah had been part of the program. It didn't do any good to hurry through the rain, so we sauntered casually down the road, singing a sea chantey, "Going Home," to drive away the rain. It didn't work. By now the water had plastered our clothes to our bodies like a second skin, and our hair looked like skull caps. Water ran off our noses like tiny water falls, and we start-ed to laugh when we looked at each other.

"I'm sure if we had been caught in a storm at home we wouldn't have found the rain all that amusing, but here in paradise it's different," I said

Bob snickered, "We don't t have to worry about our clothes, they're drip dry and so are we."

We managed to motor back to *Maria* quickly, despite the growing winds which kicked up little waves. We climbed aboard the boat, removed our clothes, dropping them in a heap on the deck. Driving sheets of water played a staccato message against the sides and decks of the boat, forcing us to close up the hatches tight. The high humidity made the boat more like a sauna than a place to sleep.

But sleep wouldn't come. We ended up talking about the history of the Marquesas. I picked up our guide book and read out loud to Bob, "The Marquesans were acknowledged as fierce warriors and head hunters. They wore their hair long, decorated their bodies with blue tat-toos, and had been known to eat their enemies." I slapped the book shut. "At least the earlier Marquesans in Nuka Hiva got to eat out. Literally it wasn't what's for dinner, but "who" was cooking."

Bob picked up the book and put on his glasses. "In 1595 a Spaniard discovered the islands on his second voyage from Peru." He stopped and read a minute to himself. He said, "Four hundred natives came out to the ship. They were allowed on the ship, but when the natives got too curi-ous it scared the Spaniards, so they shot off some guns. That frightened the natives so much they jumped ship, escaping back to their island. The Spanish captain wanted to show his power and scare the natives into sub-mission, so he ordered three natives to be shot and hung on shore. Once the killing started it went on until as many as two hundred were mur-dered. Marquesans remained cannibals for quite a while, but at some point I guess they stopped eating the priests and were converted to Catholicism. Their population dropped to 6,500 after small pox, tuber-culosis and venereal diseases." Now it was Bob's turn to close the book. He took off his glasses, putting them up on the shelf so we didn't sit on them. He slipped inside the sheet and reached over to turn off the light. Sighing he said, "What a shame. After seeing these Polynesian people we could do with more, not less."

"Unless you were the main course on the menu," I giggled.

The next morning we awoke to blessed sunshine, and I took my first cup of coffee up on deck to relax and contemplate the day. "Bob, come look at the water,"

"Why, what's the matter with it?" He came on deck, looked over the side, viewing the brown muddy scum surrounding a broken tree limb. "Oh I see. It looks like San Francisco bay after a gully washer."

When we talked with Maurice later we learned that the goats, pigs and wild horses ate the vegetation holding the soil, causing erosion problems. Torrential rains filled the rivers, and the waters whipped debris from trees, rocks, mud and carried it down the mountains into the bay. It took most of the day for the sunshine and tidal action to clear up the water.

Easter morning we awoke, eagerly anticipating the horse race taking place on the beach. For days we watched a determined band of people riding bareback, encouraging the little horses to run each morning and evening. I couldn't tell if our shower horse was one of them. At one o'clock we climbed into our dingy and anchored close into shore, just out of the wave line. Dick rowed over, "Hey Bob, can we tie up to you? We don't have a dinghy anchor."

"Sure, I'll loop the line around the seat."

Soon two more dinghies tied off of us, creating quite an audience. A hush fell over the beach; the white flag dropped and the roar of the crowd announced the beginning of the race. Screams from the people shouted encouragement to the horses and riders. A few horses walked, some refused to move, and several ran quite well. I could understand why the horses wouldn't want to run in the oppressive heat. If I had been a horse I would have walked into the water and sat down, rolling over to get rid of the rider on my back. Or maybe I would have joined the other horse in the cruiser shower. We found it hard coping with the intense heat at times.

Bob looked over at the green soccer field where a group of men gathered for a big game. The party time atmosphere brought out more families, spreading out blankets and serving food. Wild screaming and cheering followed the plays. "I can't even think about running in this heat," Bob said.

"You don't even like to run in the cold," I reminded him.

Dick untied his line from our boat, "I guess you get used to it after a while," he said. "Come on over for a beer. I want to run some ideas by you on keeping enough juice in my batteries."

"Sure thing, I'll bring over the fact sheet on my power converter. Maybe Bill can buy it for you in the states and bring it to Tahiti when he comes."

The hot climate of the south seas took its toll on both Bob and me. It was hard to watch soccer games when my whole body was operating on half speed, seemingly content to just vegetate. No wonder people talked about "jungle rot," I thought. It wasn't a physical rot, but a psychological one too. It affected ambition, work ethics and left us content to view life from under our sun shield. After years of dashing about, and Bob working his toosh off, the merry-go-round was over. We could just plain rot for awhile.

After ten days it was time to stop rotting and go harbor hopping. We stocked up on bread and fresh food, and got ready to say our goodbyes to our friends. We climbed aboard *California,* feeling lonely already. Denise and I met halfway while I gave her a hug. "I'm going to miss you and our get togethers each evening," I said. Denise, our special Kiwi, held our hearts in her hands, I thought.

She smiled, "Hey there mates, it won't be long. Soon as Dickie gets the boat back together we'll meet you in Rangiroa, or Papeete."

Dick and Bob stood looking at each other, feeling more like brothers, despite the difference in age. The warm affection in their eyes told of their mutual respect and caring. Dick put out his hand, "We'll keep in touch on the ham radio. I'll think about that power converter and let you know what I decide."

"Okay. Have a good trip yourself when the repairs are done. See ya."

We went back to our boat, tied off the dinghy and hoisted our anchor. It was hard leaving our friends so soon, but it was going to take several weeks for them to finish the repairs to their boats, and we had to be in Papeete in early May to meet Bill and family.

We set sail for Daniel's Bay, a short distance from Taiohae Bay, anxious to visit the well known wood carver, Daniel. Marquesan artists were known for their bold style in wooden bowls, stone tikis, fan handles and war clubs. Besides being a wood carver, Daniel was loved by many a yachtie as a dear and gentle man. We anchored and took our hard dinghy to shore, the rubber one having been deflated and squeezed back into the closet. We rowed until low water and rocks created a dinghy eating hazard, requiring us to carry the boat the last hundred yards. I groaned with the effort, and my perspiring hands kept slipping off.

"I'm getting too old for this job," I panted.

Bob took the major part of the weight gasping, "I'm older than you are. I wonder if this boat is gaining weight? We certainly are."

Our boat weighed one hundred forty-five pounds, and the tide receded rapidly. We were high and dry. As we struggled Daniel waded out to meet us, stretching out his arms to help carry the boat up on shore.

While we complained silently to ourselves about getting old, we noticed age had not affected Daniel's bulging muscles and strength. When he left us for a moment I said, "Maybe we're thinking old, and now our bodies believe it. We need to be more positive."

"You tell that to my knees. I couldn't do it with a straight face."

Daniel returned, and when he spoke French and met our blank looks, he gestured for us to sign his book. We picked up the black book, and turned dog eared pages, one by one. "Look at all the signatures and messages. Literally from all over the world," Bob said. with a touch of awe.

"Let's take a Polaroid picture of Daniel and his wife and give it to them," I suggested. "Pictures are a universal language."

We managed to get a picture of Daniel and his wife, posed in front of their two storied open walled house. They seemed quite pleased with the pictures, laughing and pointing to each other. Daniel went into his barn and came out with a long stick with a loop attached, lassoed a breadfruit from his tree and gave it to us. He also knocked down two coconuts. Waving his hands for us to follow, he showed us the rest of his property. We walked through jungle like vegetation as he proudly showed us his large land site. He stopped in front of a tree and pointed to a goat he had killed. The skinned carcass hung from a hook on a the tree, raw red, naked and unappetizing, except to the buzzing flies which surround it. It reminded me back home of the dressed ducks hanging in the hot sun in Chinatown. Daniel obviously didn't worry about bacteria, because he rubbed his tummy to indicate how delicious the future meals would be for his family. He explained by gestures he had six children, twenty pigs, three horses and many chickens.

On the way back to the boat Daniel took us to his artist studio where he worked on large platters and bowls, apologizing because he had so few left. He had sold most of his works. We admired his work, but the prices took his art work out of our pocket book. We shook Daniel's hand, thanked him in warm tones for his generous gifts of breadfruit and coconuts. The tide had come in, making it easy to launch and return to our boat. We looked back to see a smiling strong man, happy with his life, appreciative of his skills, and filled with love for his fellow man. What more could one ask.

Once back on board *Maria* I took the breadfruit up on deck, wondering what sort of miracle would turn it into something delicious. I turned it over and stared at the hard shell, "Why do you suppose Captain Bligh was so intent on taking these things back to England?"

"It wasn't England exactly. He thought it would be nutritious food for the slaves running the sugar plantations in the Caribbean."

"Did they like it?" Somehow I think I knew the answer.

"No, they refused to eat it, but remember the slaves in America refused to eat lobsters. They thought they were giant insects."

I cooked the breadfruit that night with lots of onion and butter, finding it tasted like onions and butter, period. On a scale of ten I would rate breadfruit a one, just above library paste and poi. I'm sure the Marquesan mothers knew more about cooking the breadfruit, and told their children to clean their bowls, just as my mom extolled the virtues of eating all my vegetables. Because of its nutritious value the breadfruit was extremely important to the islanders, as is taro root to the Hawaiians. I would have given anything to exchange it for lobster.

The next morning we decided to visit another island called Ua Pu, four hours away. The day looked promising, good wind, lots of sunshine and the assurance of new sights and new people. Then the wind died. Our listless sails were tied up and the "iron genny" turned on. We motored to Ua Pu. We were surprised to see a new breakwater and harbor on the NE side of the island, called Hukahare, dropping our anchor with assurance we were in a snug refuge. After dinner we sat on deck to watch the sunset, and nature put on one of her better shows. The reddish-orange sun painted the sky and clouds with bold sweeping strokes, appearing to capture the craggy cliffs rising up to the sky. Each minute the heavens changed to a softer, lighter hue, until night fell so quickly we thought a heavenly black out shade had been pulled down. We sat in awe for several moments in the soft dark of the night, aware of beauty in its purest form..........until the first Marquesan fly arrived. Bzzzzittt.

"Time to go to bed Bob."

"I'll race you for the sheet."

The next morning we were greeted with, SURPRISE, the rain again. I had this ugly feeling we had arrived in the middle of the rainy season, and we had better get used to being moldy and wet. I snuggled down in my sheet, and shut my eyes. Bob poked me and said, "Time to get up."

"Why?" I moaned. "Can't we check into the Gendarmerie later?"

"No, now. Rain, or no rain, we have to check in. We've been here twelve hours."

It seemed that a check in was like death and taxes, something you had to face. I looked at the wind gage showing eighteen knots of blustering wind and rain, seriously doubting our ability to launch the hard dinghy from the deck. We dressed and went forward, drenched with-

242

in seconds. Bob untied the dinghy, attached the control lines to the hal-yard, and attempted to lift the boat off the deck. This exercise in the ridiculous was met with shouts and gritted teeth, the wind trying to wrench the boat out of our hands and deposit it in some place other than the one we had chosen. I hung on to the dinghy for dear life, feeling my feet leave the deck as the boat jerked sharply from the next gust. I desperately tried to keep the dinghy from smashing into the side of *Maria*. Years ago Bob had swept me off my feet, but this was the first time I had been swept off by a dinghy. I was not a happy camper. If it had been left up to me I would have gone back to bed, but there was no one as persistent as my husband. He kept adjusting the line lower, and little by little the boat finally reached the water. We tied it securely, fore and aft, watching it cuddle up to *Maria's* side. At that precise moment the rain stopped. It was as if someone had turned off the faucet, reminding me of Dorothy in the Wizard of Oz when she said, "My they do things so quickly around here."

The wind dropped, the sun beat down on blue water, and we were back to another day in paradise. We went through our routine of putting the outboard on. We changed into dry clothes and climbed into the dinghy, ready to search for the Gendarmerie.

Once on shore we had little difficulty in locating the office because it was close to our landing. We entered the old building, finding the official with a pipe clenched tightly between his teeth, wreaths of smoke circling his head like a halo. He appeared barricaded behind the old desk, but he stood up, put out his hand, and welcomed us.

"Bonjour," said Bob. My coaching finally worked on him. He handed the official our boat documentation. "We arrived on our yacht, *Maria Elena.*"

"Bonjour," said the official. He took our documents, turned around in his squeaky chair and reached for a handful of folders, thumbing through and picking out one with *Maria Elena* in big letters. He read quietly for a minute, picking up a radiogram. Suddenly he looked up and gave us a small smile and asked in broken English. "How long you stay? Where do you go next?"

Bob cleared his throat and said, "One day. I think we'll head for Rangiroa."

"How many days at sea?"

"Hmm. It depends on weather."

"I will send a message to Rangiroa telling them you come. Merci

Beaucoup, and good day." He turned his back to us, flipped on a radio and started his message to Rangiroa. It was obvious *Maria* was being monitored very carefully, along with every yacht that entered French Polynesia.

We walked several blocks, coming upon a small store. The canned goods were different, many from China, the middle east, and of course, France. The Chinese cans had mysterious pictures of duck with "something" and a fish in different sauces. I was pleased to see coffee from Arabia, canned hot dogs from Denmark and French cheese. Although hot dogs have never been high on our list, these tasted pretty good. I tried hard not to think of them as mystery meat. At least it was a change of diet. We checked out the frozen chickens and noticed the French chickens looked like a cousin of the Mexican chickens, undersized, and little meat. I discovered some five pound boxes of chicken legs and thighs from Arkansas which looked plump and more appetizing. We decided to shop later after checking out the rest of town. The owner sent us on our way to the bakery, and soon a delicious yeasty aroma of the French loaves filled the air. We walked up to small window. Tapping lightly on the glass, the window opened, and a smiling teen-age girl said, "Bonjour Madame, no pain."

I understood the word pain meant bread, and no was no in most languages, but I could smell the bread and my stomach reminded me that food was necessary for my immediate survival. I waved my hand toward the stone oven. Her eyes followed my hand, she held up ten fingers and nodded her head up and down.

As long as we had to wait we took time to look around the outside of the bakery. The old wooden structure housed the baker and his family, a small kitchen could be seen from the little window. In the kitchen stood a large table, big containers and hand utensils. My Kitchen Aid bread mixer at home would have saved hours for this family.

I became aware of a young mother and child standing next to me, also waiting to buy bread. She smiled as I said, "Hello."

"Ah, American?" she said.

"Yes, we're a long way from home."

"We don't see many Americans. How did you get here?"

"On our boat. We sailed here."

She shook her head in amazement, and asked if we had any questions about Ua Pu.

"Tell me about the bakery," I said.

"Well, the baker gets up at 3:30 in the morning to mix up the dough and let it rise. The family collects small branches to put inside the oven, then lights them on fire. The stones that make up the oven get very hot, and stay that way all day, cooking enough bread for the whole town."

She went on to describe how the dough was kneaded and formed into long small loaves while the oven heated up. When the oven temperature was ready for cooking the embers were taken out and thrown to the side on the ground. The town people dropped their breadfruit on the pile to cook for the rest of the day. That was the second way to cook breadfruit. The green outside was burned off leaving the white inside cooked which looked more like a potato.

We all watched with growing anticipation as the baker wiped his hands on his apron, picked up a heavy towel and removed a stone, checking to see if the bread was done. Our mouths watered when he took a long tool, withdrawing the loaves one by one, and then placed them on a long wooden table. Out came our money, the first loaf went into our bag, and the second one we tore off in pieces, throwing them back and forth in our hands because the bread was so hot. Yum. There's nothing like hot, fresh bread.

The young mother took us back to her house where she gave us some pamplemousse and papayas from her trees. Our bags were loaded down, and we still had to buy our frozen chicken. We were arm weary by the time we reached the boat.

"I didn't really know what a south sea island would be like. I guess my expectations came out of travel folders, which is nothing more than a flat dimension." I said.

"True. You can't hear the voices of people, or the sound of music from a picture, much less gauge how people in a different culture view life."

"Did you think about these things when you dreamed of sailing to the south seas?"

"My dream was more of a conceptual idea, the adventure of sailing far away to a romantic setting. When I met you it became important to share the experience together."

I put my arms around him. "My romantic husband. Please don't ever change."

"I'll try not to, but don't you change either. Wait a minute. I take it back. Stop being a back seat driver."

"Oooo, you hit a nerve. I'll try, but it's a bad habit that might be hard to break."

"Right now I had better get the charts and figure out our new way points to Rangiroa. Our navigation has to be right on for this trip."

There was lots to think about and plan for our journey to the Tuamotu islands, five hundred miles away. These islands were called, Dangerous Archipelago, or low islands. Bob knew about the dangers ahead, reading stories about islands where rotting ships acted as graveyard markers for people who miscalculated. We had to be alert at all times. On that note, we went to sleep early, wishing to make the best of our last whole night's sleep.

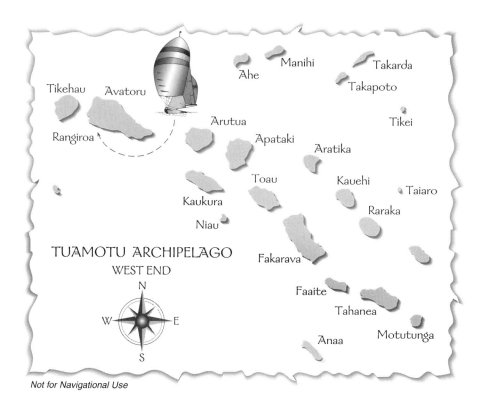

Tikehau

Avatoru

Ahe

Manihi

Takarda

Takapoto

Rangiroa

Arutua

Tikei

Apataki

Aratika

Toau

Kauehi

Taiaro

Kaukura

Raraka

Niau

TUAMOTU ARCHIPELAGO

WEST END

N

W — E

S

Fakarava

Faaite

Tahanea

Anaa

Motutunga

Not for Navigational Use

Chapter 20

THE MORAL, STAY AWAY FROM THE CORAL

"And the schooner is stranded already,
She is stranded between the surf and reef,
She is stranded, says the story,
She is stranded all for glory
She is stranded between the surf and reef."
(Sea Chantey of Norwegian origin, "Albertina")

I t's early morning, and instead of planning our trip to the Tuamotus, my time is spent trying not to scratch fly bites. It's hard to train a brain to ignore an itch. While the Marquesan islands are beautiful, the people special, the rain and sunshine were a potent aphrodisiac to black flies. I glanced at the barometer and read 29.92 inches of mercury. More rain. Could I dash through shopping before the birth of a million more flies? I handed a list to Bob.

"Besides bread, what else do we need?" he said.

"Beer. I'd buy a few soft drinks if they weren't so sweet. They must add extra sugar to the drinks made in Mexico and French Polynesia."

"I wouldn't know, I like beer."

"Me too, but my shorts felt tight this morning. Now I know why they call beer liquid bread."

We walked into town and finished up the shopping, hurrying back to the boat quickly to get under way. "Is it secure down below for sea duty?" said Bob.

"I think so, but I'll check one more time."

I went below, my eyes sliding over the empty dining table, continuing on to a quick check of our cabin, aft head, and up to the forward head. Oops, I found a drawer open, a potential mess which could have dumped itself right into the toilet. I closed the drawer and went on deck to help Bob prepare to leave. He had secured the bow anchor, but was now locked into a monumental struggle with the stern anchor, his tense face red as he pulled on the stern line. "Jeeze, it's stuck like glue down there," he panted.

"Is there something I can do? I don't think there's enough room on the stern for me to pull with you."

After a profound sigh, Bob looked around and let out some slack in the line, deciding to take it up to the big genoa winch. He wrapped the anchor line around it three times, grasped the winch handle and started turning the winch. Slowly the line inched in until the anchor popped out, sounding like a sucker pulled our of a child's mouth.

"Great job Bob. You take the wheel while I flake out the stern anchor line on deck to dry."

When Bob looked skyward an ominous black cloud appeared, releasing a drop of rain on his chin. "Looks like we'll get a wash job besides."

We dashed about, hiding from the rain under our sun shield. Bob guided the boat out of the harbor, heading toward our new destination, Rangiroa in the Tuamotus. We glanced back at Ua Pu, enjoying a last look at the magnificent spiky mountains. Waving my right hand while gently scratching my legs with my left, I shouted to no one in particular, "Bye you damn flies. Go pick on someone your own size."

The light breeze signaled the use of the MPS, and soon we hummed through the water at six knots. The wind carried a heavy cloud past us to Ua Pu, unloading sheets of rain on the people scurrying into nearby buildings. Goodbye to the rainy season too.

The fickle wind came up strong, then evaporated, dipping part of our MPS into the water. While *Otto* guided the boat we hauled in the lines, then ran forward to grip the wet sail. With loud groans we dragged it over

250

the rail. Little rivulets of warm water splashed on our legs, and the tangy ocean aroma perfumed the air. Bob pulled the lines on the dowser at the top of the MPS, drawing it down like a sock until it enclosed the sail into a single long blue snake. It coiled at our feet. I detected a sense of foreboding. I pointed to it. "Sometimes I think there should be a rattle at the end of it."

Bob laughed while rolling up the curled sail, stuffing it into the sail bag which wouldn't cooperate. The scene reminded me of a lady determined to cram her over-size foot into a tiny size five shoe. Tying up the top of the bag he looked at me with a twinkle, "You're getting paranoid about this sail. Anyone would think you thought it was alive." He tied the end of the line on the bag to the midship cleat, his face deep in thought. "But you know, there is something strange about it. I'm beginning to think it wasn't made right, or someone mislabeled the tack and clew."

I flipped my wrist at the offending sail bag, "As far as I'm concerned someone put a hex on it."

The next few hours we were chased by quickly moving rain squalls, followed by dead calm. The air's touch turned to molten lead. Bob started another sail change when I heard him yelp. "Ow, my elbow is killing me. I can hardly pull on the lines, or work the winches."

"If we were at home I'd say you have tennis elbow. But since we're in the middle of the Pacific I guess you have winch elbow. Sit down and I'll finish bringing in the gennny."

Toward evening the wind faded away and the genoa folded on itself, collapsing and fluttering like a moth. The small sea swell moved rhythmically past the boat as I rolled up the self furling genoa and turned on the engine. Bob had been sitting quietly with his eyes shut, but at the sound of the motor his eyes flew open. "We can't keep running the engine every time the wind drops. We'll put up the MPS," Bob said. "I know that will thrill you."

"Thrill wasn't quite the word I had in mind."

We opened up the sail bag and dragged out the blue snake again, attaching the end to a halyard. Bob started to raise it, but the line jammed.

"Let's drop it and go back to the genoa, it's getting dark anyway," I said.

"I want to see if I can fix it. Don't be in such a hurry to give up."

The tropical darkness appeared like a black curtain, swift and complete. Bob tried using a flash light to see why the sail stuck, but the beam couldn't penetrate the darkness surrounding the bottleneck area.

"You're just going to be frustrated," I said. "Can't we wait until day-light when you can fix it easier?"

"All right, you win....this time."

Pleased to be rid of my nemeses I purred, "I thought of a new name for the sail. How about Multi Purpose Pain In The Ass."

"Shhh, the sail might hear you," Bob cautioned. You're the one who talks about inanimate things having a life."

"Now you're kidding me. I know it's an important sail. We wouldn't have made it as fast to the Marquesas without it, but sometimes I get so confounded mad at it I want to tweak its clew."

That night on watch I thought about the MPS, musing that Pavlov would have had a great scientific study watching my reactions when MPS was mentioned. Instead of salivating like Pavlov's dogs at the sound of the food bell, my hair probably stood at attention on my neck.

During the night the waves ricocheted off the stern quarter, keeping us both awake and uncomfortable. The sound of the wind and rattling of the rigging reminded me of an English castle ghost, moaning and shaking his chains. While on watch I heard stirring down below, and was startled to find Bob at the radar staring into the screen and muttering to himself.

"That's impossible," he said. He glanced into the screen, then back to the chart, and looked up at the Sat Nav reading.

"What's impossible?" I asked.

"Come here. Tell me what you see."

I leaned down and stared into the greenish console. "It looks like an island."

"That's what's impossible. There aren't any islands where we are now. And if there were, it's on the wrong side of the boat. I've doubled checked all my navigation."

"I sure hope you're right, because it looks like another weather front is coming soon. There's just enough moonlight to see a black funnel shape on the horizon."

Bob straightened up, a smile illuminating his face. "That's it."

"What's it?"

"I'm seeing the storm front on the radar. It just looks like an island. I'll be damned. That's the first time I've seen anything like that." He scratched his head and went back to bed to try and sleep in the pitching boat.

Through a seemingly endless night the hot rising wind brushed my face with a strong insistent breath. Daylight found us exhausted, bleary eyed, and not very hungry. We managed on coffee, the last of the french bread and butter. Bob picked up Charlie's Charts guide book on French Polynesia and sat down to read. I was too tired to concentrate on anything. I grabbed a cushion and tucked it under my head. With my eyes closed tight I heard Bob turning pages, and every once in a while he would utter a "Humpt." The "humpt" didn't sound too interesting until he put down the book, saying. "We've got our work cut out now."

"I opened one eye, deliberately keeping the other one from peeking. "Why now?"

"I was reading about Rangiroa. It says we shouldn't go through either pass unless it's slack water. The tidal rips run over seven knots."

That did it. I sat up with my palms held up. "You can't go down to the nearest marine store and buy a tide book for Rangiroa."

"I know, but there's a formula in the book that shows us how to figure it out. That's why our work's just beginning. Here, you read this part."

He handed the open book over, underlining one passage with his finger. I looked down at the formulae and read out loud. "One hour before moonrise- slack water of very short duration; outgoing stream begins. Three or four hours after moonrise- slack water. Four hours after moonrise- in going stream begins. One hour after moonset- outgoing stream begins. Three or four hours after moonset- slack water. One hour before moon's lower meridian passage- incoming stream begins. These times could well be altered by heavy southerly swells or stronger prevailing winds, which by increasing the inflow of water over the reef can alter the in going and outgoing stream, even to the extent of sometimes maintaining a continuous outgoing stream."

I read it twice, feeling a headache coming on from concentrating. "You're right. Time to go below and get the Nautical Almanac. I guess we're supposed to match up the days and times and pray we do it right."

Suddenly I wasn't tired anymore. The challenge of solving a new puzzle ignited my competitive spirit. We each got our paper and pencils, positioning the Almanac between us, and little by little we came up with times and dates that would hopefully match our estimated arrival, April 18 around noon.

The next two days we dodged one line squall after another, sometimes managing to outrun them, followed by the usual calm. The cloudless blue sky outlined the yellow-orange sun, it's rays firing mercilessly down on the boat. It was ninety degrees in the cabin. Luckily we dressed in our cruising clothes shortly after clearing Ua Pu, our bodies showing a nice even tan all over. Bob usually delighted in teasing me by a pinch here, or a tickle there, but the debilitating heat spoiled any feelings of romance. If Bob panted, it wasn't over me. I wondered about couples who bragged a day wasn't a real day unless engaged in making love. Once in the tropics they might find a lot of unreal days, sweating so much they might hydroplane right off each other.

The third day out we tired of listening to the slat of the sail and Bob reluctantly switched on the engine He worried about making good time over the water and if we would reach Rangiroa at our estimated time schedule, noon on April 18. After a few minutes the engine alarm rang. "What the hell?" Bob said, bounding down the companionway steps. I followed him. He lifted the doors off the engine room and began to make his check. Perspiration quickly bathed his body, and trickles of sweat rolled into his eyes, continued on down his nose, finally dripping on his bare toes. He grunted, brows knitted in irritation and announced," The engine is overheating again. Turn it off. I'm going to try something else."

I joined Bob after turning off the engine and putting *Otto* in charge. Bob squatted near the engine, reaching over to look at the fresh water pump. "I damn near have to make love to the engine to get close enough to fix things," he muttered. I sat close enough to hand him tools. At last he looked satisfied. "I think this will do it. I bled the raw water cooling system. I think air must have gotten in there when the impeller went out."

We gathered up the tools and put them away, ready to go on deck and cool off. Both of us looked like drowned rats; my hair hung down in wet stringy locks, while Bob's looked like a greaser. Little beads of moisture stood on the ends of his beard like tiny Christmas lights. The beard! At first the beard was kind of fun, new, a different sort of look for Bob. Ever since he started it in Mexico I'd kept quiet about it. He didn't want to shave everyday, or use up precious water, but he spent so much time trimming and fussing it soon drove me crazy. The biggest drawback was the promise the beard would become soft as it grew older. I was growing older, but the beard remained the same, bristles like a sea urchin.

Back on deck Bob started the boat engine. The forward motion of the boat created a little breeze and I decided the beard wasn't so bad after all; I was crabby because of the heat. We took a bucket and lowered it into the water with a line, filled it, and took turns pouring the warm seawater over each other. The water dried quickly, covering our skin with a fine dusting of salt.

I tried several times to make ham radio contact with Dick on *California*. We figured he must still be busy repairing his new boomkin,

254

for he hoped to catch up with us in Rangiroa. We missed our friends and our daily get together.

It was April 17, and we were still a long way from Rangiroa, caught in the web of a low pressure system without wind. "That's it," Bob proclaimed. "We'll have to run the engine for as long as it takes to catch up to some wind."

I was tired of reading, and put my book down, yawned, leaned over to touch my toes several times to stretch out my back. I felt a pinch on my bare bum. "Hey," I cried, "that smarts."

"I just wanted you to know the spirit was still willing."

"I leaned over and gave him a kiss, "I love you, you bearded pirate."

"You know I could be a descendent of Morgan the pirate. My dad's last name was really Morgan, not Allen. His step-father adopted him, and both were from England."

"My Norse ancestors were probably raping and pillaging the Allens and Morgans in England. We make a great pair. How about pouring some more water over me. I'm cooking."

It was my turn for the 0200 watch. I stared into the warm velvety night, watching the ocean swells rise and fall beneath the boat, awed by their powerful energy racing across the vast south Pacific. Despite the tranquility of the night, my mind whirled restlessly, jumping from trying to learn a new sea chantey, to missing our family at home, then back to the sea chantey. I breathed a discontented breath as the three hour watch dragged on, finally standing up to make two 360 degree turns around the deck for signs of other vessels. A beginning muscle spasm in my tired bottom twitched, and my whole body signaled a disquieted feeling.

"What's the matter with me," I said out loud, trying to get a hold on my jitters. I cocked my head to one side, listening to the hiss of the water as the bow sliced through the seas. Foam covered waves radiated outward, bubbles bursting while new droplets took their place, the churning gently smoothed out into a placid quietness. My mind relaxed, and a stream of conciseness stretched outward into space toward the dazzling array of stars.

Instantly a graphic vision of my mother leaped into my mind. I saw her long face, aquiline nose, and almond hazel eyes staring at me like a doe in panic. I gasped. It had been twenty years since I had seen her alive in the hospital. I felt nauseated. Then new images unfolding in a slow, measured pace.

I remembered how dad and I stood by mom's bed after she came out of recovery from her second open heart surgery at UCLA hospital. I stared down at her. At 58 she still looked young and vulnerable.

The next image brought me to my home near San Francisco, picking up a phone and hearing mom's doctor. "I can't put my finger on what's going on, Marlene, but your mom is quite depressed," he said. "Can you fly down and see her? I think it would pick up her spirits."

I heard my voice, "Of course I will. I'll arrange for the kids to stay at our neighbors. See you tomorrow."

My mind took me back to the hospital. I pictured holding on to her hand, our entwined fingers looking like twins, slim, with tell tale veins across the hands which belied our age. "I love you mom, I whispered. "I miss you too." I remembered feeling a twinge in my stomach when I looked down into her face. As sick as she was, mom had put on her make-up, lipstick, eye brows penciled in, and the mascara artfully completed. A white towel covered her head to keep the oxygen mist away from her hair. Little wisps of auburn straggles escaped from the sides, accentuating the paleness of her skin. I felt a sudden rage at the oxygen tent that separated us, wanting to reach over the bed to give her a hug.

The vision vanished. I sat alone in the cockpit and closed my eyes, surprised to feel a gentle hand rubbing my back. Puzzling. I knew it wasn't Bob coming on watch because the touch was different. It felt more like the times mom eased the pain in my muscles when I lay sick in bed. I could even taste the milk toast she made to calm my upset stomach, enjoying the dollop of butter that swam around in the warm liquid. I opened my eyes again, the rubbing stopped, and a sense of loneliness washed over me. Tears raced down my face, quickly dried by the tropic air in the boat. I must be going crazy, I thought. But I know what I felt. She was here with me. I felt her hand rubbing my back. I sat quietly musing to myself in the cockpit, trying to understand what happened, wondering why I relieved the haunting memory this particular night. Was it possible I worried about never returning to my family at home? Am I afraid of dying too?

Shaking my head as if to knock out those thoughts, I looked for my three stars, finding them quickly. I relaxed as a warm, comforting presence again surrounded me. I felt a slight tingle on my shoulder, a gentle hand had touched it again. I blurted out "Hi mom, I'll bet you're surprised to see me out here in the middle of the ocean. If you had been waiting at home you would have been worried about me. But since you're not,

I'll bet you've been watching out over me." Tears flowed, and my throat ached with the effort of speaking. " Oh God how I miss you mom, but you don't have to worry about me. I'm going to be just fine. You know Bob, he's always taken good care of me."

My heart slowed down at the sound of my voice and a profound realization touched me. A precious gift had been given to me this night. Not only did I recall the special love between a mother and daugher, but I acknowleded the powerful feeling of trust I held for my husband

I gazed out at the sea. The same forceful body of water that years earlier almost drowned me. Yet, it felt strangely different at this moment. I concentrated on the soft lapping sounds of water against the hull, almost a whisper of a lullaby. I realized the tranquility and peace of the ocean sent me a message. It possessed two faces. I had only identifed with the dangerous one. Pay attention, I thought. This ocean could be my friend after all.

The peace of the moment became a sheltering blanket around me, like the womb that shields a child. Lost in reverie I was unware of the approaching dawn, looking up in surprise when Bob came on deck ready for his 0500 watch. He rubbed his sleepy eyes, momentarily taken back when I threw my arms around him, hugging him tight to my chest. "What a welcome for coming on watch, " he murmured.

I nuzzled his neck. "I've just been talking to mom. I could really feel her presence next to me. She touched me. Do you think I'm crazy?"

"Not at all. Maybe she was there. Who's to say she wasn't."

I hugged him harder. "Thanks for understanding." I placed my hand in his. I don't feel like going to sleep. I want to stay here on deck with you."

"I'm here for you anytime. I can't imagine my life without you. You're stuck with me."

"Like glue. And I'll never forget it.

I lay in his arms as dawn grew bolder, brandishing streaks of red across the sky. It was April 18 and we felt a flurry of anticipation, looking forward to our newest landfall with some joy, some trepidation. The Tuamotus, the oldest of the groups of islands, consisted of seventy- eight islands, all but two were coral atolls. Encircled by dangerous reefs, these worn down islands stretched out over an immense area, earning a grim reputation. Dark nights concealed fast moving currents the natives called Ati Ati. The strong flow of water rushed between islands, especially at the south end of Rangiroa, snared unsuspecting boats, drawing them onto the shallow coral reefs. They were soon gnawed to death by the coral. Until the arrival of precise navigation, such as Satellite Navigation, or getting a good triangulation of three stars with the sextant, many yachts passed by, not anxious to be torn apart. Even daylight hours didn't insure easy piloting since the tallest tree on the islands grew to only forty or fifty feet. It was difficult to see them from the deck of a yacht. The famous boat *Wanderer,* once owned by the actor Sterling Hayden, remained a broken hulk on Rangiroa. The scene appeared more tragic to us because we had been aboard her in Sausalito the night before she left for this last trip.

Today we got lucky. Bob went below to try and pick out Rangiroa on the radar. "I see it," he shouted up to me on deck. "It's sixteen miles away."

I shaded my eyes and looked forward over the deck, but only the cobalt blue of the sea saluted me. Bob came on deck to look, but he couldn't see anything either. "How about that radar," he said. "I don't use it often, but when I do, it's usually the most important times."

Later on we used our binoculars to pick out our landfall ten miles away, white beaches shimmering back at us in the hot sun. We were anxious to visit Rangiroa and experience a true tropical island. It was the largest of the islands with a circumference of a hundred miles, made up of some two hundred forty islets, and separated by one hundred thirty channels. With the sun shining behind us we could gage the water depths more easily, slowing down when we saw the light blue color of shallow water. Many a sailor has been tricked into thinking there was sufficient depth for his boat, because the reefs were only awash at a few places.

Bob looked intently through the binoculars, "I can't see a pass. Can you?"

He handed me the binoculars and I tried to find some kind of opening. "I don't see anything but a solid line of coconut palms."

Bob rubbed his beard, then pulled on his right sideburn. The hairs on his sideburn soon stood at attention, sideways, mute evidence of his agitation. "I'm going below and take another look on the radar," he said. A moment latter he returned with a smile. "The pass shows as clear as day. We must be coming in at an angle and can't see it. Time to get dressed. I'm not going to share you with the rest of the population."

"What a party pooper."

We looked at our clock, joyous to see we were approaching the pass at a time close to our calculations. Bob stood on the bow watching for any changes in the color of the water, while I steered and glanced at the fathometer from time to time. As we neared Rangiroa we saw Avatoru, the closest pass on our navigational track. The entrance loomed up before us, lined on either side by swaying coconut palms. In the middle white water churned angrily, like a giant witch's brew.

"Oh boy," Bob muttered, "I don't think we timed this just right after all, but let's give it a try anyway."

I drew in my breath, and found my jaw hurt from clenching my teeth. The pass was reported to be 400 yards wide, but in my state of anxiety it didn't look big to me. As we entered the pass currents grabbed hold of the boat, bouncing and shaking the bow back and forth like an shark tearing apart a seal. Bob cupped his hands around his mouth and yelled, "Give her some throttle." I shoved the throttle up and felt *Maria's* prop dig into the water, giving us more control. Our book said the pass had a depth of forty-six feet, probably scrubbed out by the fast moving water during changes in the tide, I thought. The fathometer read close to that and my jaw relaxed. I was pleased to see signs of civilization, a quaint little village with stark white buildings located on either side of the pass. Once out of the pass Bob signaled me to slow down because the water ahead had changed into an incredible turquoise, the obvious hint of shallow water. I reduced power, noting the fathometer read nine feet. Plenty for us. Once more Bob cupped his hands, "Keep going slow, they're lots of coral heads. It's hard to tell in the clear water how tall they are. I'll guide you around."

The next half hour we slowly made our way around obstacles, enchanted with the white sandy beaches, lush growth, and simple buildings. The lagoon bottom shown so clearly it appeared as if we could reach out and touch it with our fingers. We saw a group of three yachts lazily swinging on their anchors in front of a hotel that looked like it belonged in an ad for the perfect tropical vacation. Bob gave me the signal to circle around, then finally satisfied we had plenty of swinging room from the other yachts, he signaled me to back down to stop our motion, neutral, splash went the anchor, then I backed down more to set it.

With great excitement Bob leap frogged over the deck and jumped into the cockpit. "We made it," he exclaimed. Swiveling his head from side to side he sighed, "It's beautiful, so peaceful.... and the most beautiful water I have ever seen."

I grabbed his hand, giving it a big squeeze. "Can I turn off the engine now? Somehow engine noise doesn't seem to go with the serenity of the place."

"Of course Admiral, I was so excited I forgot." He threw back his head and laughed, sun lines crinkled around his brown eyes intensifying the color and depth. He rubbed his hands together, held one out for me to grab as he pulled me up on the upper deck. He murmured, "It's even better than the Marquesas."

We stood together for a moment, drinking in the ambiance of our surroundings. "It's a dream come true all right. It's still hard for me to believe we're actually here."

"I know someone else who knows we're here, the Gendarmerie. They'll be expecting us to check in soon."

I wrinkled up my nose in agreement, hating to jump into the reality of governmental convention when I wanted to stay in a beachcomber mode. We went below to get the lines to lower our dinghy and outboard motor. Once back on deck the job was handled easily for a change, no wind or rocking waves to frustrate us into making mistakes. We changed into our "going to meeting clothes" and climbed down into the dinghy. Bob drove the dinghy up to the bow of *Maria,* shaded his eyes and looked down into the water, following the chain down to the anchor on the lagoon bottom, noting rust had started to appear on the chain links. The forty-five pound CQR anchor nuzzled into the sand, and dappled sunlight and our shadows played patterns over it. A coral head kept guard near by, surrounded by tiny fish who nibbled at some unseen food on its surface.

Bob put the outboard engine in gear and we roared off toward Tiputa where the Gendarmerie had their office. As we went by Tiputa pass I noticed it was much narrower, not nearly so friendly looking, and with a dangerous reef acting like sentry at the north. We tied up the boat at the town pier next to several other native boats. We could see a road made of crushed coral, its whiteness almost blinding us in the strong sunlight. Looking at the coral it was hard to imagine it had once been alive with plants, inhabited by marine animals who built houses of limestone to live in. Each animal had built a house next to another, then others built houses on top of each other, creating true cluster housing. I wondered about the millions of people being born in our world who would compete for space to put up their houses. Life in the future might someday imitate a crowded coral atoll, not a pretty thought. On either side of the road stood small white houses with windows that could be boarded up during the fierce tropical storms. Shimmering heat waves poured from the open windows, and as they rose upward, they created a wavy air pattern around the house. I wondered how anyone could survive staying indoors during the day, since we were bathed in sweat just walking along the road in the open air. We looked for the French flag and found the Gendarmerie office open and ready for business.

The French official looked up as we entered, nodding his head at us as we both chimed "Bon Jour." As he stood up to shake Bob's hand I happen to notice the buttons on his tropical uniform. Two of them strained in the middle, locked in mortal combat while trying to contain a bulging belly, a thread hanging precariously from one button, ready to unravel at the slightest movement. My eyes went from the button to the official's perspiring flushed face. I worried I was looking at a heart attack waiting to happen. I feared the most exercise he encountered in the hot weather might be standing to greet people and shuffle voluminous amounts of papers.

The official motioned us to sit down, then cleared his throat, "Hummft, Your name?"

Bob replied, "Bob and Marlene Allen from *Maria Elena* sir."

The official turned in his squeeky chair to reach for a folder, picked up one and opened it. Looking at Bob he said, "Captain Allen, welcome to Rangiroa. Did you enjoy Ua Pu?"

I was amazed to see the size of the file, and being a little curious, I wished I could peek inside. It was not to be. Bob smiled and said, "Yes, we enjoyed it very much. We're looking forward to doing some skin diving here, the water's so clear."

"How long do you plan to stay and where do you plan to go from here?"

"We plan to stay three days, then leave for Tahiti. By the way, is there a store nearby?"

The official scribbled down the information Bob gave him on a piece of paper, setting it by the microphone where the message would be transmitted to Tahiti when we left. He looked up absent minded, "Go down the street to the end. On the left is a small store. If you hurry it will still be open. They close during the hot part of the day."

Bob stood up and held out his hand for the passports. "Thank you sir," he said. The official shook Bob's hand and then placed the passports in it. The effort of standing had caused the Frenchman to wheeze, accompanied by a slight grunt as his stomach pushed against the two buttons. Three pairs of eyes watched transfixed as the thread on one button unraveled, popping off and falling in an arc to the floor, then rolling through dust fuzz under the desk, coming to rest by his feet. We quickly took our leave, waving goodbye and leaving the Frenchman to get down on his knees and search for the overworked button. It might be a while before he sent the radiogram to Tahiti announcing our arrival.

As we left the office I suppressed a giggle, "Did you see the size of our file? We haven't been in French Polynesia that long. They probably know everything, including if we sing in the shower."

Bob slapped his thigh and let out a howl, " And to think I thought only the horse was watching us shower in Taiohae Bay."

We walked a couple of blocks from the Gendarmerie to the store and found the owner about to close for the afternoon rest. Bob managed to talk him into selling us a beer. I glanced quickly around the store, but decided our boat had more provisions than the shop.

After we had left I turned to Bob, "You know what I find interesting?"

"There's no telling with you." He moved back a foot because that remark invited a pinch from the Admiral.

I decided the warm weather wasn't worth the effort of teasing. "Most of the stores in the Marquesas, and now in Tiputa, are run by Chinese."

"They're enterprising people and work hard. They thrive on small businesses 'cause they can make money, feed their family and keep their relatives employed."

When we arrived back at the boat we noticed Lynn and Larry had arrived in *Talesin*. We were surprised to see them because they had indicated they wouldn't come into the Tuamotus without a perfect navigational fix. They had strict rules when they built their boat, no engine, no radio, refrigeration by ice, and only used celestial navigation. They had cruised for many years and were world famous sailors. We came along side and hung on to their gunnel.

"Hi you two, Bob intoned. Surprised to see you here. We haven't seen you since Taiohae Bay."

Larry's quick grin answered Bob, "I got a perfect fix on three stars and came in. We've been in Rangiroa for five days visiting all the sights in Avatoru. You went right by us when you came in the pass. Isn't it beautiful? We plan to stay awhile, how about you?"

"Three days, then on to Tahiti," Bob said. We talked with our son on ham radio and he and the family are flying into Papeete and staying with us on the boat. He's taking his vacation, so the time is cast in concrete."

Lynn looked over and said, "Sorry you won't be staying longer, there's great skin diving here. Too bad you have to hurry. The fun of cruising is going slow."

"We plan to dive tomorrow, I said."

Pushing ourselves away we waved goodbye and motored back to our boat. I was deep in thought, and as usual, Bob knew what I was thinking about. He put his hand on my shoulder, "I could tell you were a little bugged. I think you remembered Lynn in Mexico saying we should have sold the house and keep on sailing, more or less forget about the family."

"You're right. They don't have kids. That's okay for her, but not me. Sailing forever away from our family wouldn't have the same meaning."

"Let's check out the hotel. Would you like to go out to dinner?"

"Would I like to go out to dinner?! Does a bear s—t in the woods?"

We arrived at the hotel, looked at the name, Kia Ora, and fell in love with it immediately. The bar tender served us a ice cold beer and we looked at the menu for the evening.

That night we stopped in the bar, and to our surprise, the bar tender, Dee Dee, had placed little flowers in his beard. As each woman walked in he gave her a flower. Later we were seated by a Polynesian waiter who wore the most elaborate earrings I had ever seen. The earrings twinkled like diamonds in the candle light, but realistically they were probably rhinestones and black pearls. His graceful movements caught our attention as he moved across the floor, reminding me of New York model exhibiting a Paris gown, instead of the Polynesian lava lava. At the end of the evening we saw him ready to go home, wearing an alluring woman's outfit that fit him to perfection. He picked out a flower from Dee Dee's beard and placed it behind his ear. His earrings matched his outfit perfectly.

The next morning we heard a knock on our hull. Bob put down his coffee cup and went up on deck and looked over the side. Another cruiser from a boat anchored close by hung on to our ladder from his dinghy. He introduced himself. "Hi, I'm Dave. I see you're from San Francisco, I'm from New England. How are you enjoying Rangiroa?"

"Great spot," said Bob. "We plan to go diving today."

Dave took off his cap and scratched his head, "Say, you wouldn't have some extra engine oil would you? I need eight quarts. The store doesn't sell it here."

"I just have enough for an oil change on our boat, and I'm afraid I need that before we get to Tahiti. We've been running our engine more because of the light winds."

"I understand. My boat has a Mercedes engine and it's leaking oil like mad. I figure I won't be able to fix it until I get to Tahiti. I guess my only option is to go into town and try to bargain with someone who uses oil in their house generator."

"I'm really sorry I can't help you this time."

"Hey, if you're going diving why not try shooting the pass on an incoming tide. You can see all kinds of fish. The water carries you right back into the lagoon,....fast."

By then I was on deck listening to the conversation. "Thanks," I said, "We'll think about it." I closed my eyes and thought about shooting the pass, "No way," I mumbled. I had learned to dive, but strong currents reminded me too much of my close encounter to drowning. I shivered at the thought. I heard Bob's voice near my ear, "Don't worry, we'll just go diving down by the wreck in the lagoon. That should be fun for both of us."

We motored over to the wreck in the dinghy, the sun leaching out moisture from every pore. I splashed sea water on my suit and it dried before my eyes. We put out a small anchor and slid over the side into the clear blue water, relief coming at once as the water cooled our skin. With one hand on the boat we slipped on our fins, then treading water like a porpoise, we spit in the face mask, rubbing the liquid around then rinsing it with sea water. The spit kept the mask from clouding up and obscuring the view, but it always seemed disgusting to watch someone do it. We adjusted our mask and snorkel and placed our face down in the water, enchanted to see tiny, bright blue fish dart in and out around the wreck. Angel fish gently moved their fins, gliding through the water in an unhurried pace, stopping to feed off a piece of wood, while bright yellow damsel fish chased each other as if playing hide and seek. We spent two hours lazily searching out fish, swimming slowly, and sometimes diving deeper to check on a shell, then back to the surface to blow out the water from our snorkel. Occasionally I didn't do it right and salt water rushed into the mouth piece, gagging me. As Bob swam ahead of me his beard fluttered in the currents and appeared to be alive. When he turned to see where I was his beard floated upwards, framing his face. I felt magic in these relaxed moments, living in suspended animation in an old geological world of calcified coral, rich sea life, warm water, and of course, my love.

Back on the boat we spread out our diving equipment to dry. The time had come to plan and prepare to leave for our next destination, Tahiti, two hundred and forty miles away. Bob changed into dry clothes and returned carrying the nautical almanac, papers and pencils. "Time to figure out when slack water is again. I think getting out might be harder than getting in."

"Let me finish rinsing the salt water out of my hair and then I will," I said. "I hate it when I don't. My hair gets stiff."

Bob stretched out in the cockpit, putting a cushion under his head. "I wish we could have gotten a little more water, but there's barely enough for the people who live here. They're sure dependent on the island freighters for goods. I'll turn on our water maker when we leave."

I squeezed the last bit of water from my hair and ran a comb through it, glad to be under the protection of the sun shield. "Life here seems more simple than the Marquesas. They can't climb a mountain, hunt a goat, play soccer on a green field, but they can fish, sail, listen to music and watch TV."

Bob turned over on his stomach, resting his chin on his fist. "It's hard to equate a simple south sea island with modern conveniences like TV and VCR. I keep thinking of the natives diving for pearls and getting their feet caught by giant clams, like the old John Hall movies of the 40's."

"I used to love those movies too. Handsome boy meets gorgeous native girl, the island is invaded by blood thirsty pirates, boy saves girl and everyone lives happily ever after. Movies now either scare you to death by cutting up people with a chain saw, or the beautiful girl is eaten by an alien from outer space. I don't miss movies or TV. I'd rather like to think life could be as simple as it was today, beautiful."

I picked up a pencil and paper, tapped the pencil on my lip as I read down the familiar page, "Three or four hours after moonrise."

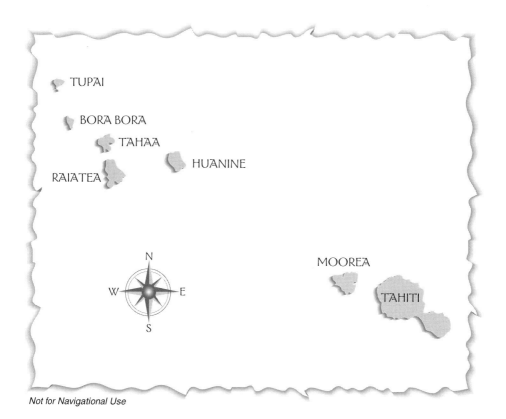

TUPAI

BORA BORA

TAHAA

HUANINE

RAIATEA

N

W E

S

MOOREA

TAHITI

Not for Navigational Use

Chapter 21

TAHITI BOUND WHILE WRESTLING A RUDDER

I steer'd from sound to sound, as I sailed, as I sailed,
I steer'd from sound to sound, as I sail'd,
I steer'd from sound to sound and many ships I found
And most of them I burned as I sail'd.

(Sea Chantey, Captain Kidd, Forecastle Shanty)

I wanted to write in my log, but I've forgotten what day it was. With every day being a Saturday, my fading memory ignored the fact the log demanded a day, time, and destination. The last two were easy, the clock read 8:30, and I knew we were headed for Tahiti. When I looked back at the Sat Nav it dawned on me jungle rot had not eaten all of my brain cells, the date showed up as noticeable on the screen as a Mexican mosquito in a wine glass. I quickly wrote down April 23 in the book. I glanced at the barometer, 29.94, noting the wind machine read, East at 5-10 knots. I poked my head up out of the cabin, "Hey Captain, how's the weather up there? I want to see if it agrees with the instruments."

Bob turned a greenish tinged face to me, "Maybe some rain, not much wind. My stomach feels like a rock."

I hurried up the companionway steps, "Sure you want to go today?. We can wait a couple of days until you feel better." I felt his face with my finger tips, definitely not his best color, but no fever.

He rubbed his hand across his stomach several times, hesitated and said, "No, let's go. I'll feel crummy no matter where I am. I want to get going and settled in Papeete."

"Can you take your watch?"

"Sure, I'm not that bad off. The bug won't last long."

He walked slowly toward the bow, starting the anchor windless. After several tries his shoulders drooped and he turned toward me and yelled something. The wind blew away his words and I yelled somewhat petulantly, "I can't hear a word you're saying."

He scowled, cupped his hands around his mouth and shouted, "Go in a circle."

After several trips of playing ring around the rosy, Larry on Talesin rowed over to see what in the world we were doing. "Can I help you guys? You're not going to get very far going around in circles."

Bob sighed and absently ran his hands over his stomach again, "I'll have to dive down and take the chain off the coral head."

Larry shrugged off the idea, "You don't look so hot. Let me dive down and do it for you."

Bob smiled, feeling better already, "Thanks, that would be a big help. My whole body thanks you."

Larry jumped overboard, swimming straight down thirty five feet, and with a thrust of his hand, undid the chain. Kicking rapidly he rose straight up, his bubbles beating him to the surface. Bob and I rolled our eyes at each other with the same look; it must be wonderful to be young and strong.

We thanked Larry again, turned our boat around, and headed back to Passe Avatoru, finding our timing a little out. We probably made the same mistake when calculating the first time, whatever that was. Despite being early, we encountered only a few rolly waves in the pass. When entering into deeper water, the turquoise color blossomed into cobalt blue, little wavelets bounced on our stern, giving encouragement to *Maria* to hurry on our way. We looked around for birds, missing the varieties which usually accompanied us back home when we left a harbor. No flapping wings, or raucous cries of the sea gulls. I realized I had also missed the squeaky songs of land birds, watching their colorful feathers flutter while hopping in short jaunty motions, their heads bobbing up and down in search of food. Even in an island paradise such as Rangiroa, our memories of home evoked a sigh of nostalgia, nudging our sub conscious to store these memories to remind us there's no place like home.

Bob went below to check his navigation since we would be passing closely to Tikehau, a chain of wooded islets standing on a circular reef about eight miles away. The Tuamotu islands made me think of a Venus fly trap, beckoning us to come closer to the fragrant flowers and white sands, then with one swift motion, capture our boat on its reef, feeding on it until nothing remained but fiberglass bones. I thought of the admonition I used to use with our children when they were young, "Look, but don't touch."

The following hours were spent reading, or lazily getting up to turn on the engine for short periods of time when the wind disappeared. Bob didn't have a lot of energy, and this was as close to being "sea sick" he would ever be. I put my book down across my chest, remembering our first crossing to the Marquesas and how worried I had been about spending twenty fours hours a day in such limited space. Looking up at Bob's relaxed face I noticed his perspiring nose acted like a water slide, allowing his glasses to slip down to his chin. As the print on his book went out of focus and his hand pushed the glasses back in place. He felt my gaze because his magnified eyes turned to mine, the skin crinkling around them as he smiled in a silent salute. It felt comfortable, just the two of us.

I stared into the warm ocean, wishing a dolphin, or a Tuna would break the placid sea. Beneath the cover of the ocean a rich variety of sea life existed, each unique in its own being. Like people on land, the sea had its fat round creatures, thin, long eels and fish, tall coral formations, and tiny varieties of plankton. I longed to watch the playful antics of the dolphins, diving and leaping in front of our hull. Their wonderful intelligence intrigued me, especially having read documented cases of them helping to save a stranded swimmer. I stared into the indigo ocean. How strange to have my life dependent upon the very sea I had feared for years. Bob broke through my thoughts, "I don't know where you've been, but your face had a far away look to it."

"I was tired of reading. I was thinking about the ocean, and that made me want some action like dolphins or tuna. Remember watching the tuna leap out of the water on our to the Marquesas?"

"You would too if you were chased by a school of sharks," drawled Bob. "They're not too smart, but they know how to get their prey."

I shuddered when I remembered the feeding frenzy in Isla Isabela in Mexico. I'm sure the fishermen were able to lure some sharks into the bay, feasting on discarded fish guts. The sector of the frothy bloody water boiling in activity, plus the sound of thrashing shark bodies as they gobbled up the food gave me goose bumps. "I hope I never meet a shark face to face, much less a smart one."

Bob and I both retreated into our own thoughts until I reached over and touched his face. "Despite storms, and our MPS problem child, I still like being a crew of two.

Bob stood up and stretched, laying his book down on the captain's seat in front of the wheel. His eyes squeezed shut as he uttered a big yawn, "Me too, but I wouldn't mind an extra pair of hands during a storm."

"Trouble is the hands come attached to a body. Wish we could figure out how to have an extra pair of hands waiting in the drawer for us to use, spooky, but nice," I giggled.

"Sure would scare the hell out of a customs or immigration inspector going through the boat," Bob chuckled.

I touched his shoulder, rubbing the raised scar he got from an encounter with a sharp edge of a stove on our first boat. "Boats have a way of leaving you with a lasting impression."

He sat back down and gave me a love pat on my bum, then stroked my arm in a lazy pattern. Contentment flowed as the sea carried us off toward Tahiti, gently rolling the boat back and forth between the waves. The mood vanished abruptly when Bob stood up again and announced, "I feel better. When's lunch, I'm starved."

Oh darn, I thought. I married him for a lot of reasons, but not for lunch.

I started my three hour watch that night at eight, conscious of the night wrapping blackness around the boat like a mummy shroud. The stars glowed in the darkness, intensifying the brilliant show the heavens presented us each night. I found my special friends, Orion's Belt, and settled down in the cockpit for the remainder of my watch schedule.

Around ten a gust of wind slammed into the side of the boat, filling the close hauled sails and knocking me off my seat. The yanking on my safety harness gave me an emotional start, and I stood up, surprised by the force of the wind. Just as quickly as it blew, the wind stopped. The black waters looked menacing instead of comfortable, erasing my former feeling of ease with the ocean. I stopped thinking about the water because the boat reacted strangely, slowing down, and then wandering off course with a back and forth motion. Darn, I thought, *Otto* had blown his fuses again. I turned him off at the main panel and returned to the wheel. I steered by hand, turning the wheel from side to side. The wheel felt like it had lost its purpose in life. If we had mechanical steering I would have guessed a cable had broken, but we had hydraulic steering, a whole different animal. Grumbling to myself I banged on the deck above Bob's head to make him aware of a problem. He appeared quickly, "What's up?" he said, the sleepy look vanishing immediately.

"A gust of wind hit us, then I checked around and found the steering acting weird and loose. I turned off *Otto*."

"Hmmm," said Bob. "I don't know quite what to think. Maybe we picked something up on the rudder. First I'll get my harness on and look over the stern, and if I don't see anything I'll check the hydraulic fluid below."

I hand steered the boat, feeling like a drunken sailor as the boat wandered from side to side. In order to stay on course the large wheel had to be turned around twice in the same direction, instead of the usual small increments. Bob came up, "Fluid level is okay. Just keep on doing what you're doing while I check the rudder again."

He hooked his safety harness to the life line and leaned out over the stern. I glanced back, treated to the full sight of his bare buns hanging over the rail in the starlight. He shined his flash light into the dark water, "I can't see anything unusual."

Meanwhile the drunken driving continued, and I realized it was going to be one hell of a long night steering by hand. A few minutes later Bob joined me at the wheel. "I wonder if we picked up a fish net and wrapped it around either the rudder or prop. Turn on the engine and back down. If anything's on there maybe we can dislodge it."

"Won't a fish net get stuck on tighter?"

"If we picked up a line on a net going forward, going backwards will unwind it. Let's give it a try."

Bob walked back to the stern as I turned on the engine switch. I put the lever in reverse and backed the boat down hard, then slowed down the engine and put it in neutral. I let out a small moan when conditions remained the same. Bob sat down and looked thoughtful, rubbing his hands across his beard several times and pulling on his right sideburn until it stuck straight out at an angle. I hoped it would give him some inspiration before he pulled it out completely.

I sat in the captain's seat, swinging my leg back and forth in frustration. One significant difference separated our personalities, causing problems between us over the years. He took his time to think things out, trying new things in a methodical, logical manner, tossing ideas out if they didn't seem practical. I would wait a little while, antsy to get going, and try something different without logic getting in my way. Sometimes it worked, but not often enough. Patience has never been my long suit. While Bob cogitated my arms began to ache from the constant turning motion, but there was no point in complaining about it. I could practically hear the gears in motion inside his head, reminding me of the old IBM machines that sorted through thousands of cards looking for the right one.

He pursed his lips and grunted, "There's no way I'm going through the reef in Papeete with the steering this way. I'll put on the Sail-O-Mat. It has it's own rudder and we'll steer with that. Once in Papeete I'll dive down and see what's wrong."

I looked out at the charcoal colored water around us, barely able to distinguish a horizon in the moonless sky. "I hate having you put it on in the dark, the rudder's so heavy and awkward. You have to step half way down the ladder to the water. Can't you wait until morning?"

Bob looked out at the water, then checked the sails. "You're right, maybe I'll wait until it's light. There's not enough wind to run the Sail-O-Mat anyway."

We motor sailed all night, trading watches one hour on, one hour off, to lessen arm fatigue. The next morning found us bleary eyed, exhausted and anxious to get to Papeete. With the rosy morning light glowing in our already red eyes, Bob went back to the stern to see if he could find anything unusual. The sunlight shone down through the blue water on our rudder, but only streams of bubbles covered it, racing and popping around its edge. Bob went below and brought out the Sail-0-Mat rudder and steering gear while I backed down the boat to stop the forward motion. He tied a small line around the Sail-O-Mat rudder, clipping it to the life line so he wouldn't lose it if dropped overboard. He climbed over the side, puffing as he lifted the rudder over the life line and fit it into place; then attached the lighter steering oar and wind indicator. As a final measure he put his foot down in the water and kicked our main rudder in place to make sure it seated correctly. Putting the gear in forward I was startled to find the steering worked properly again. I smacked my head with my right hand and groaned with fatigue, "I wish you had kicked it eight hours earlier."

"Me too, but maybe that isn't the answer. When we backed down maybe what ever had attached itself to the rudder finally got pushed off. I'm just glad it works again."

I viewed the system with a jaundiced eye because the self steering vane had to be removed when we motored for any distance. We were stuck with this unit because it was the only vane which steered with our boat hydraulics.

Bob turned on the autopilot. I sagged against the cushions, thrilled to let go and relax. I looked up at the rolling sea, and a speck of land appeared on the horizon, "Is that Tetiaroa?"

"Should be, we're about thirty miles from Tahiti on the chart."

"Doesn't Marlon Brando own the island? Imagine owning your own island paradise out in the middle of nowhere."

"All it takes is money. Pretend you're living on your own floating island. *Maria* can be paradise too," Bob said with a grin.

"An island doesn't have a rudder you have to wrestle with all night. I shouldn't blame *Maria* too much, she's been good to us most of the time."

Five and a half hours later we caught sight of Tahiti's two volcanoes connected by an isthmus, outlined by jagged cliffs rising boldly into the sky. Clouds of mist encircled the peaks, adding an air of mystery. I sniffed the air, inhaling a fragrant flower scent in the moist tropical breeze. "I love it," I shouted to Bob.

He grinned, " I hope the island is ready for Captain and Admiral Allen. As long as we bring money I'm sure they'll be happy."

Tahiti had come into prominence in the 1700's after Captain Cook had been sent by the Royal Society to observe the transit of the planet Venus. Previously the island girls welcomed sailors with open arms, trading gifts of love for ship's nails. There were so many rolls in the hay the ships started to fall apart from lack of nails. A new rule was made that sailors couldn't go ashore except in work parties, looking for food and water. But who knows how many sailors lined their pockets with nails before they searched the island.

We both looked forward to seeing Papeete, the main city of Tahiti. We were buoyed by a certain romantic notion attached to the word Tahiti, since it somehow carried a promise of beauty, culture, and of course, restaurants! I smacked my lips at the thought of fresh food.

"I can't wait to eat something that didn't come out of a can or a pouch," I said.

I watched Bob's lips move in a satisfying pucker, "I can almost taste a salad, green crisp lettuce with a bright red tomato, maybe a cucumber, and garlic dressing. Oh how I love garlic dressing."

"I want to eat something Italian, or maybe sizzling prawns I could dip into a yummy sauce." My mouth watered so much at the thought I had to swallow several time in rapid succession.

We watched our approach carefully. The weather remained helpful, clear with good visibility in order to negotiate the two hundred foot wide entrance through the reef. We were prepared for the strong possibility of a five knot flow out of the pass, also mindful of the cross currents which could hamper our passage. We had taken our mainsail down outside the pass, continuing under motor only. The busy harbor burgeoned with all sizes and shapes of vessels, ranging from Cruise ships, inter-island ferries, large and small freighters, plus the necessary tankers which supplied the petroleum products which kept the ships moving. The air around us smelled sea like, mixed with diesel fuel, and the earthy aroma of land and people. The combination overwhelmed us as we circled around, trying to decided where to drop our hook. Our first order of business meant checking in with the Gendarmerie. Bob went around in so many circles it began to remind me of a dog getting ready to lie down on a rug. He finally made his decision and I heard the satisfying splash of the anchor as it snaked itself down in search of the bay bottom. Once settled and sure the boat would stay put, we cut the engine, lowered the dinghy and outboard, hurrying below to dress up for our meeting with officialdom.

We motored over to the cement quay in town, wrapped our painter around a bollard, and climbed out onto land. An elderly Tahitian man stood on the quay, and we asked directions to the Gendarmerie. He squinted into the sun, rolling his tongue around stunted black teeth, then abruptly turned and pointed a bony finger toward a group of buildings a half a block away. We thanked him and walked briskly toward the Harbor master's office, enjoying the feeling of being on land again.

A gentleman in a starched shirt shook his head when we presented our papers, "Captain," he said, "you need to check into customs first. "We found the custom's office (Douane) down the hall and handed our ship's papers and passports over to a ruddy faced official. He walked over to a file cabinet, removed a fat folder and carried it back to his desk. What could they be saying about us that would fill that whole folder, I wondered?

His first questions was, "How long are you planning to stay in Papeete?"

Bob replied, "A month, but we will probably be going back and forth to Moorea too."

"You must let me know when you leave for Moorea and when you return. I see in your papers you carry weapons."

"Yes," said Bob. A shotgun and pistol."

"Since you will be with us for awhile you will turn them in to me right away, and your ammunition also. They will be kept in a safe place under lock and key. All will be returned when you leave Papeete for good. We also need a bank receipt for the money you deposited here, proof you have cash to return to the United States in case of any problems with your health or boat."

"How do I do that? Go to the bank?"

"Oui, they will issue you a receipt. If you hurry you can reach the bank before they close for the day."

"Can I go to the Harbormaster's office first," said Bob?

"Oui, Captain Allen. But I will expect your return soon."

He handed us our papers and we went to the Harbormaster's office. This official also showed sign of the hot climate, dark perspiration stains showed on his white shirt, while the material clung to his back between his shoulder blades. The fan in the office blew hot air across the desk, sending some of the papers into flight and on to the floor. The man reached down and picked up the papers. "Did you want to stay by the quay, or anchor out? Anchoring out is free."

"I'd like to stay on the quay if there's room."

"If you find room, and I can't promise anything, come back and tell me where you are. It is $4.00 a day American. There is electricity and water available."

We thanked him and hurried off to find the bank. We stopped several people and asked directions, finally locating the proper bank. We waited impatiently in line behind a woman tourist cashing a traveler's check. Her round pink face glistened with moisture as she struggled with a big purse, pawing through it in irritation in search of her passport. "I just know it's here somewhere," she whined. She found it at the bottom of her purse and handed it to the clerk. Turning around to us she growled, "This is the second check I've had to cash today. You wouldn't believe how expensive it is here."

We soon found out how right she was. It cost us $10.00 for a receipt from the bank showing we had placed $1800 without interest in an account six months before. Tahiti had the use of our money all that time, and while we felt we were being nickled and dimed to death, we had to add that to our "experience" in traveling on a boat. Besides, it was more important to hurry back to the customs office with the famous receipt than lose time by grousing. By the time we reached the office our clothes were wringing wet too. We handed him the receipt and told him we would be back with the fire arms and ammunition as soon as we relocated the boat on the quay.

Climbing into the dinghy was a relief to our feet, and skimming over the water back to our boat dried off our clothes and buoyed our spirits. Once back on board Bob tied off the dinghy to our stern and turned his attention to getting the anchor up. He came back to the cockpit and took over the controls, motoring over to what seemed like a solid wall of boats. "Hmmm, he said. "I'm not sure I see a place for us."

We watched another boat come in, drop a bow anchor, and back toward a small opening between tightly packed boats. In fascination we watched the boat gently push aside the rest of the boats and tie up."

"Well, if he can do it, so can we," said Bob. We saw a tiny opening, dropped our bow anchor and started backing in. *Maria* doesn't like to back, in fact one could say she down right hates to back, except into the wind. This wasn't into the wind. After several tries I kept myself busy holding the dinghy out of the way, bringing it forward by the bow. We had a group of people watching from other boats, making us try harder to look as professional as possible. Tying up Mediterranean style had been practiced by Europeans for years, enabling many boats to use a small space at the piers. But Americans were not used to this, a fact quite obvious to the crowd. We finally reached the line of boats and inched our way in, managing to slide between them without actually touching. Bob's handling of the boat made me proud. We backed up as far as possible to the cement wall without endangering our rudder and self steering gear. Bob asked permission to get on a boat next to us so he could take a line to tie to the quay. A French woman with a sallow, pinched face motioned Bob aboard, moving back quickly as he stepped down on her deck, her eyes noting his clothes, shoes in one full sweep. After Bob had run two lines from our port and starboard stern to the quay, the chasm that existed between the boat and quay made it obvious we would need a long board. At our age jumping from the boat to land didn't seem a probable answer at all. The last time I jumped any distance I had been with Lori. That was in Penang, Malaysia. I had leaped from one side of a sewer outfall, landing right in the middle like an over-aged rhino, splashing black,

"Well, if he can do it, so can we," said Bob. We saw a tiny opening, dropped our anchor and started backing in.

smelly ooze over my legs. I ran screaming into the ocean, hoping to clean it off, while trying not to think about what ingredients went into the make up of the ooze. Lori jumped over it like a gazelle, waiting patiently on the other side for me. Envy was not a pretty emotion for me.

"I'm going to need a real long board," I said.

"Jumped any good sewers lately?"

"Not funny Mcgee."

We went below and gathered up the ammunition and guns. I put the ammo and pistol in my purse, while Bob wrapped the shotgun in a beach towel. We locked up the boat and stepped aboard the boat next to us, tiptoeing down the long board to the quay. We started walking toward town. People turned around, talking back and forth to themselves, probably because our attempt to hide the shotgun was useless. It looked exactly like a gun wrapped in a towel. We reached the office and turned in the guns, trading a receipt for them. Receipts were becoming a way of life in Tahiti.

"Excuse me," said Bob to the Gendarmerie. "Is there a lumber yard nearby?"

"Oui, Captain."

He gave us directions to a yard about one half mile away. We found the well stocked lumber yard and picked out a strong plank, 2 x 12, twelve feet long, finding lumber quite dear in price also. I cringed when Bob handed me a receipt. Now that we were in civilization again we would be inundated with scraps of paper needing a home.

Bob shook his head as we left, "I should have told him I wasn't building a whole house for that price. Just a board."

"I suppose this means you carry one end and I carry the other," I said. I resisted the urge to sing, "Lift that barge, tote that bale." I gingerly tested my end, finding it rather heavy. I was sure Bob's end didn't weigh any less.

"How far from the boat do you think we are?" I asked.

"About a mile."

I rolled my eyes in dismay, picked up the end of the board, and started walking down the hot road. After two blocks I gasped, "I have to rest a while."

"No problem," said Bob. "I was just about to say the same thing."

We both set the board down and sat on it while we got our breath back. Sweat poured off us like rain. After a minute we got up and the act repeated itself at least ten times until the weary travelers reached the boat. We slid it carefully toward our boat, setting it on the stern.

"Beer," Bob croaked, "I have to have beer."

"Make it two," I said in a toneless voice. I managed to walk the plank and collapse on the cushions in the cockpit. Bob went below and brought up two beers. "Welcome to an island paradise," he said.

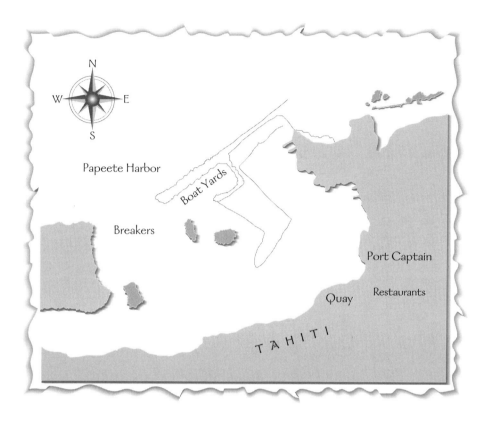

Chapter 22

TROUBLE IN PARADISE

"Come all you valiant sailors of courage stout and bold,
That value more your honour than misers do their gold."

(Sea Chantey, The Sailor's Lamentation,)

At four in the afternoon we made a horrifying discovery. The fishing fleet roared into port hell bent for home, their wakes moving like a tidal wave across the harbor, throwing boats tied to the quay into a fierce rocking motion. Geysers of water shot up between the boats, and sailboat shrouds and spreaders swung perilously close to each other, missing by inches. Bob jumped up, "What the hell is going on?" He ran to our rail and looked up at our spreaders, watching them swinging in unison like pendulums on a grandfather clock.

"Sure glad you checked their alignment when we first came," I said.

We walked over to the starboard side and checked the bumpers tied to our rail, watching them leap up like a fish on a line, then become tortured as they were squeezed tightly between the hulls. When we satisfied ourselves our boat had escaped any damage we sat down and stared at each other in utter disbelief.

"Can you believe that?" Bob said. He looked at several neighboring French boats, their occupants seemingly unaware of anything unusual happening. "Guess you get used to anything."

I looked back at the stern and jumped up, "Hey, our new board is coming loose. Quick, it's going to fall in the water."

Bob ran to the stern and grabbed the plank before it wiggled into the bay. Angrily I saw the edge of the plank had sawed into the gel coat, leaving ugly scratches on the surface. "Damn it anyway, a huge scratch. How do protect the deck from now on?"

Bob examined the scratches and went below, returning with an old towel in his hand. "I'll wrap this around the end and tie it on with some small stuff. That should keep the board from digging into the boat when the fishing fleet comes back in tomorrow.

"Speaking of tomorrow, *California* and *Starlight* should be in, but I don't know what time," I said.

Bob grinned, "On a sailboat you can't count on being on time. It's not like a train or plane you know." He stood up and put out his hand, "Now that we've got the plank secured can we go sight seeing and find out what kind of a restaurant we come up with? My salad is almost within reach."

We locked up our boat and walked down the quay, checking for sign of life on other boats. Two boats down from us we saw an American boat from Alameda, another San Francisco Bay community. The boat was filled to the gunnels with boxes, lines, fresh bakery products, looking like an explosion had taken place and thrown things in all directions. A woman popped her head out of the cabin and called to her husband, "Don't bring anymore stuff down here yet. I'm not ready." With that pronouncement her head disappeared back into the cabin.

The skipper of the boat turned to look at us, a sheepish grin on his face. "Sorry for the mess here. We're getting ready to leave for Hawaii tonight, and then it's back to the states. We've been gone three years. We hate to do it, but we've used up our all our visa time here. They're pretty strict on kicking you out after six months. We got around it the first time by going to Hawaii and then back here again for another six months.

"Why can't you repeat the process again.?"

"Not this time We want to go back to the states and sell this boat and look for a new one."

Bob put his hand out toward the skipper, "By the way, I'm Bob Allen and this is my wife Marlene. We just got in today, but I don't know if we can stay as long as you have."

"Yeah, I saw you earlier. Good job backing in. In fact, better than most guys I've seen. My name's Fred, and my wife is Bonnie. She's been canning food for our trip and it's hotter than hell below in the galley."

"Speaking of food," said Bob, "do you know of any restaurants that don't charge an arm and a leg for food?"

Fred threw back his head, laughing in hearty, choking sounds, "Nice choice of words, an arm and a leg. That's a good one skipper. Matter of fact there's a good restaurant up the street called Lou Pescadou. Nice Italian food, lasagna that melts in your mouth."

I looked at Bob's bare chest and shorts, "What kind of clothes do you wear?"

Fred eyed us, "What ya got on is fine. It isn't fancy."

"Thanks, we'll give Lou's a try," said Bob. "Have a safe trip to Hawaii, and give San Francisco Bay a hello from us. We won't be back until September or October."

"You bet. Wish we had just arrived like you instead of leaving. The little lady and I really love it here."

We thanked him for the tip and found our way to Lou's. It was every bit as good as he said, with Bob in seventh heaven as he downed his salad. I smacked my lips over the lasagna.

The next day we saw *California* and *Starlight* making their way into the harbor, eying the rather full quay. We ran up and down the cement wall looking for an opening, finally coming to a spot that looked promising. Bob waved his arms back and forth to *California* and shouted, "Dick, drop you bow anchor and come in here. We'll help you."

Dick slowly turned the 70 foot cement schooner around, dropped his bow anchor and started backing in. The tedious process went slowly, but soon he gently nudged aside the boats on either side, coming to a stop. Denise threw the stern lines to us and we secured them to the rings on shore. Dick and Denise finished tying up the boat and then stepped off on their boomkin to the quay, not needing a long plank like ours. We threw our arms around them and Bob said, "It seems like years since we left you in Nuka Hiva. We really missed you guys."

Dick stepped away and looked at us with a twinkle in his eyes. "We missed you too. We were lucky in Nuku Hiva and got everything repaired. Thank God for Maurice's lumber yard. He even let me use his tools."

We were so busy exchanging information we completely forgot about *Starlight* circling around the harbor. Jim made a pass by the quay and shouted, "Hey you guys, what about me? "

"Sorry," said Bob. "You can pull up next to me, the space is small but I think you can get in." He turned his head to Dick and said over his shoulder, "Remind me to tell you what happens later this afternoon."

After tying Jim up we explained to him about the rock and roll concert at four. He put out extra bumpers to keep from damaging our two boats. I noticed one fender seemed a little low, but dismissed it in the excitement of seeing our friends again. We grabbed beers and sat down to trade sea stories and hear about their stay in Rangiroa.

Four in the afternoon arrived, along with the fishing fleet, and soon the all the boats at the quay were doing the Saint Vitus dance. We heard a crunching sound from *Starlight* which brought us to our feet immediately. The long hanging bumper had bounced up under the overhang of the rail, ripping the starboard tow rail right off the boat. Jim and Jan stared at the agonized skeleton of teak hanging off the water. Jim finally found his voice, "Holy Christ, I thought the boat was going to jump right out of the water."

Bob eyed the damage on *Starlight,* grunting in frustration. He checked our boat for damage, but found none. By now Jim's jaw was hanging around his ankles in despair, since their budget didn't allow for too many boat problems. Bob shook his head, "I'm sure sorry about the rail Jim. Maybe I can help out by buying the wood."

"That would be great 'cause I have to get the boat repaired before I can sell it here."

"Oh, I thought you had given that up.?"

"No, I'm even letting Dick have my red avon since I won't be needing it anymore."

Jim pulled off part of his damaged rail and gave us a piece for size. Jan walked aft, "Let's forget all this sad stuff until tomorrow. Why don't we look for a fun spot along the quay for a beer. I saw a Chinese junk down the way that might be a bar. Want to join us?"

"Sure, we'll lock up and be right with you," Bob said.

The four of us walked down the quay looking at the brightly colored laundry decorating the French boats, a family's life story fluttering in the breeze from the life lines. Little children ran around the decks, some in life jackets, but mostly without clothes. We had learned the French hired their countrymen and women to come to Tahiti to teach school, or work as officials, engineers etc. Many families saved money by living aboard boats, serving their time and selling the boat to the next new arrival.

We found the dark wooden Chinese junk squatting in the water, a nondescript faded sign saying "Welcome" hung at an angle. The four of us walked up the gang way anticipating some good Hinano beer. It turned out to be, for lack of a better expression, a unique experience. We entered a dimly lit room decorated with flowers, green tropical plants and sat down. Jan looked around and whispered, "It kind of dark in here isn't it."

I peered into the gloom, "Yes, but it's a romantic kind of atmosphere, intimate and cozy."

Jim and Bob waved to a tall Tahitian waitress who glanced in our direction. Her look seemed to go right past our heads as she turned her back on us, nuzzling and giggling into the ear of a young man. We sat for ten more minutes, our thirst becoming more pronounced in the humid atmosphere. Finally the waitress passed close enough to our table she couldn't ignore us any longer. As she lingered momentarily Bob stared up at her light brown face framed by red flowers, "Could we have four beers please."

Her dark brown eyes stared down into Bob's face, and her deep modulated voice purred, "Of course sir, I'll be right back."

By now my eyes were getting used to the dark, and I realized Jan and I were the only women in the room. I leaned over, "Do you suppose us Grandmas are giving this place a bad name. All the guys in here are so young."

"Look," she said , "a couple of them are going up into the pilot house with that other sexy waitress."

Four pairs of eyes followed the young boys up the steps, watching their return ten minutes later. By then our husky voiced waitress arrived with the beer, plunking it down firmly on the table and giving us a hard stare. Bob suppressed a smile as the waitress left the table, "Drink up ladies,", he said, "It's fairly obvious we aren't wanted here."

"Why, because we're not young women?" I said.

"No, because you are women. When our waitress leaned down to put the beer on the table I noticed she had an adam's apple the size of Washington state."

We guzzled our beer, took one last look at the room full of young men, and walked nonchalantly out the door. We hoped that the people in the bar didn't think we were out making fun of them, because we learned later it was a well known local gay hangout.

Living on the quay proved exciting, dirty and noisy. We had been in quiet places for so long we loved the change, happy to be part of the main stream of life again. Clouds of dirt and exhaust covered our boat with little black speckles. We found it ingrained itself into our newly washed clothes too, but a good shaking took care of most of the problem. It was good I wasn't born a perfectionist, because the life of a cruiser had so many surprises, not all of them good. It became a question of live and let live, as well as relax and relax some more. Each day greeted us with a shining sun, warm water, blue skies, friendly people, so when awakening Bob would turn over and say, "Just another shitty day in paradise eh."

That day we saw Dick and Denise scrubbing their newly acquired Avon, making it look like brand new. Dick told us later he had just sold his old oversized, and slightly deflated dinghy, to another cruiser.

The time for our son Bill and family to arrive suddenly drew near. Despite the heat and my yearning to get back to my book, I scrambled around the boat, cleaning, polishing the stainless and humming a sea chantey to myself. "Are you going to wash down the outside of the boat?" I yelled up to Bob.

He sat contentedly in the cockpit, a beer in one hand and a book in the other. "Later," he drawled, taking a swig of beer and swallowing it with a flourish.

I laughed at the difference between how he reacted to work now, compared to how he responded for years at home. Before we put to sea he performed like a possessed "workaholic" demon, fixing everything in sight, pressuring himself to complete millions of maintenance projects, never picking up a book because he didn't have time for "that." I liked the new Bob much better. I knew he would get things done eventually, but in a relaxed manner which wouldn't raise his blood pressure, or mine. Our cruising dream had become a life saver for two people, not just one. The only problem annoying Bob at this juncture in life was the disappearance of his hair. I like to think it landed on his face in the form of a beard, but the reflection from the top of his head had became quite real. So had my extra weight.

Very early the next morning we dressed, and ate a quick breakfast. We were meeting Bill and family at the airport. I wound my blue Tahitian pareau around body, combed my hair and urged Bob to hurry up. Moments like this reminded me of my mom, insisting the world would come to an awful end if we were not on time. Bob emerged from the head smelling of shaving soap and sun screen. He grabbed his shorts and shirt, dressing in rapid motions, "Not to worry," he said, "we'll get there on time.

We padded out into the still darkness, the road empty of the usual throng of cars belching noxious fumes, driven by anxious people hurrying to get somewhere to sit down and relax. We passed shadowy trees reaching out with perfumed branches, bright hibiscus blooms decorated their limbs and seemed to invite me to pick one. I did, placing the bloom behind my ear and making me feel free, young, and desirable.

As we approached the large open market, a flurry of activity surrounded the stalls. The merchants hawked their wares as the freshest, the best, and of course, the cheapest. We knew better, nothing came cheap in Papeete. The market officially opened at three in the morning, and by now some of the best of the local fresh fish had been sold. Men and women walked with bulging bags of fresh vegetables, chicken, fish and flowers; the food for nourishing the body, the beautiful flowers a banquet for the soul. Groups of people surged toward the bright red "Le Bus," crowding up its rear steps in search of a seat by the open windows.

Bob took my arm, "Come on, we don't have time to look." We followed, carefully picking our way past large bags of goods piled on the floor, and slipped into two empty seats. Nearby a sleepy child used her mother's arm for a pillow, nestling close to the sturdy Tahitian. The girl's long black hair fell over her face, muffling the soft sound of snoring. Once the bus started the peace and quiet quickly disintegrated, having been literally shoved aside by sound waves from an American hard rock music tape played by the bus driver. I shouted into Bob's ear, "Its sacrilegious to be screamed at in a tropical paradise, even if it is five in the morning."

Bob strained his voice above the din, "No worse than what Bill used to play as a teenager. You're just out of practice."

We arrived at the airport and walked rapidly to the gate, looking in all directions for our family. I held tightly to Bob's arms, squeezing it out of shape with anticipation. "I can't wait to see them," I said. "Do you suppose he'll think we've changed?"

"Unless he's blind he's bound to see a difference. He's never seen me in a full beard, or you all tan in a Tahitian wrap." Bob caught sight of our bearded son, dropped my arm and broke into a run toward him. "Bill, we're here," he shouted.

Bill turned around when he heard his name. His eyes grew wide, his jaw dropped in total surprise as his gaze registered the new image of his mother and father, "My God, you're as brown as natives, and dressed like one too." He ruffled his dad's growing beard and laughed, "So, it's father like son huh. You two look great."

He hugged us both tightly, and when he kissed me his mustache tickled my nose. Yep, father, like son, but Bill's mustache was soft, not like Bob's boar bristles..

I saw Katie standing patiently by the luggage, holding our blonde granddaughter, Kara, in her arms. I rushed over to hug them both. I reached up and took the flower from behind my ear, placing it behind Katie's ear, "Welcome to the islands." Emotions got the best of us and Katie and I both felt weepy, our faces strained even though the smiles were trying to break through the tears. I hugged Kara, but I could feel her little body shrink back toward her mother as she looked at this completely new brown grandma in funny clothes. "It's me, Grandma Allen," I said, trying to sound like my old self.

She frowned, looked at her mom and dad, corked her thumb tightly into her mouth, and buried her face into Katie's shoulder. So much for her memory banks I thought, guess I'll just have to be patient. I missed my Kara hug.

The memory banks worked beautifully for Bill and his dad as they walked to Le Bus, arms around each other's shoulders, each grinning from ear to ear. Exhausted by the long air flight, Bill, Katie and Kara soon fell asleep after reaching the boat. Catching up on family life would have to wait.

Later we sat in the cockpit sipping beer. I saw Kara eying me from her seat, "Want to play in some water?," I said. "I can give you some dishes and a big pan."

She smiled, her twenty one month old face finally showing acceptance as she nodded her head up and down. I filled the big pan with water from the hose and set it down in the middle of the cockpit. Kara took off her clothes and sat in the pan, splashing water in all directions. She had now joined paradise too.

Bob sat back contentedly, his arms folded across his stomach. "What do you want to do now that you're here?"

Bill looked at the traffic, listened to the horns blowing, and watched hordes of tourists amble up and down the quay. "Get out of here and go to where it's quiet. How about Moorea? Can I fish on the way over?"

Bob threw back his head and laughed, "Sure, we'll leave tomorrow. It's only a few hours away. I just have to drop by immigration and let them know where we're going."

The next ten days flew by in rapid succession as we fished, swam, watched Tahitian dancing at the Bali Hai Hotel, stared in wonder at the topless French and German tourists wearing tiny bikini bottoms that failed to cover the voluminous folds of skin surrounding their bums. I envied their lack of concern about showing off their sagging bodies. They were comfortable, while I wondered if I would ever get the courage to remove my top in public. I would think it over after Bill and family left.

I hugged Kara, but I could feel her little body shrink back toward her mother as she looked at this completely new brown granma in funny clothes.

We were comfortable with the tropical heat, having become acclimated a little at a time, but it took its toll on the younger Allen family. They were reduced to wilting flowers with hardly enough ambition to breathe. When it was time to get ready for the trip back to the states we sailed back to Papeete and anchored next to the hotel Bill and family found for the night. They were eagerly awaiting a room with air conditioning in order to get a good night's sleep before their long flight. The night didn't have an auspicious start because the air conditioning broke down, reducing them to sweat the night out in a closed room instead of the open boat.

The next day we rode to the airport with them, and this time I got big hugs from Kara. It would be another six months before she saw us again, and who knows, maybe she will remember better this time. We waved at the plane as it taxied away, part sad, part glad to get back to the quiet life of a boat bum.

We rowed back to our anchored boat and the first thing I did before I picked up my book was to remove my top and brassiere. Bob blinked, "Whooo, can I believe my eyes? Right here in the harbor. You look great to me. I'm just wondering what you'll do when the first boat goes by you."

I squirmed when I heard a boat engine chugging close by. I placed my book on my chest and peered around the dodger in time to see a top-less French woman at the tiller, head held high, and breasts thrust out. Feeling flushed I put down my book, stood up on deck and waved. She looked as surprised as I felt.

My break with modesty lasted for a full five minutes. Now that being topless proved "no big thing" I went back to my original ways, but feel-ing a little braver, and less uptight. Bob enjoyed the whole show, espe-cially the good looking French woman. I pinched his rear, "You didn't have to enjoy it so much you rascal."

Teasing looks glimmered in his eyes, "Yes, sailing the south seas sure is a good aerobic activity. It keeps your heart rate up and everything."

"It's the everything I'm talking about you lecherous sweet talking husband. At least I know you're not getting too old."

"Never that old my dear," he leered. "Let's pull up anchor and head back to the quay."

"I wonder if Jim's found a buyer for his boat by now?"

"We'll know what's going on soon enough if there's room for us on the quay."

We managed to squeeze *Maria* in between two French boats, getting cocky now that we were getting the hang of this Mediterranean tie up. We found Jim and Jan pulling up a red avon over the edge of their newly repaired rail. "Get a new dingy?"

He hesitated before answering. "No, we couldn't sell our boat here, so we had to take back our avon from Dick."

Oops, I thought. Trouble in paradise. Now not only did Dick not have a dinghy, but he was short of cash, with thousands of miles ahead of him before reaching New Zealand. We chatted for several minutes and excused ourselves to find Dick and Denise. A tight lipped Dick told us about the dingy problem, while Denise stood by with a sad expression.

"I saw you talking to them," Denise said. "How's Jan? We haven't seen or spoken to them since........the problem."

"Okay I guess," I said. "It must be hard because you and Jan were so close."

"Very hard mate. Dickie doesn't understand women. Ginger really misses Joey too. They were good companions.

Dick eyed the two of us."Why don't we talk about going to Moorea. Denise's parents are arriving tomorrow for several days. I'm hoping to hit him up for a loan to buy a new dinghy." Dick shot a cryptic look at Denise who lowered her eyes. "Tom said he can't give us anymore money because he bought the battery charger Bill bought for us in the states. This whole fiasco has really set us back"

We felt badly, acting neutral so as to be a sounding board for both crews if they needed us. Later on that day Jim and Jan came over for a drink and signed our log, "Had everyone been as great as the crew of *Maria Elena* we might have continued on. Fair winds and no gales, *Starlight,* Ye ol' Gaff Rigger."

Ouch, I thought. It doesn't look like we will be able to mend the tear in the friendship between *California* and *Starlight*. We've all shared so much, good times as well as storms, island experiences, sad and funny family stories. It looked like the old adage,"no good deed goes unpunished," had come true. Life on the bounding main proved to have the same inter personal problems as life on Main Street, USA. More the pity.

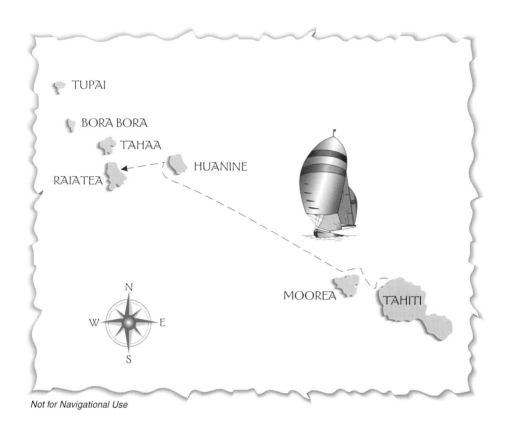

TUPAI

BORA BORA

TAHAA

RAIATEA

HUANINE

MOOREA

TAHITI

N
W · E
S

Not for Navigational Use

Chapter 23

ALLEN'S ARK

A Long Time Ago
"In Frisco Bay there lay three ships
And one of those ships was old Noah's Ark
All covered over with hickory bark."

(Sea Chantey "A Long Time Ago")

We awoke to a hot, muggy day, and as much as I tried, I couldn't put aside a nagging guilt that our boat needed some serious maintenance. *Maria* hadn't had her bottom painted for a year. Maybe the rain will come and sweep the air clean, I thought, then I wouldn't mind doing a little work. I hummed a sea chantey about Noah, thinking he probably had been too busy with the animals to take a good look at his Ark At least he only had to deal with one haul out. The fact that it occurred on top of Mount Ararat when the flood water receded might have given him a bit of a problem.

We had brought our own bottom paint with us, not knowing if a compatible paint would be available in the south seas. The bottom of our cans were now seriously rusted. We figured we had better get to work, or we might get up one morning and step into gooey bottom paint, flowing like a blue lava ribbon down the middle of our main saloon.

We located a boat yard with a marine railway to take *Maria* out of the water. Soon she glided gently up toward land, rising slowly out of the water like a graceful lady shedding her nightgown of salt. Standing near the creaking marine railway the strong odor of dead sea life and toxic paint struck a blow of deja vu, reminding me of my second date with Bob. How naive I had been at eighteen when Bob had talked me into sailing. He had been smart enough at the time not to mention who would be helping to do the sanding and painting on the bottom of the boat someday. I might have re-thought the whole thing. On the other hand, that would have meant no Bob....something I could not even imagine. I guess I'll file that deja vous experience under good news, bad news.

We inspected the bottom of the boat and found bare spots. "You can see where you scraped off the paint when you cleaned off barnacles and grass," I said. " I'm not going to ask you to scrub my back any more."

"Believe me, I'll be gentle with your back," he said with a wink, *"Maria* is tougher than you are."

Several workers chattered away in French while they blocked up our boat to keep it level. After power washing the bottom they disappeared back into the yard, leaving us to do the grunt work,....scrapping, sanding and painting. After a couple of hours in the hot sun our increasingly weary arms pushed paint rollers back and forth, salt stinging our eyes, sticky sweat rolling down our chest, backs and under arms. My tongue was so dry it felt like it had been hung on a cactus thorn in the desert. While the rollers covered faster than brushes, paint splatters of tiny blue droplets swirled in a crazy modern art pattern all over our arms and legs.

"I'm not sure if we're painting the bottom or ourselves," I said.

Bob took a rag and tried to scrub at spots on is arm."Hmm..It doesn't rub off too easy does it. The sun dries it almost immediately."

A deeply sun tanned Tahitian noticed Bob's efforts and walked over to us, scowling as he muttered in quick French phrases, punctuating his words with finger stabs at the toxic paint on our bodies. His readable sign language meant "get that stuff off quick."

I put down the paint roller and eased down in a shady spot next to the boat. "I'm getting too old for this," I panted. "I feel at least a 105."

Bob looked as haggard as I felt, and I stopped feeling sorry for myself. Misery really does like company. Abruptly he stood up, muttering to himself. He examined an area outside the galley that had remained wet, even though the rest of the boat had dried completely.

"What the heck is going on here," he exclaimed. "I know I've sanded this and painted it, but it acts like this spot is sweating." He reached up and felt it. "Cold," he announced. "This must be where the refrigerator is located inside. No wonder it takes so long to get the reefer cold. There's no insulation between the box and the hull here."

"Bummer," I said from my vantage point on the ground. "What can we do about it now"

"Nothing now I guess. I'll have to re-think things when we finally get home. Funny I never noticed the problem before."

"We've probably never had the box that cold when we hauled out. San Francisco doesn't exactly have tropical weather all the time."

He picked up a bottle of luke warm beer and poured it down his throat, leaving little foam bubbles around his mouth. "I promise from now on it will be up to someone else at a yard to do this job. I don't intend to do this ever again."

The next day *Maria* slid gently down into the water on the railway, ready as we were to get back to the real purpose of our life, cruising, snoozing and boozing, minus some cash that paid for the haul out. We pushed our way back into the quay near *Starlight,* waved to its crew and tied up our lines. Jim and Jan came over to hear about our haul out, and then hurriedly retreated back to *Starlight* when Dick approached.

Dick glared right through *Starlight* and turned to Bob. "Thought it might be fun to go to Moorea. Are you game?"

"Sure, it'll be good to get away from all the smog and noise for awhile," Bob said.

The next morning dawned with wall to wall blue sky. A perfect day to drop our lines and head out. Puffy clouds settled over the top of Moorea like a crown of cotton balls, while a salty breeze blew right down on our nose most of the way. We sailed part of the time, and used our "iron genoa" for an hour or so, hating the noise, but wanting to get anchored in a prime spot. I felt a bit unsettled, remembering the look on Jim and Jan's face when we left, so wistful and lonely. The breach between *California* and *Starlight* had not been bridged while we were gone. Money problems had a way of spoiling a lot of relationships, and tart words spoken in anger were remembered far longer than gentle words of excuses.

We watched the jagged volcanic peaks grow bigger as we drew closer. The deeply scarred weathering of the mountains showed Moorea to be an old lady, twice the age of Tahiti. We headed for Passe Avoroa, keeping the deeper blue water in front of us. We found a beautiful spot to anchor, far from hotels, and out of the way of the path of the inter island ferry.

When's California coming?" I asked

"Tomorrow I think. Dick had a couple of errands he had to run today."

The next morning in the galley I let out a scream. Bob rushed in, almost banging his head on the ceiling of the pass through from our cabin. "Are you all right?"

I pointed to the cockroach I had just squashed into brown pancake. "We've been so careful. How did it get in here?"

"Must have been waiting to hop aboard in the yard. Don't panic. I'll get the bug spray we bought in Mexico."

I scrubbed borax over everything, took out drawers and sprayed, leaving obnoxious fumes clinging to all surfaces I could reach. Not only wouldn't a cockroach want to live here, I wasn't too sure I wanted too either.

"Let's get our of here," I said gagging. "You need a haircut anyway and I don't want to do it on the boat."

"We could dinghy to the ferry landing. There's room to pull in the dinghy and set up shop. All that's missing will be the barber pole."

We tied up and I hung a towel around Bob's neck. Bob heard the sound of snickers and turned around to see several locals go by and give us a thumbs up sign.

"Hold still. The towel keeps falling down," I said.

"I am, but you nipped my ear with the scissors."

"Oh, sorry. It's hard to see the ears for the hair. When are you going to shave off that beard?"

"Maybe never...... but certainly not now."

He gave me a Morgan the Pirate look to let me know he didn't want me to tell him what to do. Rats, I thought. That damn beard is like a kissing number fifty grit sandpaper.

The next four days both California and Maria were confined to quarters because of heavy rain and I thought of Noah again. We had listened to a Bill Cosby tape last night, the one when he pretends to be Noah and balks at building the Ark. God says, "How long can you tread water," and "No, take only two rabbits, remember just two."

It must have been a hint to move on because Bob got out the charts for Huihine, our next scheduled landfall. We left with California the next day around eleven, a three knot breeze blowing its gentle breath over the boats. The bug spray smell evaporated with the tangy aroma of fresh sea breezes stirring in the sails and ruffling our hair. A sense of well being took over, and we smiled as we took out our books and let *Otto* take over the boat. It was his watch. *Otto* continued to do a good job even as the wind piped up to fifteen knots, driving us ahead at seven knots. Then just as the wind came up, it disappeared, leaving the main slatting in the motion of the swells.

"That's one noise that drives me crazy," I complained.

Bob's head turned when he heard a tearing sound. He jumped up with an oath when he found the source. "My own damn fault. The outhaul was loose and the main tore. I'll have to fix it once we're in port..... It's always one more thing."

Despite the lack of wind we arrived too early. It was only five thirty, and too dark to enter Passe Avamoa, Huihine. The reef extended a mile out from the shore and we needed some sun light to make sure we were on target. Hurry up and wait applied in this part of the world too.

When the sun shown behind us we started in slowly, keeping the red bouy to port. "It must be what happens when you get older," I said.

"You just pulled a 'Marlene.' I have no idea what you are talking about."

"You're right. I was just thinking how hard it is to rethink navigational devices when you've been used to them for so many years. They become natural. Hard to remember the French navigational aids are opposite to us."

"Great way to lose a boat though. Enough of this. Get ready to anchor."

After fussing around looking at different boats and positions Bob put down the anchor. A few minutes later he called back to me on the wheel. "I don't like the way we are anchored. That old schooner next to us is anchored with all rode. We're all chain. We won't ride the same at all. Let's move."

"We could go up ahead by that French boat," I said. "We've got eleven feet of water."

I found out to my dismay that the area proved to be the choice of the inter island ferries. Lots of them. That night instead of being rocked to sleep we careened off the bulkheads like an out of control eight ball.

But Bob and Dick thought it the best place in the world because of the special French boat at anchor not far from *Maria* and *California*. It wasn't the boat that intrigued them, it was the very nude woman who sat on deck reading a book. Much to their delight she suddenly stood up, stretched lazily like a cat, then slowly...making sure all eyes were front and center.....she dove into the water. As her nubile body struck the water a plume of water rose high, while Bob and Dick's eyes fell low.

Denise and I gagged at their performance, but it turned out we had the last laugh, or so we thought.

Later on Bob called over to Dick, "Want to take the dinghies into town? We need to pick up some fresh food."

Dick checked with Denise, "Yeah, let's do that and find a place for lunch."

The trip to town opened our eyes to the meaning of French Polynesian economics. Bob nearly fainted when he picked up a small head of red cabbage and found out it cost $13.00 American. He'd starve before he would pay that. Not me. I like red cabbage better than he does, but it stayed on the shelf due to Allen American economics.

We walked the dusty street back toward the boat, looking up when we realized a bicycle zoomed toward us. Denise and I both recognized the driver.

"Isn't that the French gal from the boat near us?" Denise hissed.

We both stared and giggled because she looked so different in clothes. She wore a flowing long dress, her stringy hair hanging in wisps around a plain, but horsey face.

"Hey you guys, look at girl on the bike," I said.

"So," Bob said. "she's not pretty at all."

"The laughs on you. That's the French gal you and Dick went ga ga over."

Bob and Dick looked puzzled. "Hey," said Dick, "We never said we looked her face."

I guess the joke boomeranged. Bob and Dick still believed in"Viva La France."

Apparently Bob and I looked at the opposite sex in a different way, but I swear you won't see me looking a man's nude bum and coyly saying, "Nice buns."

Later we learned the French nude taught kindergarten at a local school, and I wondered what my principal back home would have thought about me in the same circumstances. In the 1930's my father was told he would be fired if the principal found out he played cards! That included bridge. When dad's picture appeared in the paper with my mom at a Charity Ball he had been called into the office and told by his wooden face boss that teachers had an image to keep up with the public, and they were not supposed to have fun. I bet they had a merry Christmas staff party.

The next few days we spent time snorkeling, reading and visiting with the crew from *California*. ....and being awakened by inter-island ferries. We figured it time to move on to Raiatea.

Rain started falling in the night and I leaped up to close the open hatches. I crawled back quietly up into our bunk, aware of the change in the air quality inside, damp and close. Bob didn't seem to notice, if I believed the loud snore.

Morning crept in like a wet blanket exposing leaden skies and light winds. I didn't like the way the sky looked, even though the winds were negligible. After breakfast we made short work of pulling up anchor, and quickly setting the genoa out with a pole to keep the big sail in place. Baie Faaroa loomed ahead twenty miles away, and the normal fluffy clouds hitched to the high peaks over Raiatea were hidden in the gloom.

"I'm afraid we have to turn the engine on. We'll be sailing backwards in this wind," Bob said.

I went below to take off the shaft lock, and decided to get a new novel from the book box up forward. Near the forward head my bare toes sunk into a wet carpet. I put my hand down to the carpet and tasted the end of my finger. No salt. Oh no, I thought, I must have overfilled the water tank yesterday. Guiltily I picked up three thirsty bath towels and sopped up the water, cursing my carelessness. Bob looked at me curiously as I came up the companionway ladder with my dripping load.

"Bad mistake," I growled. "I over filled the water tank. Can you help me wring them out?"

"Sure." Bob's slow smile showed he was glad it was me instead of him as he twisted the heavy material over the side and dispersed the water. I hung the towels over the life line and fastened them securely with heavy clothes pins. I settled back in the cockpit, not particularly enjoying the lumpy seas that tossed us about. Bob had gone down below to check the navigation to Baie Faaroa in Raiatea. He's so lucky I thought, he never gets sea sick. I would hate staying down below reading with all the boat rolling around. As Bob started up the steps I stopped him.

"Could you please bring up the book that tells about Raiatea before you come up. I vaguely remember there was something special about it."

Soon I became immersed in Polynesian history learning that Raitea, the second largest island, had been the ancient religious, cultural and political center to the Society Islands. Legend had it that canoes left from this island for New Zealand and Hawaii. I thought about making a journey in a canoe to these far away places, deciding I wasn't so brave after all sailing in our forty one foot boat. I don't care how beguiling Bob can be. He would never have gotten me to go on this trip in a canoe. I do windows, but not canoes. I looked up, "Hon, didn't Dick or Denise tell us about Baie Faaroa?"

Bob thought a minute. "Yes, he lived on Raitea for awhile years ago. He said King Turi led canoes from here to New Zealand, and then Maori populated the island."

I went back to my book, but the pages started to flutter, then flip. The wind has made one of those fast appearances out of nowhere, and Bob jumped up to the foredeck to take down the pole. Before long he pulled in the genoa and we headed to wind and put up the main. Within minutes we reefed the main when the wind escalated to forty knots, blowing Maria ahead through the frothy waves like a play toy. We kept a good magnetic course because there were no leading markers to guide us into through the pass. In no time we slipped through the Passe Iriru, careful to watch for coral heads. We anchored in fifty nine feet of water in Baie Faaroa, glad to be settled and secure. *California* joined us about fifty feet away.

The next day I heard a familiar voice by the side of our boat. "Hey mate," said Denise, "how about taking a river trip. We can dinghy into the river. Dickie says it's really beautiful."

"Sounds good to us," Bob said. "Give us a few minutes."

"Make a picnic lunch and bring some munchies."

"In that case we'll be a few more minutes. We'll motor over in our dinghy when we're ready. Who's going?"

"Dick, me, Tom and Ginger."

"We can all fit in our dinghy."

After a quick packing job, which of course included beer, we picked everyone up and headed for the mouth of the River Aoppomau, the only river trip in French Polynesia.

"Better pull your motor up at the shallows," Dick said. "In fact we may have to row from here on. There's water logged tree trunks and debris that flows down in the rain storms."

Bob rowed, then cautiously put down the motor. Slowly we made our way along a natural jungle. Through the lacy greenery we spied patterns of rock rising up into the majestic walls of Mt. Tefatuaitl, making our party an insignificant speck of matter on the water. Bob turned off the motor and we drifted in peaceful quiet, broken only by the songs of birds flitting in and out of the trees. Life had slowed down and given us a glimpse of uncivilized beauty that needed nothing to add, only something to take away in memories.

Several days later in Uturoa, the main town, we took our boat into the main dock for market day. We had no sooner tied up when a man came over to wave us off, "Sorry, the inter-island ferry comes today. You can tie up further down out of the way."

We did as directed, and after tying up we met up Dick who had another man with him.

"I'd like you to meet Hugo," Dick said.

Bob looked in surprise. "We met Hugo in 1983 when he and Maeva had a feast at their home. Hello again," shaking Huggo's bear of a hand.

Hugo, burly, with a light mat of hair over most of his sturdy body, was an American insurance agent from Hawaii , married to a Tahitian. I remembered hearing his wife was reputed to be a princess. Although Maeva owned a lot of land, their spendable income had been in short supply. Hence they gave feasts for large groups and tours such as the one we attended two years before with Sausalito Yacht Club.

Dick grinned from ear to ear, "I was just telling Hugo how I used to work here and saved a young girl from drowning. He remembered it. We've been having such a good time he invited us to Pufau Bay where he lives. He even has a hand dug pool"

Hugo spoke up quickly to Bob, "Please you come too. I know Maeva would want to see you and Marlene again. But I must talk to her first about having guests ."

Hugo returned later with the good news that Maeva said "Yes." to all of us. We were excited to see Pufau Bay, this time in our own boat. *Maria* and *California* were soon anchored in a clear blue water, surrounded by palm lined, rocky shore and small homes. Many of the home owners had built sturdy rock walls at the edge of their property. Bob set up the wind generator in the rigging, a large wooden airplane propeller attached to a generator. At that point Hugo rowed out to greet us. "The pool is waiting for you," he said, "along with some rum punch."

In record time we arrived at Maeva and Hugo's house, eager for a cool drink and visit. The hand dug pool was quite an accomplishment. Hugo had built it in conjunction with a natural spring that sent cool, clear water to fill it. He claimed the natural spring had been part of an ancient religious practice. He had planted colorful flowers and greenery around the edge, but the real surprise grew out of the center. He had built an island there which now housed his bed. We cooled off in the small pool and talked about the differences between Tahiti governed by the French, and life and economics in the United States. Maeva met us back at the house and invited us to return for a spaghetti dinner the next day, and with a special treat afterwards, two French video comedies. We noticed a distinct coolness between Hugo and Maeva, but she showed nothing but kindness and joy at being with all of us. Maeva's beautiful fourteen

The hand dug pool was quite an accomplishment.

year old daughter hinted that her mother had been very angry and banished Hugo from the house. We wondered what the bed in the middle of
the pool would be like in a storm.

The next day Bob started work on a problem in our engine. He sat
cramped inside the small area, one leg tucked underneath him, trying to
reach across the engine to a cracked injector. "I'd give anything to have
full head room in here. I'm sick to death of making love to this engine."

I unwrapped one of sealed injectors we carried as spares, "I don't
know how you do it. It's no wonder you have cramps and bruises in your
legs."

I handed him the injector, relieved that I had the job of cooking and
not fixing the engine. At least the galley had full head room. "When
you're done can we join Dick and Denise on that small motu off shore?
It looked so beautiful. None of these big islands have a real beach, but the
motu does. We have plenty of time before we meet Hugo and Maeva."

"Great idea. I need to get out of this boat and cool off."

We knew paradise really existed when we sat down on the beach at
the motu with Dick and Denise, letting the clear, pale-green water wash
over us in slow moving wavelets. Fine grains of beige sand covered our
legs and laps, and we cupped our hands in the water and washed it off.

The idea of swimming seemed too great an effort. Lazy talk took place as we traded stories of growing up, working in different jobs, traveling. Denise talked of her growing up on a farm in New Zealand, working in Australia and finally meeting Dick and coming to America. It would be full circle for Denise when she and Dick finally reached New Zealand to find a place to live and work. The spaghetti dinner and French videos finished the end of a beautiful day, but the wind storm that night proved paradise had a different side.

The boat began to rock as the forty knot wind buffeted the sides, waking us up about midnight. A low moan roared out of the rigging, and the whine of the propeller whirred like a million mosquitos. The stainless section on the halyards beat on the mast like demented bongo drummers. Sleep became impossible so Bob got up to take down the wind generator before it tore itself apart. I grabbed the line to turn the prop ninety degrees into the wind to stop it, while Bob swiftly lowered it to the deck.

"Lord, do you suppose Hugo was blown out of his bed?" I asked.

"A distinct possibility. The water is so cold he would have had a hell of a surprise."

We found out later the wind had pinned the generator at twenty amps, and had actually melted the solder in the diode. We were amazed. I was more astounded when Bob produced a diode and fixed up the generator post haste.

We all had been having such a good time with Maeva and Hugo that time vanished like teenager with chores to do.

"It won't be the same when we sail *Maria* to Bora Bora." I said to Maeva. "But you won't be forgotten."

"It has been too long since my whole family has been here for a big feast. You will all join us as part of the family," she exclaimed. "It will take us two days to prepare so don't leave."

We didn't have a specific time schedule, but we knew *California* had some time constraints. It turned out they wouldn't miss this for anything. The feast would be well worth waiting for. Bob used that time to sew up the small rent in the main sail. Dick always had jobs to do to keep *California* going.

The big day arrived and the two crews dressed up for the occasion in their best island outfits. We brought small gifts, and big appetites, a guitar and my alto ukulele. The house practically burst open with adults, children of all sizes, flowers, and cloth covered tables laden with a variety of delicious smelling foods. A pig had been roasted and cut up in many pieces, fresh fruits of all kinds and colors sent sweet perfume into the air. My favorite Tahitian vegetable dish, chard, had been cooked with onions, bacon, and sweet coconut milk. There were other native dishes we didn't recognize, but devoured anyway. Afterwards we sat around and sang sea chanties, "camp" songs everyone knew, and listened to Tahitian music. A very special evening with happy people came to an end. We said goodbye with happy hearts and full stomachs. The memory of these wonderful, unselfish people will remain forever.

The next day we picked up our anchor and headed for Uturoa to fuel up, obtain water and groceries. Bob left for a haircut, hoping to find a barber who didn't nip his ears like I did. I stared at the barometer. At 1500 hours it was down to 29.9, and I didn't want to run into another front like the one we encountered the other night. Oh well, I thought, I couldn't control the weather any more than I could control Bob and his beard.

He returned sporting a pretty good hair cut, and as we pulled away our mooring lines, I thought of all that great times we had on this island. Cruising was really about meeting people. All kinds.

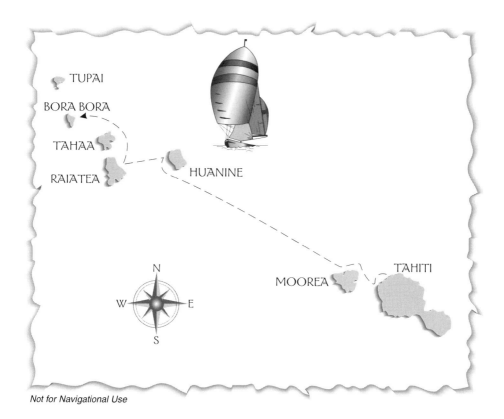

TUPAI

BORA BORA

TAHAA

RAIATEA

HUANINE

MOOREA

TAHITI

N
W · E
S

Not for Navigational Use

306

Chapter 24

WE LEFT OUR HEART IN BORA BORA

The past months of dropping mooring lines, unwrapping anchors from coral heads, and feeding thirsty water tanks had become as repetitive a job as a wood pecker jack hammering for food on a fir tree. The bird's survival depended upon his task, while ours merely created a new jewel in our necklace of adventure.

"I'm really anxious to get back to Bora Bora. Aren't you," I said.

"I hope it's as beautiful as I remember. I hated the charter boat we had in '83. I've never been on a boat that listed fifteen degrees when you emptied a water tank."

"I know. It felt like being transformed into a fly and walking on the sides of the hull."

"It won't be long before Lori arrives in Bora Bora with Brad, Terry, and Missy. We've only met Terry once, and we've never met his daughter. Sounds serious doesn't it."

"Very serious. Everything she says about him sounds wonderful though. It's good to hear her happy voice after all the bad vibes from the divorce. It's been nine months since we've seen Brad in Marina Del Rey, and almost six months since Lori surprised us in Cabo."

Bob chose the correct chart for Bora Bora and studied it, then picked up our guide book, flipping through the pages to Raiatea and Tahaa. "I think we'll go through Tiva pass to Bora Bora. It has good leading markers." He put the book down and stretched out his back.. "I'm going up on deck. I want you to steer 006 magnetic. We don't have a strong westerly so the swells shouldn't be too big." Once on the foredeck Bob called over his shoulder. "Stay far off the barrier reef until you line up with the leading marks."

"Aye Captain," I said, eyeing the breaking waves on either side "Looks like fun. Ho ho."

"You'll do all right. Just head well out and clear the barrier hump. I'll let you know when and give you a course to Bora Bora."

I kept the red-cube ballise to port and the black vertical cone ballise to starboard. When *Maria* responded to the strong currents at the inner northeast end my hands gripped the wheel to show the water flow I had claimed command. Once clear of the reef Bob set the main and genoa, and our journey to one of the loveliest islands had commenced. Our course and wind put us on a close reach, swiftly pushing us away from the fragrant earthy smells of growing gardens and budding blossoms. A pungent sea aroma replaced the blossoms as land faded into the distance. Not being close to shore didn't bother me as much as it did other people. In fact I preferred it. I joked that land appeared to attract objects like an unsuspecting boat, luring it into its night time web of reefs. I'm a daylight girl. I like to see visions of changing cloud images, seemingly transformed into fairy tale stories, thrilling sights of leaping schools of dolphins, or charging open mouthed sharks chasing several dozen tuna. The latter once grabbed our trolling line one day, ripping the high test line in two and stealing a large hook. Bob said he was glad he hadn't seen the monster who gobbled that one up. At least the shark left the pole for us.

Three hours later Bob glanced at his watch and searched the horizon. "There," he shouted. See the volcano? Isn't it something. We have to be careful going in. There's only one pass and water rushes out all the time."

"The swells are pretty good size too," I noted. "I remember from last time we had to stay out further to sea because of the reef."

We drew closer, the sails humming in the breeze, stretched tight to catch every bit of wind. Bob pulled out the binoculars and studied the landfall. "I see the pass. I can't pronounce the damn thing, but I see it."

I loved it. Old peanut butter tongue had caught him again. "It's Passe Teavanui," rolling the words off like a native. Language had always been easier for me, but impossible for Bob. We eased off and headed to wind, taking down the main and rolling up the jib. Bob went back to the bow, waving at me to head for the pass.

"Here we go," Bob shouted. "No leading markers. Course 90 degrees Magnetic. Take it off that inland big marker with a red top."

"I don't see it," I cried.

"I do, so don't worry. Leave the red markers to port and head for the lagoon."

The waters calmed, resembling mirrored glass with an upside down picture of the volcano, and palm trees lining a shore. We headed toward an open white buoy in front of a hotel called the Oa Oa. Oh joy, we didn't have to anchor in eighty feet of water after all, I thought. The wind can blow all it wants and we won't have to stay up all night checking the darn anchor. Bob looked behind us to see if he could see *California*. Only one open buoy remained beside the one we picked. Further to our left sat *Starlight*, gently rocking on its line to a buoy. We waved and shouted a hello. Jim rowed over after we tied up.

"Great to see you," he said. "We've been here a few days and scoped out the area. You can take showers at the hotel and fill up your water tanks when you leave. They have a reverse osmosis system and have to conserve water for hotel use."

"Good to see you too Jim, but a surprise. I thought you were going to sell the boat in Tahiti."

He sighed and rubbed his head. "You have to have someone interested. We've decided we have to make it to Hawaii to find a buyer. Nobody's looking for a boat like mine in the islands. Nobody with money that is."

"After we finish here come on over around five for drinks. We'll catch up on all your doing then."

Bob checked the chart and determined where the main town of Viatape was located so we could check in with the Gendarmerie. We planned to stay here at least a month or so to see Fete, the biggest celebration in the islands. It commemorated Bastille Day, July 14, in France and its colonies. There would be singing competition between the islands, as well as dances, and spear throwing. We put the rubber dinghy in the water, secured the outboard on the back, and I handed down the shot gun and the pistol and ammunition wrapped in a towel. We would have to turn these in until we left the island. A gust of wind pushed the boat back and jerked the painter. The calm mirror image divided into little pieces like a cardboard puzzle. It seemed the barometer had been telling us something, but not necessarily what we wanted to hear. Still no *California*. We hoped she made it in time to pick up the last buoy.

The wind continued to escalate, blowing salt spray over us. I kept the towel wrapped tightly around the firearms, enjoying the cooling water, but wishing it wasn't so sticky when it dried. When we arrived at Viatape we tied up and walked into town with our weapons. Two small boys ran to us waving their arms, "No, no, go back," they cried, pointing to the wrapped guns. "Gendarmerie will take away."

So much for hiding our guns. We assured them it was all right, but they thought we were nuts. The officer in the Gendarmerie signed us in, collecting our guns. His eyes coveted the pistol, holding it lovingly in his hands. His eyes met Bob's. "You sell me gun please?" He opened a locked door to show Bob his big collection. "I don't own a German officer's gun."

Bob shook his head. Not only could he go to jail for selling the gun, but it was a favorite of his. "Sorry," he said, "I've had this gun a long time. You have a good collection, but my Walther P38 stays with me when we leave the island."

The Officer gave a gallic shrug of nonchalance, stamping our papers and sending us on our way. By the time we reached our boat *California* hung on to the remaining buoy, and the wind began to whine. I made a phone call by ham radio to Lori and found out the time and date of their arrival. Two days.

Jim and Jan arrived for cocktails and filled us in on their abortive tries to sell their boat. Jan smiled, "Joey and I are glad we didn't sell. We still wanted to keep going."'

Jim's face looked gaunt and tired. "We don't have the same navigational gear you do. It's a worry." We noticed he hadn't regained the twenty five pounds he lost on the trip to the Marquesas.

Bob looked deep in thought, "Last time you didn't know how to get Longitude. You did great with Latitude, am I right?"

"Right. We never quite finished the course because we wanted to get going. Found out it was a mistake not to finish."

"Do you have plotting paper?"

"What's that? I don't remember the instructor talking about plotting paper. All we learned was how to take sights, and do dead reckoning. We can do a dynamite LAN."

"Latitude is important, but so is Longitude, Jan," Bob said, "bring your book and I'll teach you how to get Longitude and give you some of our plotting paper. Longitude is somewhat complicated since you have to take your sights, use dead reckoning to come up with an assumed position, then plot your actual position based on the sextant reading, using a series of tables with time, and date. Then you put down the assumed position and actual position on plotting paper." Bob looked at their dazed expression. "Don't worry, we'll work things out just fine."

They both looked relieved, and Bob set a time for instructions after Lori and family left for home. That night the wind howled. The long fetch across the bay set up sharp waves that spanked *Maria's* sides, waking us at times. We weren't worried because of the heavy weights that held the buoy in place. Obviously not cyclone proof, but this weather front didn't show any signs of escalating into a huge storm.

The day after we watched the shore closely, not knowing if Lori's plane had landed on time. I had about given up when I spied her waving to us from the Hotel Oa Oa's cement bulkhead. We leaped into the rubber boat and started for shore, but the wind and waves blew toward us, trying to keep us away. We made a very unsteady landing and tied up. Lori ran up and hugged us, exclaiming, "You're both so brown. Dad, that beard. You look so different."

"I'll say," I whispered in her ear.

"Big news mom and dad," Lori said with a shy smile. "Terry and I are getting married next March in your house, so you had better be home in time for the wedding."

"Nothing like a big surprise," Bob gulped.

Lori looked a tiny bit nervous and waved to Brad, "Come on over Brad." It's grandma and grandpa"

Brad gave us a look that said he didn't remember anybody who even remotely looked like us. He clung to Lori's hand, making sure he didn't get too close to these strangers. Here we go again, I thought. The price we pay for taking off for such a long trip.

Terry strode forward to greet us. He stood six feet tall, good looking, glasses, and a grin that could light up the world. He enveloped us in a bear hug, "I hope we haven't surprised you too much. I never formally asked you for Lori's hand."

Bob smiled, "The answer is yes, but thank you for thinking of us. Lori really made the choice, and that's fine with us."

Terry turned toward his 12 year old, slim, dark-haired daughter, Missy, a lovely combination of his Irish background and the exotic aura of her Thai mother. Her large dark eyes watched her father, and when he nodded, she came over and shyly greeted us.

"Well, this is just great. Get your things and we'll take you out to the boat. Can't take all of you at once, but we'll get there safely," I said.

"I hope you won't be upset mom, but we're all so tired from the long trip that we thought about staying at this hotel for the night. Terry found out they have room, and we'll all be better company," Lori said.

"Good idea. The wind is supposed to lie down tonight and so the boat shouldn't rock too much. We don't want your time spoiled by getting sea sick."

The next day we picked up our guests, bag and baggage, and loaded ourselves on the boat. After stowing all the gear we sat in the cockpit.

"I thought it might be fun to rent bikes and go around the island," Bob said. "Unless you're still too tired."

"Great idea dad," Lori enthused. "Brad will like a little more freedom to move around. He's three years old today."

Dick, Denise and daughter Ginger joined us in renting bikes. Brad rode in a small car seat behind Lori's in the rented Peugeot bike. Bob and I hadn't cycled in years, and our leg muscles stretched when we labored up a hill. Fortunately most of the terrain flattened out. Brad entertained us singing "Happy Birfday to me," waving his arms in time to the music.

We were on the other side of the island when I noticed a tall , very nude, Polynesian man standing by the side of the road. His young adult face stared vacantly into space, never moving a muscle, or giving any sign of recognition to the passing crowd. Everyone stopped talking, and nonchalantly peddled past, some a little faster. Lori's voice broke the silence. "Did you see that?"

"Yes," I answered, " It was sad to see such a blank face."

"His face?" Lori said in a surprised tone. "I didn't see his face, but I'll tell you this, he wasn't circumcised."

The old married group convulsed with laughter and Brad looked around in surprise, not knowing what had brought it all on. I decided Lori must have been have been impressed with her anatomy courses when she became a registered nurse.

A couple of days later the sun shown down on *Maria* in a golden glow, a light breeze ruffling the edges of the sun shield. It seemed like a special day for some reason, and so it was. Brad met the ocean head on. He felt about the sea like his grandma had earlier, he could take it or leave it, mostly leave it. After breakfast we all climbed into the hard dinghy and headed for a small island called Motu Iti, leased by Club Med. We knew it was private, and we only visited it if Club Med guests were absent. We landed on the far side of the island where the clear water gently lapped on the beach, picking away at the sand. Only our family occupied the Motu. Grandpa Bob took Brad by the hand to meet the water, but Brad hesitated, generously allowing just one toe to touch the water. "Come on Brad," Bob said, "nothing will happen because I'm with you. See? I'm sitting down at the edge of the water." He patted the sand. "You sit down here next to me and I'll draw your name with my finger."

Brad took a glance around and cautiously sat down, never taking his eyes off the water. Bob drew his name, then began to build a little sand castle, slowly edging forward slightly into deeper water. Brad scooted down to be next to him, engrossed in building with a small blue bucket we bought in town. Soon Bob eased himself into a little deeper water, extending the sand castle. Brad followed, pouring water on the castle until it melted and needed a rebuilt job. By this time the water lapped at his waist, and then it dawned on him. The water covered his legs and lap. His eyes grew wide as he turned to Bob. Then Brad said under his breath, "I'm all right. I'm all right." He must have convinced himself, because suddenly Brad laughed, splashed the water, filled the bucket and dumped the contents on top of Bob's head, leaving the bucket on his head like a top hat. He said, "grandpa, you fooled me."

We all congratulated Brad on being so brave. With his new found confidence he followed Lori and Missy to the other side of the island where the water came in one foot waves. He squealed and ran to meet the waves. Now a new problem took place, keeping Brad from venturing too far out in the water and getting himself in trouble. We were so busy watching the "new" Brad we missed a small boat landing with two people from Club Med. They moved quite a distance from us, splashing around in the water, giggling and chasing each other. We glanced over at the noise seeing a man taking pictures of a well endowed topless woman bouncing her boobs up and down in the water. Fascinated we watched as she pushed them together like a wonder bra, and as she jumped up, the white oversized breast came out of the water like two launched missiles. She turned and observed six pair of eyes, plus six drooping jaws, and let out a yell, "Get out of here. You're not guests of the Club Med."

He must have convinced himself because Brad laughed, splashed water, filled the bucket and dumped it on top of Bob's head.

With that we ran as fast as our legs could carry us and jumped into the boat, trying not to explode with laughter. Later when Bob and I sat in the cockpit a small dinghy with a man rowing approached us. I whispered to Bob, "That's the man at the motu taking pictures. We're in trouble."

"Hi," there said the man. "I want to apologize for my wife yelling at you. We're newly- weds on our honeymoon and she just got kind of excited."

Bob smiled,"We didn't mean to interrupt your fun. Your wife was right, we shouldn't have been there."

"I felt bad," he said, "because I knew you didn't mean any harm. By the way, I just happen to have a new Latitude 38 that I've already read. I know your home port is San Francisco, and Latitude 38 is pretty popular there."

"Great, we haven't seen too many this last year. We really appreciate your thinking of us. Would you like to come aboard for a beer?"

"No, I think I should get back to my bride. I left her in the shower, and she might wonder what happened to me. Have a great sail."

"Thanks again for the magazine. You already look like your having a wonderful honeymoon."

The days flew by with Brad investigating every inch of *Maria,* chattering about the water, and eating everything in sight. Lord, I thought, wait until he's a teenager. One night I made hot and sour soup, which I knew the adults would like, but was uncertain about Brad. He tasted it, looked up with a smile and said, "Grandma, this is delicious."

The next afternoon Terry and Lori wanted some time to themselves, asking to use the dinghy for an hour or so. Brad was down for his afternoon nap.

"I want to go," Missy announced imperiously.

"Not this time Miss, Lori and I have some things to do," Terry said.

With fire in her eyes she watched them leave, and an aura of jealousy hung in the cockpit. No wonder, I thought, she had always been the light in daddy's eyes, especially the eight years since the divorce from her mother. He had custody.

I went below and returned with pinochle cards. "Missy, how about a game of pinochle."

Her voice took on an edge and she spit out, "I don't know how to play,"

"Good time to learn. You'll probably beat me when you catch on."

For an hour and a half we played, while she kept an eagle eye on shore, searching for Lori and Terry. They returned and Missy said a few words that Terry took exception to. He took her up on the bow and they sat down and had a father to daughter talk. After a half an hour they returned, both looking like the talk did them good.

Before we knew it the time had flown by, and it was time for the family to leave for home. We had enjoyed hearing plans for a small wedding in our backyard, learning to love the man our daughter had chosen to join our family, and getting to know our new granddaughter to be. When we took them to the airport launch I didn't envy their trip home. It was a long one with several plane changes, guaranteed to produce the grumps.

Quiet enveloped the boat after the family left. "It was good to see everyone wasn't it," I said. "We had quality time to get to know Terry and Missy, but now that they're gone, the boat seems so empty."

"I really like Terry.," Bob said, "and Missy is a sweet girl. But a little jealous. Did you see her watching Lori and her dad?"

"Yes. It's natural. There will be some problems along the way, I'm sure. And a teenager doesn't necessarily want to share."

Bob took a beer out of the refrigerator and sat back in the cockpit. "Lori will try hard. She really cares about Missy. It shows."

"Brad loves her too. Things will work out, but adjustment problems will come up. Lori looks so happy, and acts more like her old self since she met Terry. Don't you think?"

"Yes, that's because he accepts her for the person she is. Mike tried to change her into what he wanted. Obviously it didn't work."

"I know. I tried to change you from being a workaholic all those years, but you didn't leave me."

"That's 'cuz I love you. But I tried to change you too. When we first married you hated ironing, and I had a heck of time getting you to iron all my shirts every week. They'd get done eventually, but I swear I was always missing my favorite shirt for at least six months."

"You did. It was a bear to iron so I hid it in the back of the closet."

The days started to run together between spending time snorkeling with Dick and Denise, reading books, shopping for food, and Bob teaching Jan celestial navigation. One day we dinghied quite a distance to a motu where we could pick up some pretty augur shells. Bob and I were already in the water when Denise slide slowly over the side of her dinghy. I gestured to her, "Be careful, there's a bunch of sea urchins on the bottom."

It was too late. The momentum of her body brought her down fast, and I saw her leg jerk when her foot found one of the sharp spines. We both came up to the surface.

"Are you all right?" I yelled.

"No mate, these things are poison. I had better get me and my foot back to *California*"

We all returned to our boats. Shells seemed unimportant at that moment.

Several days later I went over to *California* to see if they needed anything at the market. "I'm going into town Denise. Want to come?"

"I don't think so. I feel awful. When we came back after stepping on the urchin I looked all over for ammonia. I couldn't find any so I peed in a cup and poured the urine on my foot, thinking that would take care of it."

"Our cruising book says that's what to do."

"I guess so, but now I think I've got an infection. Dicky's going to take me to the doctor and get some antibiotics."

"I'm so sorry. If we can do anything let us know. You can't fool around with infection in the tropics."

Denise looked around for Dick, not seeing him she leaned down and whispered, "I saw you and Bob talking with Jim and Joey. How are they? I really miss Jan, and Ginger misses playing monopoly with Joey."

"They're doing all right. I'm sure they miss all of you too. You don't think Dick and Jim can patch things up?"

"No way with Dick," Denise lamented. "It's a closed subject. Well, have a good time in town. I have to get ready to go to the doctor."

Bob and I sped across the quiet water, reaching Viatapi in no time. We tied up the dinghy and carried twenty four empty beer bottles into the store. We bought beer, and of course salad greens, and frozen chicken legs from Alabama. We left immediately so the chicken wouldn't unfreeze in the humid air. I climbed up on the boat and Bob handed me the food to store. I came back to help with the beer. He had just placed the cardboard box full of beer on the aft deck. "Oh no you don't," I said. "There might be cockroaches hiding in there."

"Oh come off it. One cardboard box won't hurt"

I started removing the bottles, setting them behind me near the hatch. As I reached for another one a large black spider peered out of the box, one long leg extended over the edge toward me. I screamed and flicked a towel toward it, knocking the four inch creature in the water. Bob yelled as the spider gave a perfect Mark Spitz Gold Medal imitation of the crawl....straight to him. He howled and whipped his hands in the water, making the black spot rock back and forth. One had to admire the Olympic constitution of this hairy spectacle, because he continued, leg, by leg toward Bob's hand. Bob grabbed an oar and swept the inky creature into the air, placing it six feet away. When last seen the spider was swimming for all his worth away from our ungrateful boat.

"Not a spider lover are you," I laughed.

"I noticed he wasn't exactly high on your friend list either."

"Can you imagine being awaken in the middle of the night by something touching you. You reach up and find it isn't your mustache you're rubbing, but a four inch hairy spider taking a walk across your face." I shuddered.

"Okay, okay, you win. I won't bring any more boxes on the boat."

We awoke one morning to the sound of hammer and saws hard at work on shore. Small huts had sprung up like crab grass, sitting side by side. Each hut covered with palm fronds with a sign telling what would be sold inside. The beginning of the Fete had started, although it was still two weeks before July 14. In the week and a half following we listened to Polynesian singing groups from other islands competing with groups from Bora Bora, their melodious voices rich in five part harmony drowning out the noise from the pouring rain. Other days groups in brightly colored shirts and dresses, competed in dances, some of the music played in slow rhythm, others in the fast Tahitian hula. One gathering of men lined up carrying thin homemade spears, taking turns throwing long distance to stick the spear in a coconut mounted on a tall pole. We cheered along with the natives. We also frequented huts that sold warm beer, had games of chance, and watched the queen of Fete on Bora Bora perform her duties, mostly looking beautiful.

Despite all the hoopla a nagging feeling gnawed away at us, whispering phrases which included words like home, home, time to go, off to Hawaii, family, wedding, home. Dick and Denise felt the pull with us, and we noticed Jim and Jan were making preparations to leave. I guess one can only take so much singing and dancing and having fun.

"What do you think? Time to go ?" I said.

"I'm ready. There's things I need to fix on the boat that I can only get in Hawaii."

"We haven't seen a green flash yet. It seems everyone else in the Pacific has seen a green flash just as the sun sets."

"Well I'm sure as hell not waiting around for that moment."

All three boats, which included Starlight, were in frenzy of activity, loading supplies, taking on water, checking charts. Bob and I went over to *California* to see about their schedule.

"We're planning on going to Mopelia when we leave here. It's kind of tricky and I couldn't find a chart before we left home," Dick said.

"We've got a chart of Mopelia. I'll go back and get it for you," Bob said.

He left and I sat with Denise. "Come on with us," Denise said, "it would be so much fun. Then we can really show you New Zealand."

"I wish we could, but we have to go home."

I sat in the cockpit deep inside myself, not hearing the snatches of conversation that erupted around me. I felt like there were two of me occupying the same space. The universal "mother me" missed sharing love and participation in my children and grandchild's lives. On the other hand a second me had emerged over the last few months, the new "me" finding a unique bonding to mother earth, as well as acknowledging something had changed. The bond reminded me of a silk thread colored the deep blue of the ocean, resilient and strong. The further the thread pulled away from the cocoon the more liberated it became, free to find ways to weave itself into new life colors, and make itself useful, even taking a chances that might tear the tapestry of the old life. The more I thought about it, the more important it became. I didn't want to leave for my land home yet. My home existed where I slept each night, gently being rocked to sleep. We don't have to stop, I thought. Maybe we could work it out somehow. I wanted to go on with *California* to Tonga, Roratonga, and New Zealand.

Bob returned with the chart, telling Dick he could keep it because we wouldn't be needing it.

"Please, can't we go on with *California* to Mopelia too, then on to New Zealand. We could fly home for the wedding. I don't want to stop cruising," I pleaded.

Bob looked at me, surprised. "We've only planned this for a year. It's not fair for Bill to keep looking after our affairs. We don't have anyone living in our house anymore. We can't leave it empty."

Intellectually I knew he was right, but I didn't feel cerebral right now, only emotional and guilty at being selfish. I was being separated from my special friends and a way of life I loved. I started to cry and Denise hugged me, tears rolling down her face too. She took hold up my shoulders and held me away, "Buck up mate, we'll write and let you know what's going on. It doesn't look as if you'll be joining us this time."

"I don't want to go home now, please Bob, can't you think it over."

He shook his head, his face saddened. "It's hard for me too. I enjoy what we've been doing, but... " His turned his face and looked at everyone, then my Captain brushed the tears from my face, took my hand and helped me into the dinghy. He hugged Denise and Dick, Ginger and shook Tom's hand. "Have a safe voyage. We'll be thinking of you everyday."

We motored back to our boat in silence. Once inside Bob started making plans for the passage to the big island of Hawaii. I tried hard to be interested.

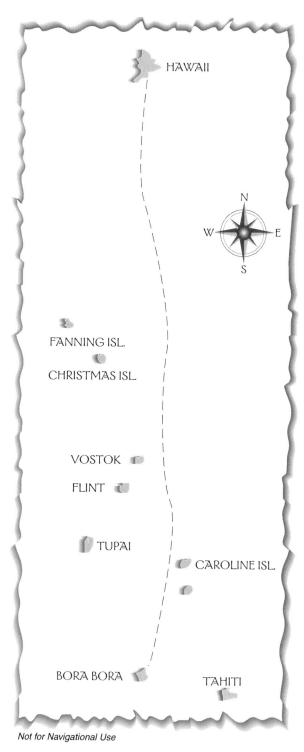

HAWAII

N
W   E
S

FANNING ISL.

CHRISTMAS ISL.

VOSTOK

FLINT

TUPAI

CAROLINE ISL.

BORA BORA

TAHITI

Not for Navigational Use

Chapter 25

SLIPPING ROUND THE HURRICANE TO HILO

Tom's Gone To Hilo
Tommy's gone, What shall I do
Hilo, hilo
Oh Tommy's gone, and I'll go too.
My Tom's gone to Hilo.
(*Halyard Chantey*)

I woke in the morning and made a pact with myself, no more whining about having to go home. Anyway, there were too many important jobs to do to get ready to leave, such as taking down the wind generator, deflating the rubber dinghy, putting on our self steering vane, Sven, securing the outboard motor, and making sure loose gear had been stowed. I went up forward and checked the space case filled with food items. Hmmm, I thought. I need to change where I keep that big jar of spaghetti sauce, but it looked protected enough for the time being. I'll get to it later.

Bob came into the cabin and stopped me, "Before we deflate the dinghy lets go over to the Oa Oa and take a nice hot shower. We won't have that luxury for eighteen days."

"Done. You sure know the way to a cruising woman's heart, through the shower."

We climbed into the dinghy and sped toward shore. I decided to take a couple of books with me to trade with the owner of the hotel, good books, because he wouldn't trade for trashy novels. The thought brought my spirits up.

Once back aboard we hauled the dinghy up, opened the air valves, and watched it wilt into a grey lump. A heavy lump. We wrapped it up in its bag and struggled down the companionway, stowing it away in the hanging closet. Bob sat down, breathing heavily, "I need another shower after that."

He returned to the nav station, and I picked up the log and wrote, July 13, 85, Saturday. While Bob studied charts I went up on deck. *California* had gone, and there were people running around on the deck of *Starlight*. I waved to them. Bob had turned the VHF radio on earlier, and after I waved I heard a voice saying, *"Maria Elena,* this is *Starlight,* how do you read?"

"Starlight, this is *Maria Elena.* I read you fine. Over"

"When are you going to Hilo?"

"We plan to leave around thirteen hundred. What are your plans?"

"I think we'll leave at the same time. We'll keep a radio watch and talk to you later."

"That's a roger. Good sailing to you. This is *Maria Elena* clear."

Around one we dropped our double line off the mooring buoy, taking a last look at the seven hundred foot basalt peaks reaching skyward, clothed in a wispy cover of angel hair clouds. We motored by tiny Motu Iti where Brad learned to swim, waving at the lush greenery and plush hibiscus blossoms. "Bye coral gardens," I said, remembering the tiny brilliant blue fish streaking in and out of brain coral formations in front of the Bora Bora hotel. Clams had partially opened up as we swam past, looking as if red sequins as been stitched to the edges. So much beauty and mystery dwelt in the blue ocean waters, portraying a microcosm of community life that lived below, some of it dangerous. Barracudas were known as the trash eaters of the sea, sometimes mistaking people for food, while gulls performed the same trash work above the water, but their focus on people was to use them as targets after their garbage runs. A variety of sharks roam the oceans and devour their prey in a feeding frenzy. Then there are different sharks on land, dressed as people tearing apart unsuspecting lives in a greed(ing) frenzy. So different, yet so alike.

Once out of the reach of the reef we put up our main, genoa and staysail, beating into a brisk fifteen knot wind from the east. The sun tried to break through the eighty percent cloud cover, and a threat of rain hovered in the dense air.

"I want you to steer 010 degrees to miss Motu Iti," Bob said.

"I'm glad we're going by it in the daylight. It's such a tiny atoll."

"Me too, but we've got radar."

By two the wind escalated to twenty knots, with the wind on our beam. *Maria* charged through the waves like a thoroughbred headed to the winner's circle, her bow tossing the foam off the wave tops and forcing it outward. I looked at the genoa, and then at Bob. "You know what I'm thinking don't you," I said.

"What you always say, too much sail."

"Have you looked at the knot meter? We're hitting nine at times."

"In that case, you're right. You gradually let out the sheet and I'll haul in the genoa line."

Carefully he stepped around the dodger, grasping the genoa line, pulling hard against the filled sail. Gradually it began to roll closed like a window shade, and the speed of the boat slackened.

"Good. We're riding easier now," I said.

"I'll keep the staysail up as much as possible. We need to make all the easting we can. If the wind dies we can put up the genny again."

By six that night the wind indicator read twenty five knots. No time to think of dinner, food would have to wait until we got the boat under control. I headed into the wind and Bob dropped the main boom into the gallows, brought the sail down part way and cranked in the first reef in the main. We kept the staysail up. Our knot meter read 7.8.

"How about something to eat," my Captain said.

"We're rolling around so much it will have to be a simple meal. I'll open up some cans of stew. We have fresh french bread though. That's all I can do."

He turned his head, "Are you feeling sea sick?"

"No, I'm afraid I've got a bladder infection. I don't understand why bacteria around here has to choose me for their convention center. This is the third time in three months."

"Oh honey, I'm so sorry. You sit up here and I'll get dinner. I'm pretty good with a can opener."

I sat down and wrapped a blanket around me. Even in the warm wind I felt chilly, and my head felt like somebody was using it for an anvil. Bob wolfed down his food, having worked up an appetite with sail handling. I barely picked at mine. After cleaning up the galley he came back to the cockpit. "Put your head in my lap," he said. "I'll rub your back for you."

The gentle rubbing eased some of the pain in my lower back, but before long I had to get up and visit the head. Blood. I searched the cupboard for medicine, praying I hadn't used it all up last time. My hand reached the last bottle of Bactrim that we bought in Mexico. That's all I can do now, I thought. Mother nature will have to take care of the rest. I hope.

Bob took the first watch and told me not to come up for mine. He would stand watch for both of us until I felt better. I went below and crawled into our bunk, feeling rotten and angry that this happened when I was needed.

At eleven I got up for my watch. "What are you doing out here," Bob demanded. "I told you to stay in bed."

"I couldn't sleep. It's stupid to stay there and roll around, when I can roll around up here on watch. Besides, you need your rest too as Captain. Admirals aren't quite as important."

"Are you sure?"

"Yes, go to bed."

At 0200 my watch was over and I called Bob. "I know I sound like a broken record, but it's too windy. We need to take down some more sail."

He looked at the knot meter and studied how the boat reacted. "You're right. We're driving the boat too hard." He dropped the staysail and I went to bed.

I may have been in bed, but the massive seas rolled me around the bunk like a marble on a glass table. For the first time since we said goodbye to *California* I was glad to be going on the first leg home. I was miserable, hurt all over and exhausted. Sleep finally came, but there were no dreams.

The next morning I dragged myself out of bed. Food helped, coffee the most. Bob and I sat in the cockpit looking like two lost souls. I seriously wondered if the good Lord was trying to tell us it was time to go home and be happy on land. I went below to get some juice out of the reefer. It felt warm.

"Bob," I called, turn on the engine. We need to run it for a couple of hours to cool down the reefer."

I heard the roar of the diesel start up. After an hour the engine alarm screamed at us. Bob shut the engine down,"Better see what's up now," he grumped.

After an hour he reappeared with a torn impeller. "I replaced the impeller in the raw water pump, but I'm keeping my fingers crossed. The brass cam is crumbling inside, so it may fail."

"That must have been a hard job with the boat is rolling around so much. I hope when we reach Hawaii we can buy a new cam. I thought for sure we could get a one in Papeete."

"Me too, but they're so many different engines from all over the world they couldn't possibly stock every part."

The rest of the morning we read books to take our minds off the weather. I heard the radio call for us. *Maria Elena,* this is *Starlight.*"

"Let's go to channel 68. How are you doing Jim?"

"Miserable. Jan is really sea sick, and the Walker Log got tangled up in our prop."

"Oh brother, that's rotten luck. Were you able to free it?"

"Yes, it took some doing, but I'm not calling this paradise any longer."

"We've had a rough time, but nothing like yours. Anything we can do?"

"Would you turn down the wind a bit, and stop the wave machine."

"Too big a job for me. Try Moses. He had good luck with the seas once."

"Thanks. We'll keep trucking' along. Sure will be glad to get to Hilo."

"Same here. We'll keep in touch. Tell Jan to hang in there. *Maria Elena* clear."

Jim must have gotten his message through. The seas calmed down somewhat during the night, and on my watch I caught sight of *Starlight* about five miles the east of us. It felt good to know someone sailed nearby. By 0340 I had to wake up Bob. *Otto* had rebelled and Bob had to replace two fuses and install a new relay while I took over the hand steering. He crawled back in bed and caught some ZZZZZ, but only an hour, 0500 started his watch.

The next morning Bob looked around, "The wind direction is all wrong. We have NW winds which is the worst. We'll have to come about and do some easting."

We came about, but *Maria* lost a lot on the tack. We stayed on a course of 60 degrees to east for awhile and waited for the wind to change, which we prayed it would. By eleven we came about again. The damn wind would not cooperate. We were now on a course of 305 degrees with the motor running about 1500 rpm. I felt like a rat running around in a cage, ending up in the same spot each time. I closed my eyes and rested for awhile. I woke up when Bob came on deck.

"How do I look?" Notice anything different?"

"You shaved off your mustache. Hurrah!"

He disappeared down below again, soon reappearing minus his side-
burns, and wearing a goatee. "What in the world are you doing?" I said.
"Playing shaving games?"

He didn't answer. He went below again, a cheshire grin on his shiny
face. Within ten minutes he stood in front of me completely clean
shaven, waiting for a big response. He got it. "At last I have my handsome
husband back again. Quick, give me a big kiss. I can't wait."

He took me in his arms and gave me a long, lingering kiss. "Ahhhh," I
said, "no whiskers sticking into my nose. And you really do look younger.
No more Old Man Of The Sea Hemingway look."

By July 18 the wind took a hike, except for a slight breeze which
blew right on our bow. The barometer had dropped to 29.90 and the
clouds began to look like there was rain inside of them. A change, hopefully good, would be on the way. I recorded the morning weather in our
log and was surprised to hear Bob yell an epithet,"Shit."

I poked my head below, "What now?"

"We just lost forty gallons of fresh water. Major problem."

"How in the world did that happen," I gasped.

"In all the heavy seas a part to the high pressure valve on the hot
water tank failed, dumping the fresh water in the bilge. I wondered why
the bilge pump went on, and that's when I searched for the problem."

"Thank God for our water maker. It may be slow, but at least it's water."

It was silly, but I suddenly felt thirsty again. Really dumb since I still
didn't like to drink water. It showed me how the imagination had taken
over, saying, "water, water, everywhere, but not a drop to drink." But I
wasn't too far off. The wind had taken a powder, leaving us floating
around on a surface so glassy calm it appeared to have been oiled.

Nighttime found us relaxed and sated after dinner. Bob picked up the
South Pacific Sailing Directions, "Tonight, in an hour or so, we watch for
one small island. I've figured out a course to take us well off the reef."

"What's it called?"

"Flint Island. It's about two and a half miles long and only a half mile
wide, but it's surrounded by a high fringe of coral reef. In fact the north
end of the reef extends out three quarters of a mile."

"Definitely one to miss. When you say fringe it sounds more like fangs."

An hour later Bob turned on the radar, leaving it to warm up. "The
book says the island gives a good radar return. I'll check it out in a
minute."

I looked down the companionway sideways from my seat. Bob's body
bent over the radar monitor, when suddenly his head came up. "Oh my

326

God, we're only a half a mile away." He ran to the chart, then checked the book. The book gave the latitude and longitude as 11 degrees, 26 minutes S, and 151 degrees, 48 minutes W. "That damn island is charted at least five miles off. I'll change course right away. We're too close to the reef at the north end."

He changed course, and then checked the radar screen again. We were all right, but the sweat running down our face had nothing to do with the heat. The rest of the night's activity went smoothly, just water ahead, nothing else.

The next day we baked like muffins under the sun shield, our bare skin cruising clothes turning a slight shade darker. Our fingers wet the pages in our books as we turned them, and salty sweat formed under us on the cushions we sat on. It helped to hear the water maker working away like a little Trojan. I could close my eyes and pretend we had our own sparkling water fall tumbling into our tank. I checked the barometer. It had started to rise. At home that would have meant good weather, but I've noticed in this part of the world it meant rain and wind. We had been running the engine to keep headway, necessitating some refueling. We added thirty three gallons to the port tank. By seven that night we finally felt a cooling breeze out of the east, thrilled to see the knot meter read seven knots with the Genoa, Main and Staysail up.

It had been six days since we left Bora Bora. I no longer suffered from an infection, and both Bob and I were adjusting to keeping the three on, three off watch. That didn't mean we weren't tired however. I took my 0200 watch, forcing my eyes to stay open. The wind had swept the sky clean, so that each star twinkled, especially those of Orion's belt. "Hello there," I whispered. "You going to keep me company on watch? If you could talk it would help me stay awake."

They didn't talk, but the radar alarm sure did, startling me out of my seat. "Beeeeeeep, Beeeep," it jangled. I jumped up and reached for the binoculars, training them on the horizon. A series of lights shone in the distance. We kept the VHF channel 16 radio on in case of emergencies, and out of the blackness of the night I heard, "Sailboat off my port bow, proceeding to Hawaii, do you read?"

"This is the sailboat *Maria Elena* on the way to Hawaii. Good evening sir, how can I help you."

"I am a Dutch freighter on my way to Papeete from Honolulu. I thought you would like to know that your mast head light is visible for fifteen miles."

"Thank you so much. That's good to know. Even though it's illegal we don't use our running lights on an ocean crossing. That's why we run with just the mast head light."

"Understood. Sailboat running lights are hard to see. What was the harbor in Papeete like. Very crowded?"

"Sorry, I'm afraid it's been six weeks since we were there. It has probably changed since then."

"Well thank you anyway. Have a good night."

"You too. Hope the harbor isn't too full and that you have a good journey also. *Maria Elena* out."

Now I was jazzed and awake. Not only did I have my friend Orion's Belt, but a friendly Dutch freighter to boot. I'm sure the crewman who called me needed a voice to cure his boredom too.

In the morning Bob checked our navigation, thrilled to see we had come 138 miles in twenty four hours. "Hey, not bad for slow poke *Maria*," I said. "These twenty knot winds are elbowing us closer to Hawaii all the time."

"I'm going to put out the fishing pole and see if we can pick up anything," Bob said.

I murmured something, not looking up from my book. Suddenly I heard the zing of the line paying out from the pole. I looked around expecting to see Bob, but he was no where in sight. "Hey," I called out, "where are you?"

"In the head. I'll be right up."

"Better hurry, the fishing line has caught something."

He came rushing up the companionway steps, past me to the stern and started to reel in the line. "Oh, we caught something all right," he said, "our trailing generator. It seems to be wrapped all around it."

"Great. That line is a pain in the butt to haul in."

Bob started yanking on the eighty foot line to the trailing generator. As he pulled it from the water the line fell behind him, coiling itself in kinks all over the deck like an arthritic snake. Between kinks and cutting filament line, it took Bob and I nearly an hour to make the eighty foot problem into a normal rope again. "Are you going to put the pole out again?"

"Yes, but I won't let the fishing line trail back as far this time."

At 2100 hours that night I heard the familiar zingggggggg again. Bob had been in bed only an hour when I went down and woke him up. "You forgot to take in the fishing line in at dusk. I heard the line pay out again. I have no idea what it caught this time," I said.

"Damn," my Captain replied, rubbing his tired eyes and rolling out the bunk. "Why didn't you bring it in?"

"Admirals do windows, Captains do fish lines."

He wandered back to the stern, not showing a great deal of enthusiasm when reeling in the line. Abruptly he called out, "What in the world do I have. Get a bucket. This thing is so ugly I'm not getting near it while it's alive. Turn on the spreader lights"

I went down below and grabbed the biggest bucket we owned, switched on the lights, and went aft. He had just finished reeling in something long and hideous. He held the pole at arm's length away from his body, and I saw a three foot black eel like body swinging at the end. Large yellow eyes stared out from its narrow head, and fang like teeth lined its mouth. Bob carefully dropped it into the bucket for the night. We turned out the lights.

The next morning Bob held the dead fish up high while I took several pictures. "I don't think it's an eel, or a barracuda," I said. "With those big eyes I wonder if it lives in deep water. I'll get our fish book and see if I can find out what it is."

We both looked at descriptions, pictures, but nothing resembled this baby at all. It looked as if the fish would remain a mystery until we got home and could take it to the Steinhardt Aquarium's ichthyologist.

The next day I called Lori by Ham radio. I felt so homesick when I heard that happy voice, and the enthusiasm it showed when I told her we were on our way home. A twinge of guilt returned when I thought how I had made such a fuss about not wanting to come home. How could I have even contemplated missing out being part of such a special wedding. We couldn't talk long because the band dropped down.

At 0700 I wrote in my log. I recorded force five, thirty five knot winds, thirty percent cloud cover, barometer 29.92. I stopped and looked around. A beautiful day, clear up to the time I walked up forward and my feet went squish in the rug. Oh hell, what now. At least we aren't bored because nothing happens. I poured a cup of coffee and took it to Bob. "Guess what. The rug is soaked up forward."

"You have such nice things to say in the morning. Let me drink my coffee before I even think about it."

He tasted the water in the rug and found it salty. We had been taking green water over the bow for days, and some of it had found its way down the anchor chain into an area that spilled down the rug. "I'll try and wrap duct tape around the chain area on deck and see if we can slow down the flow."

The next morning, Bob held the dead fish up high while I took several pictures.

By the afternoon the winds came up stronger, shipping volumes of green water over the deck and down the chain again. I took out all the beach towels and tried to build a dam to keep the main saloon from being inundated. I accomplished one thing, the towels got very wet, and so did the rug. Our crossing to the Marquesas began to feel like a trip in the bath tub compared to this one.

The next day the skies were leaden, and the seas lumped up like some Thanksgiving gravy. It took great effort to keep our balance when we tried to do anything. The winds reached twenty five knots ENE and I told my same story, "Too much sail." The Captain took down the genoa and reefed the main. I went back to the ham radio and tuned in a weather station. I copied down the report, and what I heard did not make my day. I went up on deck right away. "I just heard that a hurricane and one tropical depression right behind it is at N 14.7, 144W, moving eight knots on a course of 285. The winds were somewhere between 74 and 93 at the center, but fifty knot winds were in the fifty mile radius and thirty five knot winds were in the 134 mile radius."

Bob sucked on his teeth, frowned and went below and checked our position. We were at N 0.05 and 149.38 W. "I'm going to chart in the hurricane along with our position. We'll have to watch this very carefully. If it gets too close we'll make a run to Fanning Island." He came over and gave me a hug. "Don't worry. Things will work out. Just keep getting the weather and coordinates and give them to me right away."

By 1500 the wind abated somewhat and Bob put up the genoa again. Sort of reminded me about the whore's knickers again, up and down. He rechecked his navigation and factored in that we had SW set of 1.8 knots which tried to push us westward and backward. "It really slows us down," he said.

"I've got a ham schedule with Greg on the Seafarers Net at 0400Z. Shall I give him our coordinates when I talk with him?"

"Yes, might as well cover all our options."

At 0400Z I heard the call, "N6LDM, this WD6 EHG calling."

"This is N6LDM, WD6 EHB. Can you hear me well enough?"

"Yes, go to 1435 and down, I'll call you."

We found each other on the frequency. I explained about the hurricane and gave him our position, asking what else was new. "I talked with Bill the other night," he said. "He's doing just fine. I'll give him a call after we finish tonight."

"Don't worry him too much about the weather. It's hard on him being in one place, and us in another."

"Say, I have some good news for you and Bob. Charlie said you could use his guest house when you get to Oahu. He has a caretaker who will pick you up and bring you there."

"Fantastic Greg. First we have to get to Hilo. We plan to stay about a week and then go to Ali Wai in Honolulu."

"Great Marlene. I have to be gone for a couple of weeks. I'll try and find you again on the Seafarer's net. This is WD6EHB clear with N6LDM."

"Seventy Threes Greg, N6LDM clear with WD6EHB"

I told Bob the good news that his former boss was letting us use his home in Ohau. The rest of the night the conditions remained good. In the morning I turned on WWV on the ham radio and listened to the details about Hurricane Ignacio. It was located at 15 degrees N, 144 W. The winds had increased to 100 to 135 knots. We were presently located at 01.28 degree N, 149 W. A new hurricane arrived called Jamina, located at 17 degrees N, 114W. We were surrounded so to speak.

I relayed the "good" news to Bob. "Maybe we will be able to wait until Ignacio goes by and slip in the Hilo before Jamina comes," he said.

"Anything you say Captain. I trust your judgment. One thing though, *Otto* is acting up. I think that means reef time in the main to take the strain off the rudder."

"I think you love to get me out on the foredeck to reef and wear me out."

"Could be," I laughed. "Could be."

Each day started with the weather report, hurricane position, then our position. I think we're winning, but things can change in a short time, I thought. Sometimes the seas calmed down and gave me hope for a smoother ride, then the seas would agitate again like an old washer, swishing us back and forth. We didn't get any cleaner, just wetter below. We were now six hundred miles from hurricane Ignacio. I reached a ham operator in Kuai who gave me the Coast Guard weather frequencies, and the Hawaiian Disaster frequency. I felt like a boy scout, always prepared.

We woke up to a solid wall of overcast, unstable air. It was spooky-quiet and sticky outside. The following seas remained fairly calm, pushing us closer to our destination. Abruptly the wind hauled around ninety degrees, and put us on a close reach. The sky changed to heavy clouds arranged in a straight line, with an ominous black curtain looming behind them. Other clouds washed out of the sky and rested on the water like rolling fog. I checked the weather report, happy to hear the hurricane was moving very slowly to the west. It would miss the big island of Hawaii. But I still wondered what lay ahead.

While on watch that night a large school of dolphins leaped and frolicked in front our bow, then chased each as if they were playing tag, coming back in a few minutes for another run at us. The phosphorescence in the water made the trails look like torpedo runs. It made me laugh. More good news, we made 158 miles good in twenty four hours.

The big seas returned. I sat in the cockpit with my feet pushed against the bulkhead, trying to keep my balance while writing in our log. It was July 28, a Sunday, and the winds blew twenty five, with seas that jerked us in a fast conga line movement. The rough water whacked the hull, with some of it making its way down to join the rug. Bob yipped as he was thrown off his seat in the nav station. The violent rocking action dislodged something below, and we both heard a big crash. "What was that?" I yelled above the wail of the wind."

Bob went forward. "You won't want to know. It's a mess."

I scrambled down the companionway and was thrown immediately into the stove. "Ouch. What did you find?"

"Come here and see."

I squished across the rug and saw a blue space case, once filled with food, now empty. Ohmigosh, I thought. I had forgotten to move the spaghetti sauce. I stared down at the floor and saw what amounted to a home made omelet of two dozen broken eggs, catsup, green salsa, and that darn spaghetti sauce. The egg yoke yellow, combined with bright red catsup, salsa, and sauce ran together into a gooey ooze like finger painting material, filling in the spaces between the rough shag rug. The hot air in the cabin acted like an oven, and food began to congeal on the floor. It was far too stormy to try and clean it up. I made lunch, but we had a hard time trying to hold on to it and eat. Bob looked over, "We should have the tubes of food the astronauts use in space."

"I'd settle for some lack of gravity that didn't slam me into everything."

We continued to have harsh weather. The winds howled to thirty five, throwing green water clear over the dodger. According to the weather report we are in the midst of a tropical depression, which explained the weather extremes. Neither of us felt one hundred percent. It's either that horrible mess below cooking away in the heat, or bone tiredness from lack of rest. The smell of food and salt water organisms emanating from below was horrendous. Bob got a call on the radio from *Starlight.* They were equally miserable. Misery likes company, and if they had been having a good time, I really would have been miserable. Shame on me.

At last the seas calmed down, the storm front had passed us going west. I tapped Bob on the shoulder, "I'm going below and try to clean up that mess."

"I'll help you later. I have some navigating to do."

"I wish I did."

First I scraped up the loose stuff with a spatula, emptying it in a bucket. Then I poured liquid laundry soap on the rug, adding precious fresh water to suds it up. A pitiful amount of suds sat limply on the rug. I couldn't use much fresh water to rinse, so now we were stuck with food products, salt water, and stinky soap.

I opened my log and wrote, "0900 July 31, Sunday We can see the big island of Hawaii!" I put the book down, "With the overcast and low profile it would be easy to miss the southern part of the island, wouldn't it."

"Dick said when there's cloud cover and rain you could miss it if you're not close in. He heard of a boat searching for the island for two weeks in low cloud cover."

"The mountain is thirteen thousand feet tall."

"Yes, but covered up with clouds it might as well be two feet."

"True."

I glanced around the boat, seeing nothing but dirt. "I don't know where it all comes from at sea. I'm going to make a clean sweep, fore and aft."

For the next two hours I scrubbed the decks and cockpit with salt water, reclaiming the boat from its untidy condition. Since we were close enough we both took showers, using more water than usual, and reveling in it. We searched the horizon several times, but no sign of *Starlight*. We would try to contact them on radio after we reached Hilo to make sure they were all right. I chattered away, happy to be coming into land when Bob stopped me."Are you all ready?"

"Of course I'm ready. The boat is clean and so am I. I've thrown away all the products we're not allowed to bring in to the United States. What else is there?"

"Are you sure you want to go in like that?"

I rushed down and put on shorts and a top. It was after one when we rounded buoy #1 into Hilo Harbor. It looked like there was space for us to back in. Once in we would meet immigration and food inspector. I wondered what he would think of the mess below?

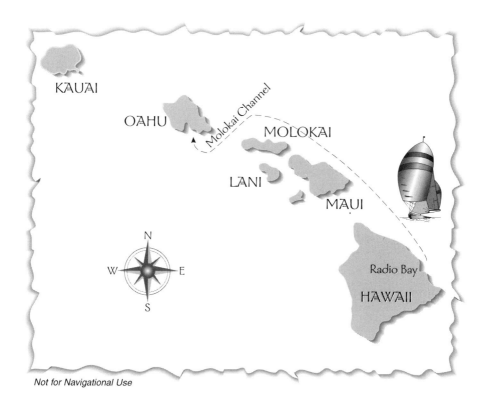

Not for Navigational Use

Chapter 26

TOO BAD WE DON'T PLAY GOLF

The Praise of Sailors
"As I lay musing in my bed,
Full of warm and well at ease,
I thought upon the lodging hard
Poor sailors have at seas.
When as the raging seas do foam,
And lofty winds do blow,
The sailors they go to the top
When landsmen stay below."

(Sea Chantey, The Praise of Sailors)

Bob herded the boat through anchored boats, circling and getting the lay of the land in Radio Bay. When he satisfied himself which position he wanted at the dock, I took over and he went up forward to take out the pin in our main anchor. We would have to back in, dropping a bow anchor along the way, just like Papeete. He signaled when ready and I backed down to slow the motion of the boat. Nothing happened.

"What's going on,?" I yelled.

Bob's stormy face turned, "I can't her a word you're saying."

Oh, I thought, we're back to that again. He appeared to be pulling, kicking at the chain, finally stomping on the deck. I never heard the anchor so I figured things were not going as planned. He brushed by me and hurried down below. He came back up, "Chain is all tangled. I have to drop the Bruce."

I waited, then heard the splash, backing down toward the dock. He watched the markings on the nylon line, satisfied at last he had let out enough scope, and returned to take wheel. "The chain lumped together in the heavy seas. It wouldn't go out at all. We'll have to pull it out on deck and redo it later."

Slowly he backed in. A man walking down the docks waved to me, offering to help. I threw him a stern line. "Thanks," I called to him. "That's a big help."

"Glad I could be here for you. Welcome to Hilo. You can call the immigration people on that phone," pointing the direction we would need to go.

He walked away, and we finished tying up the rest of the lines, making sure we were secure. Hilo Bay had a reputation of having heavy swells during bad weather. Bob left the boat to call immigration and customs. Before long a heavy set man arrived in uniform to check us in. He hoisted his big frame aboard, his large brown eyes casually inspecting the outside of the boat. He let himself down hard in the cockpit. The air escaping from the pad under him echoed like a whoopie cushion, taking each of us by surprise. Our inspector ignored the noise, and told us he played two roles, immigration and customs. Bob furnished the necessary boat papers, as well as our passports. The officer opened the packet, "I see you left from Bora Bora. You like it there?"

"We loved it," Bob said.

"I've heard it's great. Never been there myself. Now, what do you have aboard to declare?"

Bob and I looked at each other. "All we bought were tee shirts from different countries. There wasn't room to buy anything big," I said.

"No art objects."

"No, too large and expensive," Bob said.

"How about eggs, meat, cheese, fresh fruits."

"None," I said. "I threw those things to the fish before we came in."

"I see here you have guns. You'll have to take them in to Hilo to the police station and register them. Okay, I'll go below now and take a look."

I stepped in front of him. "Before you go down I have to warn you about the smell."

"The smell?" he said. "From what?"

"A space case fell over and dumped two dozen eggs and spaghetti sauce on the rug . That was quite a few days ago, and I must say it's kind of rare down below."

He started down the steps, stopped and turned to me with a sour expression, "You weren't kidding lady when you said it stunk. I'll make it quick."

He carefully avoided the discolored area, wrinkled up his nose, and swiftly walked from cabin to cabin. "All done here. Welcome to Hawaii." He made his way up the steps, glanced back toward the rug, "Don't know what you can do about that," disappearing as fast as his rolling gait could take him away from the boat.

"I guess we really do reek," I said. "We must have gotten used to it for the last week. Now that we're down here will you help me pull the rug out and up on deck. I'll need the hose so I can wash the living daylights out of this with soap and water. Hopefully the sun will sanitize it a little."

I worked a long time up topside, then went below to wash the plywood floor where the rug lived. Bob went forward and began hauling the tangled chain up on deck, laying it out in long loops. We were both exhausted by dinner time. I knew I wasn't going to cook, and Bob didn't want to use the can opener, so we walked into town and chowed down on Chinese food. We came home and slept like the dead for a full ten hours.

We tried to get *Starlight* on the radio several times. No joy. Bob went over to a newly arrived boat called *Aquarian III* to see anyone aboard had seen the gaff rigged ketch *Starlight*. When Bob returned he said the skipper had seen the boat about seventy miles out. "Jim must be having some trouble," Bob said, his voice taking on a worried tone.

We rented a car and declared our guns in town, then became ordinary tourists, going snorkeling on a boat trip, seeing Kilaua volcano in action, learning about lava tubes and cones, and passing well kept golf courses. We stopped and looked into small local harbors near Kona to see if *Starlight* happened to be tied up. No one remembered seeing a boat of that description. We felt stuck because there were not many places for transit boats to tie up, or hide.

We walked into a boat store in Hilo to see if they had some engine parts we could buy. "Sorry," the clerk said, "we have to order all those parts from Honolulu."

"You've fishing boats around here. Don't you keep parts in stock for them?"

"Like I said, we order them from Honolulu," the clerk retorted. "But if you people like to play golf we have some good courses."

"Thanks, but no thanks. Golf clubs were not on our list to bring on the boat."

Three days later we tried *Starlight* again. Still no joy. Bob set the microphone down. "Maybe they missed the island and went on to Oahu."

"I don't know, the immigration officer could have some news. I see a new boat coming in the harbor now."

A beautiful fifty foot sailboat, called *Mockingbird,* eased into the space next to us. Bob jumped off our boat to help them with their lines. He looked at the Canadian flag, "You just get in from the South seas, or Canada?"

A tired skipper looked down at him, "Canada, the weather was very rough and stormy. We're exhausted. Thanks for your help. We're sure glad to get here because my crew has to get back to British Columbia. We didn't expect the trip to take this long."

"After you've rested come on over for a drink. You can tell us all about your crossing."

"Sounds great. I'll tell the crew."

A short time later the immigration officer arrived and boarded *Mockingbird.* He climbed down later carrying a few forbidden items in a sack. Bob hailed him, "John, have you heard anything about that gaff rigger *Starlight?*"

"Yes, matter of fact I did. I got a call from the skipper in Kona. He said they had engine problems and a blown out sail. They had slipped down west so far they didn't want to beat up to Hilo. He's going to rent a car and bring the boat papers here. Don't like doing a check in that way. They should have come in here regardless."

We were relieved to know *Starlight* had made it to the island. So much can happen in the open ocean, not all of it nice.

Later we met the skipper and crew of *Mockingbird,* and traded sea stories. They left soon after to get a well earned rest. We knew exactly how they felt.

Time passed swiftly, and we realized it had been a week since we arrived. "On to Oahu," Bob said. He returned the car to the rental agency and proceeded to get the boat ready for our voyage to Ali Wai, Honolulu. "Looks like rain," he mused. "And to make it worse, no wind."

By two that afternoon we had upped anchor and motored out into rough seas. "You would complain about the wind," I said. "Look at the meter now, it's thirty five knots. Nasty." My stomach rolled around inside as acid bile walked around in my throat.

"Are you seasick?" Bob asked.

"Unfortunately, yes. I haven't been sea sick for months, and I don't know why I should get sick now."

That night the wind whistled in the rigging, and giant eighteen foot waves punished *Maria's* sides. Despite the unholy movement I slept soundly, curled up in my bunk after my three hour watch. A hand shook my shoulder, "Get up, I need you to head to wind while I reef the main."

I unstuck my tongue, "Yes Captain. Give the Admiral a second to get her bearings." I noticed it was midnight, only an hour since I had gotten off watch.

We both put on foul weather gear and headed for the cockpit. The wind swept spray off the top of the swells, throwing it into our face and covering our slickers. "Give it some more RPM," Bob yelled, as I tried to keep the boat headed into the wind. I pushed the throttle forward, revving up the engine until the boat balanced between waves long enough to drop the boom into the gallows. He pulled down the sail to the first reef. "Okay, you can fall off," he yelled back at me. He returned to the cockpit, his hair plastered to his head, white with salt. "Thanks, you can go back to bed now."

He didn't have to tell me twice.

The next day the sun shown down on us, warming up the cockpit and us too. We sat like two zombies who had been out all night scaring people. "Let out the genny," Bob said. "The wind is behind us now. I'll let out the main."

In the twenty five knot wind the boat moved ahead like she had been goosed. The knot meter read eight and a half. The swells had pumped themselves up to only eight to twelve feet, more my style of sailing.

Bob went below and worked on his navigation, bringing our position on the chart up to date. "We've been going so fast we're going to get to Ali Wai by two in the morning."

"Will we really have to stay out till morning?"

"Probably. I won't go into a strange harbor in the dark. If I happen to be able to pick out the range markers we might try it."

We sailed through the Molokai channel with relative ease, catching sight of Diamond Head. The harbor we looked for was Ala Wai, two and a half miles northwest of Diamond Head. We sailed closer, finally taking down the sails and turning on the motor. Bob stared at the entrance. "I think I see a range marker." He pointed, "See the yellow lights in those trees." He checked the compass, and picked up the guide book. "It says look for three blue neon-light rings on top of a building. They supposed to be off to the left of the range markers. I've got a good line on the markers now. Go up on deck and see if you can pick out the day markers with the flashlight."

"I'm thanking God for your eyesight," I said. "Now if we can only find a place to put this boat."

We threaded our way past the fuel dock, the Hawaii Yacht Club, both full. A little distance beyond I saw an open side tie at the end of a series of docks. "Let's go there," I yelled, "at this time of night the owners won't be coming back." I hope, I said to myself.

We tied up, dropped like the dead into our bunk and slept for three hours. Bob got up and dressed while I made coffee. After breakfast we walked over to the Hawaii Yacht Club to see if there would be any place to put *Maria*. The harbor master greeted us with good news. "You see that boat over there," he pointed to the end of the guest dock. "One of the transpac boats. She's leaving today for the mainland. You can stay for two weeks. That's all. It's a hundred dollars a week."

Bob had his credit card out so fast it almost blinded the poor man. Hurrah! We were in a first class spot, safe, showers, walking distance to most anything we would need. We reached paradise again. But first, we must find a rental car that would be cheap. Impossible, maybe, but Bob had an idea that might be creative. We had picked up a flyer in town that read, "Come to a two hour presentation of a Time Share Condominium at 11:00 at the Hawaii Sunshine Condominiums. We will give you a rental car with air conditioning for a week, only $50.00." A map showed directions to the Condo complex. Bob looked at his watch, "We've only fifteen minutes to get to the presentation. Time we have lots of, money less. Are you game? Maybe it will be interesting enough to consider a Time Share Condo."

"Sure, they can use our ears, and we can use their car."

We walked rapidly toward the complex, passing hotels, coffee shops, tee shirt shops, and bars with Hawaiian music drifting lazily out the doors. We reached the Condo complex and dashed in, sitting down in the midst of twenty five other men and women in a large conference room. A well dressed woman in her early thirties stood up, "Welcome to Hawaiian Sunshine Condominiums." her voice silky with promise. "We are pleased to have you join us, and learn about how you can own a piece of Hawaii, a vacation place where you and your family will spend many happy years."

I looked around and saw an older couple clasp their hands together, their smiles cracking through the rows of sun created wrinkles. Several other couples shifted in their seats in anticipation.

The saleswoman spread her arms out toward the audience. "I can see by your smiles that you are anxious to find out what a wonderful opportunity we are going to give you. Later I will divide you into smaller groups so that we can take you into the different apartments. As you walk through these beautifully appointed rooms I want you to think how you and your family will enjoy the views, sitting comfortably in a big chair looking out at the blue waters, having a Mai Tai on the balcony, just relaxing in one of Americas most famous vacation spots. Think about whether you want a one, two, or three bedroom Condo that will just fit your special needs."

Some people moved in their seats, ready to follow the saleswoman anywhere to see this place in paradise. Bob looked at me and rolled his eyes. "Hard sell," he whispered. "Wait till they get to the kill."

A man stood and took the woman's place. He was tall, blonde with an athletic tan, a picture of health and happiness. I looked down at his shoes, suede. Oh, oh, I thought. Beware of salesmen wearing shoes of suede. His smile seemed to incorporate everyone in the room, pulling you into some secret that he held just for you. "Now is the time to buy before the prices go up. You buy today at the present value of money, not tomorrow's value, when you might not be able to afford these beautiful places. It's that word inflation. You and I know first hand what inflation does to each of us, eating up our income, then rising again the next year. After your initial investment all you will have to do is pay for incidentals like upkeep, and a few condo fees. Renting out your time share will pay for that. I won't keep you any longer because I know how anxious you are to see these apartments. Follow Miss Mahafty and me to the thrill of your life."

We stood with the others and trailed after a group of five, wandering in and out of different apartments that somehow all began to look the same. We did appreciate the view from the windows of the outside apartments. Little giggles wafted out the doors as people imagined themselves living like kings and queens in their own condominium, drinking those Mai Tai that would never taste the same back in Iowa.

Very soon we were rushed back into the big room, each small group sitting around a table set for six. An earnest young man, looking hot in a suit, tie and vest, greeted us. "I have some costs sheets at each place. I'll give you a few moments to look these over." We picked up the papers and read through the fact sheet. Afterward Bob's face looked quite serious. "Now," said the young man, who is ready to buy the first unit?" He stared at Bob.

"Not me," Bob said. "I don't think I'm interested. I've read over the fact sheets and it's not as good a deal for me as you make out."

"Tell me," he went on hurriedly, "if you did want one, which one would you choose, one, two or three bedroom?"

"No bedroom," Bob said, no condo, no nothing."

Several people looked at Bob as if he was some sort of a traitor, frowning, and making little clucking noises in the back of their throats. Others looked uncertain, as if they missed something. The embarrassed young man rose, muttering out loud, "I wonder what I did wrong," hurrying over to the tall, athletic salesman, Mr. Haggarty. The two of them returned to our table, Mr. Haggarty addressed Bob. What seems to be the problem?"

"I don't have a problem. I've read over your financial fact sheet, and I agree that thirty percent of the costs would be stable, because that includes your initial investment. But the other seventy percent would definitely be subject to inflation. That would include all the services, upkeep and taxes. Quite a hunk of change."

The salesman furrowed his brow and licked his lips, "I'm sure the others here don't believe that number, but you have a right to your opinion."

Bob pulled out the slip saying we would get a car for $50.00.

Mr. Haggerty tossed his head, "If you'll just step over there by the window I'll get back to you after I finish with these fine people. You will just have to wait."

Bob and I got up slowly, wandering over to the window. I whispered, "Now what? I feel like a kid who's been sent to her room for bad behavior."

"Mr. Haggerty didn't like my numbers."

"You could have told him you had been the chief financial officer for a major company and knew how to number crunch through hype."

"That would only antagonize him. He didn't want me influencing other people."

After twenty minutes of wandering around by the window, staring longingly out at the blue ocean and totally ignored by the sales manager, Bob cleared his throat and said in a loud voice, "Can't see how anyone could fall for that seventy percent being anything but an inflationary item."

Heads snapped in our direction, chairs scraped as people shifted uncomfortably, looking hard at the salesman at each table with a questioning look. Mr. Haggarty leaped from the table and went directly to Miss Mahafty. In a low, but distinct tone he snarled, "Get that couple out right now. They're ruining it. Give them the damn car."

She strode quickly toward us, her high heels clicking like castanets on the wood floor. With an icy expression she handed us the coupon we needed. We smiled and thanked her, leaving silently. One car coming up, I thought happily. It was worth the lecture. Indeed it was, red in color, and a dream to drive. Paid for with present value money.

Now that we had a car we became tourists again, going to Pearl Harbor for the Arizona tour. Bob had been eleven, and I had been nine when the Japanese bombed Pearl Harbor. In the early forties the war had an unreal quality to us as kids, never having heard a bomb go off, or been shot at and seen people die. But adults had memories of past wars. Unlike some of his friends who's fathers had to go off to war two, Bob's father had died two years before Pearl Harbor. My father had been too old. Our family war effort had been taken up in wrapping tin foil in big balls, buying, or selling war stamps, or helping to plant a victory garden. My garden mostly grew what we fertilized the soil with, potato and carrot peels. I did get a few carrots and tiny potatoes, but giant worms ate up the tomatoes. I secretly would have paid my mother not to plant peas. When forced to eat them I swallowed them whole like pills. I also remembered the big gas ration stamps, not being able to buy beef often, and rationed butter. The closest to war I felt had been during the blackouts, and one time when we heard the air raid siren and had to move our beds into the hallway. I had shivered all over thinking our house would be bombed any minute. Later people said a Japanese submarine had come into Santa Monica Bay. So when we arrived in Pearl Harbor I didn't know what to expect. I had seen old movies of the raid, but now we were actually here in person. We boarded the tour boat, listening to a tape that depicted an attack. We heard the whine of bombs and rapid explosions, visualizing the horror of sailors and civilians screaming, bodies being blown apart, men buried alive under ship decks, dying, trying to get help, failing. As the tape ended silence struck out as a physical blow. Slowly, solemnly the guide stretched out her arm, dropping the flowered lei into the moving water in memory of those who died. Both Bob and I had tears running down our face. He remembered these awful sounds of war in Korea. I was just beginning to hear and understand the impact.

On our way back to the boat we both retreated into our thoughts. Quiet refreshed our spirits us as we passed commercial shipyards, big and small shopping centers, and an old clipper ship called *Falls of Clyde*. If anything could perk Bob up it would be a clipper ship, smelling of old tar and hemp, huge masts reaching to the sky, with yard arms out-stretched, waiting for sailors to embrace them while trying to wrap a cumbersome, flapping sail. He smiled, "I guess it's time to go back to our own time frame and get ready for the trip home. Let's see if we can find the cam for the pump."

"Do you know which pump it is?"

He reached into his pocket and pulled out a slip of paper. "I brought the serial number with me."

Within a mile we saw a sign, "Ship Chandlery," where we might be able to buy the cam for the raw water pump. Bob took out the slip of paper and handed the serial number to the clerk. He opened up a draw-er where dozens of cams lay piled up on top of each other.

"Why doesn't the manufacturer put new cams in the major rebuilt kits?" he asked the clerk.

"Beats me. They leave that out, and put in a part that has to have spe-cialized tools to be pressed on. The guy that thinks out these things does-n't have a boat in salt water. You don't have any tools for pressing on a bearing do you?"

"Of course not. I'll take four of those cams. Now that I have them I'll probably never need a new one again."

"You're right about that," laughed the clerk.

"Let me ask a silly question. Why have I seen so few marinas in the islands."

"Ali Wai is the only big marina, and it has a waiting list of several years. Some of the other harbors are wide open. They could put in a breakwater and build a marina, but instead they keep carving out more golf courses. Sure makes it hard to sell boats."

We shook our heads. Politicians must play a lot of golf.

Back on the boat I noticed the wash had begun to build up. Civilization had one big drawback, we had to wear clothes that would require a washer and a dryer. I suggested Bob call the caretaker and visit his old boss's home. "We were invited you know."

"I know. I feel a little funny about it, but my curiosity is too much. The place was always one of Charlie's favorites."

After the phone call we packed the car with clothes, and the multiplying wash, knowing that the house would be equipped with all the emenities. We arrived at a beautiful five thousand square foot home with a pool, located next to the beach where white sands carpeted the area, and crushing waves pounded the shores. Heaven, I thought. We unpacked the car and went inside. Culture shock shook us as we stared at the king sized bed, a bathroom the size of two thirds of our boat, long hall ways, modern kitchen with lots of water, pictures that didn't need to be screwed to the walls, long couches beckoning someone to sit down and relax. It was too much. We, who had been used to forty one feet up, and forty one feet back, held on to each other as if we might get swallowed up in this immense space. Later that night in bed Bob sat up, "I forgot to get my water and the kitchen is miles away. Pack me a lunch to tide me over on the trip."

The two days we spent flew by at mach speed. It was time to get back to the boat, and make lists of things needed for the trip home. The real voyage lay ahead, returning to a different life, our home which would need repairs, to family, to hugs and kisses from grandchildren, to old friends. Leaving behind adventures, new friends, new experiences, more chances to experience nature and life, and how they co-exist. Once again I felt like two people, but on thinking it through, mostly one. Something deep inside of me really did want to go home.

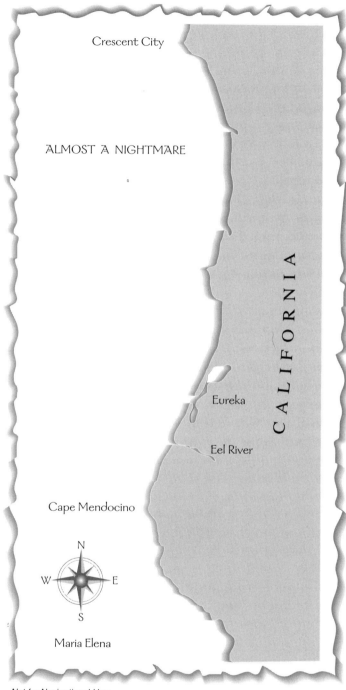

Crescent City

ALMOST A NIGHTMARE

CALIFORNIA

Eureka

Eel River

Cape Mendocino

N
W — E
S

Maria Elena

Not for Navigational Use

Chapter 27

HOMEWARD BOUND

Goodbye, fare-ye well
"Oh don't ye hear the old man say?
Goodbye fare-ye-well, goodbye fare-ye-well.
Oh don't you hear the old man say?
Hooraw me boys, we're homeward bound."

(Sea Chantey,)

At 0630 I opened my eyes. Sunlight filtered through the hatch, bathing our bunk in the soft glow of dawn. I closed my eyes again and curled up closer to Bob, putting my arm around his middle. He stirred, "Better be thinking of getting up," he murmured.

I snuggled closer. "I know, just a few more minutes. We won't be sleeping together for the next three thousand miles. Sounds weird doesn't it?"

"Sounds like a long way home to me."

Home. It did sound long, I thought. "Up and at'em," I said, pulling the covers off as I rolled out of the bunk. "I want to turn on the weather radio station. They predicted water spouts yesterday."

We dressed and ate a quick breakfast. The excitement of starting home apparently robbed us of our appetite. No great loss since we had been grazing Hawaiian food like a horde of cannibals in a nudist camp.

The radio crackled to attention with the weatherman predicting good weather, no water spouts, light trade winds and diminishing sea swells . On deck the gentle wind seem to sigh as it blew its salty breath out of the ESE for a change. Bob put down his pencil, "We'll have to east as much as we can the first part of the trip, just like last time from Bora Bora."

We went up on deck to take off the sail covers. Bob looked out toward the end of the dock, making a "hmmmm" sound. "I think I see someone I know from work," he said, "a man I used to see at quarterly staff conferences. He worked in Europe."

He jumped down and headed for a pudgy, balding man who gazed intently at a fifty foot cruising boat tied to the end dock. "Hey John, haven't seen you for a long time," Bob said, extending his hand.

John turned, and his jaw swung open in surprise, "Bob," he gasped, "is that you? My God, what are you doing here?"

"I retired from the rat race and took off on my boat to cruise," Bob laughed. "How's everything going with you?"

"Oh, you know how it is. Never enough time, meetings that go on forever, jumping on and off airplanes, and putting up with people that think by twisting our balls we will sell more product."

"Ouch," Bob said. "The ultimate stress."

"I heard you retired, but I didn't know about the boat. You look tan and fit. Must agree with you."

"Indeed it does. When are you going to retire?"

"Oh, I don't know. Can't do it now. I still have one kid in college, and the wife want to redo the house and get new furniture. You know what that's like. I'll have to keep working until I drop. He studied Bob's face, "You look ten years younger than when I last saw you.....and we're the same age." He frowned and patted his paunch, his face a series of stress lines outlining his eyes.

"Thanks, I feel younger too. But I understand about retiring. It took me awhile to make the big decision. Real hard to let go of pay checks. Are you looking at boats, or just dreaming? "

"Both. I'd like to get a boat, but the wife is afraid of them."

"I'm lucky. My wife didn't like them at first either, but she finally got over being scared. Now I trust her with my life. Couldn't have made this trip with just two of us otherwise. Sorry to cut it short, but I have to get back to our boat. We're leaving as soon as we can to sail home."

"Fantastic. How long will it take you?"

"Depends on the winds and where the high is located. Probably three weeks. Marlene and I are both getting anxious to leave. We've been gone for almost a year. Say hello to people at work for me."

Bob waved goodbye and jumped back aboard our boat, a smile spreading over his face. "I'll bet I looked that stressed a year ago too. He's my age, but looks a lot older."

"That's because you have taken so much vitamin B," I said.

"I don't get it. I don't take extra B vitamins."

"I'm talking about a special compound B Vitamin. This B stands for boat, guaranteed to change your life by giving you more get up and go."

"You're bad!"

"I know, but you smiled. That makes me good."

"I have to admit your crazy sense of humor helped both of us through some unpleasant times."

"Neither of us is exactly the crabby type. We both tend toward the positive thinking side of things."

"I guess that's why we get along."

"It's because we're both Sagitarians."

"You know I don't believe in that stuff."

"I know, but you must admit we are a lot alike. We match in what I feel is even more important. You're just as sentimental as I am. If you were the kind of macho guy who stepped on my feelings all the time, we wouldn't have lasted."

"Aha, thrown me out eh?"

"On your ear buster."

We finished securing gear, and packing away supplies. By 1100 we were ready for a hot shower and lunch, both at the yacht club. The last task before heading out to sea was to refuel at the Texaco dock. Between the tanks and jerry jugs we could carry a hundred and eighty gallons of diesel fuel, plenty to carry us through the high when the winds disappeared. We motored out the channel toward the open ocean, headed for the Molikai Channel where conditions were good for sailing. Instead of the usual thirty five knot winds and eighteen foot seas, we found fifteen knot winds and eight foot seas, a pussy cat by comparison. The warm wind picked at our clothes and hair, while the sky mirrored the blue sea below. Our genoa sail puffed out like a male pigeon chest, bowing and raising as if following an ancient courtship dance with the rolling waves. A good start, I thought.

Bob brought up the binoculars and trained them on a boat ahead of us, "It's *Lois Lane*," he said, "one of the last Transpac boats to go home."

"Give them a call on the VHF radio. I think that's the boat Mark and his wife are aboard."

Bob called and talked with Mark, discovering that another couple was helping them to deliver the boat back to the owner in San Francisco. "Maybe you can radio us and relay the weather," Bob said to Mark.

"Glad to Bob. We will be moving faster than you, and may be out of VHF range in a day or so. Tell Marlene I'll meet her on the ham radio at 1600 each day, 1413. She has my call sign, but I didn't write hers down. What is it?"

"N6LDM."

"Good. Got to go now. I need to change the headsail."

The winds continued steady, but by nightfall they increased to twenty five knots. We dropped the genoa. Wonder of wonders, it was Bob's idea this time. "We're over driving the boat," he said when I smiled.

The next day the seas bumped up to only two feet, but very short in between wave sets. It reminded me of riding a hobby horse as a child. *Maria* moved along at six to seven knots when suddenly a rogue wave came out of nowhere, whacking the bow and sending a wall of green water over the dodger.

"Wow," I cried. "What a sneaky steam roller that was. Glad it didn't come over our stern."

"Right. A wave that size would have flooded the cabin below."

Not a pretty notion, I thought. Waves like that also wash people overboard, reminding me of the *Overboard* story I read earlier. Wearing my harness with the tether attached to the steering station sounded like the most beautiful accessory in my whole wardrobe.

That evening my captain said he had a wonderful idea, "We could have just one glass of wine after dinner when all the dishes are done, and toast the sunset . Then we could see who could make it last the longest."

"You are desperate," I said laughing. "I guess one glass won't ruin our judgement."

Bob was so excited about the one glass of wine he volunteered to do the dishes. He must have set a record, because I could hear the dishes and pans clattering together like an old Spike Jones record. He handed me my glass and we sat back against the cockpit cushion. He reached over and took my hand. A fiery red sun hung just above the ocean, then dipped a sunbeam toe into the water and slipped behind the horizon to turn off the light. We languished in the twilight, enjoying our time together, not speaking, just sipping carefully. My glass lasted thirty-five delicious minutes. Bob persevered for thirty-six.

On my 0200 watch the time stretched out so slowly it felt painful. It was all I could do to stand the long passage of time since we had made up our mind to go home. Other passages had been as tedious as this one, but it bothered me more because I wanted to be in my home NOW. My three stars winked down at me, but it brought no smile to my face tonight. I made my two 360 turns to check on hazards, set the kitchen timer for twenty minutes, and closed my eyes. "To hell with everything," I grumped. For twenty minutes I succeeded in feeling very sorry for myself, until I became bored with such dull company. Don't be an ass hole, I thought. There are people who would give up everything just to do what we've been doing. I opened one eye and looked at my three stars again. They looked back and glittered. An old nursery tune stuck in my head and I made up new words, "Twinkle twinkle little star, you probably wonder what I are. I are a whiner on the sea, looking foolish, silly me. No more moan and nor more groan, it won't help me getting home." I snickered, feeling better. Especially when I checked the clock and found my watch was over.

All the next day the winds blew, carrying us further north. We had been using the trailing generator for several days to pump up our low batteries after using the ham radio. Bob went below and pulled off the panel to check the bank of batteries. They were charged all right, so much so the water had almost evaporated. He poked his head up the companionway, "Pull out the trailing generator. We're cooking the batteries. I need to refill them with water."

I hauled the eighty foot line in, and spent the next forty five minutes untangling the twisted dacron, then went back to reading my book. The rough seas made the printing jump up and down. At 1700 my Captain joined me wearing a I'm starved expression. Cooking in the rolling seas didn't appeal much, but I pulled out one of the dried Yurika food packages that a cruiser had given us, dropping it into boiling water. Voila! Instant dinner, and pretty good too. No dirty pans to clean, more time to study the sunsets.

By August 30 the winds charged out of the NE, stirring up rough seas and creating mountains out of waves. Breakfast was going to be a challenge. I started out by spilling the coffee grounds on the rug and into the sink. I gritted my teeth and decided that even Mother Hubbard would have screamed "shit." At 1600 I talked with Mark on the ham radio. "I don't know about you," I said, "but I've been slammed around the boat so much my natural color has become black and blue."

"Roger that," said Mark, "We have to be careful not to put too much strain on the sail rigging. Very light weight, and we don't want to lose our mast. It's been hard controlling the wheel in these mixed seas, so we've gone to a one on and one off watches for the time being."

"I don't envy you having to hand steer. *Otto* may act up once in a while, but he still works."

"You've also got the dodger to keep the wind and spray off you. I checked your position and I figure we're about 180 miles ahead of you now. The weather is turning worse. Twelve foot seas. If you haven't reefed you had better do it now. It will be easier."

"Thanks Mark. I wish you didn't have to send your crummy weather to us. We don't want it. I'll talk to you tomorrow. Hope the night goes well for you."

The trailing generator went back in the water, following us like a homing pigeon. The further north we traveled the colder the air turned. No more bare bodies, just bare feet. We bundled up in pants, shirts and jackets. Later on in the evening Bob and I had to finally put on shoes. If anyone had listened to us they would have thought we were being tortured and burned at the stake. "Owww," I cried, "either my shoes have shrunk, or my feet have grown, or least think they have grown. Damn, I can hardly walk."

"Me too," Bob groaned. "It's like my feet are stuck inside an iron maiden."

We limped around like the walking wounded for several days. When I talked with Mark he said they were so cold that they had to get up a half hour earlier before watch to put on enough clothes to keep warm. "I'm worn out dressing before I go on watch," he complained.

I put down the microphone. He's getting paid for it, I thought, which makes us look like a couple of masochists. Of course our payment wasn't money at the end of the trip, it was something far more important, home. During the night the wind howled, tearing at the rigging with ragged fingers, forcing water down the chain again and damaging connectors located at the bottom of the mast. The masthead light shorted out. Bob got out the hand pump and sucked out the water in the small sump area. This had long been a problem area because it didn't drain into the main bilge until it was full. He fixed the connectors early in the morning.

For some unknown reason we were both cheerful this morning. Maybe we're getting into the routine of it all, accepting the rough weather and lack of sleep. A shower really made our spirits soar. Bob put up a smaller headsail, staysail and reefed the main. The ride smoothed out, and we seemed more balanced. During evening twilight we toasted the sun going down. In return for the toast we saw our first flash of green, lighting up the sky, as the sun set into its bunk on the horizon. We sat stunned, for we had given up hope on the seeing the phenomenon of Auroa Borealis. God sent another little goodie to brighten our rough days, beautiful electrical discharges in ionized air.

The seas calmed down enough for me to cook a special Sunday breakfast. While I fried the corn beef hash and fixed eggs, coffee, and biscuits, Bob pulled up the trailing generator again. He called to me. "A manta ray took up residence on the end of the propeller. It was keeping it from turning."

"How do you know?"

"I saw it through the binoculars."

"Guess he was one of the teen-age mantas looking for a thrill ride."

Days went by and still we headed north. The high we sought evaded us, so the winds wouldn't allow us to head toward land. We zipped along at six and a half knots, with breezes blowing about eighteen knots. We were at 38.12 N and 154. 44 west. In San Francisco home was roughly located at 38. N and 122 W.

Bob became frustrated with the lack of progress reaching the high. "I've been trying to catch the position of the high, and now I just found out it's moving north again. To make matters worse we are going west, which is absolutely the wrong way," Bob said.

Feeling silly I sung, "We can't find the high, we can't find the high. High Ho we're feeling low, we can't find the high'."

Bob stared down at me with a wry look. "Well, it's corny enough to bring out a smile. Maybe I'll try a port tack toward land. I'll see if we can make any headway."

Fours disappointing hours later Bob came about. "We're going nowhere. We'll east some more and go north. We don't have a choice."

I turned on Coast Guard radio and listened to the weather report. "The high is now located at Latitude 44 North," I said. "Hurrah," we're at 43.30 North. Another thirty miles and we should be in it. My song worked."

"Sure," said Bob, "and pigs fly."

We turned on the engine and powered through the seas, trying to make those degrees of longitude get smaller. I flicked on the ham radio and tunned it to twenty meters, hearing Mark's voice boom out on the manana net. He was at 44 degrees N and 147 degrees W, with NW winds, which was just what we were looking for. Bob looked jubilant when I told him. "After we get through the south east tip of the high we'll get the north west winds, and then it's homeward bound for us."

How sweet the sound! We were still fourteen hundred miles off the coast of Coos Bay, Oregon. What a joke. We had originally planned to turn when we were off the coast of Point Reyes.

A new day, a new problem. Winds picked up to twenty seven knots and Bob took down the headsail. We were flying at eight and a half knots. He yelled back at me, "Way too much sail for these sea conditions."

Even with the sail down we chugged along at seven and a half knots. Then as the Lord giveth, he taketh away. No wind. Bob shook his head in dismay, "Turn on the engine. We have to keep from heading south and getting carried past San Francisco. There's no way I want to beat back up."

The one good thing about the lack of wind proved to be calm seas which made sleeping after watch a pleasure. No tossing about banging into the bulkheads, just sleep, sleep, sleep. Ahhhh.

Bob checked the barometer. "Going down. We going to catch something pretty soon."

All I could think of was we were about six days from home. The eighteen knot wind blustered from the NW, good sailing for *Maria*. The weatherman spoke of early fall weather pattern. Boom.....no wind. What's going on, I thought. It's enough to drive one crazy.

Bob looked around, "Feels like we're in the high pressure zone. It's hot and the barometer is still falling. Turn on the motor. We've got lots of fuel."

During the day the wind gradually returned, gusting again to eighteen. *Maria* almost skipped across the tops of the waves. After our nightly toast Bob bent over and took off my right shoe. Years ago I had taught him some Shiatsu reflexology massage, and now he rubbed the sole and sides of my foot with strong fingers. I was in heaven. "I know how relaxing that is," he said.

"Good, then I'll try it on you. Give me your foot."

We each took turns massaging each other's feet. By the time my watch started I was so relaxed I could have sailed for years.

Early the next morning Bob snoozed cozily in our bunk while I sipped coffee on my watch. At 0715 *Otto* went on strike and I went below to wake up sleeping beauty. By the time he dressed and came on deck I was clinging to the wheel like sucker fish. The winds had freshened to forty knots within fifteen minutes. Bob yelled through the roaring gale, "Turn on the engine and head into the wind. Make sure you keep enough RPMs going for control. I have to put on my harness."

He crawled up on deck and clipped on to the life line, but before he could do anything the genoa started to rip at the leach. "Want me to pull in the genny?" I screamed at him, noticing the wind indicator read fifty knots.

"He glared at me and screamed, "I can't hear a word you're saying."

His look had been so lethal I screamed back, "Good you bastard."

He pointed toward the wind. Both the genny and the staysail flogged like massive pumping wings, putting him off balance. I raced the engine trying to keep the boat headed into the wind, but mammoth rollers kept pushing the bow off to one side, or the other, and it felt like *Maria* was being slapped in the face by a powerful fist. Shrieking winds lifted the spume from wave tops, flinging it so hard it stung like needle pricks when it reached our face. Bob grabbed hold of the furling line and pulled as hard as he could to get the genny wound around the inside cable. The wrap on the drum jammed itself so tight it left the clue of the sail whipping in the wind. Carefully he unhooked his tether, and re-hooked it to the mast so he could begin lowering the staysail. He grasped the edge of the sail with one hand, and hung on to the halyard with the other, dropping the genny as fast as possible. A wall of green water swept across the deck and engulfed him, twisting his body backwards away from the mast. His hand tried to grasp the edge of the staysail, but it tore it away from his grasp. His tether jerked, and his hands reached out and clutched the mast again, both of them sliding up and down trying to get a purchase on the slippery aluminum. We heard a ripping sound as a small portion of the staysail material came apart. I could hear Bob yell obscenities into the wind, his mouth open when sea water found it. He coughed and gagged as he returned to the cockpit, collapsing into the seat beside me. With two sails down and the main already double reefed the boat became easier to control.

I looked at the water logged Captain next to me, watching him try to get his breath. It scared me to think how easy it would be to lose him over the side. The tether could have broken, or the life lines given way due to corrosion. The expression on his face made me think the same idea crossed his mind. I felt a stab of relief that he was okay.

He remained thoughtful as he rested. "You know, I really should have put the topping lift back on when we built the gallows. I guess I thought

I wouldn't need it, but without it I have to head to wind to get the main sail down. Bad deal." Bob's breathing slowed down and he closed his eyes, "By the way, I'm sorry I yelled at you," he said.

"Then I'm sorry I called you a bastard."

"What?", he said with a shocked look. "I can't believe that."

"Well, believe it. I never said I was perfect."

He went below to check on the auto pilot, and got it going again. I picked up the log and started writing down the latest events. I surprised myself when I wrote in large letters, I'm tired of being a good sport.

Bob fixed the auto pilot, and by 1615 we were moving right along under a doubled reefed main. We surfed along at seven knots with following seas. Bob joined me in the cockpit and looked astern. "You may, or may not, want to look at the waves following us."

Being the curious person that I was, I couldn't *not* look. at the waves. My eyes bugged out at the eighteen foot mountain of green water hanging behind the stern, complete with a sudsy breaking waver curling over the top. *Maria* didn't seem to mind. She rose up like an elegant queen as the water rushed under her. The big sigh came from me, not *Maria,* but I wasn't afraid.

That night we mentally rested easier with the double reefed main and a storm jib Bob put out. We took precautions because the weatherman had reported another low was due to pass with thirty to forty knot winds. Wonderful, I thought. But by 1400 we started the engine because the batteries were low, and we wanted to reduce the roll from the following sea. Our bodies and mind ached with exhaustion.

I normally looked forward to a new day, but with all the little surprises of late, I wondered what was next on the agenda. The winds dropped to fifteen. Good! We tried to get a weather report on the ham radio, but the bands were terrible and noisy. Bad! I listened to the mañana net at the latest front had passed us by. Good! I confessed to Bob that I was tired of being a good sport. Bad! That night me both were able to sleep and be rested. The happiest part of my watch came when I searched the heavens, thrilled the skies had been swept clean of any cloud cover. My three stars winked at me.

The next morning I tried to call Mark on ham radio. I called three times, finally deciding he must have reached San Francisco. The radio crackled, and I heard, "N6 LDM, this N6 DQN."

"Peter," I cried, N6 DQN, this N6LDM."

"Hi Marlene. I heard you calling Mark and he answered you. You two can't hear each other. I'll relay if you want."

"Where are you Peter."

I heard him laugh, "I'm sitting here anchored in Bora Bora."

"What a quirky thing radio is. Here Mark is only a couple of hundred miles away, and we can't talk to each other. And you're thousands of miles away and sound like you're next door. Ask Mark about the weather. Are there big seas where he is?"

Peter came back. "He said yes. He thinks they're generated from Hurricane Rick coming out of Mexico. He also says he hates to tell you, but they're about to go into San Francisco Bay."

"I expected that. After all they're on a racing boat."

I waited, then heard Peter, "Mark said that was true, but there were many times he wished he was on your boat. You had more comfort and a stronger rig. He'll see you around Sausalito in a few days."

"Thanks Peter, I appreciate your help. I know you're loving the cruising life, but right now we're tired and anxious to get home. Have fun. We'll be thinking of you. This is N6 LDM clear with N6 DQN."

The next day the barometer rose. We had a twelve knot wind out of the west and were blessed with a beautiful day. Somehow I thought we deserved it. Later a few rain showers swept by us, and I was sure God wanted to remind me to be more humble. Earlier we had put up the infamous sail, the MPS, because we were having to motor too much. I watched it carefully, but it behaved itself and came down like it was supposed to at 2200. That should have been a clue that things were moving too well.

At 0100, on my watch, all hell broke loose. The winds escalated to thirty knots, and the steering seemed out of synch. I wondered if *Otto* had become paranoid again and refused to work. I had to turn the wheel several times before I could get any action from the boat. Was the hydraulic pump leaking, I thought? No matter, time to get superman, namely the captain. I explained the problem and he tried steering.

"You're right. It feels very strange. "I'll go below and check on the hydraulics."

I heard a cry from below after a wave hit us, but I couldn't leave the wheel. I screamed, "Bob, what's going on? Are you all right?"

He yelled back, "I'm trying to put on the emergency steering, but when the wave hit us, it threw me and I cut my head. I'm all right. Don't worry."

Don't worry, I thought. That's ridiculous for Mrs. W. Wart.

"Don't touch the wheel he called. Come down here."

I went below and found Bob with his feet pushing on the emergency tiller attached to the rudder, blood running down his face from a small cut on the side of his head. "The following sea is so strong it's putting too much pressure on the rudder," he panted. "Let's put the regular steering back together and a second reef in the main. All I need is the pin to the rudder. Can you see it?"

"No. I don't see anything." I poked my head down into the rudder well and searched all the nooks and crannies of the bilge. At last I came upon where the errant pin had rolled. "Here it is," I said, trying not to sound triumphant. "How about your head?"

"Forget that for now. We need to reef the main and get some control over this boat. Go take the wheel."

I ran up topsides and grabbed the wheel, ready to head into the wind. Bob came up harnessed and ready for another round on the upper deck. Neither of us liked the idea of trying to reef in a moonless sky in rolling seas. Please Lord, I thought. Don't let anything happen to him. He put on the spreader lights so we could see.

Again I pushed the motor to its limits, trying to keep the bow into the wind. It helped that I could keep track of Bob on deck in the strong light. He winched down the sail, so that only a small portion remained, wrapping a line around it to hold the bulk of the sail in place. He finally finished and came back down into the cockpit. "That's it for now. I'll clean up down below and put a bandage on my head.

I stayed at the wheel and thought about getting home. Somehow that calmed me down. Well, it helped until I heard Bob give a furious yell, followed by more obscenities. He came up and told me the $600.00 Tamaya sextant in its case had fallen into the bilge next to the rudder post. The case had been severely squeezed and wrecked. Later on I opened the tortured case and found the sextant hadn't been damaged. We were both too tired to care. No sleep at all.

September 15, I wrote in my log. We were close to San Francisco Bay now, maybe another twenty eight hours away. Even though the barometer was falling, the twenty five knot winds and swells were moving the boat closer to home. It felt like a sleigh ride, whoooooosh.

We both looked like we had been in a war zone. Bob bandaged, bags under our eyes, sleep deprived beyond belief. But the ridiculous feeling of happiness remained. We were almost home. We could stand anything for that. Bob slept peaceful in the cockpit for an hour. I tried, but adrenalin surged through me like a gigantic dose of NoDoze. I fixed the last dinner of the trip, a quickie spaghetti and sauce from the Yurika supply. "No wine," I said. "it would hit me like a sledge hammer."

"We'll wait and raise a glass when we came under the Golden Gate Bridge. Okay?" Bob said.

"You bet okay."

At precisely 0200 Maria slipped like a ghost under the dark shadow of the bridge. The moon cast shadows of cable marks across the decks, while stars reflected in our raised stainless steel wine cups.

"Here's to my captain who sailed the seas to different lands, and brought us both home safely. It was a wonderful experience, and I thank you from my tired heart."

"Here's to the admiral who helped make the trip possible, and fun. You're truly my best friend. I love you very much."

I put my arms around him, hugging that sweet body close to mine, "I love you too."

He held my chin with one finger, "It's funny. We've both changed since we left. I've learned to relax, and you made a friend of the ocean."

"The nicest part is we've grown much closer. This last year we've had time to talk about our lives, and feelings. As long as you worked it seemed we never really told each other our most intimate thoughts."

"True. But I think that it's our working together twenty-four hours a day, and always being there for each other, that has made the biggest difference."

"All I know is I never want to be very far from you...... ever.

At 0300 we rounded the curve in the channel and caught sight of a lonely house on the hill, as if waiting patiently for someone to make it a whole and a happy place again.

Bob glided into the dock and I jumped off with the bow line, securing it, then taking the stern and spring lines from his hands. All was secure and quiet. We noticed something white stretched along the length of the top of the garage door, puzzled by its presence. When we drew closer we could see a long computer print out banner saying, "Welcome Home Bob and Marlene"

"Who do you suppose did that?" I said.

"I don't know, but we'll find out." He looked up at the dark house. " I think we'll have to sleep on the boat tonight. We won't have a bed set up in the house."

"That's all right. At least the bed won't be moving around."

We crawled into the bunk and sank down in the sleeping bag with a sigh of happiness. Bob rolled over and whispered, "We made our dream come true. Now that we're home it hardly seems like we left."

"I know." I put my arm around his waist and squeezed. "We'll remember these days even when we're really old and grey. But then I wondered if we would be content to stay put after all the adventures we've been through. Life might seem kind of dull."

"It can only be dull if we let it. Besides, who'se to say our dream is over just because we're home."

"You're right. I like that thought."

Bob closed his eyes and stopped talking. Silence filled the cabin, broken only by his gentle breathing. I lay back down, but my mind pranced about like a restless gazelle. Just a year ago, I thought, I sailed away as housewife, trading my fancy kitchen for a galley, my king sized bed for a bunk. I returned home a sailor, satisfied lover, and experienced traveler. Now the term housewife sounded so blah. But there was so much more. The fears which had made me Mrs. W. Wart all my life had also stifled the freedom to experience abundant life, strangling true intimacy. Somewhere in that big expanse of ocean I let go of those worries, and found that love and zest for life filled my heart, as well as our boat, to the gunnels. My excitement at this realization made me want to wake Bob up and kiss him all over, for he had gently guided me through the letting go process, showing me I had skills and strengths that I could be proud of. Good sense prevailed. Instead I blew him a kiss, and closed my eyes, knowing the dream we had achieved was only the beginning.

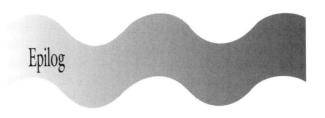

Epilog

LIFE GOES ON
GO TO SEA ONCE MORE

"Come, all ye bold seafaring men, and listen to me song'
When yiz come off of them damn long trips I'll tell yiz what goes wrong.
Take my advice, don't drink strong drinks, nor go sleepin' wid a whore,
But get married, lads, an'have all night in, an go to sea no more.
Look here my brave young sailor lad, there's no more work ashore,
But here's your chance; take ten pound advance, and go to sea once more.
So I shipped me aboard of a whaler that was bound for the Arctic Sea
Where ice and snow and the cold winds blow, froze my toes all off'n me."
(Sea Chantey, Go To Sea No More)

The year after we returned we heard *Starlight* had been sold when she reached Honolulu. The owners moved back east to the United States, eventually buying a new boat seven years later.

California suffered more problems with the boomkin. When leaving Tonga the boomkin ripped a hole in the hull just above the water line, and the sea seeped into the bilge. The crew managed to get back to Tonga and make repairs. While sailing about one hundred miles off the

363

coast of New Zealand the ferro cement hull struck an unknown object. The boat abruptly rose up underneath them and then shook like a wet dog. They had lost all rudder control. They surmised that they hit a whale, or possibly a container from a freighter. Without steering they called for help. New Zealand Coast Guard refused to come out that far, but fortunately a nearby fishing boat heard the call and towed them the hundred miles to safety. They plan to go cruising again.

After returning home we spent time fixing up our house and getting things back in order. But of course the sea called in an accusing voice "So the house is done. Why are you staying land-locked so long? We replied, "We decided to do short trips, instead of long trips that would mean moving out of our house again." (See what happens when you get older? You start talking to yourself.)

We made trips up and down the California coast to the channel islands, with Bob managing to break three ribs while trying to board the boat during a storm at Santa Cruz Island. The next few years found us chartering boats in different parts of the world; a canal boat in England, sailboats in Yugoslavia, Bay of Islands, New Zealand, Tonga, Turkey, the last charter a canal boat in France. All fun but someting missing.

Then the sea called in a louder voice, "No wonder. You are not on *Maria Elena.*"

Well, here we go again, yearning for another ocean experience with the two of us, albeit, twelve years older. We worked furiously getting *Maria* ready for the hard sail to the Pacific Nortwest. We added a GPS, Trimble, side curtains that zip into our sun shield to keep out the rain, and a new auto pilot, an Alpha. Poor old *Otto,* our Sharp auto pilot, died of aging parts.

It took us two weeks to sail the rugged coast of Northern California, Oregon, and Washington, including a week of waiting out bad weather in different anchorages. We finally sailed into Port Angeles, Washington, resting and going on to Vancouver Island. We spent four months cruising the American San Juan, and the Canadian Gulf Islands. We left the boat in Canada for the winter. 1996 found us cruising to Alaska and the Queen Charlotte Islands, a 2500 mile round trip. It felt good being on *Maria* again, experiencing the sea roll under her, smelling the rich salty air, seeing the sky filled with birds as they dipped in and out of clouds. I picked out my three stars from Orion's Belt on night watch, respecting the massive power of twenty-five foot tides, but most of all, rejoicing in being one with the open ocean we both loved.

Big changes in our life started after our Alaskan trip. While shortening sails in heavy weather Bob discovered his once sturdy legs wobbled doing the foredeck "dance," and he panted like a teenage lover. Now that might not be bad if the panting had been while making love, but it wasn't. He was shortening sail. We came to a decision, almost unthinkable for old-time rag sailors like us. The time had come to sell *Maria* and buy a Trawler. As usual Bob had his heart set on one special boat, a trawler under fifty feet with full headroom in the engine room. He was tired of being hunched over "making love to an engine" in a small space. The boat he craved was a forty-six foot Cheoy Lee, alas none for sale on the west coast. We found ou boat, a 1979, Cheoy Lee Trawler, in Detroit. It was love at first sight. We decided there could be only one name for our new/old boat, *SEA CHANTEY*. We named the rubber dinghy, *CHANTEY MAN*. The boat was too tall to be shipped by truck, so once again the Captain and Admiral took over the cruising duties of bringing this yacht back to San Francisco. More adventures, fulfilling more dreams, proving life was still radiating excitment and wonder at any age. But I like to think, *especially for the very mature* adults. *SEA CHANTEY* is home now. But knowing us, there is no telling for how long..."Ahhhh, Bob, did you hear something calling us?"

CHANGING THE
BOAT FOR CRUISING

W hen we bought our Morgan 41 OL in 1974 it
came with basic equipment such as: a Westerbeke 4-107 engine, compass, mainsail, genoa sail, 35 pound anchor, two toilets, an alcohol stove,
and a gaping hole called an ice box.

The Westerbeke 4-107 grew older and more cranky. So cranky in fact
that the actual crank broke in half, resulting in the ultimate demise of the
engine. The engine blocks of the Westerbeke and Perkins were the same
so we installed a new Perkins 4-108, then proceeded to pirate as many of
the 4-107 parts as possible to carry as spares. We kept two injectors with
mounting brackets, a raw water pump, transmission oil cooler, and
engine oil cooler. I had looked at the old greasy parts with a jaundiced
eye, wrapping them up and placing them in Tupperware containers to
keep out moisture. We were fortunate we followed that line of reasoning
because we ended up needing an injector with the cast iron mounting
bracket. We had brought new injectors with us, but never dreamed our
almost new engine would have a cast iron bracket failure. Boats are as
perverse as some crabby people. I won't ever cast a hostile eye at old
spare parts, instead I will lovingly wrap them with care.

Earlier we had added a club jib to our sail complement, with the boom moving on a traveler. When we made our cruising plans we were advised by our sailmaker to take the jib sail with us, but not the boom. He said the boom would be like a loose cannon on the foredeck, either inflicting serious injury, or knocking one of us off the deck into the water. We converted our club jib to a free footed one. After being in the tropical storms with winds changing directions in a matter of second, I heartily agree with him. We also purchased a new heavy duty cruising main, since our old one suffered from sagging sail shape and vanishing thread. We took the sail with us as a back up since an old sail was better than no sail. Later we replaced that sail with a full batten main, a much superior sail which really worked well. We installed a baby stay and running back stays. The running backstays would support the mast on long hauls, and the baby stay was for the staysail.

The sail maker also advised us to check our rigging carefully, because losing our mast would be an astronomically expensive, as well as difficult to replace. The tropics take a debilitating toll on rigging, with one year of sailing equaling ten years at home. We had seen several cracks in our ten year old shroud swedges, and felt it would be prudent for us to replace all our standing rigging. We ordered the new backstay to include the two insulators needed for the ham radio antenna, since the main frequencies we used were in tune with our backstay length. (20 meters)

We talked with as many returning cruisers as possible, and they advised us to carry good ground tackle, meaning you couldn't have too many anchors in case of a disaster. We had replaced the 35 pound CQR earlier with a 45 pound CQR. We added a 65 pound Bruce (which actually weighed 71 pounds) to keep the 45 pound anchor company on the bow. The Bruce had proved its worth by holding the North Sea oil platforms in place during violent storms. We stowed the 35 pound CQR on board behind our main saloon companion ladder.

We also learned we should change our alcohol stove to a propane or kerosene one, because alcohol was not readily available outside of the United States. This was also true of natural gas. Kerosene and propane were plentiful world wide. We searched for a solution to the storage problem, since propane containers on deck could end up tripping us or interfering with the operation of the boat. Our problem was solved by a local marine outfit, Margas system, who invented a self contained propane system that didn't require a built in air tight compartment. This meant we could safely put the propane below decks in one of the hanging lockers, venting the unit over the side. We bought the first one ever sold. At the same time we also purchased a propane Dickinson stove with three burner and an oven. The oven worked well, but was not used much in the tropics because of the heat. I baked bread on top of the stove instead. (see Appendix 7)

The next area we concentrated on was the icebox. The box was so deep and dark that I practically had to climb inside to find our food, often feeling like a spelunker exploring a cave. The supreme mystery, which I never solved, was what happened to the food I put in, and never saw again. It reminded me of searching the washing machine for the elusive missing sock. If I believed in the tooth fairy, I should also believe in the ice box fairy, one who either consumed the food, or changed the molecular structure into some unrecognizable smelly form. Bob finally built a refrigeration system that incorporated a truck hold down plate which ran off the main engine with an air conditioning compressor. By running the engine an hour a day in moderate climate, or two hours a day in the tropics, we could keep our favorite food cold. Beer. This system finally crashed about ten years later, replaced in 1996 by a Swedish self contained 12 V DC, water cooled unit called Isotherm. A much more efficient unit which runs off the batteries instead of the engine..

In the main cabin we converted sea bunk into a series of cupboards for food storage and kitchen tools. The bunk had been used only once in ten years and required you to climb up quite high. I figured it was only useful to an ape, or a six foot six basketball player.

Another concern of Bob's was the amount of fuel we carried, one fifty gallon tank for diesel. The more he thought about the long ocean passages the less comfortable he was with the inadequacy of fuel storage. He searched the boat for space to add a tank, finally choosing to removed a fifty gallon water tank and replace it with an eighty gallon stainless fuel tank. We also carried four five gallon jerry jugs filled with diesel fuel, giving us a capacity of 150 gallons. Another five gallon jug was filled with outboard fuel. All jerry cans were lashed on deck to the life lines. This was purely personal on Bob's part, because many cruisers would prefer to keep the extra water.

We added a Sea Gold water maker, installing it under the sink in the galley. This small desalinization unit pumped four gallons of good tasting water an hour, running either electrically, or pumped by hand. We didn't use it in harbors because petroleum products destroy the special membrane filter.

On an earlier trip we found one very important item aboard another Morgan 41, a gallows. No, this wasn't to be used to hang mutinous crew, this gallows supported the mainsail boom. Before we installed the gallows on our boat we had some wild and terrorizing rides around Point Conception. Bob had tried to reef the mainsail while tumultuous wave action shoved the boat back and forth, causing the big sail to swing viciously back and forth. Bob hung on so hard he felt like his fingers had etched out holes in the boom. After that trip he designed a beautiful stainless steel and teak gallows, consisting of three slots for the main boom to rest. Depending on the tack, he could choose the appropriate slot to drop the boom, reefing the sail as it stayed in place. We also found the stainless steel supports on the gallows a handy spot to grab when going aft.

We bought an anchor windless which had two options, one using electrical power to raise the anchor, or raise it manually if the power failed. Remember redundancy? We had been used to anchoring in twenty to thirty feet of water in the bay, or along the coast, but in the South Pacific we had to anchor in 80 to 90 feet. This meant lots of chain had to be set and I do mean chain, not line. Coral heads in the pacific will tear a piece of line to pieces in a relatively short time, so chain is the better option if one plans to stay in one place. No one in his right mind wanted to pull up 250 feet of 3/8 chain by hand, so the electrical option will save a back , but not a buck. Because the windless drew a lot of current it was important to keep the batteries well charged. (See Appendix 3). Bob ran the engine while raising the anchor.

Trying to see inside our anchor locker, engine rooms, or work areas, was like peering into different caves. Bob installed work lights in each difficult area. That freed up a hand holding a flashlight since boats seemed to require at least three hands to work on any problem.

When we decided to cruise with just the two of us we had some "special crew" in mind. Our chosen crew would be *Otto,* the automatic pilot, and *Sven,* our Swedish self steering vane. Of course we added a few prayers that the auto pilot wouldn't gasp into electronic fits. Bob carried spare parts and knew how to make most of the repairs needed. Later we changed the Sharp auto pilot for an Alpha Spectra. Excellent choice.

Most sailboats had mechanical steering but ours was blessed (?) with hydraulic steering. Due to our hull design and steering, the only practical vane for us was the Swedish Sail-o-mat. Money-wise, it was like buying a Rolls Royce instead of a Chevette.

These welcome crew members became two important parts of our family. Compared to real crew they didn't eat, drink, or bitch about their work load, get seasick, and only occasionally suffered a part ache. They couldn't talk our ears off, brag about being accomplished sailors, steal the candy we had saved, or sneak the Irish whiskey, all salutary behavior.

Lastly we mounted a manual bilge pump in the engine room at the request of the insurance surveyor. This was a boat steeped in redundancy, but for a very good cause. Bob wanted lots of options because our lives depended on it!

Appendix Two

EQUIPMENT

AVON ROVER

AVB 23423M84S   SEAGULL
                     MARINE 1851

AVON LIFE RAFT   #17388   MC GRAW AVE
                                        IRVINE, CA.92714
                                        (800) 432-7275

SEABIRD DINGHY   #DN6109338C84   NEW ZEALAND
EVINRUDE 8 HP   # E0326898
                     MOD. E8RCRM

SAILOMAT
WINDVANE   MOD. 3040 L

HYNAUTIC STEERING   P.O.BOX 668
                                        OSPREY, FLORIDA 33559
                                        813) 966-2151

SHARP AUTO PILOT   MOD. MK2   (714) 646-7115
                                        COSTA MESA, CA.

LORAN TI   MOD. 9000   P.O.BOX 226080
                                        DALLAS, TX 75266

MAGNOVOX
SAT NAV   MOD. 4102   2829 MARICOPA
                                        TORRANCE, CA.90503
                                        (213) 618-1200

FLUX GATE COMPASS	MOD. 332	SAME AS ABOVE
HORIZON VHF	MOD. 862 S 10 AMP FUSE	
MODAR VHF	#449CDE0696-49 MOD. 440	
ICOM RADIO	#02439 MOD. 720-A	HAM RADIO OUTLET 990 HOWARD AVE BURLINGAME,CAL 94010 415) 342-5757
MAXI COM	#31006021	
HUSTLER	20 METERS 40 METERS	SAME AS ABOVE
ICOM RADIO	#001115 MOD. 725	SAME AS ABOVE
TUNER	MOD. AH 3	SAME AS ABOVE
AQUA GUIDE RDF	#11800161 MOD. 712	MARITIME ELECTRONICS SAUSALITO, CA.
RAYTHEON HAILER	#4143 MOD. 250	MARITIME ELECTRONICS
RAYTHEON RADAR	# LH 21232 MOD.	MARITIME ELECTRONICS 300 HARBOR DR. SAUSALITO, CAL 94965 (415) 332-5086
LOCATO WATCHMAN RADAR DETECTOR		WEST MARINE 295 HARBOR DR. SAUSALITO CA. 94965 (415) 332-0202
DATA MARINE DEPTH SOUNDER	# 031436 MOD. 2730 RD	MARITIME ELECTRONICS
DATA MARINE LOG	# 02060	MARITIME ELECTRONICS

DATA MARINE WIND	#013085 MOD. LX360	MARITIME ELECTRONICS
DATA MARINE KNOT METER	#010092 MOD. S0200D	MARITIME ELECTRONICS
WIND GENERATOR RED WING	OUT OF BUSINESS	
ADLER BARBER COLD MACHINE	#7988 MOD. DCM12	WEST MARINE
AMANA RADAR RANGE	#K50602005 MOD.	AMANA REFRIGERATION 1601 ADRIAN RD BURLINGAME CA. (415) 697-9435
DICKINSON PROPANE STOVE	#LPG8308 (MARINE STAINLESS FITTING LMT)	71 MORRIN RD MT WELLINGTON AUKLAND, NEW ZEALAND 572-226, 572-697
MARGAS SYSTEM CONTROL PANAL	SER. 083 MOD. 20V	
DIESEL HEATER	D3L EBERSPACHER	EDINGER MARINE 399 HARBOR DR. SAUSALITO, CAL 94965 (415) 332-3780

PROPS

MAIN-	12X24	PICHOMETER PROPELLERS 2516 BLANDING AVE. ALAMDEA, CA. (415) 522-2616
OUTBOARD 8 1/2 X 9	PT.#390237	

TRAILING GENERATOR	8 1/4 X 5	
ANCHORS		
CQR- 45 LBS	3/8 HT 250 FT	GREEN MARK 1-40FT GREEN YELLOW 50-90 FT YELLOW MARK 100-140 YELLOW RED 150-190 RED MARK 200-250
BRUCE 30 KG	3/8 PROOF- CHAIN	50 FT+ 300 FT 1/2 INCH LINE-
CQR-35	3/8 PROOF	210 FT 3/4 NYLON
DANFORD-25	32 FT	
DANFORD 5		
DINGHY	100 FT LINE	
BINOCULARS		
FUJINON 7 X 50	# 1101	
EVERTITE 7 X 50		
SEXTANTS		
TAMAYA		
DAVIS MARK 25		
ACR DISTRESS	# 10097 MOD.565	ACR ELECTRONICS, INC 3901 N. 29TH AVE HOLLYWOOD,FL. 33020 (305) 981-3333
FIREFLY LIGHTS 2 ACR	SEE ABOVE (Personal light to be worn)	
WINCHESTER SS SHOTGUN	# L1377818	
SMALL MAXI COMPASS	MOD. 350T	WEST MARINE
RARITAN HEAD	# 26139 MOD.	1025 NORTH HIGHT ST. MILLVILLE , NEW JERSEY 08332

READ SEWING MACHINE

ORRICK VACUUM

LIGHTS

RUNNING LIGHTS	1004 GE	
COMPASS LIGHTS	X 2	1487 GE
MAGNIFYING LIGHT-		
FLASHLIGHT BULBS		

Manufacturers equipment may have changed names and addresses. This partial list is just an idea of how to keep track and know your gear. It also helps in case something is stolen. (I hate to say it, but it happens.)

Appendix Three

ELECTRONIC EQUIPMENT

Maria Elena had a good navigation station where we could easily wire in all electronic gear in plain view. The depth sounder read up to 600 feet in meters, fathoms, or feet. We had a distance log, VHF radio (2) Magnavox Satellite Navigation, Loran, GPS, Global Positioning System, (later) and a hailer. The VHF radio had an emergency antenna if the mast came down. The hailer was used as an automatic fog horn, a loud speaker, or as a listener. We had two horns installed on the mast, one faced forward, the other aft. By turning the unit on to the listening mode during dense fog we could hear the direction of a bell buoy or breaking surf.

Our Magnavox Satellite Navigation system proved outstanding and reliable during the trip to the South seas. Before leaving on our trip to the Northwest we purchased a GPS, a global positioning system. It is by far the most accurate and worked beautifully for our 2500 mile Alaska trip. While extolling electronics, we must keep in mind that nothing is perfect or incapable of **FAILING** at the worst possible moment.

We also had a radar detection device. The alarm worked only when a ship in the vicinity had its radar turned on. It paid to be on watch and awake, because we encountered big ships without their radar functioning. We called them on the radio and asked if they saw us. There seemed to be a wait while they either turned on their equipment or looked at the screen. The detector proved useful when transiting out to sea near a shipping lane, but we had to turn it off when sailing down a busy coast. The constant ringing of the alarm kept the person off duty awake instead of asleep.

My favorite piece of electronic equipment was the ham radio. We installed it in the aft cabin away from the busy navigation station, so I could conduct my radio work and not interfere with Bob's work.

Our radar worked well, but we seldom used the Loran since it did not work in Mexico or the South Pacific. We didn't use our radar a lot over the year to the south seas, but the times we did were critical, such as during fog conditions along the west coast, or picking out a passage through the Tuamotu islands, and tracking storms. In our travels to the Northwest and Alaska it became an essential piece of equipment. I wouldn't leave shore without it.

We put a radar reflector in the rigging to alert ships of our presence, with the assumption that big ships could pick up a small boat on their radar. One day while visiting San Francisco Marine traffic control we discussed the radar reflector with the operators. We learned that the freighter and tanker's radars were set high to pick up large ships, passing over a small boat. Suddenly we felt very small. I remembered once monitoring a call from a thirty foot yacht to a super tanker just outside of Morro Bay. The yacht said, "BT San Diego, I want to know if you pick me up on your radar. I'm just off your starboard side".

The tanker radio operator replied, "I am sorry we don't see you. We don't have small target acquisition radar".

I think the word target almost set the yacht into a panic. We still carry our radar reflector, but are aware we might not show up on their screen. Therefore, we drove defensively. Many cruisers dislike complicated electronic gear, preferring the KISS theory, KEEP IT SIMPLE STUPID.

To augment our electronics we took two sextants, the Tamaya Jupiter for Bob, the plastic Davis for me (lighter to hold). Bob had used celestial navigation in the navy, but was very rusty. Since I needed to learn the whole theory we took a course from a retired Coast Guard Commander. Sometimes there are courses given at the local Community colleges, but they were not available at that time.

Keeping in
Batteries Charged

Because of the vast array of electrical equipment we put on board, we used two D-8 deep cycle diesel batteries. Later we added one more D-8 that we kept off line for emergencies. We had several ways to charge the batteries.

1. Shore power through a 70 amp marine battery charger
2. The Onan 7.5 KW generator, using the battery charger
3. The engine alternator, which was equipped with a Max Com that caused the alternator to charge a maximum rate until they reached a predetermined level and then returned alternator control back to the normal regulator.
4. A trailing generator we threw over the stern when sailing at least 4.5 knots. Any slower than that would cause us to lose at least one half a knot in speed. The small generator itself was mounted on the stern. Attached to the generator was eighty feet of line which had a stainless rod and propeller on the end. The stainless rod kept the prop in position as well as deterring sharks from biting off the prop. The trailing generator could charge up to 12 amps. When the generator was not in use we stored it inside the boat.

5. When in port at anchor we used the small generator with an airplane propeller, hanging them up in the rigging. The wind turned the propeller, sometimes generating up to 20 amps, and our biggest problem ended up being the danger of cooking the batteries by boiling out the water. We have since determined we needed to add a regulator to prevent this. This the same generator we used as a trailing generator, but with a prop instead of a propeller.

The new kid on the block for cruisers now is solar energy. To keep mold from forming we have solar driven fans in each head, which worked quite well in ventilating the boat. New improvements in solar cell theory are taking place each year. But solar cells alone would not have kept pace with the amp drain when transmitting from my ham radio.

HAM RADIO GROUND PLANE ADVICE

When we investigated ham radio installations we talked to ten different hams who had installed ten different ground plane systems. This was due to the uniqueness of each boat, but the principle remained the same. The following is what worked best for us in our sailboat. We installed a grid of three inch copper strips in the aft cabin under our sleeping quarters, soldered all the joints, and then fiberglassed over the entire grid. Taking a copper strip down from the grid to the engine we soldered a woven copper battery cable to the strip, attaching that to the engine. This grounded the system. We installed another three inch strip from the grid up the wall to the automatic tuner on the ham radio. When we had our new back stay made we added two insulators, the distance between them had to match the frequency we intended to use the most. (twenty meters) thereby turning our back stay into an antenna.

My radio was in ICOM 720-A. It had a great signal and I was able to make contact with the United States most any day if atmospheric conditions were right. My call sign is N6 LDM. I have since added an ICOM 725, using the 720 A as a back up. Didn't I tell you this was a redundant boat?

In Alaska I talked every day to two hams on 3.55 frequency, at seven in the morning, Alaska time. They were Joe May, AL7IK and Dave Walton, AL7DJ. They provided weather, information on anchorages and things to do and see. I also let them know where we would be each day in case of emergency. Wonderful, helpful people. When we got down into Canada I reported in each day to a Northwest Boater's net on 3.65 at eight thirty in the morning.

SAFETY AND EMERGENCY EQUIPMENT

1. Two Horseshoe life buoys, both with boat name, and one with strobe light and flares.
2. Two safety harnesses, his and hers.
3. Two personal small strobe lights (firefly) which pin on to clothing.
4. Eight life jackets
5. Halon automatic fire system in the engine room.
6. Three fire extinguisher, 1 halon, 2 dry chemical.
7. Sixty five pound Bruce anchor with 250 feet of 3/8 chain, mounted on the bow with its own bow roller.
8. Forty five pound CQR anchor with 50 feet of 3/8 chain and 250 feet of line, also mounted on bow with its own bow roller.
9. Thirty five pound CQR with 50 feet of 3/8 chain and 250 feet of line, stored midships below.
10. Twenty five pound Danforth anchor with 30 feet of 5/16 chain, and 150 of 1/2 inch line, mounted on the stern with its own roller for a stern anchor.
11. Two big Constellation compasses, one located at the steering station on deck, the other located in aft cabin below in the emergency steering area.
12. Safety line, 3/8 nylon, running chest height from bow to stern on both starboard side and port side of the boat. We used this line to

clip on to with our safety harness tether when going forward on deck at night, or during daytime storms. When in port these lines were removed and put away.

13. Emergency tiller used below. Tiller was the same pipe used as the manual handle on our windless. The emergency tiller was used once during a storm.

14. EPIRB, emergency locator. We also had an extra battery.

15. Eight man life raft, automatically actuated when in water.

GET AWAY BAG

Each boat's survival bag may be unique to the people who need it. It consists of a bag large enough to hold the extra EPIRB battery, water, prescription drugs, eye glasses, fishing equipment, knife, and special survival food. The dry food we took had been given to us from a freighter's commercial life raft supply which was being replaced by fresh provisions. I'm glad we never had to use it because it was awful tasting, but it could have saved our lives. Later we discovered a couple of rats had taken up residence and tried the food, one small bite. I wonder how a rat said "yuk." We got rid of the rats with traps, not poison. Our concern was the rats might die in our headliner where we couldn't get at it. It is a good idea to carry rat and mouse traps. These are the stowaways that will bring the most grief.

Appendix Seven

MEDICAL CONCERNS

We didn't want to spend all our money on equipment for the boat, and forget the boat needed a well person in charge to run it. Boat equipment breaks down, so it should become as no surprise that the same thing can happen to a sailor, no matter what age. We took responsibility for ourselves.

BEFORE WE LEFT
1. We each had a full physical from our primary doctor.
2. We went to the dentist for a checkup and cleaning. (We bought an emergency dental kit at a marine store.
3. We took an advanced first aid course which included CPR.

Our doctor wrote prescriptions for our daily medicines, plus medicines to fight infections internally, as well as, topically. We made copies of these prescriptions and kept them on board, so officials in other countries would not think we were in the drug dealing business.

The following is a list of what we took in light of our own physical condition. It should not be contrued as a positive buy, only a guide in organizing your own medical chest. Because we would be sailing off shore we had to be self sufficient. If cruising along coastal waters your list would be shorter because of being closer to medical help.

SEA SICK

Scolomine Patches- This medicatiion may not be available anymore, but if it is, you must have Doctor prescription. Works well as long as you don't mind having cotton mouth. Very important not to use more than a week at the most. We met one woman who used them for a month and went into severe depression when she stopped. A doctor also told us never to put the patch in the same place as it doubles up on the drug, causing psychological problems.

Merazine-I like it because it doesn't make me sleepy.

Promethazine- Must have a doctor prescription. Phenergan 25 mg. with Ephedrine 25 mg.

Ginger Tablets- Natural, but it worked for me. Watch for the ginger burp.

Accupressure Wrist Bands - They work.

FUNGUS

Athletes Foot- Tinactin , or other over the counter medications

Hair- DHS Zinc, or Excel shampoo

Body - Burrows solution for hard to heal.

Vaginal and Groin Fungus- Wear cotton underwear. Use mycostatin ointment, or for women, gyne-lotrimin. For vaginal thrush use Betadine Solution. This is a common problem in the tropics.

URINARY TRACK INFECTION

Cystitis- Woman seem more prone. I used Bactrim. Gantricin is good, but I was allergic to sulpha. Drink lots of water to dilute the urine. New medicines are being introduced so check with your doctor. The above medications need a doctor's prescription.

DIARRHEA

This can ruin your whole trip. The cause may be contaminated food or water. This can include your own water if you are not careful. I took **lomitil** (RX) with me. The **BRAT** diet works well. That stands for **bananas, rice, apples, and toast.** If fluid loss is gross the electrolytes need to be replaced. I used gatorade in a powdered form.

CONSTIPATION

Can happen on long ocean passages because of decreased exercise, canned food, and lack of fresh foods that offer fiber. I took Metamucil.

You can grow sprouts in special jars, or take along dried prunes and other dried fruits.

BURNS

The galley is a where burns can occur when pots spill in rough weather. I had an **oil cloth apron** If I had a minor burn I put my hand in cold water. (hard to find in the tropics unless you have ice.) I used clean sea water, then put on **Silverdine ointment.**

CHECKING YOUR WATER

I was given good advice from a Naval Ship's nurse. He told me to get a swimming pool test kit. When chlorinating the water we were to check in twenty minutes using the chlorine section of the test kit to see if chlorine remained in the tank. If it was gone we were to put in more chlorine because bacteria was still present. Test again in another twenty minutes. If you don't want to use chlorine, use iodine tablets according to directions, and forget the test kit.

JELLYFISH STINGS

We saw small and medium size Jellyfish along the coast, huge Portuguese-Man of war in mid ocean. We looked for them before we went in to swim. I kept **Adolph's Meat tenderizer** for that. You can also use ammonia, or a deodorant that contains aluminum salts.

EARS

In warm sea water it is easy to get itchy ears from bacteria. We used **Synalar drops** for itchy ear, but some people put alcohol in the ear to dry it out. That's a bit harsh for some people. Bacterial infection we brought **Cortisporin** ear drops. True ear infections have to be treated with antibiotics like **Penicillin** or **Erthromyicin**. Both these need a doctor's prescription.

EYES

Polynesia has out breaks of **Pink Eye**. It is very contagious. I brought **Maxitrol.** There are prescription sulpha products in ointment form which will stay on longer. Boric acid powder mixed with water can be used for sore eyes. Follow the directions on the package carefully.

FISH POISONING-CIGUATERA

This is a very real problem in the tropics where fish feed on the coral reefs, then people feed on the fish. The best rule is not to eat any reef fish. Sometimes one fish on an island is poisonous, but not on another island. Even locals make mistakes. We were told that some locals leave fish out to see if ants or flies come to feed. Too risky. There are books that describe harmful fish for different areas. If someone gets Ciguatera you should give them an emetic to throw up, but that might not work. It is serious enough that some people die.

CORAL CUTS

These are very important to take care of because they tend toward **staph infection**. Bob got a cut from the boat, and then went swimming in a coral reef area. Because there were coral particles in the water, the cut became infected. We treated it with **clorox** first, and then with **hydrogen peroxide.** We had to follow up with antibiotics because despite our quick work, infection set in.

SEA NETTLES

These are long tranlucent strands. I treated the sting with 20 percent vinagar.

LICE

Not a nice subject, but it happens. Treat with **Bornate Solution**

BUG BITES

Campho Phenique and **cortizone ointment**

PAIN

Severe pain we used **tylenol** and **codine.** (requires a doctor's prescription) The problem with the codine is that it may cause constipation. Muscle pain we used **Norgesic,** or **Flexall.** Muscle spasm we had **Quinine Sulphate.** (also for malaria) **Asperin, Ibruprophen** for minor pain.

WOUNDS

If you receive a cut that **requires stitches,** and you can't do the stitching yourself, bring **Steri Strips**. They are used in holding surgical wounds together. Use **alcohol prep packets** first. Stiching should be done only if a doctor cannot be reached within a short period of time.

ALLERGIC REACTION

If we had an **allergic reation** to drugs we would use **Benedryl.** With hives I used **Atarax**, and we also carried a bee sting kit with a **hypodermic needle**. All above medications require a doctor's prescription.

ANTIBIOTICS

This is a very personal choice that should be made by you and your doctor. I have several allergies, therefore I am limited to what drugs I can take. Bob can take anything. We brought **Penicillin** for him, **Erthromyicin** for me, plus **tetracycline.** We also brought **Nystatin** for infected wounds.

USEFUL MEDICAL SUPPLIES
Thermometers: rectal and oral
Chemical heat packs, chemical cold packs
Triangle bandages
Scissors, scalpel, (disposible blades) tweezers, forceps (artery clamp)
Aluminum splints for fingers
Bandaids of all sizes
Adhesive tape in all sizes
Sterile plastic gloves,
Safety pins
Gauze squares, 3 inch, 4 inch (five each)
Elastic velcros rib belt, an elbow and knee slip on ace bandage
Neosporin ointment
Cortizone ointment
Multi Vitamins

BOOKS
Ship's Medicine Chest

Advanced First Aid Afloat, **Peter F. Eastman, M.D.**

HYPOTHERMIA
Hypothermia is a condition when exposure to cold air or water lowers the body core temperature. At its worst, it can cause death. This may not seem to be a concern in the tropics, but you have to go through a lot of cold water to reach the warm water, and surprisingly even warm water is not problem free. Mild hypothermia can occur in warm water, causing shivering, cold hands and feet, numbness in limbs, loss of dexterity causes decreased crew efficiency and increases the chance of accidents. I experienced mild hypothermia. Remember, the only clothing I wore at night on watch was a tee shirt in the tropics. When howling winds and rain pummeled me I started to shiver. In all that hot weather I became quite cold. At that point my thinking process was stressed, which could have led to some loss of reasoning and affected my efficiency. Bad news when trying to navigate. Obviously my putting on more clothes alleviated most of the problem.

According to experts one of the most important preventative measure to start with was to get lots of rest (I wish the expert had been with us during nights of equipment failures). Because of those interruptions rest wasn't possible, even if we rotated our watches often. Logically that was a reason to have another crew member, something we really didn't want, and a purely personal choice. Many insurance companies considered this unwise. Life taught us we had to live with the consequences of our choices.

When we attended the Safety At Sea Seminar in San Francisco, we learned if someone went overboard it was important for the crewman to stay near the boat. The person should keep clothes and boots on for some insulation and flotation. If possible a hat helps the heat escaping from the body. The person should keep his head out of the water, including the back of the head. The arms need to be held close to the sides, chest and PFD. The legs need to be crossed, knees raised as much as waves and stability permit. If more than one person ends up in the water they should hold each other, chest to chest. Have the legs intertwined as much as possible.

These hints on medical concerns are meant to encourage you to learn more about the subject through medical seminars, and books on the subject. I also encourage you to take Red Cross courses in First Aid and CPR. Everyone is different, so the medical concerns must fit individual people. All of the above information was meant to fit our needs, not necessarily someone else's.

I am sure I haven't covered everything. There are some good cruising medical books that cover the subject more thoroughly. There are also cruising courses on medical problems offered in some major areas such as San Francisco. There are also different Safety At Sea Seminars given in different locations around the United States. I definitely recommend a cruiser look into these seminars.

Appendix Eight

TIPS ON PROVISIONING

When it comes to food, what is one person's delight is another person's poison. Knowing what to bring along on a boat becomes a subject of personal choice, due to simple taste differences, as well as medical concerns, diet standards, and allergies to certain foods. Another consideration could be the area you intend to cruise. If one is coastal cruising you may not want to load up your boat with too many supplies, but off shore you need to plan more carefully. You can easily obtain canned food, fresh food, paper products, cleaning supplies etc. if you cruise along the coast of the United States, Canada, Mexico, many parts of the Caribbean, major South American countries, islands like Tahiti, Pango Pango, European countries, New Zealand, Australia. Paper products in French Polynesia are very expensive. In Mexico paper products are not expensive, but not very good quality. Dry goods, such as flour purchased in Mexico, Caribbean, South America, can contain weevils. While they may be a form of good protein, they sure ruin a good meal. If you are a person that must have Stove Top Stuffing, then you should pack what you think you must have to last the trip. Cardboard packaging of Stove Top, cake, or muffin mixes draw moisture into the package, and after a period time, it won't be edible. This can happen in a shorter period of time in the tropics where humidity inside the boat can be high. We solved that problem by buying a vacuum packer and repacking those items inside the sealed packages. You may use the same thing with flour, and baking materials. Weevils, or cockroaches can't get into these packages, and since no odor can emanate from them, mice and rats won't be attracted and get into them either. Different cruisers had rats and mice aboard at one time or another. Carry a rat trap, as well as a mouse trap, plus roach poison. Don't bring cardboard cartons aboard since roach eggs may be hiding in the folds.

Space is usually a problem on sailboats, especially when it comes to cooking utensils. We used a pressure cooker as an oven. Don't put any water in it because once the lid is sealed it becomes its own oven. Use only low heat. We baked bread in this manner, by inserting a stainless bowl that fit inside the cooker, and then placed the raised dough inside the bowl. You can also cook rice in the pressure cooker. You use one part rice, and two parts water. We didn't add salt. Cut up dried fruit will plump up nicely and give the rice or more festive look, as well as being more nutritious. Instead of using dried fruit each time, we added dried beans. This helps to add fiber to the diet. We had a regular oven, but in the tropics the oven heated up the cabin too much.

Keep a note book detailing where food and paper products are located. It is so easy to forget when you are tired. Even when you're rested it's easy to forget.

WHAT WE TOOK

Dried packaged mixed fruit, raisons, nuts
Black bean, lentils, red beans in tupperware
Rice, pastas (variety) in tupperware, or vacuum pack
Freeze dried meals (Get at camping stores) Beef stroganoff, chicken chow mein etc. for rough weather meals)
Top Raman dried soups with noodles (type)
Salad dressing packets
Coffee, tea, dried gatorade, small fruit juices, long life milk, single packages of hot cocoa
Dry packaged sauce mixes
White vinegar, vegetable oil, catsup, mustard
Sugar (in tupperware)
Quick cooking oats (for cookies as well as hot cereal)
Cereal (tupperware)
Hard candies (good for dry mouth on long passages)
Baking powder, baking soda

Bisquick (in tupperware)
Lots of Parmesan cheese
Corn starch (tupperware)
Spices, salt, pepper, dill weed, allspice, Italian seasoning, paprika, garlic powder, cinnamon, curry
Noodle and sauce mix packages
Dried mushrooms (shitake)
Dried tomato
Soy sauce, hoi sin sauce, oyster sauce, sesame oil, chili oil (for my Chinese cooking)
Cake mixes (vacuum pack) Brownie mix
Chicken and beef bouillon cubes
Honey
Syrup
Peanut butter (lots)
Crackers (tupperware)
Moisture proof matches
Jam

CANNED GOODS
ALL CANS SHOULD BE MARKED WITH WATER PROOF PEN, DATE, CONTENTS

Due to lack of storage in our first small sailboat, we kept can goods in the bilge. Naturally water got in there at times, and the cans lost their wrappers. Picking out something to eat created some hilarious meals.

Personal choice for food types-Remember the salt content is high in canned foods
Soups, all varieties
Tuna, corned beef, spam, hams
Fruits, variety
Beans, chili, Boston baked beans with canned bread
Ravioli, spaghettio's
Stew
Green beans
Olives
Mushrooms (small cans)
Enchilada sauce
Corn
Potato
Onions

Cherry pie filling, apple pie filling
Hash, beef, and corn beef
Evaporated milk, dried milk (packaged vacuum pack)

PAPER PRODUCTS

Toilet paper, kleenex, paper towels, some paper plates, napkins, aluminum foil, zip lock baggies, (different sizes) trash bags

FRESH FOOD HINTS

Eggs can be a problem if you don't have refrigeration. We cleaned each egg and covered it with Vaseline, putting them in plastic egg cartons. They also can be covered with paraffin. They will last three week, sometimes more. Buy the freshest eggs possible. Unknowingly we bought some older eggs in Mexico that almost hatched. The smell was terrible.

Carrots and cucumbers last quite awhile. Potato, onions, and garlic last well if air can get around them. Fruits rot easily in hot climates.

Cabbage lasts the longest on an ocean crossing.

CLEANING SUPPLIES

Joy soap (cleans dishes, decks, bilges, and will lather in salt water
White vinegar in the heads keep them smelling sweet
Boat soap, cleaning pads, lots of rags
Bleach

HELPFUL HINTS

Water is a precious commodity, so don't use sea water for clothes washing. It takes twice as much fresh water to get the salt out. Let dirty clothes sit in soapy water for the day, then wring out the soapy water well before putting the clothes in rinse water. Some cruisers brought along a hand wringer. Bob was my wringer. Salt draws moisture to it, so keep as much salt off your clothes, and keep it away from living quarters if you can.

We used a sun shower for bathing until water was used up. We also carried water in used box wine liners and refilled the sun shower. We hung the shower on deck and used a soap that didn't leave a scum. After that we bathed in a small bowl. It's not wonderful, but better than nothing. We installed a foot pump for water in the galley. We used that instead of the pressure water system.

We tried to air our blankets, or sleeping bags. The sun keeps the mold away and makes things smell better.

We kept a spray bottle with a dilute combination of bleach and water to spray areas where food was prepared. Especially when cutting up chicken or fish. It killed the bacteria. Wooden cutting boards were better than plastic ones. The bacteria on wood has been known to dissipate faster.

My captain says "a place for everything and everything in its place." The admiral says that too, and cleans up after the captain when he forgets. We tried to remember to return tools to the same place. Otherwise we would spend more time looking for them than fixing things.

We kept a written record of where spare parts and tools were located. I forgot to write down where I put a small plastic Christmas tree before we left cruising. It was hidden so well we didn't find it for three years.